D0558368

"JANIS JOPLIN was one of the seemingly triumphant symbols of the counterculture of the '60s—a rock star who was so into feeling that she and her audiences shared a heavy communion of emotional tripping. Then Janis died, at 27, of an overdose of heroin. Why, riding so high, had she succumbed to that drug that most effectively *kills* feeling? *Buried Alive* not only tries to answer that question but also provides an unsentimental dissection of the self-indulgent life styles of many in the shaky rock pantheon."

—*Playboy*

"MYTHS CLING . . . NOT SURPRISINGLY, SINCE JANIS CULTIVATED THEM with the same passion she collected 'pretty young boys' at her favorite bars. Two biographies since her death—David Dalton's worshipful *Janis* and Peggy Caserta's trashy *Going Down With Janis*—have added only confusion. Myra Friedman's intelligent, deeply felt book should set the record straight."

—*Newsweek*

Buried Alive

The Biography of Janis Joplin

By Myra Friedman

BANTAM BOOKS
TORONTO · NEW YORK · LONDON

In her memory

BURIED ALIVE
THE BIOGRAPHY OF JANIS JOPLIN
*A Bantam Book / published by arrangement with
William Morrow & Company, Inc.*

PRINTING HISTORY
*William Morrow edition published August 1973
Bantam edition published August 1974*

*Bantam Books are published by Bantam Books, Inc. Its trade-
mark, consisting of the words "Bantam Books" and the por-
trayal of a bantam, is registered in the United States Patent
Office and in other countries. Marca Registrada. Bantam
Books, Inc., 666 Fifth Avenue, New York, New York 10019.*

PRINTED IN THE UNITED STATES OF AMERICA

Acknowledgments

Many friends of Janis were helpful to me in gathering material. I am especially indebted to Linda Gravenites, Vince Mitchell, Pat Nichols ("Sunshine"), and Dave Richards, whom I myself have known as friends and whose openness of heart and understanding concerning the motives behind this effort led them to speak to me without the slightest reserve or caution.

For their time and cooperation, I am indebted to Sam Andrew, Toby Ben, Brad Campbell, Richard Bell, Peter Cohon ("Coyote"), John Cooke, Lyndall Erb, John Fischer, Dave Getz, Nancy Getz, Diane Gravenites, Nick Gravenites, James Gurley, Richard Hundgin, Richard Kermode, Kris Kristofferson, Seth Morgan, Bob Neuwirth, George Ostrow, Ken Pearson, Clark Pierson, John Till, and Eddie West.

I am no less grateful for interviews with Kip Cohon, Clive Davis, Sam Gordon, Bill Graham, Elliot Mazer, Joe McDonald, Gabriel Mekler, John Morris, Toby Ross, and John Simon.

For their warm assistance in providing me background information, I owe special thanks to Philip Carter, Bob Clark, John Clay, Arlene Elster, Ellen Harmon, Chet Helms, Julius Karpen, Janice Knoll, Jim Langdon, Eyde Mattison, Dave Moriaty, Johnny Moyer, Tary Owens, Julie Paul, Travis Rivers, Powell St. John, Yvonne Sutherlin, and Ken Threadgill.

I am particularly grateful for the contributions of Karleen Bennett and Jack Smith.

Finally, for giving me the benefit of their knowledge and experience and for providing me contributions of indispensable insight, I want to express my unending gratitude to Bernard Giarritano and Dr. Edmund Rothschild.

For his faith and patience, I thank my editor, Jim Landis, and for her encouragement, my agent, Ellen Levine.

To Dr. Marvin Hurvish, I owe the deepest thanks of all.

Part One
Bluebonnets

1

Port Arthur is an oil refinery town in the southeastern corner of Texas where the Sabine Lake blocks it from melting into Louisiana and where the Neches River, running along the northeastern rim of the town, twists down from Beaumont some twelve miles to the northwest. Rolling east on Interstate 10, it's the darkest of drives after sundown, the night cracked only by the glimmer of an occasional highway motel. Route 73 is blacker still, except that one thin beam soon slits the dark, opening, on Port Arthur's outskirts, into the massive expanse of the refineries. Closeness dissolves the illusion of some futuristic city in space as the brightness gives way to the reality of steel. The refineries are just that—a sprawling network of jumping jacks, drilling rigs, towers, derricks, and squat white round kegs for the storage of oil.

There is the smell of petroleum. There is the pall from the chemical plants despoiling the banks of the Neches. There is shipping and the Intracoastal Canal. Cutting up from the Gulf of Mexico, the waterway shoots straight along the downtown section parallel to a street called Procter, at one time Port Arthur's main avenue. Business has splurged out east, and Procter remains a desolate strip that is haunted by sailors at night and is less than bustling in the day.

The Lucas gusher spurted twelve miles away in 1901, and in the decades that followed, oil was what

3

made Port Arthur. Oil is what moves it today. But the fabled Texas oilmen live elsewhere, and while a few millionaires and a number of wealthy professionals make their home in the town, there is little ancestral grace to speak for a South of rich, landed gentry. In the residential sections that spread out to the east, there are rows of decent slat houses, noticeable for a modest consistency. The area was built on marshland, the architecture limited as a result. Still, the streets curve nicely, and the town is lush with marvelous green-heavy trees that mesh at the top and form caves of sanctuary from a murderous, sweltering sun. The suburbs, in fact, are blandly pretty, and a wistful gentility comes through. But the land is flat as a mesa. The air is gummy with humidity, and it howls—heat, mediocrity, boredom.

Some sixty thousand people live in Port Arthur, but the sixties have scooped it dry as a dust bowl of its adventurous youth and spleen. That fate has befallen any number of small American towns. However, the younger residents who have left dispute any similarity between Port Arthur and other locales. The unions, they say, are mighty, and the struggle for power brought to the town a series of strikes that erupted in hellish battle. Those unions too drew a great number of people into the southeastern corner of Texas, able to make good money from oil but ill-educated and primitively hard. Some were drifters from East Texas. There were Cajuns from Louisiana, Chicanos from Mexico, and blacks from everywhere. Only the blacks have stayed poor and segregated. The nicer residential areas flowered, with the white laborers living in the same neighborhoods as the professionals and the industry's executive personnel. The result was an abrasive cultural clash and an undercurrent of mean hoodlum toughness that smashed right into a mode of life styled by gracious ways.

"When we were growing up," a former resident reflected, "right next door to some doctor whose son was working a paper route to save money to buy a nineteen-fifty Ford, there'd be a family who just handed their kid a fifty-seven Chevy and told him, 'Now don't take no shit off nobody and if somebody looks at ya wrong, hit 'im in the fuckin' mouth.' It was a very tough place to grow up, a lot of violence *always*."

Cultural clash has brought part of that violence. Some seethes right out of the Texas character. Right down to the fellow who still signs "X" on his paycheck, Texans know their bloody history, and the spirit of it has stuck. They are a people quick to anger, their infamous bluster the swagger of pride. Then there is the fast money from oil and the independence of the range. Only a hundred miles from Port Arthur sits Houston, with one of the highest homicide rates in the country, and there is more to do in Houston than in the industrial towns on the Louisiana border. To further fire a swinish temper, there is the soggy closeness of the heat and the venom of the inch-long black mosquitoes that thrive in the thick, dank bayous.

A visitor sees the scratch in the surface of docility only in a surprising number of smashed headlights and dented fenders among the taxicabs in town. And the cautious person steers clear of Procter at night. The seamen come in from the docks, and they are dangerous when drunk which, since the whorehouses were shut down in 1962, they usually are, having nothing else to do. And the blacks have caught the "fever," though the white citizenry doesn't talk too much about it. Nor about the violence at all.

Few older residents of the "respectable" community admit that their young people have included that seamier world in the scope of their experiences. Fewer recognize that something might crawl into the minds of the more curious that could give that world some savor—because it is fundamental and

gritty and because there is little else in Port Arthur
to interest a restless mind. Neither does the "respectable" community admit to the allure that lies in a
strip of dusty bars over and across the river in the
state of Louisiana.

The southeastern corner of Texas is primarily
French Catholic and Baptist, with the Southern Baptist Conference probably the most powerful political
force in the state of Texas after the Democratic party.
It is the Southern Baptist Conference that formerly
dictated the Texas liquor laws. Prior to 1971, the
saloons could serve only beer and wine. Hard liquor
could be gotten in clubs that charged a membership
fee. The drinking age is still twenty-one, but gosh-
awmighty, it is eighteen in Louisiana, and any soul
with imagination would have been bound to scoot fast
at the opportunity to get across that river and live
it up or live it down, depending on the point of
view.

But in Port Arthur, there is the "good" as opposed
to the "bad." The fancier families from Louisiana raise
their children to perpetuate tradition, and damned if
they don't succeed. Their daughters are proper
ladies; their sons are southern gentlemen. If the
economic stratum is middle income, that has never
meant anything to people whose ancestors got high
on orange blossoms and cologne. The goals of life?
Cultural standards may divide the town, but the
aims of existence unite it.

Education is functional and ascends in a regulated
pattern. Most of Port Arthur's high school graduates
go to Lamar State College in Beaumont, a technological institute geared to serve the region. It makes
schoolteachers and nurses out of the region's daughters and prepares its sons for work in the oil industry.
That is what shapes the vision of the future for the
majority of Port Arthur's population and, at least in
the past, as one person put it, "They hated anybody
who didn't want what they wanted."

Heedless of all that, Port Arthurans like their town, They have a new city hall, and their churches are modern. They take pride in those structures and also in the way of life that Port Arthur represents. They are a good people too, unless they are threatened, and the citizen of lively mind can go unnoticed, if quiet enough. Some people live there for convenience. Some because they are trapped by the inertia of habit. Others? There is a sad charm about a man who sighs, "Ah was born on this heah land."

All the same, roots, habit, and convenience are secondary matters for the majority of the population. For many, there is the contentment that comes from sureness of thought. In that corner of Texas, the boiling complexities of other worlds need not intrude to confuse the mind. The people are exposed to little. Most make do with the *Port Arthur News* and leave the rest to Washington and God. Or maybe just God. Washington is in disfavor because HEW according to them has come and messed up their school system which, before that happened, was working out its integration just fine. Also, Washington is near New York, which is the central location of the National Broadcasting Company, which is just as bad as the HEW.

In February of 1971, NBC-TV sinned against Port Arthur. A segment of "First Tuesday" that had to do with Janis made a hasty reference to Port Arthur as "drab." As if that was not bad enough, the cameras had zoomed in on Procter for a quick scan of the town.

"That show!" one lady indignantly cried. "Why, who ever went around there took pictures of saloons and lounges that I bet Janis, even in her last year here, didn't even know existed! That part of town where decent people don't walk when they don't have to! Not anything about the good side . . . the churches! Nothing about the kind of homes! Nothing about the library! Our new city hall!"

A copy of the *Reader's Digest* and a book titled *The Psalms Speak to Us Today* sat on an immaculate coffee table.

"Now let me ask you," she whispered, "how long had she been drinking and taking dope? And I read somewhere that her house was decorated in such good taste that you would *never* reconcile it with what she did for a living!"

No, they didn't like "First Tuesday," and letters of objection poured in to the *Port Arthur News*. The NBC affiliate even canceled the show for all-time future viewing in the area. There are citizens who harbored a suspicion that the program just might have been the reason Port Arthur stayed only a finalist that year in the national competition for "All-America City." If, for some, there could be a double edge to the meaning of that honor, it would surely slip by the good solid stock that make up the All-American people of Janis Joplin's birthplace.

2

Seth Joplin moved to Port Arthur from Amarillo in the Texas Panhandle to work as an engineer for Texaco shortly after receiving his degree at Texas A & M. Gentle and introspective, he has said of himself that he would have made an excellent monk, and there is about him the aura of a man who has segmented his life into exquisitely separate planes. One has been devoted to the duties of job and provider, with strong, loving bonds to his family. The other has been nourished by his profoundly ascetic nature. He has neglected neither, but in the soft, telling quiet of his eyes is the sacredness of a private reality, and he has leafed through his days as he has through his books, with philosophical absorption. Janis always referred to her father as a "secret intellectual," and she was terribly disturbed as it became apparent that the years had been harsh to his body. He suffers from an agonizing arthritis, but still works, now as a supervisor in the Texaco package division. His day begins at five-thirty in the morning.

Dorothy Joplin comes from Nebraska. Her father was originally a rancher, then a farmer until the depression wiped out his farm and he became an export salesman, settling with his wife and four children, first in Kansas City and then Los Angeles. Financial necessity brought him to Amarillo, where Mrs. Joplin went through her senior year in high school. She moved to Port Arthur when she was twenty-two. There, she was courted by Seth Joplin for a year before the couple was married in 1936. She is an industrious and disciplined woman, with an aggressive temperament and an unwavering decisiveness to her very shrewd intelligence. Rather worldly in some respects and quite insular in others, she expresses her stalwart opinions with brisk, metallic precision. Too active of spirit to remain a homebody, she has worked as a businesswoman and also as the registrar at one of the local colleges. Mrs. Joplin is well-liked. Graciousness shows in her smile and a warm hospitality in her manner, through something more distant remains in her eyes. They are an unreadable blue nickel-gray.

When the Joplins were first married, they bought a home in what then was the country. Billowy fields burst free across the street from 4048 Procter, and with the opportunity afforded by the oil industry, the living circumstances were about as pleasant as you could find in those days of the nation's recovery from economic disaster. Their home was close to the grade school, and the children they planned to have, as soon as they could afford it, would be within walking

distance of the school. The first of those children
was Janis Lyn Joplin, born in St. Mary's Hospital on
January 19, 1943, at nine forty-five in the morning.

One day when Janis was seven, Mrs. Joplin took a
snapshot of the junior Girl Scout pack to which Janis
then belonged. The Bluebirds, as they were called,
lined up for the picture in front of the grade school,
Janis standing among them demurely concealed in
the second row. Quite suddenly, while her mother
was peering through the shutter, Janis skipped out in
front of the group. The shutter clicked; Janis bowed
a deep dainty curtsy—and grinned.

Mrs. Joplin said the incident was atypical. If Janis
had a tendency to chatter more than usual when the
Joplins were having company, she seemed to have
no special design for putting herself front and center,
certainly not as a youngster. Indeed, nothing in
Janis's childhood stood out to the Joplins as an intimation of what would come; she was a normal little
girl whose earlier years went by in ascending ridges
of happiness and very few dark pitfalls.

A wan and tiny baby at birth, Janis weighed only
five pounds, eight ounces. She developed rapidly,
however, a healthy infant who sat up at six months
and stood at eleven months, one week. Anything exceptional, Mrs. Joplin believes, showed in the area of
motor skill. She handled a fork and spoon with agility
by the time she'd reached a year; she preferred milk
from a cup as early as eleven months. "She cut her
food like we did and ate it like we did," Mrs. Joplin
said. "She didn't smear her face with food, and
friends came to take her to other homes to show the
dexterity she had in eating." She was, in fact, an easy
child to care for, neither too docile nor too active,
and all in all, the Joplins remember, she seemed a
cheerful youngster. An effervescence springs right out
from the character of her early pictures, in which she
is all white-blonde and cherubic, smiling that incomparably marvelous smile—radiant, as if it had been

scooped on by a merry gremlin enticed by her wonder-filled eyes.

A fuzzy strip of well-trimmed hedges hangs like an inverted cornice beneath the front windows of the Joplins' unassuming home in Griffing Park. They have lived there, in one of the better municipalities that make up greater Port Arthur, since Janis was about six. Trees shade the house, which is meticulously kept, a blend of beige off-white and cream.

I sat in the Joplins' living room, thumbing through old scrapbooks as Mrs. Joplin told me about Janis's earlier years. A few of Mrs. Joplin's books lay on the coffee table: a Toynbee volume, *Giles Goat-Boy*, and *I, Claudius*. Hanging on one living-room wall was a large crewel embroidery, a Shaker Tree of Life done by Mrs. Joplin.

In the study there is a painting of a faceless young man. The silhouette is sharp, the style all jagged on a canvas of two-shaded brown and very opaque taupe. One of Janis's paintings also hangs in the home of another Port Arthur resident. Its lines are equally angular, its colors the darkest of purples, lightened by fields of violet and an icy needling white. Furious slashes of black outline two female figures, one clothed, one nude. Both paintings are startling. Janis's references to her artwork had always been rather flip. "I read poetry and I painted," she'd say with no more than a disinterested shrug.

The fact is that Janis's interest in art had once been quite serious; she began to draw almost as soon as she could hold a pencil, and, pleased by her obvious interest, Mrs. Joplin arranged for her to have some private art lessons when she was in the third and fourth grades. As for her musicality, any signs were restricted to the habit of singing herself to sleep when she was a young child. Though she was a member of the church choir and the glee club in junior high, no one, including Janis herself, paid any particular attention back then to her musical gifts.

Mrs. Joplin herself used to sing, though not professionally. "I didn't like the scene," she said grimly.

From her earliest days, Janis displayed a churning intelligence and an insatiable demand to *do*. She took to reading before she entered school and had a library card as soon as she could walk. Mrs. Joplin read to Janis frequently, but only as a matter of course. "It wasn't to make her precocious or head of the class or anything of that sort," she explained. Being an especially bright and curious child, Janis simply learned. Later, it was no secret to Janis's friends that she was a voluminous reader, although she went out of her way to keep that hidden from her public.

Mrs. Joplin also said that Janis took quickly to magical tales and is convinced that Janis unraveled her whole life as one spinning yarn that curled endlessly in circles and circles of made-up stories, similar to the gleeful fantasies of her childhood. "You have to understand," she pleaded, "what kind of things appealed to her. She studied about the theater. She studied 'tall-tales of America.' She'd spin these tales. It was so far out that you were supposed to understand that it was that way. She tried the same thing with the press—in my opinion. And it backfired. I overlooked that marvelous capacity of hers to trust people."

Mrs. Joplin stopped her narrative and pointed to a snapshot in the scrapbook. "This little boy and Janis went to the same Sunday School class, and when they would have a game where you all marched clockwise they would march counterclockwise and just twinkle about the whole thing."

Janis was six when Laura was born. Besieged by colic, the newest member of the family demanded for the first three months of her life the special concern of her mother. It was an exhausting period for Mrs. Joplin, during which her attention to her other daughter was inadvertently affected. The situation did not seem to ruffle Janis. According to her friends, only as she grew older did her feelings appear to be complicated by any jealousy, and then it

was not hostility but forlorn regret that Laura, unlike
Janis, was able to do everything "right." When
younger, Janis showed only the greatest affection for
her sister. "She had a very very protective relationship to Laura," Mrs. Joplin said. "She watched her
with more concern than I did."

Janis was already doing exceptional work at school
when she was accelerated in the third grade. If there
was any strain due to her being the second youngest
in the class (she was a month older than her close
friend Karleen Bennett), it didn't show at the time.
She progressed as a "normal" child with all the normal joys and all the normal traumas—as far as anyone could tell. Her brother Michael was born when
Janis was ten. As she had Laura, she accepted him
happily.

Mrs. Joplin, however, remarked that Janis did seem
to need more attention than her other children. "She
was unhappy and unsatisfied without it. The normal
rapport wasn't adequate. She still had to have more
attention than the other two." It was also clear that
Janis pressured herself toward achievement. Whether
it was height, grades, or activities, she had to be
ahead. "This was not something her daddy and I
did—'you must excel, you must excel.' I don't remember even mentioning it."

Janis had begun writing plays when she was in the
first grade, and so that she could stage them with her
friends, Mr. Joplin built her a puppet theater. The
Joplins' backyard was a busy gathering place for all
the young children on the block. There were trees,
a sandbox, and animals, which Janis loved always. She
had dogs until high school, when a high mortality
rate discouraged the Joplins from owning any more.

Unfortunately, a number of Janis's friends moved
out of town when she was in the sixth grade. The
Joplins' Griffing Park home was some distance from
the junior high, and Janis, for a while, traveled by
bus with children she didn't know. She was a strikingly timid child. Rowdy youngsters were present,

and she complained of being frightened. A car pool alleviated the problem, and Janis returned to being happy at school. She had adjusted well throughout the early grades. Mrs. Joplin stressed repeatedly that Janis trotted cheerily along, comfortable in her environment. There were no "behavior difficulties." Everything, as a matter of fact, was perfect. "I even worried about it a little," Mrs. Joplin said. "She never did anything for me to correct!"

One intimation of the future occurred over a meal when Janis refused to eat some turnips her parents thought she should try. "She sat at the table until bedtime rather than eat them!"

Commenting on Janis's stubbornness, she agreed that her daughter "came by that honestly."

Another issue had Janis very obstinate. She sucked her thumb obsessively. She was still doing it at the age of eight when her father decided the day had come, she had to be made to stop. There was a radio show of which Janis was especially fond. Persuasive efforts hadn't worked. On this particular day, he gave her a choice: she would be denied permission to listen to the show unless she gave up her sucking. Janis thereupon threw a tantrum. She wanted the thumb in her mouth; she also wanted her radio show. She shrieked, kicked, cried, screamed, worked herself into a frenzy. The Joplins could recall nothing like it in Janis's childhood ever before. The behavior was most unusual, as it was unusual for either of Janis's parents to be punitive during those years. The entire episode was almost forgotten.

With the ages of the children so dispersed, activities done together by the entire family were perhaps a little less frequent than ordinary. There were the limitations of Port Arthur as well. Fortunately, Mr. Joplin was an imaginative man; he often took the children down to the post office to look at the Wanted Men posters.

"It was a little unusual," he pondered, "but it was somewhere to go. That wasn't the real reason, the

Wanted Men. We'd just roam around the deserted building and read about all the people who were wanted for murders. We'd go any unusual place we could."

Mr. Joplin also took the children to the library, and Karleen Bennett often went along.

Recalling those browsing afternoons, Karleen said, "Mr. Joplin is very educated. When he'd take us there he'd say, 'When you want to check out a book, you pick it up and weigh it. If it's heavy it's going to be a good book, because they spent money for the paper. If it's not, they didn't think that much of the book.'"

Mr. Joplin later explained. "I did use that as a criterion for books I didn't know anything about. I just liked the feel of books, so I wanted a good heavy book anyway, and if I took out a book from the shelf and it was lightweight, I'd put it back. I always liked long books too."

The children, Mrs. Joplin said, were encouraged to think and also to discuss their ideas. "We included the children in all our conversations," she stated, "and we wanted them to voice their opinions and ideas about everything."

Janis herself recalled her early childhood as being nearly idyllic. "Then the whole world turned!" she said. "It just turned on me!"

It was Easter week when I visited Port Arthur. The schools were closed and some of Janis's former teachers were out of town. That, or on the golf course for the better part of the day. One lady had put my request for an interview on the altar of her church, and God, I guess, had turned me down. There were others not available for who knows the reason. Nonetheless, from the people to whom I was able to speak I got a similarly cheery portrait: Janis helped out in the library; Janis helped out at the church. Janis won an artwork contest for the cover of a junior high publication; Janis did posters for the library.

Janis was cooperative; Janis was shy. Janis was "just like everybody else."

"When Janis became well known," one of her teachers told me, "and the children would hear her over the TV or something, well, I would tell them the *plus* side that I knew. But one time she was on and they asked me, 'Did you hear Janis on TV?' and I said, 'No.'" The woman tightened her lips and shook her head somberly. "'You wouldn't have liked it,' they said, 'you wouldn't have liked it.'"

Some of the praise was surely more enlightened than that. "Her intelligence was *so* much," one woman said, "that the school didn't recognize it."

But the over-all tone was really quite strange. It was not because the praise betrayed a love for the ordinary and unprovocative, which most of it certainly did—everything was fine when Janis was "just like everybody else." What bothered me was something much more insidious, a vision of safety in dreary evenness, beyond which there is unmentionable danger. Then I realized that Janis had held exactly that vision and that she'd been true to her roots till the end. She'd gone out and proven it to be absolutely right.

3

The revolt began unnoticed, likely in Janis's own mind to have been nothing more than an unfamiliar shadow, a longer look at the sky one night, a poem, a troublesome twinge of the flesh, any or all gone quickly enough and fading with the drift of buried memory. Perhaps a question: "Why not?" An answer: "Because." Outwardly, for a while at least, everything continued as before. Mrs. Joplin said that Janis's behavior was not strikingly different from the other children's until her senior year in high school, although her intelligence and imagination were quite another matter. Of that, the Joplins were very much aware. Janis's grades were consistently excellent, and when they were slightly less than that, it was because she was not particularly challenged.

By all accounts, Janis was an astonishingly naive and gullible girl, a leadable child ready to do anything in order to please other people. Arlene Elster, who was a year ahead of Janis at Thomas Jefferson High, admitted that sometimes she and Karleen made up preposterous stories, which they showered on Janis to tease her. Invariably she believed them. Her language, at least until her junior or senior year, was free of gamey embellishment. Karleen laughed at the memory of the "cussing contests" that Janis lost, a forlorn and pathetic contender. Her white-blonde hair had toned down to a brown. She was chubby, and a smattering of freckles across her features gave her the air of a church-going innocence endearing to the town's adults.

"Probably about the ninth grade," Karleen remembered, "she started having opinions of her own. A question about integration came up and all Janis said was she though integration was fine. You just didn't do that in Port Arthur. You *still* don't! For the rest of the time, there were these two boys, they followed her around and called her 'nigger-lover' everywhere."

Mrs. Joplin felt that it was a question of the belligerence with which Janis expressed her ideas, thought the anger was brought on by her strident tone. Others would say impossible, that in Port Arthur, Texas, in the 1950s, the song-and-dance required to express that opinion with a cotton-mouthed softness would reduce it to no such opinion at all. Karleen indicated

that the constrictions of conformity were almost unfathomable in those days, and any challenge to that
rigidity was regarded as an intolerable threat.

Yet Janis was not the only one who spoke her mind
on such issues, nor the only one to be called names.
In a sense, Mrs. Joplin was right, more so than she
actually knew. Had Janis been especially pretty in
her classmates' eyes, had she a daintiness to decorate
the gristle of her rebel spirit, all might indeed have
been well. Such was not the case. Janis was clashing
with hostile surroundings and building a style to cope.
As so often happens in the impatience and mystery
of a sensitive heart, the way became confused; the
effort to keep her balance turned back like the independent demon, running her through with perverse
and terrible cruelty. Janis cloaked herself in that which
appeared more strange—all very gradual, but ultimately abrasive, an alienating style that made things
worse. By her early years in high school, her differences were noticeable to her classmates, if not yet to
her teachers and parents.

Janis's former high school companions are scattered. In Port Arthur, only Karleen remains. But from
all of them came the theme of her difference, Janis
as "one of the guys," some failure to meet the standards of southern lady femininity that showed itself
in a roughness of manner, a coarse defiance, a willingness to play buffoon, to subject herself to verbal
abuse, anything to be noticed and belong.

As early as the tenth grade, Janis began to establish some peculiar identifications, gravitating at
first toward a tough hoodlum element at school. They
were tentative. Tary Owens in San Francisco and
Jack Smith in Austin indicated that her behavior was
a trivial dalliance with the world of the outcast, a
straining for acceptance from any quarters she could
find. Janis started to assume the dress and mannerisms of the senior high girls who dated the town
thugs. Jack Smith thought it only play-acting in that
particular stage but bound, if continued, to get worse.

"Still," he added, "I'd say that in the ninth and tenth grades, Janis was happy and popular in that nothing world that high school creates." Tary Owens knew too that Janis didn't belong with those people or, it must have seemed to her, anywhere at all. For a while, she seemed to seesaw, dating boys who were acceptable to her parents and generally toeing the line.

Jack Smith now teaches art history at the University of Texas. He met Janis when they played bridge together in the seventh grade. "In the Ladies Aid Society's 'Bridge for Cultural Improvement'! So help me!" Later he and Janis became close friends. Clearly, he said, Janis was not forced through the routine of bridge clubs and other activities. "She *liked* that club and nobody made her join. There're an awful lot of people that deny any communication whatsoever between her and her parents, but they're wrong."

Some of Janis's friends thought that especially so with her mother. Mrs. Joplin, they felt, was both indulgent and controlling, the dominant psychological force in the Joplin family. Mr. Joplin by contrast was more permissive, less punitive, and demonstrably gentler in manner. But Jack, reflecting on Mrs. Joplin's nature, saw her as quite a bit different, not essentially cold at all, only determined herself by a cultural outlook that had nothing to do with her fundamental character. "Like a Victorian father," he described her, "*wanting* to be close, but duty-bound and obligated to 'prepare her child.' She just couldn't give that last inch, but Janis was the apple of her eye. It was more that Janis wanted her mother to be something and her mother wanted Janis to be something and they kept conflicting."

Karleen, who admires the Joplins greatly, spoke in a similar vein, stressing that the Joplins were extremely liberal in some ways, but very strict in others. Mrs. Joplin, she claimed, wanted Janis to conform and was anxious about social disapproval. Her parents, Karleen said, watched what she read, what she did, where she went. She recalled that Janis once painted a nude silhouette on a closet door and was made to cover it up, which she did with neuter fishes. "You could see something was going to happen. Either she was going to bend to what they wanted or it was going to blow up the other way." Karleen did not question that Janis was loved, only the way it was displayed, and as Jack Smith said, "It's just nonsense to say if Janis's mother couldn't accept existentialism for instance, that she couldn't be a caring mother! Janis was more of a family type than people want to believe!"

As a blight on an adolescence that was already rocky enough, Janis lost what prettiness she had in those ways so judged by children. Her chubbiness bloated to a hefty bigness; she developed a terrible skin condition, far beyond anything that could be termed a teen-ager's siege of acne. It was severe enough to require sanding. Jack Smith, however, was certain that her skin condition did not really affect her popularity, but that Janis herself withdrew, self-conscious and ashamed. Depression and conflict can themselves contribute to physical change. Mrs. Joplin had Janis's thyroid function checked in connection with her gain of weight. While her metabolism registered high, no medication seemed needed. The correlation between thyroid function and weight is not always present, but a high metabolism would more likely exist in a person tending to be thin.

Parents are notoriously blind about the physical appeal of their children. That is particularly so with mothers when the offspring is a girl. Mrs. Joplin mentioned casually that Janis put on some weight in her senior year, but that otherwise she was "beautiful." That was not so in the eyes of her peers and hadn't been before. Janis would have needed a charm of incalculable dimensions to compensate and a granite-strong inner security. She had neither. Moreover, her assets—her intelligence and talent—were handicaps in the mindless monochrome of Port Arthur.

Before her senior year, Janis had found some kind of a niche in a cluster of five boys, among whom were Jim Langdon and Dave Moriaty. The others were Adrian Haston, Randy Tenant, and Grant Lyons. They leaned toward the different, or thought they did, anyway. Jim Langdon, for example, played trombone. All of them had a tendency to fight the conformity of the town. Perhaps they were more intelligent than the average; certainly they were more adventurous.

By Port Arthur standards, the whole quintet was somewhat on the odd side, behaving, as its members did, in a mold that had no precedent. Rebellion, as it had been acknowledged before in Port Arthur, existed as old-time "delinquency." Historically familiar, the delinquents of the town, while not liked, were at least understood. But the Langdon crew was Port Arthur's first flush of the fifties revolt. They read books unassigned in the classrooms; they listened to jazz, and they did some other unacceptable things in which Janis participated as she became part of their adventures. They climbed the water towers.

"You just didn't *do* that!" Karleen snickered.

They climbed the Rainbow Bridge, which sticks up like a crazy hairpin some three hundred feet above the waters of the Neches. They climbed everything, obviously because it's so goddamn flat down there they had to get *up!* They had beach parties, they spooked around an old abandoned Coast Guard station. They drank a lot of beer. And they sang, although no one seemed to give that much thought. As they got a little older, their adventures got wilder, but in those early high school years, that was all they did on a dull summer night, which, given the Port Arthur weather, much less its opportunities for fun, was any night of the year.

Janis began to associate with that group by in-

sinuating herself in its midst. Initially she was
hardly welcome. Sometimes the boys would try to
escape before she found out what they were up to
and tagged along. They did not view her as they
did other girls. She was neither pretty nor charming.
One did not date a girl like that; and what then
could be the terms of a friendship? In time, their
attitude changed. Janis demanded no courtesies;
anything went in her presence. She was merely "one
of the boys," and none of them would have thought
of considering her in another light. "Then," Dave
Moriaty reluctantly explained, "everybody began to
realize she was fun to have around because she raised
so much hell. By the time we were in mid-high
school, she was one of our favorite characters. I hate
to think of how we treated her sometimes. She occupied about the position of court jester!"

Janis's friendship with Jack Smith temporarily dissolved. "I didn't like the things she did to hang
around that crowd," he remarked.

Janis was loud, boisterous, and crude. "Loud as
hell!" Jim Langdon proclaimed, his eyes bulging like
purple grapes as he paced the floor of his Austin
living room on stumpy, confident legs. He remembered no breathy quiet in her speech and no stran-
gling agony in her eyes.

"When Janis was outrageous," Jim continued, "she
was totally outrageous. Like it was unheard of for
a woman to yell, 'Well, fuck you, baby!' It even
embarrassed *us*. At the same time," he went on comfortably, "we used to also use it to our advantage
when we wanted to freak out people. For the express
purpose of doing that, we'd always bring Janis along.
You definitely wanted her there, because you already
took into account what each person was going to do,
and you knew Janis was going to drop a bomb. She'd
drop a bombshell and you knew it would be a joy
and a delight to watch. It was always the most fun
talking about how Janis had blown them out!"

Whatever her relationship to the five boys with whom she'd palled around, Janis had gained from them a modicum of acceptance. An arrangement of real cost and imagined gain is a hideous bargain by any measure, no matter that she penned it herself. But the boys were a buffer against the rest of the students. She was occupied with her studies, and she was enjoying her painting. She had Arlene Elster and Karleen, at least until her senior year. Arlene and the five boys graduated. Most of them went to Lamar, and she continued to see them frequently enough, but in the halls and classrooms of Thomas Jefferson High she was suddenly on her own. Karleen had a boyfriend and spent less time with Janis than she previously had. There was Janis's weight gain. Her defiance had stiffened tremendously. She had begun to dress outlandishly by Port Arthur standards.

Janis became as hated as an epidemic of horse fever. The students threw things at her, they mocked her, they called her names, of which "pig" was the favorite.

"Janis would laugh," Karleen told me, "you know, playing along to get along. But she'd go home and cry."

Just why the assault was so savage is complex. Karleen intimated that Janis appeared to draw the hatred to her, behaving as if she didn't care what people thought, although it was obvious to Karleen that she cared a great deal. Mr. Joplin said that it almost seemed as if Janis would find out what other people didn't like and do just that.

"She dressed sloppy," Tary Owens agreed, "she was overweight, didn't wear makeup, just refused to do anything to compromise."

Not everybody concurred in the opinion that Janis had been subjected to extraordinary mistreatment. "I think she chose her lot," Jim Langdon announced, "and like anybody who's different—or an *oddball*— or a *freak*—or a *creep*—she was persecuted."

The fact is that the situation was far easier for the males in the rebel junta. Grant Lyons was a star on the football team, and nobody in Texas is going to mess with that! Jim Langdon was winning prizes for his trombone playing, an asset to the school, and Dave Moriaty was editor of the high school paper. Presumably the others had something that made life tolerable too. Their transgressions were also overlooked as the old sowing-wild-oats business, which boys are expected to do, and girls are most definitely not.

Above all, none of them seemed to yearn for the security of the very things they defied. Through the glib reminiscences of the days when they were shafting the Port Arthur establishment, I heard no anguished heartbeats. As for Janis, she craved acceptance by those more ordinary people, longed to believe what they believed, and somewhere, like a blade cutting through her heart, that beast of belief was always there.

"You saw the listings of what she said she was in," Jack Smith exclaimed.

I certainly did. Right next to her graduation picture in that absurd yearbook full of the Basketball Sweetheart, the Posture Queen, the Sweetheart of this, the Sweetheart of that, was the whole works: Future Nurses Association, Future Teachers Association, and some sort of social club called Psi Lambda, which offered the credentials of properness.

"She just didn't join those things and not show up," Jack said. "She was involved in 'em and believed in 'em at one time."

Things became even harder for Janis in her senior year. Mrs. Joplin suggested that Janis take drafting, thinking the class would aid her in developing more precision in her art. Janis, it turned out, was the only girl in the class.

I didn't realize I was putting her into a bad emotional setting, but they began saying she was chasing the boys and that sort of thing. It hurt her terribly."

Then there was the trip to New Orleans. Permission had been denied. Mrs. Joplin thought Janis too young to go wandering around that honky-tonk gloss. Janis was not in the habit of lying, but burning with an eagerness to hear some of the Bourbon Street bands, she created a ruse and deceived her parents. Telling them she was spending the night at Karleen's, she hopped instead into the old family Willis and shot off to that glittering pool of excitement outside Port Arthur. The intention was to come back in the morning with no one the wiser except, of course, Janis and the three boys she took with her. Jim Langdon was one. The other two were not close friends. The other regulars in the group had refused to go, a bit wary of the escapade, which was strictly limited to a tour of the jazz joints and a few other bars.

"We roamed around," Jim said, "and in the morning we headed back."

With Janis too tired to take the wheel, the car was driven by a super hot-rod driver named Clyde, and slow, on a wet pavement, they skidded into another car. Banged in, the radiator wrecked, the car wouldn't move! And yes, they had to wait for the cops! The boys were eighteen, Janis a year and a half younger.

"You ever heard of the Mann Act!" one of the policemen snarled.

"Huh?" Jim grunted. "What's that?"

No one was charged with the Mann Act. There was no basis for any charge at all, but there was surely a basis for gossip, the shudder, "disgusting," the delicious *dream*, of what must certainly have occurred. Mrs. Joplin believes that Janis's problems multiplied to disastrous effect following that adventure. Let us say that it brought Janis's differences into sharper focus and puffed out the fantasies that all along had been the real root of the hatred.

Philip Carter, who was in Janis's class, but did not become a close friend until after their high school days, implied that it was exactly that. The focus of the ostracism was indeed sex, the foundation in reality irrelevant.

"Sex," he said, "is a big hangup down there. They're hypocritical because they say one thing and do another, but as long as they're conforming, justifying it by the front of a lifestyle on the basis of, say, the Baptist Church, it's all right. Really it's amazing to try to comprehend the heads in Port Arthur. I've never been able to do it."

The heads, of course, are easy enough to comprehend. There's nothing new about the whore who's conjured in the swampy suck of the minister's private fantasies. Janis was "different"; she became a girl with a "reputation." The vocabulary may be archaic. Not so her suffering.

Later, Janis became positively grandiose in her claims about her past and, God knows, her then-present sexual escapades. But I could find no substantiation of her "precociousness" among any of her Port Arthur friends.

"Listen," one girl insisted, "she walked in on me when I was in bed with my boyfriend and I had to go into this long explanation to keep her from knowing what was going on because she was so naive. You can hear all the stories. I've heard them all. All I can tell you is that after high school, there was a party and she came charging in and screamed, 'You lied to me! Now I know what you were doing that afternoon!' And I was about to die laughing because nobody there knew what she was talking about. The guys in Port Arthur are still saying they had her, now more than ever. But it's not true!"

That girl is fairly certain that Janis remained a virgin until the summer after high school. A few other friends contest that. But without exception, males included, all were firm in stating that the Rabelaisian stories going around Port Arthur were totally out of proportion. Whatever she did and whenever she did it, she seems to have done it later than any number of her classmates.

"She was probably more innocent than nine out of ten of the girls who graduated from high school with her," Jack Smith said. "Any given high school cheerleader put out more than Janis."

Even Jim Langdon agreed that Janis's earlier behavior did not include what was assumed. "I remember a couple of guys trying to make her at some party her sophomore year. I remember her trying to come on very tough, very experienced, but actually folding in the clinch. She maybe even cried."

All in all, it would appear that many of those sugary southern belles—from the "right side of the tracks," not to mention the other breed—were balling in the oil fields when Janis was still climbing the Rainbow Bridge!

Yet to "come on very tough, very experienced" was her way, partially in defense and more crucially in an inexhaustible confusion—it was there until the end—about sexuality. If it had been brewing, which certainly was so, it couldn't have been helped by the torment to which she was subjected as a result of the itchy loins of her classmates.

"Here," Karleen said, pointing to a simpering face in Thomas Jefferson's 1960 annual. "He's a very successful man now, one of Port Arthur's fine citizens! He used to call Janis after he'd taken his girlfriend home. He never went out with her, but he'd say he made her. He'd call her up and just say things like 'You wanna screw tonight?' and stuff. No matter what she'd say, he'd keep it up. Sometimes she'd get upset; sometimes she'd act as if it didn't bother her. Then after a while, she'd go into a terrible depression and it would take time for her to come out of it!"

Parents warned their chaste children not to associate with Janis. The teachers? Janis's friends made it clear that the faculty was hardly inspiring. To most, her grades, her brightness, her painting meant nothing. Their attention was to her other activities. Mrs. Joplin was called over to the school and asked why she couldn't get Janis to be "average." Janis herself was brought in and admonished for her behavior. She got louder, she got cruder. Again, she began to seek companionship with the hoody toughs and their girls. Karleen said that in the bombast, the extroversion that seemed to increase, there was an acute withdrawal behind, as it would ever be, the center, a depression that foamed up as the whirlwind of a constant hysterical display.

Janis had a need to exhibit, and it could not be that she exuded no seductive aura. The beginnings of what would be no control over most of her impulses was splurting up back then, held in only to the extent that her parents could cap the explosion. The unorthodoxy of her ideas, the differences in her interests, her rejection of Port Arthur mores, all stemming from sheer brainpower, increased the hostility of the community. But much of the interest in Janis seems to have been fundamentally sexual. The contempt was for her physical appearance; the hate was for her body mannerisms. And Janis, to protect herself from disintegrating under the pressures, handled her conflicts, terrifying as they were, by simply acting them out. Tary Owens said, "She was like the image of everything the students disliked. It just reached a thing where most of them hated her."

Still, Janis had some friends and if, in view of the over-all attitudes, it took some guts to claim that friendship, they did so nonetheless. But only once, after all the dull-minded praise of her regretfully gone "normality," were there some words that were fired with verve.

"My grandmother!" Arlene Elster cried. "She used to say to me, 'How come you're not like Janis!' Because to *her*, Janis seemed bubbling and happy and cute from *inside*. She didn't see those others things. To her Janis was *alive!* A girl who was really *alive!* She *loved* her!"

"Good grief! What was your grandmother like?"

"Oh," Arlene said, "she was just a little old lady who did a lot of baking around the house."

4

While Janis continued to make excellent grades in her senior year, she was at a miserable sixteen, hardly living up to her potential; but then her teachers were more concerned with her peculiarities than with her obviously high intelligence. Nor was she attending school full-time. As the atmosphere became more intolerable and it was clear that she could meet the requirements for graduation without the full-time burden of classes, she began to reduce her attendance. She took a job as a waitress and worked, for a while, selling tickets at a local theater. Sometimes in the evenings she dropped in to Pasea's coffeeshop, where Port Arthur's "beatniks" hung out. On the walls of the coffeeshop were some of Janis's paintings. She had begun to sell a few of them, and she had found one other means of brightening her days. She had started to sing.

Right before the folk music boom, the "in" people, if anyone remembers, were listening to jazz. That was in the good old days when "in" was "out" and the masses were the masses. No taste. They were listening to rock and roll. Janis and friends were listening to jazz, qualified by Jim Langdon—"progressive jazz." As folk music got under way, they switched to that. Through Grant Lyons, Janis had heard some Leadbelly records, but the Kingston Trio was favored by the group, and by Janis, Odetta.

Karleen remembers Janis singing on some junior high auditorium program in a piping soprano like a wobbly flute. The adults loved it. "She *sang*," one of her teachers protested. "Not that caterwauling she did later."

It was in her sophomore year that Janis began singing along with records; she had an ingenious gift for mimicking voices. "You couldn't tell one from the other," her mother nodded, "she did it so effectively."

When she'd perfected a flawless imitation of Odetta, she did exactly the same with Jean Ritchie, able to flick her timbre from the heated entreaty of the one to the clean falsetto of the other.

A story of Janis's that she happened upon her Odetta voice at a party is hard to confirm. Jim Langdon merely remembered a call.

"Hey! Guess what! I think I can sing!" Janis cried.

He ignored her. Thinking back on the incident, he explained his reaction. "I mean, Janis was the painter. *I* was the musician."

"She painted when I met her," Bob Clark said.

Bob Clark is from Beaumont and became friendly with Janis in her senior year through those of her friends who were over at Lamar. Being a member of the intelligentsia, so to speak, he fit in immediately.

"She didn't sing at all as such," he added. "I remember her sounding like Odetta all right, but she just sang along with the rest of us."

If there was a moment of discovery, it was Janis's alone, lost to the others in a hundred hours of song and many a wild night on that zany Rainbow Bridge. Bob, Janis, Grant, and Jim would make their way along the fragile catwalks, their arms out for balance like gliders in the breeze. Only the moon was cool, its reflection spiraling down to kick frosty caps over the dirty face of the Neches. Like little mannequins on that monstrous bridge, they'd dangle their feet off the edge, and the burning nights got damper as the steam of danger formed droplets on their skin and their lungs burst with the exhilaration of the forbidden. They sang, the rest of them, and Janis scorched the stars with a secret.

In May of 1960, Janis graduated from Thomas Jefferson High. College presumably would be a relief. She would meet people with different viewpoints who would surely appreciate her ideas, her artwork, her interests. Of course the college was Lamar, in Beaumont, although Janis's parents can hardly be faulted for urging her to attend that school. With the horrendous difficulties she'd had in high school, they felt it best she remain nearby, at least until she was a little older. They were actually grateful that she went at all.

Considering the size of Port Arthur, much less its grim proprieties, the criticism of Janis had to place dramatic strain on the Joplin household. "Here we have a precocious kid who's been selling oil paintings," Mrs. Joplin elaborated. "We're not big Chamber of Commerce people, but we were contributors to our community. Anybody in this kind of a category and then one of their children has some trouble and that's going to be a favorite source of gossip."

Surely, along with the realization that Janis was troubled and that she had been literally battered by the cruelty of her schoolmates, was the discomfort of being subjected to that gossip. Mrs. Joplin must have been frightened too by the character of Janis's behavior. Karleen witnessed some fiery arguments, and Mrs. Joplin did not deny them. Moreover, Janis and her mother were locked in an intractable knot tied by a similarity of temperament. Mrs. Joplin was as forceful as Janis; the collision was head-on and hard. Janis refused to do anything her parents thought advisable. When she finally agreed to go to Lamar, it was not in a spirit of willingness.

For a year, until the summer of 1961, she remained in the area. She went to her classes at Lamar; she took courses at Port Arthur College and learned how to work office machines. Sometime during that period she also ran off to Houston and, in a few days of hanging around The Purple Onion Coffeeshop, managed to get herself quite ill. She drank a great deal and ate hardly at all. Distraught and sick, she stumbled back home and had to go into the hospital, Mrs. Joplin said for the treatment of a kidney infection. After Janis left the hospital, she saw a psychiatrist for a short period of time in Port Arthur and also, during that year, a psychologist in Beaumont.

Mrs. Joplin said that they had permitted the psychiatric sessions without objection. Indeed, Janis seems to have blown that whole episode out of proportion. One of her friends got some impression that she'd had insulin shock at the time. (She would mention to a few of her friends, including myself, something about an early "nervous breakdown.") A few years later, she had some extended sessions with a psychiatric social worker in Beaumont, a man of extremely high caliber. Although that is another matter, he told me that Janis had discussed the earlier counseling but made no reference to any kind of psychotic episode. Her public talk was apparently untrue.

She did, however, land up in a hospital in Beaumont. "She was cutting classes," Mrs. Joplin said angrily, "and her conscience was bothering her!"

That Janis was tormented is certain. With that restive infidel thundering at the gate! It might at least have had the bloody kindness to possess her. Janis always had two devils, the visible one no more ferocious than her demon saint from heaven, come down to rake her over the coals of hell.

But it should have been a decent enough year. The hub that had formed around Janis's Port Arthur friends had expanded to include new members, one of whom was a fellow named Johnny Moyer. Wally and Tommy Stopher were two others. It was, in fact, Tommy Stopher's painting that ultimately so affected Janis that she stopped her own. She decided her gift was short of genius, and as Tary Owens remarked, "If she couldn't be the best in the world, she wasn't gonna do it!"

There were female friends in Beaumont, too. Janis roomed with the girl who later became Adrian Haston's wife, and she was friendly with Jim Langdon's fiancée Rae, whom he married in May of 1961.

Nonetheless, Janis was discontented, and in the summer of 1961 the Joplins paid her way to Los Angeles, probably not certain that it was the correct move, but willing in any case to give it a try. Mrs. Joplin had a sister in Los Angeles; Janis could stay

with her until she found a job. Janis did, in fact, live
with her aunt for a few weeks, in the meantime getting a job as a keypunch operator with the Los Angeles Telephone Company. Mrs. Joplin said that
Janis, upon getting her first paycheck, moved into a
nice little apartment within commuting distance of
her job.

"Then," Mrs. Joplin added with a muttering reluctance, "she moved from there to a more economical
area and . . ."

"She moved to Venice," Mr. Joplin said firmly.

". . . got a close-to-the-beach place," Mrs. Joplin
continued, "which is the kind of thing that would appeal to her. My sister was upset. It was an area of
which she didn't approve." Mrs. Joplin added hastily,
"It was the beatnik area."

Powell St. John, who later became one of Janis's close
friends at the University of Texas, remembered his
astonishment upon meeting Janis when she returned
from California. "I'd had no experience with beatniks!
I'd read their stuff, but I didn't know if I'd ever *seen*
one. After talking with her, I had to go back and con-
sult the glossaries and find out what she was!"

"Well, doesn't anybody around here ball, man?"
she'd asked loudly.

Powell said, "I had to stop and think and then I answered, 'NO! NO! As a matter of fact, they don't!'"

"What's the matter with everybody?" Janis had
yelped. "I want to turn everybody on to that!"

"I mean," Powell said, "we were just kids from
straight middle-class families . . . of course, so was
she." He gagged as a sly, knowing laugh stuck in his
throat. "But," he added, "Janis had transcended all
that, you see."

Actually, Janis's Texas friends knew little about her
Venice experiences, although a few of them are certain that she spent at least a few days in San Francisco around the same time.

"That's where she got that sheepskin jacket," Rae

Langdon remarked. "I'll never forget that. She had on
that jacket, and my sister, who is very straight, like
to died when she walked in. Janis was lounging
around on the couch next to Jim and my sister just
freaked!"

Janis apparently had stopped off in Beaumont to
advise her friends of her newfound worldliness,
which very likely had something to do with her blast-
off greeting to Powell. From most of the people in
Texas I got the impression that Janis's flamboyance,
that awesome braggadocio in her carriage and
speech, so shattered their senses—unhinged them,
really—that they were quite incapable of suspecting
so much as the slightest exaggeration. She did everything she said. And did it bother her? Never.

I asked Powell if he hadn't been slightly intimidated by his introduction to Janis.

"Good Lord, yes!" he chuckled. "Nobody knew
what to make of her! You didn't have a *chance* to
think about it. We just accepted it, I guess. I mean, it
was neat! It was cool! It *was!* Because it was fucking
brand new!"

Whatever had happened to Janis in Venice, it
could hardly have been so thrilling as she claimed. "I
met people just like myself," she would say. True, she
was only eighteen at the time, but had the Venice
escapade provided her with such a sense of identity,
it is somewhat peculiar that she returned voluntarily
to Texas. After a few days at the Langdons', she
showed up at her parents' home, unexpectedly, and
stayed in Port Arthur until the summer of 1962.

It was during that year that Janis began to sing in
public. The first time was New Year's Eve right after
her return from Venice when, encouraged by Jim
Langdon, she performed at a Beaumont club. By that
time, Janis had started listening to Bessie Smith.

Dramatic it would be if her listeners had been
smitten with ecstasy and had risen to their feet to bel-
low for more. But they knew the crests of a Chris
Connor freedom, and the blues to them was Anita

O'Day. Janis was met with the limpest response and applause that crackled about as loudly as crumbling old yellow paper.

What is interesting is that the disaster of that night apparently didn't deter her; she started singing at the Half-Way House in Beaumont and at The Purple Onion in Houston, where a year before she'd pressed herself into the crowd as a pathetic runaway on the loose. Also in 1962, she cut a tape, a commercial for a bank in Nacogdoches, Texas. Jim Langdon and Tary Owens set it to the music of Woody Guthrie's "This Land Is Your Land," and Jim wrote the jingle:

> *This bank is your bank*
> *This bank is my bank*
> *From Nacogdoches to the Gulf Coast waters.*
> *Sixty years of savings*
> *Sixty years of earnings*
> *This bank was made for you and me.*

There it was: the first recording Janis Joplin ever made.

5

That is one thing that happened that year; another was a curious shift in Janis's personality.

Those days in Port Arthur began with relative constraint. Janis returned to Lamar in the spring of 1962 and was conscientious in her studies. During vacation periods, she took a job as a waitress at a bowling alley in nearby Port Neches. She lost weight, and at work, one of those tight white little aprons wrapped trim

and starchy around her waist, went placidly about
her business. She wore makeup. She took her long
crimpy hair and, to the delight of her mother, pinned
it up so that it puffed out in a soft nestling mound
above the nape of her neck.

Janis's job ended at midnight, and usually, when it
was over, she'd drive calmly back to Port Arthur.
She'd pick up Jack Smith and they'd go to the beach
with a six-pack of beer, which they'd split evenly.
They'd talk and Janis would be home by one-thirty
or two, everything simple, serene. On nights when
Janis wasn't working, they'd frequently go dancing.

She was worried, she said, about the unfeminine
things, the coarseness that sometimes plagued her
that she didn't understand—and some of the things
she was doing. She could not imagine the why of it or
what in her she had to find to stop it from happening
again. So her manners were not gruff, but even delicate, requesting Jack please to light her cigarettes
and open the door. Jack would respect what she
seemed to need and performed those formalities with
an understanding gentleness, though when they
danced it cost him his own personal comfort because
he was awkward on the dance floor, felt gawky, and
did not like to think that anyone might notice. So
Janis, grateful for the way he treated her, never
asked him to do that except when the music was very
slow.

As for going to the beach, when they reached the
water, they very often drove onto the pier. Janis
would talk about being buried by the sand as if that
were to be all of her life and say that Jack, who was
writing poetry and painting experimental things, was
doing *that*, but the main thing he was doing was being Jack and Nova (Nova, whom he later married
but who was not in Port Arthur at the time).

The beach has an eluvial shore at the particular
coast where Janis and Jack most often went. You can
walk out a quarter of a mile before the water begins
to tickle your waist, and where the bottom sinks in a

gradual slope the sea is luminous with plankton. Young couples would roll and splash in that plankton and let it tint their bodies. All up and down the beach, there would be figures lying about like macabre lamps in the dark. Janis and Jack did that a lot. Then, very slowly, the dreamy hours that floated so sweetly changed and began to tumble and jolt with anxiety. The six-pack of beer turned into a bottle of Thunderbird for Janis, and from Thunderbird to bourbon.

Janis abandoned the placid mood that had lasted at least a few months, left it as if it hadn't been there at all. They kept going to the beach, though the quality of her ways had changed. Sometimes the fog would come in and swallow the beachline, making the area dangerous indeed. But Janis would drive as if she and Jack had been spun out of a compression cylinder of some sort, jagging at sixty, seventy miles an hour in that fog where you couldn't see the hood, much less the water, and screeching, whnnnnh, to a stop, would brake it there just where the waters would tease at the tires.

The days and nights began to jar, and from the beach Janis and Jack started to move again into the Louisiana bar scene, which had been a hectic fury before. The escapades got wilder and the franticness resumed, then increased. It was like jet streams, Jack said, maddened and frenzied gropings, and her words a brutal harangue. Suddenly, to him, it was unnatural, and nothing like it had been before.

"It became some phenomenal energy thing that had to be sated and some tension that she couldn't release." Jack gasped at the memory. His Lincolnesque face turned ashen. "It reminded me of some later Van Gogh self-portraits, like Vincent in flames! The swirling brush strokes all around and this cool blue and his flaming red beard and those strange, strange eyes. As if it were going to *smash* out at you! You could see it in her! Like an incredible frenzy! You could just see it!"

"Didn't the 'nice kids' in Port Arthur go across the river?" I asked.

"No" Jim Langdon claimed. "That's where you went to do your sinnin'! It was late hours, booze, women, violence, all that good ole luscious sin. We had the chance to see something really important—like somebody killed! Most of the kids who went were dumb-assed, mean-assed, mother-fucker kids. But *we* went in a different spirit . . . uh . . . like Hemingway awe!" Strutting around the room, he nodded somberly, "Kind of the spirit of *The Sun Also Rises*. It was the nearest we could get to going to Pamplona for the running of the bulls!"

It was mostly Lou Ann's, but the Big Oak too, and Buster's, maybe one or two more, all beer joints pasted on a roadside strip across the Sabine River on the Louisiana side. Not much difference among them, all big and barren with dulled wooden floors, their homely bareness relieved by the fussy swirl of dark greasy patches, a mosaic made by large clacking feet. A good stomp and a film of gray swims up to settle on the face, and only a strong barking cough can move the taste of it from the tongue and scratch through the coating on the roof of the mouth. Along with the dust in the air is a bristling danger, the still meanness of poolhalls in the back and the omnipresent evil of knives in the pocket. It's code-of-the-hills country, and they don't take to Texans in those bars. If the strip caters to those who slip over the border to have a drink and a dance, the Louisiana clientele likes it no better for the fact that the cash is green and good and plentiful. The rednecks are wary, with the slyest of eyes and lips that curl down suspensefully at the corners. A menacing white engraves their cruel knuckles: a stranger is your enemy till he proves he's not.

"I saw a guy get his stomach cut out from one side to the other," Bob Clark said blithely, "fell right out in his hands. Three o'clock in the afternoon it was and my girlfriend," he laughed, "just kept on knitting."

Janis loved going across the river. They all did, but if the "nice kids"—meaning well-behaved boys—didn't go, it was even less customary for Port Arthur or Beaumont girls to frequent the area. Janis? She was just "one of the guys," so she charged into the Louisiana bars with a style honed by the roughest grindstone she could summon. She shot pool with the rednecks and a dance if you please, along with a very risky come-on and words Louisiana toughs don't like to hear from women, and if they do, it's a quick one on a grimy mattress and don't try kidding around about it, don't try that at all.

"She'd get them to pay her way," Jim said. "She'd take beers when they wanted to buy her beers, and when it was time to go, she was ready to go, all right —with *us!* It took four or five of us to make sure we'd get out of there alive!"

Jack Smith chuckled sweetly, "One to keep the car running, one at the door, one to watch Janis, and one to yell when it all started happening!"

One Sunday night began a typical madness that got even madder than most.

For many a church-going citizen in Beaumont, Texas, it was another good day with the Lord. For Janis and her friends at Lamar, it was the dullest day of the week. On Sunday, the bars in Louisiana don't open until midnight, and this Sunday was particularly boring. The weeks before had passed too quietly, and the torpor of inactivity, longer than usual for them, had weighted their bodies and cramped their nerves so that there was an especial tautness to the mood when they struck out for Louisiana shortly before midnight.

"Let's go in and dance," Janis urged huskily when, after a tour of the other bars, they finally hit Lou Ann's. "Come on, let's go!"

"I'm broke," Jack said. "Had enough anyway."

Philip Carter slouched in the back of Dave McQueen's secondhand Olds, vintage '56, "It's three in the morning, for chrissake," he said wearily.

"Anybody coming?" Patty Skaff yelled. "What's this waiting around? Lez go!"

Stepping out of the car, Patty thumped with determined footsteps toward the entrance. She was Dave McQueen's girlfriend, prone to outdoing Janis in the Louisiana saloons, and Dave did not cotton to that manner of habit.

"If you wanna go, you get somebody to pay your way," he barked angrily. Dave sat with the car door open, his left foot uncertainly on the ground.

Jim Langdon stood near the hood of the car. Johnny Moyer and Jack remained in the back seat, waiting for the developments.

"Fuck you." Janis glared. "We'll do it! You don' have t' pay for us." She stomped after Patty.

Janis and Patty got the rednecks to pay and to dance with them too while the others watched and got drunk. Dave McQueen slumped in a chair, seething, and got drunker than the rest. Then, when the sun began to rise, they piled back into the Olds and Dave McQueen crashed his foot down on the accelerator, as if he would mash it right on through the bottom of the car.

"Goddamn this piece of junk," he growled. "It's crawling like a fucking cow!"

Janis, Johnny Moyer, and Jack sat in the back seat, with Philip Carter squeezed in on the left, half of his body in Jack Smith's lap. In the front, Jim Langdon plopped shotgun next to Patty.

"Look at your speedometer, Dave!" he cautioned.

"Look at it, hell," Dave hissed. "The dashboard light doesn't even work! Gimme a match!"

"Man," Johnny Moyer warned, "jes cuz yer mad at Patty don' mean ya have t' try t' kill all of us! Ya better slow down!"

Janis's wild cackle peeled through the car as Jack pleaded nervously, "Take it easy."

Dave McQueen took his right hand off the wheel and bent a match back to whiz it to life with his

thumb. "It only says a hundred n' ten," he said grimly.
"I'm gonna get it to a hundred n' twenty!"

Terror quieted everyone else, and the only sound
was a snap in the front as Dave McQueen lit matches
to keep an eye on his speed.

"Ouch!" A thread of fire snuck down the matchstick
to bite his busy thumb. Striking another match, he
ripped over from the access road onto the freeway
and twisted the wheel crazily with his left hand. He
careened the wheel back, but it was too late. The car
bounced once, then shuddered sideways and stuck
one second on the precipice of motion before it
vaulted.

'Hey, don't spill my beer," cried a voice hanging
from the ceiling of the car.

"Good God, we'll all be killed," someone shrieked.

Three times over and smack, the car shot across the
spread of freeway and rolled into a ditch.

For a minute all was still.

"Anybody hurt?" Dave gasped.

"Not a scratch," they said as they climbed out of the
ruins one by one, stunned, panting, and astonished.

Jack Smith said, "While that car was moving, I
thought I heard someone say, 'I hope we'll all be
killed!'"

As the year went on, the parties accelerated, and finally one night, after another crazy scene in Louisiana, Janis and Jack roared back into Texas, drank up
the state, and drove on to Austin. They arrived at a
rundown set of tenement apartment houses called
The Ghetto at five thirty-seven exactly. In one of
them, sitting on top of a refrigerator, was a gangly
young man with fierce blue eyes. He was singing
loudly and well, and also strumming a banjo.

Janis clasped her hands together. "I love it!" she
cried. "I love it! I'm going to stay!"

6

"Oh! *Now* it's jumping!" John Clay agreed about the change at the University of Texas in Austin. "They're fixin' to build a wall around the campus *now!* It wasn't like this *then!* No sir-ree!"

When Janis came to the university in the summer of 1962, the fraternity and sorority conglomerates had the campus wrapped up in a toxic conformity. It was worse than in Port Arthur. Bubble hairdos were imperative for girls, and black suede loafers were demanded. Kneesocks that were white and of a special ribbing were rolled back just so many inches to hit the assigned proper point on the calf.

John sneered dryly. "The frat guys wore black *leather* loafers, and wheat jeans, tan, with a wave *al-*most suggesting corduroy."

John Clay comes from Stamford, Texas, smack in the middle of church-dominated country, and his rebellion against it is evident, partially in those fierce blue eyes (it was John Clay sitting on the refrigerator that weary Texas morning) and partially in his pugnacious speech. He slams into the t's of his words, branding them just like cows, and is still busy telling Cotton Mather he can take his hell and shove it where it belongs. An emphatic "you know" punches his sentences, and he ricochets from one subject to the other as fast as the bullets that whizzed down from the Texas Tower when Charles Whitman went mad.

"What did you major in?" I asked him in amazement.

"Linguistics," he replied quickly. "It was on Nineteenth and Nueces."

"Your linguistics classes?"

"*No!* Janis's rooming house! But she hung around The Ghet-to!"

At the end of a very sallow decade, the color of the San Francisco beat scene touched Texas as it did everyplace else. Throughout most of the state it faded as fast as a cool spell in Juarez. In Austin it stuck. By the early sixties, there was an established "beat" milieu, and The Ghetto was its center of gravity.

A dingy apartment complex six blocks from the campus, it was approachable only through the alleys in the back; the apartments rented for thirty, thirty-five dollars a month, and they were a scummy mess. Living there were Powell St. John, Jim Langdon, the Stopher brothers, John Clay, and, for a while, Jack Smith. Mostly it was a place of revolving residency, home ground for the campus rebels, no matter where they slept. Bob Clark, Dave Moriaty, and Tary Owens frequently made their way through the falling plaster, and Johnny Moyer zoomed up from Beaumont on weekends. A whole crowd of people circulated on the fringes. There were Fredda Slote, Julie Paul, Winn Pratt, and Robert Shelton, the cartoonist who, along with Dave Moriaty, was kicking things up on the campus paper, the *Texas Ranger*. Then there was a fellow named Bill Killeen, with whom Janis lived when she first hit the campus. Their affair didn't last.

A disdain for campus norms was one of the themes of The Ghetto crowd, but just as important was music. Austin was the center of a tiny, extremely intense folk music movement, and that too was distinguished from the tastes of the other students. Naturally, the division followed the lines of general conformity and defiance. The straights were hung up on the Kingston Trio. At The Ghetto they cared about ethnic folk. The advocates of country and blues were a smaller and scruffier bunch, to be sure. What they had were a terrific enthusiasm and a persistence that was powerfully effective. It was they who held unchallenged control of the folksings that took place in the Union Building on the campus.

The night after Janis arrived, she was singing with that crowd, backed by Powell St. John on harmonica and Lanny Wiggins on bass. There would be no more ignoring of Janis's talent—not by *those* people. She and Lanny and Powell made a musical unit called The Waller Creek Boys. That was the name they already had; they didn't care to change it. During her University of Texas days, they stayed a permanent trio. They performed at the Union Building on Sunday afternoons and at a converted yellow filling station called Threadgill's on many a Wednesday night.

"It looks the same here more or less," Ken Threadgill drawled. Cocking his head, he eyed a lightbulb that protruded from a crumbling tinfoil shade. "Yep, it ain't changed."

Behind the bar was an autumn-toned painting, all umber and olive, its gilded frame straddling a shelf at a peculiar precarious angle. It was an ancient-looking thing but strong, its drama of cowboys and Indians determinedly flaring through a blotchy shield of soil. At ten-thirty in the morning, the day was working its way painfully through a mustard-colored blind. The light began to spread and drew a gray sheen from the felt Stetson of an early customer downing a Lone Star beer.

"Had this place nigh on thirty-eight years," Mr. Threadgill murmured. He touched a thickly veined hand to his thin silver hair and leaned his large body over the decaying linoleum countertop. "Music here since 1946." Nodding proudly, he pulled himself to his full height and patted the apron that covered his paunch.

Mr. Threadgill himself sings in a high country purity that bears a resemblance to Jimmie Rodgers, but his speaking voice is deep and sentimental, as is the cast of his wise blue eyes.

"You wouldn't ev'n rekinize this place on Wednesday nights," he said, "them kids just come packin' in."

Piles of old seventy-eights were stashed beneath the epic tale of the white man and the redskin. A sign dangled higher, advertising soft drinks for fifteen cents, wine for thirty-five.

"I giss I bridge the generation gap," he continued. "I git a real bang out of 'em, the kids. Other people sometimes say. 'Well, whadda ya *see* in 'em!' I don't know as I c'n rightly say. Thar jes nice 'n' friendly. And Janis! She was singin' bluegrass in that high shrill voice of hers. Most of the time she didn't use anything, but lots of times she played an autoharp, right up at that round table over yonder."

A thousand signatures had been burned into the surface of the heavy oak table. Hers was etched in with the others, right over a large heart, its fragile lines pierced by the stabs of those hard tough J's. Above her name was scrawled, "Mr. Threadgill. I love you."

"Yep," Mr. Threadgill said softly. "She was jes' like one of mah own kids." He looked at me questioningly. "She *drank!* I know that, but she never took to no drugs. Only thing I c'n imagine is . . . recording is reeel hard." He shook his head thoughtfully. "At the Newport Festival in sixty-eight there was a party and I sang and she took a sofa pilla and sat right down at mah feet. When she died I . . ." His voice trailed off. "I thought the world of that girl."

Mr. Threadgill removed his rimless glasses and poked at the inner corners of his eyes. Glancing down at his apron, he carefully smoothed it out. "I loved her," he sighed.

During her Austin days, Janis was not very comfortable about singing in public. She was shy, for one thing, and really without a commitment to any particular style. She sang blues like Bessie Smith, with her notes as open as the Texas sky. In ballads she'd turn to her Jean Ritchie voice and a xylophone purity, no toughness. She'd slide from that to a whining country and wring it dry, Rosie Maddox. There was this style and the other; the one she chose depended upon the extent of audience acceptance.

It is a contention of Mrs. Joplin that Janis, with calculation, settled on blues and rock, varnishing herself an image she thought befitted the music. Her belief has some foundation. Janis had enrolled at the University of Texas as an art student and then gave up her painting because of Tommy Stopher's work and her conviction that she was not destined to be a painter of true greatness. Even more to the point, as Tary Owens remembered, she almost gave up singing when a girl came to Austin who sounded like Joan Baez! "She always said it," he insisted, "she didn't want to do it unless she could be the best there was in whatever sphere she was in."

A few years later in San Francisco, she said to her friend Bob Clark, "You know, I'm trying hard to make it and I feel like there's one other person. If she makes it, I won't; and if I make it, *she* won't."

Bob Clark astonished me by saying, "That person was Judy Collins!"

The Austin crowd was almost unanimous, too, in the belief that Janis actually lost her voice before she joined Big Brother. Hearing Janis in a thirty-foot room backed by a harmonica and bass may have been deceptive, but they are adamant in that view. Her voice was piercing and clear, with none of the rasp that strafed out of her throat later on; her volume and range were unfathomable.

"It got to be a whiskey voice," John Clay fiercely insisted, "from drinking all that goddamn hard liquor! She'd pretty well lost her voice by the time she was really famous. That really gets me! Janis Joplin was blowin' America's mind at half power!"

There are some among the Austin crowd still resentful that Janis never spoke very much of those days. It was, they feel, the first time she received any true recognition as a singer, and their hurt is genuine that she failed to give those who encouraged her some credit for so doing. "About the last thing you'd ever expect Janis to do," John Clay snorted, "if you knew her real good, was to tell how many people helped her."

The suggestion that Janis was egocentric was hardly unwarranted. Janis's emotional world was small, consisting almost entirely of her own desires and needs. Rarely did she talk of her Austin companions, nor did she mention their encouragement. Still, Janis's tendency was to linger only on the experience of the moment. Perhaps more important was what that Austin experience basically meant, the encouragement of her talent quite secondary in her mind to some very bitter memories. Excepting the gratification from her singing, Janis was wretched, a great deal more than seems to have been known.

She was treated as a figure of ridicule by the student body at large. Her torn-off jeans, her tennis shoes or bare feet, her long hair, her autoharp, drove them crazy with anger. She provoked as she had in Port Arthur, purposefully gruff in the presence of campus regulars. But as in Port Arthur, her participation in her own unhappiness did not diminish the pain.

It is significant that Janis never failed to speak of Ken Threadgill when chatting about her past. She was certain of his affection. Nor was her relationship to that endearing old man marred by the character of her other associations. The supreme summary of that? "Our attitude," John Clay said, "when she became famous was 'one of our boys made it!'"

She partied, she drank, she percolated vulgarity. The trips to the Louisiana bars continued.

Winn Pratt had a similar temperament, and one time at the Shady Rest Motel Lounge an across-the-river tough saw Janis as fair game, then made a remark that heated up Winn. There was a fight, and "YOU TEXAS SONOFABITCH!" the man shouted as he whopped a fist into Winn Pratt's face. Janis and the pack scrambled to the safety of their cars. Still, a bottle made it to Johnny Moyer's jaw, and a crunch thundered through to his brain as the bone in his face splintered and his vision, for a minute, went very black.

Jim Langdon said this was an important incident, because Janis was being "her usual self" . . . "a catalyst for trouble," he called her. But the victim steamed through with thoughts of his own. "I don't think she was her *usual* self," Johnny Moyer reflected. "Everybody gets louder and more belligerent in that kind of environment. . . ."

Jim: ". . . but it was very easy to get into troub . . ."

Johnny: ". . . and you're influenced by whoever you're with!"

It was somewhat beyond a matter of influence. Janis had perpetuated that arrangement begun long ago in Port Arthur, now firmly fixed in the weird labyrinth of expectation and fulfillment.

You stumble awkwardly on greeting a neighbor; the next time you stumble again. It is understood that you will do that. A mutual understanding of your clumsiness has been reached, agreed upon by both. And wanted too. In the presence of that person, you are ever after a bumbling fool. So it is that relationships can become bizarre transactions, the seed of some minor behavior blossoming into an irrevocable commitment.

At The Ghetto, Janis showed the face of a boisterous, partying hell-raiser. She bounced loudly around, calling herself "a jive chick." She hit John Clay over the head with a toy bucket. She was generally wild.

"One time," John Clay said heatedly, "she was wrestling this guy and she started screaming and I came in to say, 'Stop screaming!' She sounded like someone being raped! She's going, 'Shriek! Shriek!' Then I banged her on the head! And she screamed *louder!*" He dropped his voice. "She would occasionally drive people to the point of attacking her back then."

She often got very drunk, and on one occasion threw Julie Paul down the stairs. She brought grass into The Ghetto.

"That was a damned risky thing to do!" John Clay flared up again. "We were being watched." Gritting his teeth, he added, "I actually thought she was very corny."

As for Janis bringing grass into The Ghetto, John Clay was right. She had smoked a few joints in high school, but it is well known by all of her friends that she never really liked grass. Assuredly, bringing it into The Ghetto was to impress people with the hipness she'd acquired in Venice.

Actually there was no drug scene to speak of at the University of Texas back then, though peyote was legal and some of the crowd ate it from time to time. Janis tried it, then stopped because of adverse reactions. Never did she take to psychedelics or, for that matter, to any of the peripheral philosophies they spun. What she did take in Austin was Seconal; the first mention of that came from Julie Paul.

"She'd take a whole lot of it and run crazy. She'd walk the streets at night and try to get run over and run into buildings with her head."

I told Julie that no one else had indicated Janis had been so depressed.

Julie grimaced. "I don't know where everybody *was!*"

Well, she yakked like a crow and laughed like a loon. That was what most of them remembered, the hell-raising and the nuttiness and the wild, brawling times. There was no failure to recognize her unhappiness, just a crude incomprehension of its depths.

"What I *do* remember," Jim Langdon remarked, "was one night when Janis said, 'There's Jack and Nova, there's Jim and Rae, there's this one and that one, but there's always just Janis.'" His face fell for a second, then brightened. "Actually, though, *she* was the one who was included, and our girlfriends were excluded. Janis was one of the guys! I never knew her when she had a steady man. She was always independent and freewheeling!"

"You really think she was independent?"

"That's a silly question," he replied brusquely. "Of course she was an independent girl. I mean, she had a large ego to gratify. She certainly sought and needed other people's acceptance, but she was very definitely an independent person. There was nobody else controlling her destiny! That's for sure!"

On an overcast day, Jack Smith drove me around the hills of Austin, rich with mounds of bluebonnets, the state flower of Texas. We went by the spot where Winn Pratt, after leaving behind a suicide note, drove off a six-hundred-foot cliff. He shot the car so fast, it went clear over to the other side of the river below. We drove up on a mountain and turned the car around where the shrubs are crusted with lime, their scraggly branches glistening like oddly misshapen bones.

Jack said, "Janis was supersensitive to human frailty, both to notice it and to soothe it. She never caused a hurt in somebody who was vulnerable. I never saw her throw the first punch or jump on anybody who didn't jump first."

Sometime during the winter, Janis was publicly pilloried for the benefit of the entire student body at the University of Texas, nominated for the lofty position of Ugliest Man on Campus. The Joplins received an anguished letter. If she was different, well, she was different. But what right, she wanted to know, did man have to be so inhuman? Was there some God-given sanctity for certain people that she hadn't understood? What could permit her to be treated the way she'd been treated by the students on that campus? Janis explained that she had to leave. Mrs. Joplin called the Dean of Women, but Janis had gone. Inquiries were made, and finally the Joplins were informed that Janis had taken off for San Francisco.

Part Two
The New Jerusalem

7

"The God's truth, man! If anyone says she played that autoharp in Texas, they're living in a dream!" The carrot-red ropes of Chet Helms's hair flipped wildly about as he shook his head. "Maybe she strummed it a little, but she always chose accompanists or sang *a cappella*."

Once Chet Helms had been an engineering student at the University of Texas, and as proper as they come. It was the civil rights movement that kicked off his conversion and a need to get out of Texas. The emerald city was San Francisco, until wanderlust grabbed him again. In the winter of 1962, he headed back for Austin and skidded right into The Ghetto crowd. "A can of bullshit there!" he said. "The whole alcohol mudra! You know, everyone gets drunk and says, 'Ho, ho!'"

But Janis! She seemed—well—liberated. The embodiment of sexual freedom, he thought, available of an instant, without inhibition, simply beyond the repressions that so bound others, or certainly Texas girls. He could *talk* to her, he said, as if she were "one of the guys."

It was the vision that appealed, a stretching out of his fantasies, because Chet was shy and lacked the courage to deal very comfortably with Janis's bluntness. No physical intimacies ever occurred, as he made it very clear. Still, she *seemed* so free, and for that alone he was enamored of her presence. And

53

what a marvelous companion on the road she would be, a vagabond like himself.

He had also heard her sing, and knowing the San Francisco folk music structure, which he did, he was able to convince her that opportunity lay in California. That, but mostly the awesome unhappiness climaxed by the Ugliest Man Contest, stirred Janis's decision to leave. On a Wednesday night in January of 1963, she sang one more time at Threadgill's and, shortly after midnight, hit the road.

She had, of course, gone everyplace and done everything and hitchhiked many a time. Jim Langdon claimed that her parents hardly ever knew where she was. She'd just be off, her head pounding, her blood churning, a fire inside, and it was the call of the wild that would get her.

Some twenty miles from Austin, Janis cried out forlornly, "Chet! I've never hitchhiked more than twenty miles in my life!"

Recalling the incident, Chet chuckled, "I'll never forget that. Her confession! She talked to everybody like she was a 'man of the world,' and there she was, terrified!"

They continued on to Fort Worth. Chet's family lived there and would provide them with one night's shelter, or so Chet hoped. They were out of there in an hour. Janis was grubby with dirt. Her mannish attire shocked Chet's folks. Their son and this strange loud girl were not married either and were hoofing it across the country. "It created a crisis in my mother's religion," Chet sighed.

The rejection upset Janis terribly: Chet discovered many things about her he hadn't realized before. One was the fact that she was very well-read, which was not quite in keeping with her guttersnipe style. Nor did she yawp with the competitive desperation that was usually so apparent. "She had a fantastic mind really," he nodded. "I didn't see those things initially."

It took them fifty hours to get to San Francisco. All weary and crusted with filth from the road, they went straight to North Beach without a rest. Janis sang that very first night at Coffee and Confusion on Upper Grant Avenue. Her voice was blue and gold and blazing, bringing down a rain of audience gratefulness and coins dredged up from skimpy pockets. Janis was endowed with fourteen dollars. No collection had ever before been permitted at the club.

In the winter of 1963, the North Beach area of San Francisco was in the throes of transition. The weakened remnants of the beat culture remained. Through the steamy windows of the coffeeshops, one could catch a glimpse of a poet or two intertwining a verse with the scale of a saxophone or the muffled thump of a drum. The terrain abounded with painters. The jazz enthusiasts, the artists, and the thriving practitioners of folk music jangled along compatibly. If the beat movement was dying, there was still a surge of excitement in the activity, the early spasms of something about to be born. But because the times were transitional, there was no visible form to any of it, and the media lapsed into relative silence about American bohemia. Spawned by the civil rights movement, the folk music trend was seen as a music linked to politics, but somehow separate. Rebellion did not appear self-conscious; certainly no *putsch* was under way. So for the next three years, it was the best of times, with the exception of the two years after, which were even better than the ones before—or so they nostalgically say.

Janis began singing at The Coffee Gallery, occasionally at Coffee and Confusion. She sang alone, using her autoharp or backed by an accompanist, who was sometimes Jorma Kaukonen, later of the Jefferson Airplane. Word spread fast in North Beach. There was this chunky girl with witchy brown hair. Her skin was scarred and knobby. She wore a dingy man's shirt and ragged jeans. But she could burn out the spine with her voice.

Janis and Chet, in the meantime, crashed at a friend's apartment. It was not too long before Janis moved in with a girl known as JJ and fell in with a North Beach crowd of bluegrass and white gospel-music fans. Ellen Harmon, who would later be an important figure in the creation of the San Francisco dance hall scene, also became her good friend.

Janis held a few jobs off and on (her mother thinks with the Philco Corporation; a companion said the American Can Company), but she was hardly working consistently. Money from singing was strictly petty cash gotten from passing the hat.

"She was living on the dole," Mr. Joplin said. "Unemployment, but there isn't any difference if you don't ever *work*!"

He was right; the trick of staying on unemployment was developed as a job unto itself by many an explorer on the streets of San Francisco. Quite common then, it is a still flourishing practice, although few of the true poor have ever succeeded in polishing the procedure with enough refinement to get away with it. For Janis, in any case, there was some work, some unemployment, some cash from the hat, and some just getting along. She was set apart from the other street people only because she sang, and well, by God, a penny earned is a penny saved. Not Janis? When Julie Paul came to visit her that spring, she found out Janis had a bank account, a mighty hard thing to manage from grubbing on the streets.

Janis was in the habit of saying that when she first went to San Francisco, everything she did was in the headiness of experimentation. Thus she told reporter David Dalton in the summer of 1970: "I wanted to smoke dope, take dope, lick dope, suck dope, fuck dope, anything I could lay my hands on I wanted to do it. . . . Hey, man, what is it? I'll try it. How do you do it? Do you suck it? No? You swallow it? I'll swallow it." Gobs, grabs, bites, swallows, an oral assault if there ever was one, and vivid speech indeed.

Just the same, it must have been a heady experience too to find everything that was deplored in

Texas, now, all of a sudden, *de rigueur*. No one shunned her; no one laughed at her clothes. Everyone was outside. Their regulations—and well they had them—were at least their very own. One of them was the use of drugs. If Janis's impulses were palpitating, so was her empty hurt heart. Dope would bring her *belonging*, and that, above all, was what she was after, always.

For a while she stuck to alcohol, the guzzling of Red Mountain bourbon. Ellen Harmon remembers it well, the days when she and Janis hung out at the coffeeshops and drank on the corners with the winos. "I mean, from the word 'go,'" Ellen reflected, "from the time she hit the street with Chet, she juiced constantly. I could never understand it myself." Ellen's black hair swept over her face as she picked up her youngest son. "I do other things. Not as physically damaging." Not now.

In May of 1970, the Haight-Ashbury Clinic released some data on the course of the drug scene in San Francisco, indicating that the amphetamine craze bloomed between 1967 and 1969, heroin starting around the end of that period in the cyclical syndrome of up to down. On the publicity-reflected scale that is surely true, but nonetheless Janis and everyone she knew was using speed heavily in the early sixties. There was *plenty* of it around. There was a little smack, and naturally, lots and lots of grass.

"Everybody's head is fucked up about dates," Chet apologized, "because we did so much dope. I mean, we walked right into a speed crowd."

A few people say that Janis did not use speed until the summer of 1964. Their misinformation is very likely the result of Janis's tendency to block out from her past what episodes she chose to deny. Her claim was always that liquor and drugs later destroyed her memory. But as a close friend put it, "She'd *say* she couldn't remember. But if she was talking about a specific thing and she *wanted* to remember, she could remember ev-er-eee-thing. Every detail down to which pants and how tight. She had an *incredible* memory."

When Chet met Janis, she was involved with a speed user in Austin, and there is some contention that she may have tried speed even in Venice. Regardless, both Chet and Ellen state that Janis, in San Francisco, took rather rapidly to the rituals of the street. While Janis admitted her involvement with speed, she apparently chose not to remember how early it began and to obliterate entirely one other matter.

Friends who were of major importance to Janis in the late sixties insist she hadn't tampered with heroin at an earlier time. But some months after Janis died, Mrs. Joplin received a call from a girl in Beaumont who'd been witness to Janis's using smack back in her coffeehouse days. And Julie Paul, who was attending Sacramento State College the spring and summer of 1963 and saw Janis on weekends, was emphatic in saying that Janis, at first, was using not speed but heroin. The facts are somewhat sketchy. Julie saw Janis only twice a month and is uncertain how extensive her experience was. Before developing a real heroin habit, she seems to have gone on to speed.

Janis went through that year reaping a host of disasters and seemingly clutching at ways to ruin opportunities. She appeared at the Monterey Folk Festival in the summer of 1963, at least as John Clay was sure, and somehow could not avail herself of the offers that were stimulated by her performance.

One night, walking home, she got brutally mauled by a bunch of speeders in a back alley. Another night, she had a serious motorbike accident. Her relationships with men followed a similar pattern, Janis fulfilling her self-ordained despondency with tragic regularity. She'd been lonely at the University of Texas. She was lonely in San Francisco. Janis struck Ellen as always uneasy with men, the nature of her relationships suggesting an inverted enjoyment, the melancholy bliss of passion forever unfulfilled.

"When you've got a family," Ellen said, "and an old man, it's just not full boar all the time! He's there! But it's not romance! It's something else! It's what keeps families together and it's what's keeping the world together, whatever's left of it anyway. She *liked* to be uncomfortable in a relationship."

Janis's misfortunes continued with a suspect consistency, and so, she must have thought, she'd travel, escape, and find. She jaunted to New York and back and may, at that time, have hit Memphis. Then in the summer of 1964, she decided on New York again. "Searchin'," Chet shrugged. "That was her favorite song."

In New York, Janis took an apartment with another girl somewhere on the Lower East Side. She told her parents that she was working for a data processing company, and for a while that may have been true. Janice Knoll can only remember that Janis was continually at the Knolls' apartment and that she was singing occasionally in a tiny East Village club called Slug's. She wore black Levi's and a black V-neck sweater always. A huge gold watch dangled on a clanking gold chain she drooped constantly around her neck. She had acquired a guitar and sang folksy blues. Her voice was as tough and sleek as the hide of a two-year-old mare. Still, in New York she was hardly noticed.

Janice Knoll is an amiable girl who talks rapidly, accenting, as she goes, unlikely words and syllables. There is an odd, distorted rhythm to her speech.

"Never weeeent outside," she giggled. "Laaaauuuu-ughed a lot."

Janice Knoll does certainly laugh a lot. Her speech is littered with "right?" Both "right?" and a tittering laughter filtered through her insistence that Janis had never used speed before that memorable New York July.

"I'm positive," she exclaimed. "It was the way she was about it. Because we were so loaded, we were just turning on people right and left. We didn't force anyone. Somebody would have to say, 'Lissen, would you turn me on?' Right ? And she wanted to be turned on. Right? And we said, 'Groovy,' right? And we had a pound of the shit. Right?"

Nonetheless, there is no doubt about what happened after. Janis and a group of people sat in a filth-infested apartment on the Lower East Side and shot speed all summer. What did they talk about?

"I don't know," Janice Knoll giggled. "We were reeeeally stoned. I never asked her anything. We were together and we flashed."

It is true that in the early days no one knew very much about speed, but it was a bit hard to swallow Janice Knoll's claim that none of them gave it a thought. "There was no fear, no embarrassment, no nothing."

Yet Janis was very subdued, inside herself and shy, suggesting fear perhaps that she would never have expressed or some kind of conflict she was unable to fathom. Janice Knoll got the impression she was close to her parents. What Janis seemed to stress was an inability to gain understanding, particularly from her mother, but an estrangement born of hostility was absent. She remembered a drawing that someone did of Janis at a mother's breast.

"It was the epitome of her," she whispered.

There was correspondence, and Mrs. Joplin sent Janis clothes—which Janis refused to wear. Evidently she had led her parents to believe she was making progress in her career. Evidently Mrs. Joplin had decided that if Janis was determined to be a singer, she ought to dress for the stage. She had quite a conception of costume. It is a fascinating twist that Janis found the clothes too garish!

There was a blouse, black but embroidered with a flaming orange and glimmering all over with tiny mirrors. There was a robe that was long and tapestry-plush, its white emblazoned with a design of rich scarlet, its lining a voluptuous satin. She gave them to Janice Knoll. "So help me," she remembered, "she said they were too flashy for her!"

In the fall of 1964, Janis returned to San Francisco. Arlene Elster came to town in November and was appalled to find her living in a rooming house on Geary Street in a bad-smelling, dirty small hole. It was, of course, some years before Arlene would have her own infamous reputation as owner of the Sutter Cinema and a proponent of "erotic" film. Back then she represented Port Arthur, and, as she stressed, "Janis didn't seem to want to have anything to do with me."

Before Janis had gone to New York, she'd become friendly with a girl named Linda Wauldron. Later, Linda would marry her boyfriend Malcolm Godfried and move to Hawaii, but prior to that she and Janis were roommates. When Janis left her Geary Street room, she and Linda took an apartment on Baker, in a basement. Janice Knoll showed up that January. "It blew my mind!" she cried. "She was so far into it—a speeed freak!"

As anyone who gets deeply into dope will do in order to buy it, Janis began to deal, which is how she met a girl who would later become a close friend.

Sunshine is blessed with a marvelous sense of humor in spite of a severely depressing background. Part Indian, she was born in a police car in Milwaukee and grew up on a reservation. She rarely sees the child she had when she was only thirteen. She and Janis were drawn together by their similar vitality and also some mutual difficulties. Being blunt herself, Sunshine accepted Janis's thundering directness as one of her assets. It did not always reap favor with others.

Sunshine also remembered that Janis was very uncomfortable about what she felt was her physical unattractiveness, her marred, pitted skin, her bulky body. Her concern was obsessive that men wouldn't find her appealing.

"At the same time," Sunshine said, "she didn't try to impress people. . . ." Modifying that observation, she remarked, "Well, she did, but it wasn't the same way. You know, a lot of people just viewed her as their connection." Flecks of blond peeked through the strands of her dusky brown hair. She shook her head mournfully. "Janis refused to acknowledge that she had something inside her a lot of other chicks didn't have."

If they didn't want her, they would want her dope. For Janis, dealing speed—all the other reasons aside —was another curious tool for the gaining of acceptance.

They say it's the greatest flash that can sprint through the body, the most indescribable rush to heaven that can hit the brain. When the rush subsides, the amphetamine high floods through the system like a celestial choir glassily intoning visions of breathless optimism. The world is incandescent, fantasies of accomplishment overwhelming. People on speed are notorious for doing a great deal of nothing. Twenty thousand motions to walk across the room and the illusion that vast amounts of knowledge are being consumed— and dispensed. It is sexually stimulating, although it is said that extensive usage can have an opposite effect. Methadrine, the most popular of the amphetamines, is non-addicting in the strictest sense of the word, producing no physiological withdrawal, though chugging back into the gray depot of life is a depressing trip that most find unbearable. On the other hand, it builds tolerance almost immediately and the compulsion to keep the world glowing forces things upward to a necessity for phenomenal quantity. Then the effects change, and the downward course begins. It leads not to death but to hideous physical and mental deterioration.

"It was a ver-ree high trip," Janice Knoll gurgled happily. "Right? We were really more, I'd say intellectual speed freaks than what you see now—common everyday street speedfreaks! Our trip was not that base. We used it for an *aesthetic* thing!"

"Janis too?"

"Uhhh . . . we never talked about it. We laughed about it. She *loved* speed! She *loved* the life! She was *exhilarated* by it! Right?"

Somehow Janis's exhilaration failed to convey itself in the letters she sent to her father at times during that year. To assuage her parents' fears—they knew nothing about the methadrine—Janis fabricated some tales concerning the way she was living. (Janice Knoll said, "Are you gonna write and say, 'I'm strung out on speed and eating at the Salvation Army!'?") But while she hardly revealed the source of her problems, she was open in telling him she was acutely troubled.

Mr. Joplin poignantly recalled their correspondence. "She just felt nothing was good and she wanted to know, 'Is this all there's gonna be?' And I explained, 'Yes, that's all and you've got to find out how to live with it. This *is* life, and you've got it.' Of course that didn't make her any happier, but she was a brooding type, and she had to come to the conclusion that if this was all there was, why, it wasn't worth it. She never did build on any wider basis than that either, I don't think."

Janice Knoll could only recall the mental heftiness of the speed experience. "Janis had a seer. He was really on to a very heavy, aesthetic, intellectual trip. Uhh. Nietzsche . . . uhh, Hesse. Truth! Life! Zen! Right? That kind of life, ya know what I mean? Using speed for fun, but for *truth* . . . I mean, it wasn't let's just get high and go in the park! It was, more or less, let's get high and uhh—do! Uhh. We read incredible amounts of books. We discussed a lot of really heavy intellectual kind of stuff like—uhh—and that's where the trip was really at!" She added hastily, "I mean there was this other kind of half-assed

drug trip, true, but that was . . . I mean, a lot of it
we were into but, uhh, we were into *beauty! Aesthetic
beauty!* Right? I'd do it all over again!"

One day in May of 1965, Janis returned to the
Baker Street apartment and sank howling on the floor.

"What's the matter with you?" Janice Knoll cried.

"I'll . . . I'll tell you . . . I'll tell you . . . later,"
Janis gasped.

"What is it, for chrissake?"

"I went to the hospital . . . I went . . . I told
them I was CRAZY!" Hysterical wheezes boomed up
from her stomach. "And they said I wasn't!"

Janis had tried to commit herself to San Francisco
General. What with the hospital wary of those trying
to scam off the state, she'd been denied admittance.
Janis may have roared over the irony of the situation
then; never did she recall it with humor. She had
been deadly serious; she had been frightened and
deadly ill.

Bob Clark visited with Janis several times that
year. She told him she was shooting meth. "Bob," she
confessed, "you learn a lot from it, but you can't learn
a thing from it you won't learn from time and it's not
worth it because it hurts your body too much. . . .
Don't let anybody ever get near you with a needle!"

Janice Knoll continued to look fondly back on those
days. "This scene we were all in, in the beginning,
was *the* beginning. It was very exciting! Everybody
was alive! It was wonderful! Right?"

I asked her if Janis had been able to continue with
her singing during those inspiring years.

"Well, yeah . . . but . . . for a period of time
there, she wasn't really heavy into it. She had a
guitar and stuff, but most of it for her was a really
heavy *head* trip!"

It was a common enough attitude; there was the
hippie culture, which gained so much attention in
1967. Then there was the beginning, which was—
better.

"It was beautiful," she said. "It was the flower

generation! Oh, what a disaster! And I know *exactly* what it was. There was a certain group of people, they were happy, they were turned on! By Zen! And once you've been turned on to Zen, you can never turn it off. Heavy . . . spiritual . . . psychic . . . uhhh, trips—uh—gain knowledge—gain wealth. . . ."

"Wealth?"

"Uhh, gain love . . . turn the world on, learn where truth is at. I mean knowledge was really important, right? Uhh, like feelings, the hereafter. Uh, how to live. Enlightenment! That's where it's at, right?"

"Right," I grumbled.

"What blew it was, a lot of people freaked out on the outward manifestations of the inward trip and they found *those* things. Which is not valid. Too many people were happy! Too many people had flowers! Flowers meant jackshit. There were people that didn't have a clue in the world of what they were doing in that crowd, except they were with *those* people."

A girl from the other side of the room said, "OOOOooooh! It's wonderful!"

"I know it!" Janice yelped. "They had done it naturally. And these people saw them being happy, right? And they picked up *that* part!"

"I want to know you forever," the girl across the room murmured adoringly.

"I've had satoris, right?" Janice said. "My first satori convinced me that everything I had worked for was a reality beyond the reality. If I smashed that TV, that reality is not as real as a satori. I got turned on to *feeling! Being!* It didn't matter what anybody else did in the whole world. It just mattered what *I* felt. Now those other people, I came back from Europe. It got sooo superficial. And it died. But in the beginning, that's what our trip was, you dig? And later? Only twenty percent touched it. The rest were escaping, whatever. Just out for good times, right?"

Ellen Harmon cut right through to the bone.

"Nobody was on any spiritual quest back then. What it was, was getting away from mother and father so you could do whatever you wanted which, in most cases, was just lying around and getting as high as you could! Then what happened was, everybody took a bunch of acid and got all wired. *That's* what happened to the scene! They got serious!"

As for Janis, she used to say that her speed experience was induced by a man. *He* had been the cause of it. *He* had brought her lower than she had ever been in her life.

Ellen Harmon drilled near the heart of Janis's complexities when she speculated on the agony of the Joplins over what had ultimately happened to their daughter. "Her mother is probably making herself real unhappy over something she had no control over. *Nobody* had any control. Janis hardly had control over herself. In fact, she might not have had any at all."

Always, Janis was inclined to put the responsibility for both her salvation and destruction on the strength or weakness of other people, as if, somewhere inside, she was an inert object to be moved at the will of the wind, her clamor and racket no matter. It was dependency that was at the basis of her attraction to strong personalities (noisy ones would do) and at the core of her astonishing naiveté, gullibility and trust, a stunning example of which occurred when she was sixteen.

"What's the quickest way to drive home?" she'd asked Arlene Elster one night.

"Well, go down Eighth Avenue," Arlene had told her, "because there are no stoplights and you don't have to wait five minutes for the lights to change."

Janis had gone her way and then had had an accident. The next day, she'd called up Arlene in tears and had sobbingly protested, "You didn't tell me I had to stop at the stop signs!"

That is exactly the way Janis went through life, rippling lightning all the way, but depending on people to make her stop, as if she could neither read nor observe the signs herself. It is an ugly truth that her careening madness was a vicarious experience, not only for the public but for a great many of her "friends" as well. Then it was she who chose them.

But as for her own feelings, she did not accept responsibility for what happened to her on speed; she blamed it on the man she loved.

When Janis returned from New York, she swung into a few affairs, and typically none was sustained. Her involvement with the young man in question started sometime in the spring of '65. She had possibly met him the previous summer. He'd also visited the Knolls; he'd had the dope!

By all accounts, he was a soft-spoken charmer with a very sharp brain and questionable character who, before he met Janis, had been engaged in some rather odd activities. Neither his name nor his history was his own, for one thing, both adapted from an adventurer he'd met when he was seventeen. Added to that were a number of frills to increase the drama of his personality. What was not an invention was a fraudulent international pharmaceutical company he set up in Canada to obtain drugs. That was the young man Janis claimed to want as a husband. Her choice was not bad luck. If she didn't know about the pharmaceutical company (and she may, at that, have known), she certainly knew about the women.

"Listen," a friend of Janis's said, "he lived with one girl and he got her pregnant. Then he lived with another one who had a child and made the first girl sleep in the living room while he slept with the other one. He was such a con! Unbelievable!"

Hardly looking like the kind of man one would associate with Janis, he had short hair and always wore a blue serge suit and black Oxford shoes. He was also a methadrine addict and, it would seem, psychotic. Janis had one experience of retrieving him from a Seattle hospital and having to take him back when he saw spacemen on the assault.

Nonetheless, he seems to have been very bright and, in spite of his erraticism, he had some fetching ways. He was gentle and exceedingly romantic. Janis was an exceptionally vulnerable girl. Whatever in the world it was all about, Janis was going downhill rapidly, and he was along on the ride.

"When a speed person can't get it together to cop speed," Chet recalled grimly, "you're a goner. You get to where you don't remember things. Janis would change her mind two hundred times before she got to the door. She was emaciated . . . almost catatonic, just not responding. Things were happening and she could *not* respond. That's like terminal speed."

Janis's young man was in better condition at that point than she and was instrumental in helping her recuperate, at least to some degree. She managed to gain a bit of weight. If she didn't stop speed entirely, she must have been able to decrease her use. The decision had already been made that she had to go back to Port Arthur. Chet was sure that Janis's boyfriend had a hand in preparing her for the trip. "She was incapable of functioning on that rational a level herself," he said.

It had taken Janis about seven months from the time she'd returned from New York to degenerate into a vegetable, an eighty-eight-pound spastic speedfreak, hoveling in a corner and trying desperately to focus her eyes on a somehow still terrible world.

8

In the summer of 1965, Janis returned to Port Arthur sufficiently recovered to distract her parents from the real reason she was there. Ostensibly, she had come home to prepare for getting married, which was, in fact, the case, but secondary to her need to put herself in an environment where she could permanently stop the use of speed. She registered immediately as a sociology major at Lamar. She wore prim and practical dresses, the kind with stitched gathers at the waist that plump out the hips but conceal the ripple of enticing movement—and they had long sleeves. The tracks on her arms covered, Janis commenced a ten-month period of attempted conformity that even surpassed, as her friend saw it, the demanded conventions of the town.

Janis was always puzzled by people who, being unique, could still maintain some order to their souls. For herself, there were only extremes; a world of primitive, unbridled impulses; that, or a realm to police her. She simply *could not* contain herself without the most rigid of impositions, or so she felt. If she could dress like the others, act like the others, think like the others, then and only then would she be safe.

Bernard Giarritano, the psychiatric social worker Janis saw during that period, tried to help her understand that life need not be like that. She could see it no other way. "Really," he reflected, "it was like trying to say, 'I want to be like Port Arthur,' and, of course, she couldn't."

Along the same lines, Bob Clark remembered an evening when he took Janis to the ballet at her request. For the occasion, she had her hair done all up in curls, in a packed little bun just so, exactly as she'd piled it during that peculiar winter of '62. She wore a proper dress with a wee bit of proper neckline graced with the proper amount of ever-so-proper jewelry. "She *still* looked different!" Bob laughed. "There was just no way that girl could be like the kind of people who run for Miss Texas! She couldn't believe in that, so she had to blow it all!"

Janis told Mr. Giarritano she had been terrified by her experience with drugs. She was also depressed of heart. It was more than the physical damage that had laid her so terribly low. The acute awareness brought about by speed she found intolerable, and she was ridden with anxiety about the effects of coming down. Everything grated on her nerves; she was edgy about driving, hypersensitive to sounds, scraped to the bone by sudden images. For a while, she was on some medication, but appeared more comfortable without it.

The focus of Janis's conformity was the desire to stay off drugs. Still, she referred constantly to doing "the right thing" and saw that image in her sister Laura. Janis seemed jealous to the extent that Laura was able to "adjust," whereas she could only fail. Janis tried unsuccessfully to cultivate some acceptance from the conforming elements in the area, tried to assimilate their ways and views, but she was afraid to approach those people herself, and they were wary of her. "She cried for them to be friendly," Mr. Giarritano recalled, "but to them, she was a 'weirdo,' and they would have nothing to do with that." Even her intelligence was a problem; traditional teachers did not take kindly to her quick and challenging mind.

"Janis suffered," he emphasized, "and she *knew* she suffered. She talked about how fucked up her head was and she thought coming back here was a way to get out of that, but there seemed nothing that could satisfy her that she was becoming 'straight' or doing 'the right thing.' She specifically used those words."

For the entire year that Janis remained in Port Arthur, she kept a calendar, just-so-neatly penciling in the date of her parents' anniversary and the celebratory occasions for everyone in the family, birthdays and the rest. She recorded the dates of all her appointments and all her tests at school. At the bottom of several pages, she scrawled the fluttering emblems of love, adjoining her name to that of the young man she supposedly would marry soon. But as time went on, it became obvious that no wedding

was impending. Janis's alleged fiancé had also left
San Francisco, promising her that in New York he
would find his way to a stable existence. He had gone
so far as to call Mr. Joplin in observance of the
ancient formality of asking for Janis's "hand." He
had come to Port Arthur to see his "bride-to-be."
What he was really doing was running out, although
it is likely he intended that all along. Mrs. Joplin was
sewing a wedding dress for Janis, and Janis was
making a Texas Star quilt when he went his dis-
oriented, solitary way.

The trauma caused by the desertion was horrible.
For all that, Janis apparently viewed marriage as a
symbol, a cast of "straightness" she could take on as
another restriction in that seemingly impossible
venture of self-control. Janis, Mr. Giarritano said, was
worried about her adjustment to her surroundings,
frightened of it all, but mostly of herself, and for that
control she felt she could not exert alone, she looked
to her environment, to marriage, and to him. "That's
why she came to me," he nodded, "and even though
she'd put down a lot of what I would say, she wanted
me to restrain her."

Restricting herself as much as she possibly could on
her own, she was reluctant to go to parties, and when
she did, she left shortly. A few people recall a gathering in Houston at which she refused to drink, finally
succumbing to a few sips of wine under considerable
pressure.

Most of Janis's friends took it for granted that she
knew nothing of guilt, nor are there many who think
that drugs and liquor were catalysts for her sexual
adventures. If she had conservative periods, that was
because she was an extremist, and that, as they say,
is that. Jack Smith had some other thoughts on the
matter: "Not that I've taken any Masters and Johnson
survey, but it's common with couples we know that
came out of this background that the girl won't
participate in some acts, but after a couple of drinks
will literally demand them. Janis never went through

any 'please Lord, forgive me,' but her pendulum
swung oddly. That's like the person who gets the bad
hangover and then the next day says I'm going to
stop drinking, then I'm going to stop smoking, then
after that I'm going to stop coffee, then I'm going to
study and do God knows what! I mean she got so
straight, people didn't like to be around her! She was
downright *dull*!"

Thus did she discuss her sexual behavior with Mr.
Giarritano as if it were all a matter of course, but
what she said was revealing. So he recalled her words.
"She said she enjoyed it, but she would come in
terribly disappointed that her night's liaison didn't
work out so very well. She'd say it was just about a
fifteen-minute lay and that wasn't worth a damn, but
she'd shrug it off as 'this is one of the things you
get.' "

She dwelled on the breadth of her experiences.
And she talked about the women.

Janis reported her first homosexual experience to a
girlfriend in Port Arthur as having occurred shortly
after high school. During her sophomore year at
Lamar, she had enraged a young male friend who
had stumbled into a room at a party to find her
embracing his wife-to-be. He had become violent,
throwing a bottle at his girlfriend, which had missed,
smashing instead into Jack Smith's mouth and causing
him to lose most of his teeth. When Janis returned
from Venice, she was seen also with some lesbians
in Beaumont; that may have brought on the fears
she had expressed to Jack on the beach and the dainty
style she'd struggled to assume. At the University of
Texas, she'd had homosexual contacts and a number
of such relationships in San Francisco. At least one
lesbian affair took place during the summer she'd
spent in New York shooting speed with the Knolls.
Later there would be far fewer escapades.

These activities with women, those earlier and
later, were neither the minor phenomenon that some

of her friends would like to believe nor the basis for
a *cause célébre,* as the militant lesbian groups would
have it. Janis, the latter hold, had she been a proud-
hearted lesbian able to withstand social condemnation and willing to accept an orientation toward
her own sex, would then have been not so compelled
to self-execution by liquor and drugs. Besides, she
owed it to them to declare herself, thereby lending
support to their movement and freeing from bondage
the lesbians throughout the world who needed the encouragement of an example. The view that Janis's
difficulties stemmed from an inability to glory in a
homosexual pedigree has been most stridently expressed by Jill Johnston in *The Village Voice,* who
spumes forth with an almost weekly declaration that
all women are basically lesbians anyway. Those who
dispute her words are ipso facto guilty of intolerance
toward lesbianism and/or a fear-ridden failure to
perceive that only the social system with men holding the power of the world brings women to engage
in sexual relations with males in the first place. Some
of Janis's friends, on the other hand, would have her
lesbian tendencies dismissed as utterly insignificant,
never to be spoken of at all; or proclaimed part of an
enviable freedom she had so stupendously attained.
If the last views are somewhat less totalitarian than
those of Jill Johnston, they are also even more juve-
nile. After all, no one need heed her premise about
woman's fundamental nature to presume that a denial
of an existent homosexuality could brew up severe
internal disruption.

But to the truth. Janis was consumed and driven
by a need for love that was preposterous in its magnitude, her excessive narcissism the result of bitter
frustrations and the very stuff of her insecurity, her
desire for constant attention and her gluttonous
hunger for approval. She was in fanatical pursuit of
affection while rendered incapable, by the self-
direction of her feelings, of establishing intimate
relationships. Like a longing child crying for love, her

aim was to receive, to take into herself a comforting warmth of which, for whatever reasons, she felt acutely deprived. With an obsessive and insatiable need such as that, what sex would fill it became a secondary matter and the physical demonstration of affection a substitute gratification for what she essentially craved. "She just wanted to be close to someone," said one of her wiser friends. That many women were maternal figures to Janis should have been evident to all who knew her. That was so in non-sexual as well as sexual friendships. Janis's relationships with men were always pre-eminent, as was her heterosexual proclivity in general. In those early years, however, a homosexual woman who approached her was not likely to be rejected. At that time, she may even have initiated some of those relationships herself. What affairs there were later were undertaken with Janis as a passive party for the most part, as I have understood it. An individual so terrified of losing love might well yield to a sexual approach in order to preserve the contact. In the affair of which Janis spoke to Mr. Giarritano, that seems to have been the motive, human intimacy the aim rather than sexual release. Something especially poignant exists in the fact that those relationships were more frequent in her earlier days. It was then that she was most locked in the fortress of lovelessness, then that she felt especially denied. Fame had its drawbacks, but it fulfilled a crucial function, satisfying to some degree her need to exhibit and to be sexually admired. Anxiety about exposure might have led to a decrease in those lesbian contacts. Nonetheless it is likely that other emotional factors were very significant.

There is another related and most crucial aspect of Janis's liaisons with women and to her entire sexuality. Doubtless any emotional disturbance to which the homosexual is victim because of homosexuality alone is the result of society's attitudes.

Were there not such condemnation, homosexuality could represent a sexual adjustment no more troublesome than that with which the majority of us, by virtue of acceptance, more comfortably live. To say it's a matter of simple preference, substantially no different than the matters of taste that dictate a fondness for green over blue, may be stretching a point. But if it results from a childhood development gone askew from the norm, that is ultimately quite irrelevant. Given the near-infinite potentials of infancy, it is really impossible to make generalizations about what lies behind sexual practices. This, however, is probable: to become clearly homosexual, to make the choice that one honestly prefers relations with one's own sex, no matter the origins of such preference, requires a certain integration, a stability of psychic development, a tidiness of personality organization. The ridicule and the humiliation that took place at that most delicate period in her early teens, her own inability to surmount the obstacles to regular growth, devastated her a great deal more than most people comprehended. Janis was not heir to an ego so cohesive as to permit her an identity one way or the other. She was, as Mr. Giarritano put it, "diffused"— spewing, splattering, splaying all over, without a center to hold. That had as much to do with her original use of drugs as did the critical component of guilt and its multiplicity of sources above and beyond the contribution made by her relationships with women. Were she so simple as the lesbians wished her to be or so free as her associates imagined!

Despite her attempt at conformity, Janis began singing again several months after returning home. Jim Langdon, by then, was writing for *The Austin Statesman;* he had a contact with the owner of a club in that town called The Eleventh Door. Janis shocked her old friend Powell St. John the first time she performed there, appearing in a black suit and heels and

her hair in that neat, proper bun, a schoolmarm with
a voice raging out in a gorgeous swelling sea. "So
tight she looked!" he said. "Then her voice came out
like Bessie Smith!"

Expecting to hear someone like Joan Baez, half the
audience greeted her coldly; the rest adored it. And
Jim Langdon reviewed the performance: "Texas has
been a hard place for a good many blues singers from
Leadbelly on, but because of this it has produced
some great ones. In my mind, Janis Joplin is one of
the great ones."

A friend of Mrs. Joplin saw the review and, shaking
her head glumly, said, "Dorothy, you don't have a
chance!"

Sometime during the fall of 1965, Dave Moriaty,
who'd been traveling around Europe, returned
briefly to Port Arthur, and found Janis hideously
depressed. "She thought my bumming around was
great, but she said her bumming days were over. She
was going to be a keypunch operator, get a secretar-
ial job, and not be 'a bad girl' ever again. I was
shocked. I knew Janis was no keypunch operator and
nobody's secretary!"

It was simply like this: singing was Janis's salvation, the only happiness she ever knew; she began
to go to Austin more frequently.

John Clay still feels that Janis never sounded as she
had in the old days when she was a student at the
University of Texas. "She'd toned down her style for
the Houston coffeehouses," he grunted disapprov-
ingly, "fitting herself to commercial taste."

That criticism aside, Janis felt generally encouraged. Her mood appeared to lighten, and she continued to perform at The Eleventh Door. In early
March of 1966, she played an Austin benefit for
a sick blues musician named Teodar Jackson. She
sang Buffy St. Marie's "Codine," "I Ain't Gotta
Worry," and "Going Down to Brownsville." The
audience shot up in a wall of deafening applause.
A week later she wrote to Jim Langdon:

Hope you don't mind the lilac stationery. It's left over from days of writing _____. Sigh.

Would you do me a favor, please? When any of those pictures that were taken of me last weekend are developed, could you send me some copies? From either the 11th Door or the benefit. Would really appreciate it.

How's my career coming along up there? Oh, if you reviewed the benefit in your column, would you send me a copy of that too? If my engagement for the 25th and 26th is definite, would you let me know, so I can start hustling a ride? Oh, I wanted to thank you . . . blush . . . for everything you've been doing to help me. It really is important to me. I don't think I could have done it without your confidence so, if it doesn't embarrass you, I really appreciate it.

Janis

Regarding her singing, Mr. Giarritano said that her only anxiety about it concerned the prospect of drugs. There was no doubt, she told him, she was burning for that career. She was able to say, "I want to sing," but uncertain that she could do so without destroying herself, an attitude without question sucked in from her Port Arthur environment. It is no coincidence that most everyone there associated her singing with disaster, nor an accident either that their animus toward her style had to do with its erotic character, as if there could be only a step from that to annihilation. "She was successful here," one woman said angrily, "and she left to do something that killed her!" That is patently untrue. Janis did not die from singing. Mr. Giarritano tried to assure her that it need not lead her where she feared it must.

Except for four or five of her old friends, Janis refused to associate with people who were in the least bit unusual. The use of psychedelics was starting in Austin, and Janis wanted nothing of it. "She was afraid she'd get dragged into it," Tary Owens said, "and that *it would kill her!*"

As it became more apparent to him what Janis wanted to do, Mr. Giarritano tried to help her understand, "that being like Port Arthur wasn't her. This wasn't her style. This wasn't where she felt and that is why I said, 'Go do what you know and what you want.' I stressed that she could do it *without* drugs. She didn't want to turn on to *any* drug, ever again. And I said that since she *knew* that, her awareness could act as a deterrent. Surely, in Austin, in San Francisco, there'd be some agency or person she could talk to. She was absolutely miserable here!"

"When did she start to snap out of it?" I asked.

"Oh, she had ups and downs," he remarked, "but she never snapped out of it. Never."

By early May, Janis nonetheless appeared in a considerably better state of mind. On May 10, she wrote another letter to Jim:

> The 11th Door was really a gas this weekend. I got an encore Saturday night too.
>
> Listen, I am seriously contemplating moving to Austin for the summer. This would probably be a disaster, but I think I want to. Moan! Of dire importance—could you get me enough work to keep me from starving? Please let me know what you think. . . . Also would you please do me a favor? I sent your money . . . find out from Tary or from Powell what Powell's house address is—not his P.O. Box No. in the signature, house signature. And send it as soon as you can. I have to write J.B.
>
> Oh! And another thing. Tary said you mentioned the concert in your column. Have an extra copy? Or Tary said I could have his.
>
> Doncha think I'm a nice lady, here's your money. . . . Thanks.
>
> Janis

Soon afterward, Janis went up to Austin. She was planning to join an Austin rock group called the Thirteenth Floor Elevators when Travis Rivers came to town. Chet had sent him to lure Janis back to the Coast one more and final time. She was needed, Chet said, to forge the last dazzling link in a circle of musicians called Big Brother and the Holding Company.

It was an article of faith for many that Janis's openness was one of her greatest virtues. Her frankness was indeed refreshing at times, one of her most lovable qualities, though often it leaped up only from an eerie inability to restrain what she felt and was quite beyond the realm of choice. Thoughts, feelings, flashes, impulses, hit, spill, bubble, bang. Albeit breathtaking, that is the chatter of candor and should never be mistaken for the real thing. Like a dream, such verbal gyrations may contain the thrust of an emotional truth, but always the truth of event or reality.

As it happened, there were many matters about which Janis was not honest at all. One was surely ambition.

Janis's father had a dear friend, tragically killed in a fire, whom Janis had adored. Long ago, he had told her she was destined for more than was there in the dreary grounds around her, and Janis devoured his words. "The majority of those students," she once said to her mother, "they'll look back and this is going to be *the* high spot in their lives. I don't intend it to be mine."

The fact is that Janis made much of having stumbled into a singing career. An accident it was, a quirky affair that turned out to be, you know, sort of put on her and then she got all caught up in it—the crowds!—the screaming!—the applause!—and it all kind of went to her head, got all messed up and things like that.

That wasn't supposed to happen. She was just a "beatnik." That's what she set out to be, a street person—"just like everybody else!"

Well, it all depends on the constituency. For hers, it was another article of faith that she was seized by the glories of stardom only when her fame was a *fait accompli.*

"She didn't want to be a star," Janice Knoll insisted, falling for that line. "She just did it because she was hurt after the marriage fell through, and that was all that was left for her." That there were any number of accidents that led to her celebrity is quite beside the point. The question is one of desire. Janis's lack of it was sheer fantasy, created, in part, by her own indulgence in an especially curious deceit.

Not a deliberate lie, it was an elaborate self-delusion designed to protect herself from an essential and pulverizing guilt. Beyond that was another court of judgment to which Janis submitted her aspirations. Competitiveness and ambition were ugly propositions to a culture hooked on the idea that those were the evils of another generation and that they, the people of the new dawn, had divested themselves of those drives. Of course, in the new catechism, sex, on the other hand, was elevated into the First Commandment, the heavy-handed imperative, Thou Shalt. Janis's extravagant claims on that score were sources of awesome admiration to the "revolutionary" culture, and well she knew it. And if they were not always true, damned if she would ever have admitted *that*! But the ambition for stardom was another matter. So that just along those lines, Janis devised a peculiar story to guard herself against that charge: her excuse for joining Big Brother and the Holding Company was sex!

Shortly after I met Janis and was gathering information from her for publicity purposes, we were sitting in a large New York restaurant, chatting about her past.

"How I happened to join Big Brother?" she murmured. "Well, Chet Helms sent Travis Rivers to get me. What I usually say is that I wanted to leave Texas, but that's not what really happened." Janis suddenly raised her voice. "I didn't want to leave." Then slowing her words and booming them out, in case anyone in the restaurant might miss them, she

added, "But he was such a *good fuck!* How could I
not go!"

Janis perpetuated that story in her interviews with
David Dalton, insisting that she was "no star" and
telling him with raunchy elaboration that she was
"fucked into being in Big Brother."

To Jim Langdon, at the time that she made her
decision to leave Austin, she said the same. "In her
words," he told me, "the reason that she went out was
that she hadn't had a good ball in an awfully long
time and Travis was a good ball!"

Travis may be a "good ball" or not, but his sexual
prowess had absolutely nothing to do with her
decision to leave Texas. Her ambition—stirring, nag-
ging, persistent, screaming ambition—was there all
along. It was clear in her conversations with Mr.
Giarritano; it was clear in her letters to Jim Langdon;
and it was decidedly, unmistakably clear in her phone
conversations with Chet Helms. Janis's only reluctance was the fear of drugs.

"When Travis got there," Chet said, "she called me
from Austin to reaffirm the proposal that she join the
band."

"Chet, is it all right?" she'd asked. "Will I make it?"

"Look," he'd replied, "I know you think you're
gonna meet all the people you were into speed with,
but I'm happy to tell you most of them ain't into
speed anymore. There's a whole new renaissance,
and it's beautiful. The world wasn't ready before, but
it's ready now, and you can't imagine that sitting
in Austin."

Janis asked only for reassurance that if things
didn't work out, Chet would buy her a bus ticket
home. The excuse of Travis's seductive genius, drawn
to respond to the needs of others as she sometimes
accurately guessed them to be, was unadulterated
sham.

On the twenty-seventh of May, Janis saw Mr.
Giarritano for the last time, and shortly afterward

told her parents that she was leaving. This was the occasion on which Mrs. Joplin claims that Janis stated her calculated plans for the future.

"She had read this piece this guy Langdon wrote, which was just like the Pied Piper of Hamelin. I wasn't going to let her go with hard feelings, so I went out to the car and she said, 'Mother, I've given a lot of thought to this. The only way I can anticipate any success is if I utilize a type of music that's not going to be the same as every good singer on every block. The one type of singing where there are the least type of good singers is blues. I'm going to try that format and I'm going to have to package it so it'll sell. Just like Daddy packages oil!'"

Blues cut right into Janis's tormented heart; her personality was ready-made for the image. It is questionable that she spoke in exactly that way. On the other hand, in view of her ambition, Janis may have said something very similar. Moreover, it is true that at least prior to that time Janis had not exempted other styles of singing.

"I don't think," Bob Clark agreed, "that Mrs. Joplin was just whistling 'Dixie' when she said that Janis could have been anything!"

Whatever had occurred in her conversation with her mother, Janis departed with reassuring words, and shot with Travis right back to Austin to announce the decision to her Texas friends. They were not enthused. A few thought she needed more time to regain her equilibrium. Jim Langdon had also booked her for some Austin performances, which she would now be unable to fulfill. More generally their reservations were based on the feeling that things should be done in a standard way. "You know," Dave Moriaty smiled, "working up through channels, but that's the way everybody thinks. That's *not* the way anything really gets done."

Janis left Austin on May 30 with Travis and a carload of people. On May 31, while traveling on the

road, she wrote the following letter to Linda Wauldron Godfried in Hawaii. The letter was never mailed.

Linda!
　God, you can't imagine where I am! Moan. I'm sittin'
in the back seat of a car (excuse writing) . . . and
going to San Francisco. Well, I don't really know what
happened. I came up to Austin and saw this guy I used
to know here, Travis Rivers, who is now living in S.F.
He was bearing word from Chet Helms, who is now a
big man in S.F. who throws big dances. With great
new rock and roll bands and Bill Hamm does his light
shows and he runs two bands and wears mod clothes
etc. Wanted me to come out there and sing with this
blues band he has. So I called him this morning and
he verified it very enthusiastically and also told me if I
got freaked out, he'd at least give me a ticket to go
home. So I thought I'd just go. Been talking to people
about the city—Travis and this guy named Mark who
is a friend of [Sal's] I met on Pine Street. Remember
Pine Street, God! So anyway I decided to go. Talked
to all kinds of people and no one discouraged me!
Everyone thought it was a good idea! Moan, and I so
wanted to be discouraged! Well, so now I'm in this very
packed car with Travis who is kind of a madman but a
groove! (Like a less refined Pat Cassidy if you know
what I mean.) And he's huge and hairy and this little
tiny S.F. man in black. And guess who else we're
giving a ride to? SARLEK! Some really freaky methadrine person (terrible and nervous and ugly and omnipresent with lots of dope and points [which he mailed
there] and he sometimes sits *next* to me and is really
bitching about everything MOAN)!! Haven't even left
Austin yet and I'm really freaked out! Very humorous
actually—it's the one thing I wanted to avoid—very
uptight about it!—finally assured myself I wouldn't
have to be around them, and here he is! God, he's
another George the Beast only not likeable!
　Well at any rate, it's unbelievable! But the singing
thing seems nice. I really want to try to do a new rock
and roll thing and Chet says he already has the set up and
really wanted me to sing, says the guys who make up the
band have all heard me and think it would be a gas.
So I'm going.

After all, I say to myself—it's summer—I could call it a summer vacation and go back to school.

We'll see. Right now, it's too much! I've maneuvered my way into the back seat laden with duffle bag and I can be away from that guy and get to dig traveling—again and (me) and have lots of grass and it's really kind of nice. Sorry for the handwriting—it's the car etc.

Wow, you're going to have a baby in four weeks! God, I'm really thrilled! I sent you a shower present. I hope you like it. As soon as I get an address I'll send it because I *really* want to hear from you and so that Malcolm could maybe write me or something (I guess he wouldn't do that . . .) Well so I can hear somehow about the baby! God I'm so excited!

Boy, things sure are different. I'll write more when we're not moving and I can think. Sure do wish you were around though. Little afraid of the city, wish I had a friend there. God, I'll probably go see the Knolls. Linda, can you imagine the knot this all brings to my stomach! Whew, I am scared to death. More later. . . .

Janis marked on her calendar that she arrived in San Francisco on June 4, 1966. Chet was right. San Francisco had most certainly changed. Janis had no idea how much. The rasp of Bob Dylan's words had turned its music upside down. Electricity had punctured to its gut. Dylan! The Beatles! The Byrds! The Stones! Janis had been studying for a history exam at Lamar when the first rock dance was held at the Longshoreman's Hall and the move began from North Beach to that area surrounding an intersection where Ashbury crosses Haight and mecca was born.

9

A magical town, San Francisco, with enchanting green parks and the bluest of bays, where the fog settles down in mysterious puffs and the embers of the day heat its waters till they flash with mirrors of emerald and gold. The land of toy streetcars and skittery hills and funny gingerbread houses, sugar and spice and everything nice and creamy clean in the afternoon sun. It is the most breathtaking city in the country It is soaked in artistic tradition and a grand tolerance for nonconformity. It is a heavenly haven for dreams.

The believers in this one thought they could love everybody and that the mechanized designs of modern society need not extend to all. They would purge themselves of envy. They would cleanse their hearts of greed. The separate boundaries of the self they would erase, so that they would lovingly dissolve into the egoless mass. They would hold only populist sentiments. Art was an aristocratic concept, so life would be art and everyone an artist. Politics? There would be none, except for the politics of ecstasy, and there would be plenty of ecstasy, since energy would go into a Dionysian explosion of the body and make things whole once more, as they must have been before civilization came down to squeeze the heart out of the sensual center of life. They would turn to the past but revel in the present: neon, day-glo, electricity, chemicals—all would bring the Kingdom of God.

It was thought of as an experiment, and the ones who joined it came from everywhere. They belonged to the most affluent generation in American history; still, they wanted no part of the American dream. They were somewhat the result of a system that had prolonged their childhoods and had relieved them from the pressure of quickly assuming customary roles to perpetuate customary values. They were also the heirs of a liberal rearing, which had fostered

their self-expressiveness, then had put them at bay
in a society that was compelled to protect its institu-
tions against the very ideas that rearing had helped
to develop. They had been brought up to the swelling chorus of black liberation. As was the case with
their white activist counterparts, the conditions of
despair that were part of the black experience were
in no way their own. Nonetheless, they were bur-
dened by a sense of futility, an alienation from their
middle-class backgrounds, and a desperateness that
was emotionally vivid for all the lack of a true oppression.

Poverty, racism, pollution appeared part of the
country's fabric. Their private lives seemed to hold
no tolerable prospects. They were helpless to stop
a horrible war that they felt no one honorable would
willingly fight. They were products of ranch-house
tedium and split-level traps or more ostentatious
suburban deserts with sterling silver, merger marri-
ages, and oases of country-club pools. What could
they do about a society in which the acquisition of
needless goods was the end-all and be-all of existence? Dull community, dull jobs, dull sex was all
around them, in the lives of their parents and their
parents' friends. Camelot had ended in Dallas; the
civil rights movement had let them down.

These were the ones who came to the community
of the Haight-Ashbury in its beginning. They came
because they were disillusioned, frustrated, lost, or
bored. They came because they saw no alternatives
and were ill-prepared for choices. They came to rebel.
They came because others did. They came because
they were already there. It was their little society, "just
like a Christian community in Rome," and if its current
was visceral entirely, that was more spiritual still. At its
best, that current produced some of the most marvelously energetic, celebratory popular music the world
has ever known. It also brought about a verbal sodden-
ness by which measure the beat generation was

positively scholastic, and it brought the abuse of some
very destructive drugs.

As Ellen Harmon remembers it, from 1961 through
at least the end of 1965, San Francisco was the most
beautiful town in the world. As yet there were not
enough obvious eccentrics to upset the city government, and San Francisco was downright paternal-
istic to its offbeat adventurous young. If, in the
earliest of those years, there had been some horrendous casualties because of speed, that memory was
overshadowed by nostalgia for the exuberant days
that preceded the great hippie migration of 1967.

Back in the early sixties, Ellen had been part of an
urban commune called The Family Dog. It members, or four of them, were responsible for the stupen-
dous event on October 16, 1965, at Longshoreman's
Hall, which was the first rock dance the city knew.
The music was provided by The Charlatans, the
first of the city's rock bands, the Jefferson Airplane
(without Grace Slick), the Great Society (with
her), and a group called the Marbles, which immediately afterward disappeared. The Dog was up to
two or three more dances. Then Ellen and her friends
took off for Mexico and left the San Francisco dance
scene to Chet Helms and a very ambitious wild-eyed
maverick named Bill Graham. By the time Janis
arrived, Chet had the Avalon Ballroom; Big Brother
and the Holding Company was its house band,
and he was managing the group. Bill Graham had
what was to become the most famous rock palace of
the sixties, the Fillmore Auditorium.

In the first days of the Haight, there was only a
cluster of San Francisco bands. The core was Big
Brother, The Grateful Dead, Quicksilver Messenger
Service, the Jefferson Airplane, and Country Joe and
the Fish. By December of 1966 there would be some
fifteen hundred bands flourishing in the Bay Area,
all of them drenched in the influence of blues.

Blues spoke the pain, the urgency, and the estrangement to give voice to their own frustrations. It spoke
a rebellion and a sensuality that was strained through
their music as it was through the surrounding milieu.
"Like the same cats in the Haight," someone explained it, "I'd known when they were in the black
scene. It's like we know who we are, but we don't
want to be white! Like black culture was really sexy
and white culture is like celibate—whew!"

And it was blues, amplified and transformed by
the screaming colors and inward messages of acid,
that shaped the San Francisco sound. With a shattering electricity to burn the mind, it was screeching and pounding and maniacally loud. It was
intuitive and unpolished and rhapsodic and endless.
Like its environment, it was meant to consume,
hemorrhaging in a bleeding dazzle of strobes, posters,
slides, and lights that whipped right back into the
center of sound in a writhing, inseparable oneness.
Big Brother was an aural and visual crash, a kinetic,
deafening, freak-rock total, and a symbol of it all.
It had been that already when its members made the
decision to work with a female singer.

After auditioning vocalists for several months, they
thought of trying out Janis. Two of the band had
heard her before, and Chet had not forgotten.

Just a short time before Janis reached San Francisco,
Dave Getz had a luscious dream: the girl who was
coming to join their group was incomparably beautiful, causing sparks of passion to flare in his heart. In
the midst of his dream there was a sequence of love-
making to seal his adoration.

Dave was the drummer in Big Brother. Unlike
guitarist James Gurley, and Peter Albin, who played
the bass, he had never seen Janis when she sang in
the coffeeshops of North Beach. Guitarist Sam Andrew
did not know her either. All of those who constituted
part of the Big Brother family—the wives and the

girl-friends and the companions—were expecting her to be somewhat glamorous.

Janis arrived, homely and fat, a plain Texas girl with an atrocious complexion who wore rough-and-tough jeans and mannish tops. She bound her hair in a ponytail or pulled it up tight in her Port Arthur bun. When it fell down, it looked like the fur of a mangy cat that's just been stung by a wasp.

Nor was their musical rapport very smooth at the beginning. Their initial rehearsal was hardly marvelous, with Janis completely terrified, for one thing, and unaccustomed to a rock band, for another. Her voice, of course, compensated for whatever was lacking in the way of a compatible style, which they all expected would eventually develop. Nonetheless, Janis was still very shaky on June 10 when she performed with the band at the Avalon Ballroom. Most of the doubts *she* may have had, at least along musical lines, were brought to an end that night—or so she frequently recalled. "It happened the first time," she claimed. "I just exploded. I'd been into a Bessie Smith type thing. I stood still and I sang simple. But you *can't* sing like that in front of a rock band, all that rhythm and volume. You *have* to sing loud and move wild with all that in back of you."

Janis's memory of instant glory was not shared. There were a number of people who didn't care for the new Big Brother in the least. James Gurley heard repeated complaints: "Ged rid of that chick! She's terrible!" Janis's country-blues was a bit in the teeth of the band's sonic fury, and the result was foreign to San Francisco ears. But her musical style would change in time—as would assuredly Janis herself.

After staying with Travis Rivers for a very short while, Janis took a room on Pine Street. She had, perhaps, a pact with herself, and for a while was able to keep it. Dave Getz's dream was ruined. What he conceived didn't happen, for Janis betrayed a nervous reserve, unlike the creature of his wish, and there were, in the back seat of his car, necking games that Janis would call to a halt. Maybe, Dave thought, it was because of Travis; but it could not have been Travis, whom Janis, by then, didn't care about much anyway.

She kept her calendar too, a symbol to tie her to the restraints of home, and she marked the dates of performances just as neatly as she had her tests at Lamar and all her family's birthdays. Big Brother knew nothing of such things, nor did they suspect she might be greatly frightened of her environment. They had adjusted to her lack of glamor. She was funky, raw, and headstrong. If, on occasion, she expressed some anxiety, anxiety is not what they remember. She was just whining. "We used to have to endure her saying things like, 'I'm going back to Texas!'" Dave Getz snorted.

Sometime that summer, Tary Owens visited the city and found Janis doing a great amount of leatherwork in her room, a hobby to keep her from touching speed, the busyness of her hands a relief from tension. She had resolved to stay away from drugs. It had been a year, and surely she could manage.

Jim Langdon saw her that summer as well when he came to town with Tary. "There was a moment when I first got out there of her being almost defensive," he said. "I have no idea why!"

While Janis was truly disturbed by the dope in the Haight, she found an appeal in the fantasy life that those around her were leading, because it so stimulated her own. Here was an unending stream of people without strong identities either, who found them in playing roles. They were Indians; they were blacks; they were gypsies. Their clothes were funny. They had funny names, anything to discard their pasts. There could have been no environment so appropriate to meet her psychic demands, not until fame would replace the rewards of those surroundings. The efforts to maintain restrictions were fading. She noted on her calendar the day of registration for summer school, but let those plans go and moved instead with Big Brother to Laguanitas, a rural town in San Geronimo Valley. There the change began.

In time, there would be lace and beads, bracelets and rings and the discarding of a Texas bareness. Already, Janis had run into her old friend Sunshine, who had frowned on her dull Texas garb and had set Janis thinking. In Laguanitas, the vision grew as Janis took in the glow and ornamentation in the apparel of other girls. Those girls were Nancy Getz, a frequent visitor named Suzy Perry, and above all, James's wife, Nancy Gurley.

Beautiful and charismatic, Nancy Gurley seems to have been possessed of a very special vanity, not reluctant about exuding the presence of some powerful gypsy queen. So she was envisioned by others. She dressed in long gowns of lace and velvet. Many, many necklaces draped colorfully from the porcelain gracefulness of her neck. The days when the clothes Mrs. Joplin sent to Janis had struck her as too sumptuous seemed very far away. She could be like *that!* There would be appropriate rituals too and ways to behave, things to believe in and things to say, expected, approved, and noteworthy of attention. The clothes would take money, which Janis didn't yet have. But the image was begun.

Janis was incredibly taken with Nancy, as she was with her husband. Not able to copy her clothes as yet, she followed in her footsteps by making love to James. Janis was competitive even with those she mimed. Furthermore, James had a kind of lean, tender attractiveness, although Janis had a strange way of describing men, including James, in terms of their sexual abilities. Such talk was mightily enjoyed by others, and so she would persist. Just the same, Janis had a tendency to talk of herself in a similar vein as if there were some secret definition being sought through it all.

Naturally, the situation with James created some serious conflict between the two women. Somehow it was resolved. She and Nancy remained exceedingly

close, Nancy continuing to exert great influence on
Janis's transformation.

"When you were around Nancy," Richard Hundgin
explained, "you always *felt*." Later Big Brother's road
manager, Richard was an old friend of the band and
all the people on its periphery, a number of whom
are now dead from drugs. "She symbolized the Earth
Mother in the Tarot," he said. She was also, by
Richard's account, an educated girl with a masters in
English literature. Whatever she gained from that,
she couldn't have thought it much; she dispensed
with it by using a lot of acid, which she liked to mix
with speed. Negative about heroin, she died of just
that in 1969. She was pregnant at the time.

As the central figure in the Laguanitas house and
the leader of its ceremonial rites, Nancy instructed
all the girls in the art of beadmaking which, to be
done just so, required putting the beads on wax
leather thread with knots on either side. There were
other rituals. Cindy Albin was the only girl in the
house who didn't use speed. The temptation for Janis
was terrible, particularly because she was once again
in the midst of couples and dreadfully lonely.

Peter was with Cindy, Sam with a girl called
Speedfreak Rita, and while David and Nancy Getz
have since separated, they were together at the time.
Her involvement with James did not amount to
separating the Gurleys as a pair. There was a girl who
visited the house on occasion with whom Janis had
relations. That did not seem to be what she wanted.
Essentially, Janis was left with nothing to do but shoot
pool in the local redneck bars and hang out with the
Grateful Dead who, it happened, lived down the
road. That made her no less alone. The nights of
drinking with the boys—and Janis drank always—
were not enough to ease her unhappiness. What they
did was increase her sorrowful recognition that
nothing had changed at all.

Finally, after a valiant struggle, she did what she
swore she would never do again, although her speed

habit did not reach the hideous proportions it had
before. It was some help that she was occupied with
her music, and if speed engendered a lot of busy
beadstringing activity on the part of the others, Janis
did it to contrary purpose, to diminish shooting up
dope. Once, however, Nancy Gurley, Rita, and Janis
sat around making a fifteen-foot-long beaded curtain
in the frenzy of a speed high. Dave Getz said,
"Speed really makes people creative. People were
doing stuff behind it like posters and music."

It was, of course, acid that was the principal drug
in the peak days of the Haight-Ashbury, affording
that holy glimpse, its users still insist, into the
infinite mysteries of the universe. What they learned
no one who has not taken the drug can say, because
the psychedelic experience is beyond translation by
mere words. Its proponents claim merely that during
those hours in which they have been transported,
they have experienced a "oneness" with the universe
and have returned to this earth with an acquired
wisdom which, unfortunately, they cannot express
because of its awesome depth. Yet, while granting to
LSD the power for such illumination, they are positive
that it has not the power to inflict any damage to the
brain. Suggestion of that sort—toxic psychosis or
brain lesions—come only from the medical establishment and are, accordingly, false. The worst that acid
can do, they are sure, is force to the surface an
already existing condition, and if that happens, that
is fine. All of it is worth the risk, in any case. The
psychedelic journey, they say, is akin to the mystical
experience, and if discipline is the very crux of that
experience, the true believers of the new consciousness
have found a way to get around it.

Janis had taken acid once in North Beach. During
the early days with Big Brother, she took it again—
inadvertently. Grabbing at a magnum of wine being
passed around a room, she slugged down three gigantic swallows of a powerfully dosed potion.

"Oh!" someone cried. "You must really dig acid!"

"ACID!" Janis shrieked and, jumping up, ran to the bathroom, there forcing herself to throw up.

That was the first night she heard Otis Redding. His effect on her was enormous. Bill Graham cannot forget the eagerness with which Janis attended every performance Otis gave at the Fillmore that weekend. An hour before the show, she'd be on the dance floor and would place herself in the middle, very close to the stage. While he sang, she watched, transfixed. She absorbed his motions, dwelled on his shouts, and in her imagination perhaps could hear her own voice in those corrugated rasps. Later Tina Turner was to be a major influence too, but it was Otis Redding who changed Janis's concept of singing. "Her high-energy trip started right at that moment," Dave Getz declared.

It had not taken Janis very long to throw off her Port Arthur restraints in any number of ways. As many saw her, she was tough and loose, the intensity of her needs splurging out with astonishing directness. Alternately, she was warm and demanding, quiet and raucous, insecure and grandiose, the character of the moment so without disguise as to be interpreted as a special gift of honesty. Above all, she seemed without sexual inhibition, adopting the hippie ethic in caricature. And thus her belief: do what you want, feel good when you want, take the moment, experience all there is to experience. Everyone admired her words.

Sometime that summer, Chet Helms and Big Brother had a parting of the ways. Nothing personal was involved; Chet was merely preoccupied with the Avalon and The Family Dog productions, and the band was feeling neglected. For all that, the divisiveness was sharpened by another issue. Long before a split between Janis and Big Brother actually occurred, she almost left the band!

Janis, it happened, was approached by a representative of Electra Records with a large contract

offer to join another group. Running off to a meeting
to discuss what Big Brother assumed would be a proposal to them all, she returned and gleefully announced the bid she'd received, which included no
offer to them. To Peter Albin, she was as possessed
as a fifties teen-ager, panting in a fifties movie house,
coveting a fifties dream. "He's gonna make me a
star!" she cried. "He's gonna give me a car and a house
in Hollywood!"

Obviously she didn't leave, but until that was
settled, the possibility of her departure caused quite
a stir in the ranks of the band. Perhaps they should
just break up. Chet protested: they could go on without her well enough. Janis undoubtedly got tremendous enjoyment from the thought that she was so
indispensable. She was very angered by Chet's opinion that the band might still have a future. Nonetheless, it was certainly Chet's attention to other matters
that was the prime source of conflict.

Big Brother was without a manager when they
went to Chicago in August of 1966 to fulfill a four-
week engagement. Songwriter-singer Nick Gravenites, who was a friend from San Francisco, was in
Chicago at the time. He roared at the recollection of
the audience response, which was amazement of the
negative brand. And the group? "They were just too
freaky! This chick had this hair hanging down and
she was dressed in this *bedspread*! And the
jewelry! Chicken bones! Voodoo shit! And this
Patchouli perfume, *reeking*! Her complexion was a
wipe-out. She had this sore throat and she was
screeching like a wounded owl! I didn't really like
the sound, but I was impressed. They were aliens
and they were sticking it out!" Nick also remembered
a record producer in the audience who muttered with
distaste, "Too bad, no one's gonna pick up on 'em."

One record producer was lurking around who had
some other ideas. Misfortune had it that the manager
of the club did not come through with all the money
the band was supposed to receive. Big Brother was

broke and vulnerable when Bob Shad of Mainstream
Records plunged in with a contract offer which,
under the circumstances, they accepted, rather than
wait for the possibility of signing with a larger and
more prestigious company. There was more than
naiveté to the band's foolishness in making the
decision to sign Shad's contract. Janis wanted to
record, her restlessness carrying the implicit threat
that Big Brother had better come up with something
to prevent her from going elsewhere.

The band returned to Laguanitas. They made the
album, and with no one to protect their interests it
was cut in a rush to cost a minimum and not released
until Big Brother was nationally known. Afterward,
a fellow named Jim Kalarney took over for a short
while. Then, in January of 1967, Julius Karpen
became their manager. His first action was to move
them into the city. For Janis that was particularly
fortunate. She had been so terribly lonely. Most
important, the move took her away from a situation
in which she was constantly tempted by speed. She
used no dope during the period that she lived in the
city with Joe McDonald, then of Country Joe and the
Fish.

The affair lasted for three or four months; it disintegrated. It was that casual, which is to say Janis
treated the whole matter with a moderate importance that may have limited his own response. As he
told *Rolling Stone* after her death, "Just one day
I said, 'We're not getting along so well,' and she said,
'Yeah, I know it,' and I said, 'I guess I'll leave,' and
she said, 'Yeah.'" Like all of her relationships, it was
dommed—for one reason or another—to imperma-
nence. If her air when he left was one of indifference,
it is likely that she was merely resigned, accepting his
going as another one of her strangely inevitable
burdens of disappointment.

As for her behavior during those days, he remembered that once Mrs. Joplin came to visit and Janis
went about the apartment, subdued and proper.

Janis fixed a Chinese dinner and set the table neatly, serving the meal with quiet pride. He remembered too that Janis, even when her mother had returned to Texas, was sometimes like that, gentle, say soft, but that some puzzling fire would suddenly well up to overwhelm her, dislocate her attempts at balance. Then there would be sheer raunch and toughness and crazy things—such as the Hell's Angels.

It went back to the highest days of the Haight-Ashbury and before. Allen Ginsberg turned the Angels on to acid. Ken Kesey and his Merry Pranksters embraced them. And in all the' naiveté that pervaded the Haight was the belief, for a while, that a wondrous conversion could be worked on the bikers, that their Neanderthal instincts could be softened, the whiz-bang wheels of their Harley-Davidsons tamed. Why, an Angel named Chocolate George died at the corner of Haight and Belvedere when he swerved his bike to avoid a kitty-cat who was pussyfooting it across the street! Wasn't that a sign of the tenderness that bubbled under the surface of violence? As for that, it was at least *open*, unlike the violence that runs the rest of America, and that, they claimed, made it better. The Angels were "upfront" and loose, although actually they were a tribal unit with astonishingly inflexible codes of behavior. Perhaps there was appeal in the rumble of their bikes, the martial pageantry, the brutishness. Some Haight residents were merely afraid. Others believed; part of the rock community believed. If they dismissed the Angels as a horde, one, two, or three Angels together were "beautiful."

There sprung up a camaraderie of sorts between the Angels and a few of the San Francisco bands: the Airplane, the Dead, and especially Big Brother, with whom the Angels felt a special affinity. So if Janis became friendly with some of the gang, it was only natural. They were part of the environment, and Janis was adapting to that environment more and more by the day. As some saw her, she was "heavy" and got on with the bikers because they shared with her an honesty—of instinct and belief. She was untorn by serious conflict. If she drank, shot dope, traded men like cards, that was because she believed in experiencing all. "She had no conservative side sexually," said one of the members of Big Brother, "and the only thing she believed in was getting stoned right now!" Said a member of the Big Brother family, "She was a *hard* lady. She was totally, funk, totally get it on, totally pleasure of the moment, totally I will take everything I can get to be as high as I can get and fuck as many people as I can get, and she kept radiating energy into this, and that is what made her become her image."

Joe McDonald's opinions were strikingly different, as he expressed them in the *Rolling Stone* interview after her death: "They wanted to see her shoot up, they wanted to see her get loud, they wanted to see her scream and yell and screech about. . . . I don't know what happened to her in Texas in her childhood, but I got the feeling that she was just the wrong person in the wrong place and got treated in the wrong way."

Julius Karpen insists that he saw Big Brother as a similar unit, with no one person more musically notable than any of the others. But Janis, by the time she broke up with Country Joe, was already someone special in San Francisco. She was also getting her first vague nibble at national fame. "Guess what," she scrawled on a poster of herself she sent to Tary Owens. "I might be the first hippie pinup girl."

Behaving with the egocentricity of a star is an altogether different matter. Janis was easily threatened; in her efforts to get her way, she could be forceful and intimidating to the extreme.

"Well, you're pretty heavy, Janis," Julius said once, following a disagreement.

"I just don't sing that way, you know," she retorted.

Similarly, Dave Richards remembers that his hiring

took place on a battleground of challenges, tests, attacks, and retreats, all in the process of his simple employment as someone to help out with the band's equipment. Although in time he became one of Janis's dearest friends, he reacted, at first, with terror. "I mean, it was like, 'Are you gonna ball me?' But it wasn't even *that!* It was like, 'What're ya gonna do?' She was testy, testy about masculinity, about femininity, about *everything!*"

Sometimes Janis pitted herself against those who really liked to play the game. With all stops out, she tried, one time, to tackle Bill Graham by throwing a scene at the door of the Fillmore. Bill promptly barred her forever—meaning that evening—from entering the hall again. Reports came backstage to Nick Gravenites, who was performing at the Fillmore that night, that Janis was crying on the street. More likely, she was cursing for beginners, then fell apart in defeat, although the humiliation seemed definitely to give her pleasure. "When Bill screamed like that," Nick agreed, "she was like a little girl, and she *dug* that!"

Even so, Janis's dramas gave the impression of a very self-centered girl, still possessed by a need for constant reassurance—that she could sing, that she was liked, that she was, above all, noticed. She worried constantly about reactions to her performances, though certain that she was destined in this world to attain some special place. "She was a lot looser in the beginning." Nancy Getz said, "but still she was harsh. It was 'fuck off,' and if you don't like it, split."

She was never really cruel, just thoughtless, defending herself before the attack that was sometimes not even coming. When she became aware of other people's feelings, she could be winningly sensitive, generous of heart, and touchingly sweet. Frequently, though, she was simply oblivious to the needs of others.

The San Francisco sound, by the time Big Brother moved back into the city, was at its most enthralling, a full burst of exotic thunder that herded to its rhythms the march of the Haight-Ashbury community. The bands were functioning as part of a free-wheeling, noncompetitive society; managers were friends, united in an effort to conjoin the evangelical spirit of all the bands; there was dancing in the streets, and concert after concert was free, with the music rising, it seemed, right out of the quivering earth of the Panhandle and Golden Gate Park.

By that time, too, the national media had started to write about the music coming from the Bay Area and, needless to say, about its accompanying environment. That environment had undergone some change and was now a haven of sin, according to the city government. From one side of the mouth, it was "this wild movement akin to Sodom." From the other, the city sanctioned the Gray Line tours of the area—the bus passengers just shaking with horror all the way.

The impoverished Haight, on the other hand, had started to show some unimpoverished ideas. On one level, there were the Diggers. Taking their name from a group of seventeenth-century English farmers who raised food for the poor, the Diggers of the 1960s took it upon themselves to clothe, house, and feed the thousands of runaways who were flooding into the Haight. Two of its members, Emmett Grogan and Peter Cohon, became friends of Janis. As for the Diggers as an entity, there are still some suspicions that there was less purity in their motives than met the eye. Some recall methods that showed another face than love, suggesting a pent-up violence. Their position was one of enormous power, and there were those among them who enjoyed it. Ostensibly, however, to feed, house, and clothe was the Diggers' function and, for the most part, it was fulfilled.

The hustle too was common on the streets. "That's the gypsy trip!" Richard Hundgin insisted. It was also not very difficult. "Any kind of working!" he agreed. "Musicians are finding out they have to work. That's not the most pleasant side of the music business. Like it's not as pleasant as sitting around at parties having groupies stroke your body, you know."

"Like there's no way," Dave Getz added, "for some people to make a living. There's no place to *pay* you for playing the tambra. There's no place that will *pay* you for standing on your head in the full lotus position."

Some of the hippies found that craftsmanship paid. Good hippie garb cost money. Jewelry stores and clothing boutiques began to line the streets near the Haight. The biggest money came from other sources. The economics of the community revolved heavily around rock, and with the exception of heroin *then*, the dealing of dope.

Most did it casually and made little profit. Others were able to turn dealing into an extremely lucrative enterprise, copying with great ingenuity the crafty capitalism that makes for the power elite. There is no question that they were sincerely convinced of their benevolence.

"I *believed* in dope," a former dealer proclaimed. "It was a kind of revolutionary thing. With a big dope organization, you could hire people that were poor. I mean, it was very easy to become *extremely* wealthy. Make a couple of grand a day and become *infamous* —all over the country!"

This hippie dealer thought little of the virtue of poverty. "Fuck poverty! I *luv* money," she whooped, "but my trip is getting it and spending it, ya dig? Ya don't work till you've got a heart attack with two million in the bank. Ya get it, ya spend it! And after a point, ya *stop!*"

Several matters brought her activities to an end. One had to do with the law. Another was a painfully earned discovery.

"See, after a while," she sighed, "you realize your number is getting close. Then, I don't use drugs now, not even grass. I had a nervous breakdown. From speed and coke. You can shoot cocaine every ten minutes, but you can overdose on it. I've seen it and I've almost OD'd on it myself. I had convulsions. See, I got strung out on speed and cocaine. Then what happened was that I got out of that by taking a hell of a lot of LSD. Acid saved me from the needle! It really did! But then I went crazy on the acid!" She started to laugh. "So I did DMT to stop the acid! Then I went nuts on the DMT! So after that, I smoked grass and hash because I did too much DMT and sniffing cocaine! Then after a while, I just flipped out!" She stopped laughing abruptly. "It was horrible," she trembled, "just horrible."

If their house capsized, however, say the original members of the Haight, it had nothing to do with such phenomena. It was the media that did their heaven in. Before the press discovered the Haight you could walk down that street and there was nothing but love.

"The Haight-Ashbury was our town," Nancy Getz said. "It was sunshine and flowers and love. And the media got ahold of it and ate us and fed us back to ourselves."

There were rumors too that the crime syndicates had moved in to take over the drug market, but certainly changes began as the tons of verbiage poured out from the press. The alarming print that announced the migration of one hundred thousand to two hundred thousand young people to the Coast surely helped to bring them, although there were stories that the press had been fed the figures by the Diggers themselves—as a warning or an invitation, no one was ever sure. In any case, it was the members of the Haight who staged the Human Be-In of January 1967. The frivolity of thousands of people in the most outrageous holiday parade in history could do no other than create the influx of almost every confused teen-ager who could manage the way to a road. With them came problems that the original members of the Haight had never known.

There came violence, exacerbated by the anxiety of the police. There came trouble with the poor black

community, which did not think much of white middle-class kids declaring the wonders of poverty. There
came a character to the use of dope that upset the
aesthetics of the area. "*We* weren't shooting dope on
Haight Street," protested one resident who kept her
habit indoors. And so their house was weakened. The
beams turned rotten and the walls came tumbling
down.

But first, there was Monterey.

10

Never again was there a festival such as the one that
took place that June weekend of 1967. Never was
there another event where over thirty rock groups
were inflated by no more than the joy of an enrap-
tured audience and the gorgeous pleasure of performance itself. There were eight, there were nine, there
were ten times as many people overrunning the famous rock festivals taking place only two years later.
There was never another Monterey.

For three days that California coastal town trembled to the apocalyptic vision that shook its County
Fairgrounds, exhorting it up from its bucolic compla-
cency and pulling it into a mind-boggling voyage as
giant electronic waves washed over its serene terrain.
Only twice the glint of Götterdämmerung. The Who
set off smoke bombs on the stage and smashed their
instruments in the rites of destruction; a musician
named Jimi Hendrix made a funeral pyre of his guitar. But the images went quickly, the burlesques of
free-form tumult, speaking more wit than anything
like terror. The weekend was too intoxicating, too
radiant, too pure.

On the second day, Big Brother and the Holding Company mounted the stage. The band fumbled with their instruments, and a few minutes later their lead singer bounced out, all gleaming in a silver-white pants suit made of a sleek lamé. She snaked in a small circle in back of the mike. She seized it as if by impulse. A desperate foot stamped down on the platform. And Janis Joplin let loose the first astounding note of a performance that shook with more energy than the rest of the entire festival. The roar that followed could have been a fissure opening in the earth.

The Fairgrounds of Monterey had been packed with many other people besides the hippies, who were the most visible part of that splendid panorama. Present too was every major recording executive in the country, a multitude of record producers, booking agents, concert promoters, and any number of managers. Most of them were wearing beads, but it was their money that was jangling. A few of the San Francisco bands had already signed contracts with major recording companies. Yet their captive audience was still on the home ground of the West Coast, and the great majority of the Bay Area bands were functioning in a self-sustaining community, far away from the mechanics of industry. Those musicians were as green as the leaves that top the California redwoods and, not incidentally, just as high. But they surely had aspirations. And Lord, were they grabbed by the messianic spirit! So when the industry swooped down, they were eager to be plucked—and fattened and basted and fed to the public—as the newest products in the very big business of entertainment. For the country as a whole, the era of acid rock began with Monterey. Actually, it was the end.

As for Big Brother, they heard howls of enthusiasm from *Newsweek* and *Time* and more howls after they performed at the Monterey Jazz Festival just a few months later. Moreover, Clive Davis, the president of Columbia Records, had made his interest clear. He invited Julius Karpen to attend the CBS Records convention, and also Big Brother's lawyer, Bob Gordon, who had become the group's attorney the previous spring and would later be Janis's as well. Bob ran smack into the problem of extricating Big Brother from the five-year exclusive contract they'd signed with Bob Shad and Mainstream Records, but to the band the future seemed clear. There was more in the offing than could be had in the meadows of Golden Gate Park. That had been Janis's dream; she should have been ecstatic.

A few months after the festival, Janis met a brilliant clothes designer named Linda Gravenites, Nick's former wife. With Janis's physical metamorphosis nearly complete and her financial situation improved, she asked Linda to design her an outfit. There was an instantaneous compatibility between the two women. In her turbulence, Janis reached out for the serenity evident in Linda's dark, almond-shaped eyes, for the strength that showed in the high cheekbones of her strikingly attractive face. Linda's calm is a bit deceptive, but she is warm, compassionate, and intelligent. In the lingo, she'd be "together," and she takes to life unstoned. She became Janis's roommate sometime that fall. Thereupon began a friendship unmatched by any of Janis's other California associations. When she first moved in, Linda had a conversation with Janis that struck Linda as particularly memorable: "Janis said the funniest thing. She said, 'Linda, how can you be so happy? You don't have anything!' I didn't, but I *was* happy, and I said, 'Janis, happiness is a subjective attitude and what you choose to pay attention to. I have friends. I have what I do. What *more* do I need?' Janis didn't seem to understand at all!"

The differences in attitude notwithstanding, the friendship between them was strong. Janis consulted Linda about everything of importance, which, of course, included her career. Changes in that were obviously impending.

During the period following Monterey, the relationship between Big Brother and Julius had begun to deteriorate. Julius was idealistic to a fault, but more important in building toward a split was the conviction on the part of the band that a manager with greater experience was what they needed now. A fiery argument concerning a concert at the Hollywood Bowl brought everything to a climax. Afterward, Big Brother was left with a situation assuredly more serious than ever before. There were a few options, and one day Janis asked Linda what she thought they should do.

"Well," Linda replied, "that depends on what you want. If you just want to play and laugh a lot, then you ought to sign with another San Francisco manager. But if you want to be an international star . . . you sign with Albert Grossman!"

"That granite face," Nick Gravenites chuckled. "You could see Albert as capable of most anything, because he hardly ever changes in appearance. He can one day be talking to a maharaja, and a Japanese transistor king the next. And always looking the same, so you can imagine him doing anything. He *is* a little sinister, because he's sinister to the point where you can *see* him being sinister!"

To many of the San Francisco musicians, Albert Grossman was indeed a sinister figure, and perhaps a little worse. At the time of Monterey, when the San Francisco bands were guided only by local businessmen claiming spiritual bonds with the hippie community, Albert stood ominously as the Emperor East— sly, cunning, powerful, and possessed of the satanic qualities inherent in the materialistic civilization of New York City. Nonetheless, as the man who had played the managerial role in the career of Bob Dylan, he was by no means someone to be lightly dismissed.

Nor to the public at large was Albert much different. To that part of the population concerned with folk and rock, he was the overstuffed, hoary-headed villain in a documentary movie about Dylan called *Don't Look Back*. In that film, the portrait of the scheming manager was intensified by the assumption, on the part of many a Dylan-worshiping viewer, that their poet laureate cared nothing for money and that Albert had been captured in all his evil secrecy, unaware of the cameras that were whirring away in his face. There he was, just as they imagined, long-haired but crafty, amusing but manipulative, the totally money-minded businessman, maneuvering sneakily behind the scenes and gleefully trading Bob Dylan's innocent pound of flesh for pounds and pounds of corrupting cash. A book by Tony Scaduto about Dylan later tarnished the idol's image; the impression of Albert remained.

The truth about Albert Grossman is an entirely different story, or certainly more complex. Endearing and formidable, shrewd and compassionate, droll and sarcastic, open and enigmatic, he is one of the last great eccentrics to which the music business can lay claim, commanding from many of those who know him well both unwavering respect for his brilliance and taste and tremendous love for his fundamental warmth. But like the Buddha to whom he bears some physical resemblance, his is the manner of taciturn ambiguity. Indeed, with his great grizzly head and his long, iron-gray hair, with his looming posture and cryptic speech, he certainly conveys the air of a man around whom one must be very careful. It is all of an attitudinal stance, part shyness, part doubt, and very much the cunning caution of a toughened man who keeps a determined eye on his own vulnerability.

Skimpy with words, he is not all that generous with gestures either, restricting himself to an odd juggling motion with his arms and a weird habit of twisting his left fingernails against those of his right. One reads many of his thoughts by guesses and the obscure mechanism of an intuition that becomes sharpened with experience and time. After a while, his rimless glasses cannot hide the twinkle in the impenetrable coldness of his large blue eyes. On the other hand, he can be contemptuously blunt toward those he doesn't like and uncomfortably direct about many of his opinions. His concept of management is totally without the embellishments of a soft-pedaling hypocrisy. His job is to protect the interests of his clients, and toward obstacles to that goal he can show an alarming lack of mercy. One of his admirers put it well: "On the score sheet of who's done what, he is the heaviest in the business. There are people who despise him because he says 'No' to them, which he will do even if nobody else would dare. I mean, I heard him tell an important film guy who wanted Dylan in a movie, 'Well, Mr. Dylan's price is a million dollars. If you can come up with that, then we have something to talk about!'"

It is incidences like that that lead people to believe Albert has no interest in anything but money. Tony Scaduto, in fact, stated that the main charge against Albert was something called "commercialism." He was wrong. The most well-founded charge against Albert is a tendency to become overly involved with the tomato patches in back of his Woodstock home. He could hardly be said to hate money, but he is not a man of all-pecuniary aims. He has been known to reject managing the careers of some very famous artists whose box-office power is large but whose talents leave him bored and unaffected. Adding to his reputation is the fact that once given his interest, he is icily clear as to the terms of his counsel. Some musicians have found that alienating. There are people in the industry, too, who prefer more garnish to the matter of making contracts. Although he is consistently respected throughout the music business, there are a number of people who react to him with distaste. One of his clients insists that any dislike is attributable to envy and that alone.

"It's jealousy," he nodded with conviction. "I know a lot of people who don't speak well of him who don't *know* him. Then Albert drives a hard bargain. I was glad to have him on my side. He's a *terror* to have on the other side of the negotiating table."

Albert was at Monterey because it was an event and also because a few of his groups were scheduled to perform. Rumors to the contrary, he did not pursue Big Brother. There is even some question about his reaction to their sound. Typically he never said what it was, and who could judge from his appearance? Responding to the report of one person's insistence that Albert was "absolutely overwhelmed," Nick Gravenites just giggled. "Christ! I don't know. I mean, how would Albert Grossman look being *absolutely overwhelmed!*"

The fact is that Albert would never have signed the group had he not been mightily enthused, though it was not Albert who made the approach. That happened on a multibarreled front covered by Bob Gordon, Bill Graham, and Julius himself. Finally, a nervous communication from Janis brought Albert to California.

Albert's initial reluctance was due to several factors. For one thing, the split with Julius had not yet occurred when word of Big Brother's interest was first relayed. Even after Julius had made it clear that he was no longer handling the group, Albert remained aloof. "Just wanting to make sure," Julius said, "that whatever caused our breakup wasn't something he couldn't relate to either."

The other matter that affected Albert's hesitancy was very likely the situation in his own office, an unsettled ship of personnel and clients who were multiplying in tremendous number.

The combination of those factors gave rise to a slowness of developments that had Big Brother stunned at the prospect of the signing. "We were just so jazzed at the thought of Albert managing us, lowly *us*," Dave Getz explained. In retrospect, Dave also believes that Albert was cool from the beginning to everyone in the group but Janis. Bob Gordon heard nothing from Albert to that effect.

Whatever his feelings, which very likely were just not totally formulated, Albert flew out to San Francisco in November. The signing was in part a ridiculous ceremony, at least as it was recalled by the members of Big Brother. That was because they had no idea of the monetary potential in the kingdom of fame.

By 1969, when rock music had been stretched to its most commercial boundaries, the amounts of money that could be accumulated by performers reached outrageous proportions, with the acute irony of that situation in the call for revolution coming from some of the richest of them all. But even in 1967, the money to be had was mammoth. A figure of fifty thousand dollars a night was, and is not, uncommon, even though there is an enormous fluctuation in payments. For instance, a large concert in a major-sized city can bring not only a sizable predetermined fee but a percentage of the total gate. College dates are more frequent, however, usually bringing a flat payment only, the range of money anywhere from thirty-five hundred to ten thousand dollars. There is money from records royalties and music publishing, the latter the richest gold mine of them all. At the same time, the cuts into that basic money are innumerable and huge. There is a percentage due the management, another due the booking agency. There are accountants and lawyers and the costs of travel and hotel accommodations as well as electronic equipment. There are salaried employees who travel on the road. There are *taxes*! Most of all, income is consolidated in a terribly short period of time. Certainly one can become rich, but had better be careful about lavish expenditures; and musicians, thrust overnight into an income bracket to which they are unaccustomed, are more than usually extravagant.

All that aside, the financial stakes are sizable. Like

five serfs in the land of Cæsar, Big Brother had no
conception of the empire's wealth. Still, Albert laid
down no demands that they make him a fortune.
Dave Richards said that Albert clearly stated the
group could determine their own aspirations. As
Dave put it, "It was 'Money? Okay. No money? That's
okay too.'" It was Big Brother that set a minimum.

"You have to make us seventy-five thousand dollars
a year," they insisted. "We want to make sure that if
you're gonna take twenty percent you make us a lot."

"Okay," Albert replied. "I'll make you a lot."

"Yeah, well, we want *at least* seventy-five thousand
dollars a year, and if we *don't* make that, the contract
isn't valid!"

"Yeah," Albert shrugged. "Make it a hundred thousand dollars."

Dave Getz thinks that Albert's attitude was the sly
awareness that a hundred thousand dollars was a
trivial figure and that their naiveté made the arrangement hilarious. It was actually written in the contract! Bob Gordon, however, said that it is amusing
only in hindsight. "Albert's position, in all seriousness,
was that if he couldn't do any better for them than
they'd done before, he didn't really deserve to manage them."

So much for Albert's motives, and if, during that
afternoon, he grinned and said, "Don't ever trust me,"
it is likely that his words meant nothing at all and
were no more than the moment's flash of his ever
enigmatic style.

There was nothing ambiguous about his one adamant condition for going ahead with the contract. He
set it down before one pen was lifted that momentous
afternoon. "We might as well get it straight *right now*.
There's one thing I won't have anything to do with
and that's smack. I've seen terrible things with it and
if anybody here is messing with it at all, there's no
point in going any further. We can call it quits before
we start!"

Every member of Big Brother nodded in innocent-

faced agreement, assuring Albert that, under no circumstances, would they ever have anything to do
with heroin.

Janis's Lyon Street apartment had a quaintly curved
balcony that soaked up the rays of the afternoon sun.
In the front room of the flat, which cost all of seventy-
five dollars a month, Linda Gravenites slept on a
large, comfortable couch and, by the great natural
light of the day, did all of her sewing. A tiny kitchen
jagged off to one side of a long entry hall, and in the
back was Janis's bedroom, all dark and draped with
the emblems of seduction, the final enrichment to
Janis's image. Velvet and satin swathed her bed; her
windows were veiled with lace and silk. One wall
stood clear of sensuous enticement, its attraction a
series of posters, Janis protrayed by her photographer
friend Bob Seidemann. There were animals, always
essential to Janis's happiness. A romping half collie
named George enhanced the charm of the apartment;
an aloof cat named Sam stalked possessively about.
There were friends and laughter and Linda. All in all,
it was, or should have been, the best year of Janis's
life.

Rehearsals occupied her days, performances her
weekend nights. Most of all, she had attained acceptance. She had trimmed down to a slight and attractive figure. She had acquired the aura, which, while
not of a conventional beauty, had the irresistible radiance of energy. No longer an outcast, at twenty-four
she was a queen, and if the regal chamber of her bedroom saw no permanence, wasn't she too young for
that anyway, and wasn't her lofty status the reason,
and didn't a revolving but continual solace to her
flesh cushion the wilderness of her heart a little—just
a little? Besides, what the hell, it was just one jazzy
trick after another.

One day, just like any other day, Janis took George
for a walk through the Panhandle. Resting on the

grass for a while, she broke her boredom by throwing a stick for the dog to chase and return to her feet. Tired of the game, she pulled herself up and continued through the park, then stopped as a familiar female figure came sauntering over the grass.

"Man, haven't seen you in ages!" Janis smiled.

"Yeah, long time. How's it going?"

Janis shrugged, going on to chat about her music and a number of other matters. "I need somethin' new," she sighed. "What've you been doing?"

"Oh, this and . . . a little smack. I'm kind of strung out, though."

"What's it like?" Janis asked. "I've done it a couple of times, but I didn't like it, cause I always got really sick."

"Yeah," the girl nodded. "Well, I got sick the first couple of times too."

Janis peered at her curiously.

"The high's a groove, ya know . . . but it's a drag to be strung out. Listen, I gotta meet somebody. See ya around, right?"

Janis waved as she turned around to walk back in the direction of her apartment. George dipped his head toward her feet and pranced happily behind her as she headed home.

Janis of course had tried heroin before. This, too, was to be no more than an occasional experiment. And, true, Janis was clear-eyed when her smiling "never" met Albert's stern admonishment. She was clear-eyed that night when the signing was celebrated over an imperial dinner at an imperial restaurant in Chinatown.

A gay occasion it was, although there were a few nervous giggles about Albert's droll humor and some edgy laughter that accompanied someone's question: "Albert! What'd ya mean, don't ever trust you?" and more edgy laughter when Albert, for an answer, smilingly spooned a pile of rice onto Janis's held-out plate.

Also there were the hostile reactions, throughout the San Francisco community, which Big Brother would have to face.

An iron curtain separated the music worlds of the West Coast and the East. It was not merely business; it was musical too. From Albert's view, he was bringing no more than professionalism to the careers of Big Brother once they had decided, quite on their own, to leave their enclave of innocence. As he saw it, the first order of business was recording, and his choice to steer Big Brother through that was a very professional musician and producer named John Simon. John was present at the dinner that evening. For himself, the highlight came when Dave Getz voraciously gobbled the eye of a huge fish that lay majestically across the center of the feasting table. "I thought that was indicative of San Francisco liberated minds," he snickered. "The liberated San Francisco mind could eat that gray eye!"

No recording plans could be undertaken, naturally, until the contract with Columbia was finalized, and that involved the delicate situation that remained with Mainstream. Only a hunk of money would pry loose the teeth of Bobby Shad. Eventually Albert got CBS to shove out $250,000 with only half of it recoverable from Big Brother's royalties.

The signing with Albert completed, Janis went home that Christmas to visit with her family. At a huge party in Beaumont, she saw some of her old Texas friends, a few for the very last time. She returned to San Francisco to find herself pregnant by the fellow who'd gotten her back on smack. Shortly after her twenty-fifth birthday, she went to Mexico for an abortion. The experience was gruesome, with the physical effects bad enough, but the emotional trauma by far more severe. Her reaction was one of moral horror. "It was *wrong!*" she cried to Linda. "It was *wrong!*" An obvious depression lasted for about three days, then simply seemed to dissipate. At no time, except to physicians, would she ever mention it again.

By the time Big Brother was ready for their national launching, Janis already had her public style. "I remember," Bob Clark remarked, "that way back when she was living with Linda Wauldron, she told me she didn't want to mix her life with her image or something along those lives, but it must have been that first year with Big Brother that she started to develop her stage personality. She wasn't like that earlier—not quite so hard."

If that had happened before—the hardness, the flamboyance, the conspicuous consumption of everything that could feed the senses—the style had been thickened by the San Francisco mystique, the layers to hide her desolate heart. It remained for the treachery of fame to render her isolation utterly complete.

Part Three
Count Your Fingers

11

I am far more certain of the events that followed, but as I vaguely recall, it was around the eighteenth of January, 1968, that I went to work for Albert Grossman. The date doesn't matter except for this: it was approximately three and a half weeks before Big Brother and the Holding Company came to perform for the first time in New York.

Ostensibly, I had been hired to handle press relations, not only for Big Brother but for most of the other performers Albert had as his clients. And back in those days they were many and mighty: Peter, Paul, and Mary; The Band; Richie Havens; Mike Bloomfield; James Cotton; the Paupers; Odetta; Paul Butterfield; Ian and Sylvia; Gordon Lightfoot; and, the most famous, Bob Dylan. Actually my connection with Peter, Paul, and Mary was to be formally nonexistent, developing, what there would be, out of a close personal friendship with Peter Yarrow and his wife. I was to have no contact with Dylan at all. At that time, he was untouchably ensconced in the rural environs of Woodstock, New York, but his presence, specterlike though it was, hung heavy in the Grossman office and was, in part, responsible for the peculiarity of its atmosphere. When I came there, that office, in the rock hierarchy, was like the Vatican, just as powerful, and shrouded in just as much mystery. And, in the same sense, Albert Grossman was its pope.

Certainly, as I tried to interpret my surroundings, I saw them as almost that foreign. My musical background was classical and my dedication to the piano all-consuming from the days of my Midwest childhood. Events and God knows my limitations had altered all that, but there was the core of my sensibility, so that being in the very center of the rock world had me far adrift from the universe I knew.

The course of that had already started. For the five previous years, I'd worked in the publicity department of Columbia Records and, toward the end, as the industry followed the shift of the cultural wind, so did my life begin to change. Then, around August of 1967, when the corporate character of Columbia had just about driven me mad, I left, pressured by inward necessity, but quite indefinite about my plans.

To be sure, if one could write, there was a market. A host of new publications had come with the explosion of rock, diminishing the perils of free-lancing for many an unpublished writer. And so I took a fancy to that idea and even followed through in one or two instances. Still, I was possessed by a personal malaise, long since passed, but unconquerable then. I could generate within myself no real enthusiasm, nor a cynical relish for blood, both of which, as I saw it at the time, were required to tackle the new journalism with any determination.

Moreover, my attitude toward the cultural revolution was mired in doubt. For its rebellion, I loved it. I loved its music and I was wonder-struck by its abandon. Still, I was disturbed by what it might unleash and definitely offended by some of its silly slickness. That was when I considered it. Really I was not considering very much at all other than the state of my personal life and my paralyzing mood of indifference. It was in that frame of mind that I decided to get a job. A friend named Charlie Rothschild told me there might be an opening in Albert's office. Thus, I embarked on a three-year adventure unlike anything I had theretofore experienced. There was much glory in those years; there were a lot of laughs and a marvelous wackiness through it all. I suffered too, but I learned a great deal more and I regret none of it—except the agony to which I was witness and the hor-

rible anguish in which it all came to an end. Still, I
fell there by chance, and it was the last time, or so I
pray, that I was to let life take me where it would.

When I started off working for Albert, I was filled
with all sorts of anxiety and foreboding. That was because I was hired, not by him, but by an amiable girl
named Arline Cunningham, his assistant at the time.
While she assuredly didn't intend to scare me to
death, she intimated that Albert was none too happy
about the whole business. Notorious for what was assumed to be a disdainful attitude toward the press,
Albert, I gathered, was reluctant to take any step
that would make his outlook appear otherwise. As I
got to know him, I learned that basically wasn't the
case. Some managers court publicity for themselves;
some do not. Albert is among the latter, and the media were after him always. Moreover, part of his style
is to hold his response to unfamiliar people in abey-
ance, until rapport is clear . . . or altogether out of
the question. That makes him appear suspicious
which, on occasion, he has reason to be.

Albert now spends all of his time in Woodstock, occupied with a mammoth recording studio, the management of some performers, and a record company
named Bearsville. Then, his location was in a converted apartment building on East Fifty-fifth Street
in Manhattan. And if Arline had scared me to begin
with, his own private office completed the job.

I used to be terrified to walk into that room. The
drapes were usually drawn and the lamps barely flickered, so low was the wattage of their bulbs. At a certain hour of the day, though, the sun would streak
through and the whole room would remind me of a
Vermeer painting, old and burnished in tone, with
one of those brilliant shafts of brightness slanting in
from the left to cut a precise golden circle on the
floor. All Louis XIV, his office seemed, forbidding and
imperial, which was exactly the effect of his presence.
That his clothes were country apparel—rumpled

sweaters, clumpy boots, frazzled jackets, and the like
—made no difference in his imposing manner. In
front of his desk there was a great red leather chair,
very soft and ever so comfortable, but sinking into its
recesses used to give me the feeling that I was disap-
pearing and that Albert, looming behind that expanse
of mahogany and all the papers that covered it, was
getting bigger and bigger and bigger. In time, my
fear of Albert gave way to great affection, but never
did I take willingly to the enveloping arms of that
terrible red leather chair.

If Albert's own office was dim and mysterious,
weighted with the tone of something from the past,
the rest of the place was a well-lit concentration of
1960s oddity. It was not that the people were so terribly strange, but they were all wandering about with
aimless looks, their functions undiscernible. Reorgani-
zation was constant, the number of personnel changes
astounding.

Albert's first partner, John Court, departed a few
months after I arrived. Arline was gone by midsummer. No one could stick with the job of handling itin-
eraries: the booking of flights, the renting of cars, the
hotel arrangements for some one hundred musicians
and roadmen that were involved in the tours of ten or
so acts. There were clerks and mailboys who came
and went. Secretaries changed constantly; the suc-
ceeding switchboard operators couldn't be counted.

Also, the power of rock generated an in-and-out
flow of people, for the most part the jet set of the
avant-garde, cultural adventurers of the rock-pop-
new sensibility. And sometimes political adventurers
as well. Cultural or political, it was all show business,
or so it seemed to me. A carousel, that office, with its
riders speeding by in a blurry whirl—hair, beads,
beards, and color—a freaked-out cinema of the sur-
real. In time, I realized that the over-all weirdness
was deceptive. For all the trivia of the hipness about,
Albert ruled with tremendous class and great business
acumen.

I speak of my reactions at the time, and in my first few days I felt acutely displaced, dropped helpless and struggling in a netherworld of the bizarre. Though it was only the first of five offices I was to occupy during the course of those years, the room I was stuck in completed the picture. It was as gloomy as an underground dugout and scooted right off a small entrance lobby decorated with a sagging yellow loveseat and an insanely busy switchboard. I was only glad that I didn't see much of Albert, trembling in fear of him as I did.

On occasion he'd be in my office, just materializing like a body of ectoplasm. He'd stand there, his long silver hair knotted in a pony tail, a colonial apparition, making that winding motion with his fingernails. He'd mumble a little, then disappear as stealthily as he'd arrived.

"Is he always like that?" I kept asking Johanna.

"Oh, you'll get used to it," she'd laugh.

Johanna Beck was my secretary, and I was quite content to deal with her and Arline and several others around with whom I felt comfortable. There was, above all, Sy Rosen, who was frequently at the office. Albert's accountant and financial consultant, he served in that capacity for a great number of Albert's clients and would do the same for Janis. His sanity and warmth were also to be my salvation in many a frantic moment, but I hardly knew him then. Generally, I was ill at ease and showed it in my own particular mask. I was all nerves and jumpy aloofness. Nor did the assurance of Albert's secretary, Liz Clarkson, do much to dispel my anxiety. I simply tried to stay busy, going through the files and attempting to establish some procedure in the function of my office. I was also contemplating the arrival of Big Brother. The photographic genius of Irving Penn had already etched them into the pages of *Look*, and a rock critic named Bob Christgau had put it down in *Esquire* that he'd been mesmerized at Monterey by Janis's left or right "erect nipple." I can't remember which.

The day before Big Brother arrived, a particular call came in for Arline, which she happened to receive while in my office.

"Hello . . . yes . . . this is Arline . . . yes . . . but . . . yes . . well . . ."

I watched the distressed expression on her face as she tried to stumble through the conversation.

"You don't have to yell!" she cried, grabbing a pencil and scrawling something on a scrap of paper she promptly threw on the floor. "Listen! Will you stop yelling!" Gritting her teeth, she held the phone at arm's length away from her ear. She jerked it back. "All right . . . yes . . . all right." She went on like that, trying to interject her comments until, the call completed, she plopped wearily into a chair.

"Good grief!" I said. "Who was *that*?"

"*That*," she replied, "was John Cooke."

A Haaavad graduate, a former member of a very Cambridge folk trio and the son of Alistair Cooke, John is as patrician as a leftover from the Roman Senate and every bit as committed to his own ideas of order. When he became Big Brother's road manager in December of 1968, he suffered no such intimidation as Dave Richards described. No, the hounds of hell couldn't scare John Cooke, not as he would have it. He'd bare the perfection of his startling white teeth and tweak at his suave mustache; he'd summon the hauteur within his easy command and fix them with the ice of his cutting black eyes. Then he'd *count* them! And the poor slavering beasts, cowed by his exacting evaluation of the odds, would turn to run howling for the safety of distance.

"You were a member of that organization," said Mrs. Joplin. "Knowing you had somebody who had talent and who had a problem, *why* did they hire a business major to be the road manager instead of a sociologist? The man from Harvard. John Cooke."

"Well, he was a Spanish major," I grinned.

"Was he really? I thought it was business."

A road manager has a difficult job, a regimen that

few can handle. It is his whistle that gets bleary-eyed musicians out of bed in the morning, his order that packs them in the limousines. He must zip them to the airports, drag them to their concerts. He must soothe the nerves of uniformed guards, collect the money from promoters. He must get his hairy caravan by the staid gray suits that host the bleached-out desks of all those Holiday Inns. A road manager is as crucial to a rock group as a Fender guitar. John Cooke was the best in the business by virtue of his amazing efficiency, not to mention what always looked like an absolute passion for holding a post of command.

He got off to a bad start with Big Brother. It was the precision of his manner that did it, that and the very careful attention he paid to every word that came from his own mouth. Both of those things stayed with him. Big Brother's attitude changed. Gradually, they developed a fondness for qualities they believed lay underneath, and they learned to respect his assets. Moreover, as his association with Big Brother progressed, he became, at least by the measure of his previous tightness, considerably more relaxed. He was marvelous with promoters, saving his condescension and dyspepsia for special occasions and people. John can be quite pleasant, particularly when he thinks it expedient to be so. He was also, in his fashion, devoted to Janis Joplin. In any event, whether initially intimidated, he was relatively subdued when the group arrived in New York.

It was Arline who met them at the airport, she and Vinnie Fusco. A wiry young man with dark, nervous eyes, he also had been hired by Arline, his expected function slightly unclear. Nothing was vague about his charm, however, or for that matter his ambition, but he held that back in those early days and accompanied Arline to the airport because he had little else to do. I was still in a mood to remain out of the way. Albert had been low-keyed about their arrival and had suggested no more than a modest party on their behalf, that is, if they should want it. We would be having a meeting with Big Brother to discuss it, and I was perfectly happy to postpone our introduction until what seemed an appropriate time.

That meeting took place in Albert's office only a few days later. I still thought of that office as a somber room, sort of a mausoleum wherein lay queer and ominous secrets. Of course, it was nothing of the sort, but merely Albert's sanctuary, its dark quietness a reflection of his personality, which is rich with understatement—sometimes. Certainly he was understated during that afternoon's discussion, which was kicked off by Arline's blithely-put question to the group: "How do you want us to promote you?"

A moment of awful silence followed her words, and I turned to look at Janis. She was sitting next to Albert, and the sun—because it was that hour of the day when its rays came through the curtains—drew a thin white line across her profile and made the pallor of her complexion more starchy than it was by nature. Wriggling uneasily, she made a nervous motion with her head, and the light ran through her drab brown hair as a curlicue of red. The members of Big Brother glanced at each other blankly.

"I mean," Arline continued, directing her words at Janis, "what kind of image do you want?"

The effect of that was worse. Albert said nothing. Vinnie Fusco stared at his feet. Someone in the room said "Huh!" No one in Big Brother had understood Arline's question, and neither, in fact, had I.

In all the time that I had spent at Columbia Records, only once had I witnessed an "image" calculated over a round-table discussion. Nor was it conceived by the publicity department of Columbia, but rather by the very Broadway manager of the subject in point. It had been disastrous as well, the performer bearing, in the essence of her personality and in the style of her singing, no resemblance to the creature who was fabricated out of that plotting that I had overheard. Once a superb jazz singer, the girl was obliterated and reconstructed into a cocktail music chanteuse with a personality to match. Her career lasted approximately six months. I found the whole process chilling. That, I had thought at the time, must be what happens in the factories of Hollywood, and I wanted nothing to do with such procedures.

In the case of Big Brother, the whole idea struck me as especially bizarre. A bunch of beaded musicians born out of the San Francisco hippie milieu to be made into *what*? As for Janis, she looked as though she'd climbed out of a Louisiana swamp. There was her energy, so forceful that it seemed to spring out and literally part the air around her. There was her speech, which tumbled from her lips as if it were one with the never-ending mobility of her body and the restless darting of her blue-gray feline eyes. If I sensed some clinging need—the way she looked at Albert, the manner in which she struggled to sit regally in her chair—if there was a tissue of pathetic dependency visible underneath her commanding style, there was still her presence: grand, raw, powerful, simply bedrocked in defiance and sexuality. There was the already completed immortalization of her "erect nipple." There were the libidinous phrases that described her singing. Everything about her rang sheer theatrical genius. What athletics of transformation Arline Cunningham had in mind, I simply could not imagine. The subject was dropped as Albert steered the conversation back to the main topic of the day: Big Brother's forthcoming first performance in New York and the planning of the party to introduce them to the press.

During the few days that lapsed between that afternoon and the third week of February, I had little contact with Janis or the rest of Big Brother. They were cloistered at the Chelsea Hotel, legendary as a haven for visiting and resident bohemia. Their evenings they spent at a New York restaurant called Max's Kansas City, which catered to the pop world and all its flashy configurations. Nor did the band

come to the office too frequently at first. Dave Richards and the other equipment manager, Marc Bronstein, were around much more, always bouncing
about with warmth and good humor. Of John Cooke,
I can hardly recall a thing.

What is vivid in my memory was my immediate reaction to Janis. If I had been struck by her magnetism,
I had been equally affected by the painful urgency in
her eyes. Something about her had edged my own
restlessness uncomfortably forward to connect with
her nerves, tingling and shredded and as hazardously
open as an exposed electrical wire. With that had
come a protective response for which I simply could
not account. It was all of a fleeting nature, and I
hardly gave it a thought. I'd not been particularly impressed with Big Brother's Mainstream album. Neither had I been present at Monterey, nor seen D. A.
Pennebaker's film of the event, so that my personal
reaction was a separate matter, my concern that perhaps it was the aura of Monterey that had settled
around her talent as a deceptively sulphurous glow.

In another day, when Second Avenue stretched
through what was always called the Lower East Side
and never the East Village, great old Yiddish plays
used to be performed on the stage of the Anderson
Theater. On the night of February 17, 1968, it was a
rock hall, though destined to close soon after, unable
to withstand the competition from the Fillmore East,
which Bill Graham opened the following month, only
a few blocks north.

Back in the Anderson's cramped dressing room, I
watched Janis as she studied herself in a three-way
mirror.

"Do I look old?" she asked.

She had just turned twenty-five, but the plowmarks
in her forehead as she fretfully scrunched her brow
seemed to justify the question. When no one answered, she turned to grab at a bottle of Southern
Comfort and tilted it to her mouth. Smacking her lips,

she slammed the bottle back on a table and followed Dave Getz out to the orchestra pit to listen to B. B. King. In a few minutes, she returned, commenting anxiously on the marvel of the black blues guitarist with processed hair who was out there in a sleek navy suit playing a down-home black blues which, she said, could not possibly be matched by Big Brother.

"We're just a sloppy group of street freaks," she muttered; then, smiling childishly, she snuggled up to Albert, who was sitting at one end of a couch.

During the sound check that afternoon, she had sat in the auditorium with John Morris, a member of the Anderson staff at the time. "I ain't so sure we're ready for New York," she'd noted.

Dave Getz was more awed still, wilted by the feeling that they had no business being the headline act, wondering really why they were there at all. The other members of the band wandered back and forth, listening for a while, then attempting to relax backstage which, because the dressing room was small and packed, was a somewhat difficult matter. Arline was sitting languidly at the other end of the sofa and Vinnie was staring at his feet again in one corner of the room.

"Hi!" Sam Andrew said, as the rock world's classiest groupie squeezed through the door. Linda Eastman was so classy that she landed up as Mrs. Paul McCartney, but that night she was merely a classy groupie, an especially nice one too, there with a camera to protect her pride. Another girl trailed in as well. Robin Richmond's cover was a reporter's notebook, a job with *Life*, and a self-conscious habit of hissing her s's as in "yesss," which whistled off Vassar, between-the-teeth. Other people popped in and out, some with a purpose, most with none, but that is the way of backstage settings and it bothered no one and certainly not Janis, who was the main reason for the influx.

She returned to peering at her reflection, fidgeting with the seam of her tight satin pants. "Do I look old?"

she repeated. Again, no one responded. "I think I'm getting fat," she worried, then clutched at the bottle of Southern Comfort once more. Looking back into the mirror, she made stage movements to herself, snapping her pelvis a little and raising her fists with a synchronized jerk. She grinned with pleasure. Suddenly, to me, she looked like an impish four-year-old in grown-up masquerade.

Peter Albin sat in a corner writing out the sequence of songs.

"I wanna do 'Catch Me, Daddy' first!" Janis commanded.

"Yeah," he said, "that's what I got."

Janis turned toward Sam. "You love me?" she pleaded. "Oh, I wish ya loved me!" His long blond hair dropped in a clean angle across his profile as he leaned toward Janis to give her a quick kiss on the cheek.

John Cooke stalked into the room. "O.K.," he barked. "Let's go!"

I reached the back row of the hall just as Big Brother, silhouetted against a bluish darkness, began to take their places and the equipment men fooled with the amplifiers before shooting back into the wings. Swiveling out with the sass of a fan-dancer, Janis stood motionless behind the mike. She crouched for a second and I jumped up in astonishment as the entire theater blazed open.

Never before had I heard a sound like that! She was a headlong assault, a hysterical discharge, an act of total extermination. It was as if some invisible claw had risen up from her throat, its talons hooked to tear unmercifully at the outer reaches of the auditorium. She lunged into "Catch Me, Daddy," and this unearthly inferno smashed back into the whirling colors of the light show behind her, paroxysmal movements, yells, wails, moans, screeches, crashing dizzily against a distortion as angry as an amplified hive of buzzing hornets, the scream of Big Brother's instruments. She yearned through "Summertime," her voice like a bow

stuttering on a sooty viola. She beckoned through
"Piece of My Heart." She shuddered and stomped
and provoked and flogged, the range of emotions
transcendent of lust, but she was naughty and down,
and the sex of her pounded on through in a graphic
heightening of it all. In between songs, she rested,
panting with exhaustion, but not too weakened to
beam as she received the pandemonium that burst
forth in her honor. Four encores were wrung from Big
Brother before the audience would let go. The last
was Big Mama Thornton's "Love Is Like a Ball 'n'
Chain." Yelps from the hall pierced the uncanny wails
that soared up from her throat near the end of the
song. A stunned pause followed. Then the crowd
reared back like a huge stable of just-branded horses
and heaved forward with a shrieking charge to the
stage.

Many months later, I was on occasion to be alternately
amused and irritated by the speculation from some
quarters that Janis's career had been launched with a
colossal campaign by the Grossman office. The fact is
that I was totally unprepared for what happened at
the Anderson Theater, an embarrassing admission,
but nonetheless true. The house had not even been
sold out, and while most of the critics had responded
to my invitation, I had not anticipated anything so out
of the ordinary. Then did I *like* what I'd heard? Well,
who could think in such terms? I was standing in the
lobby trying to figure out my reaction when Bob Shelton, then the rock and folk-music critic for *The New
York Times*, came dashing up the aisle.

"She's fantastic!" he cried. "Let me have her picture!"

Mortified, I slumped against a wall of the lobby
and told him I didn't have one.

"Whadda you *mean*, you don't have one!" he glowered.

" 'Cause this is all I've got!" I ripped a photo of Big
Brother off the wall and thrust it into his hand.

"I don't *want* this! I need a picture of *her!*"
I pleaded, "Let me run backstage. Maybe somebody's got one."

"I don't have *time!*" he said. "Forget it for now and
tell me who plays what."

Bob readied his pencil; I smiled bleakly and had to
tell him I wasn't sure.

"Don't you *want* me to write this review?" he
snarled.

"I'll check the facts . . . I'll call you in twenty
minutes." I dashed backstage as he marched off into
the street.

Linda Eastman, it happened, had a photo of Janis,
which I brought to Bob's apartment at eight-thirty the
following morning. He was still seething, and to make
his mood worse, Linda's photo was too dark to be
used. Bob's justified anger was strictly of the moment.
On Monday, he had Janis at the top of the *Times'* cultural page. They'd taken the group picture and
cropped it down. There she was, crowned by a glaring
two-column headline and set in the center of an enormous two-column rave.

Two things happened on the day the review appeared: Big Brother signed their contract with Columbia Records; that completed, they went over to a
Greek restaurant called Piraeus, My Love on Fifty-
seventh Street and met the New York press.

A select audience had occupied the seats at the Anderson Theater. Even the critics who attended were
of a special group. If they had not been at Monterey,
they were no less aware of who Big Brother was, and
with a few exceptions—Bob Shelton and one or two
others—they were extremely young and representatives of an exclusive press. No matter the variance
among its members and the publications that carried
their words, they were united in this respect: they
had grown up listening to rock; they identified with
its lifestyle. For some, rock literally defined the terms
of their existence, and certainly it defined their

journalism, much of which blasted forth with a sputtering frenzy that jangled and writhed as spasmodically as the music to which it paid homage. It was that, the tactile nature of the style and not political oppression, that marked the "underground" press, where most of such writing appeared.

As a major media phenomenon, however, rock journalism had been started in the mid-sixties by a magazine called *Crawdaddy* which, by 1968, was nearly defunct. Indeed, Paul Williams, its original editor, had dedicated himself to rock with the commitment of Robert Craft to the works of Stravinsky. Doubtless he saw rock as every bit that lofty because he went at it with a vocabulary that placed it somewhere in the aesthetic province of the Huxley Variations. I could take it until the term *Sprechstimme* popped up in an article on The Supremes. For sheer gall, nothing in rock journalism has ever rivaled the equating of a vocal technique indicated in the scores of Alban Berg and Arnold Schoenberg with the droning of "ma momma warn' me 'bout men," or something like that, to a Motown beat.

Overriding such silly pretentiousness, however, was a sincerity that was anything but laughable—at least as the record companies saw it. *Crawdaddy* was the first publication to prove that those companies were prepared to take rock journalism seriously. They did so by advertising, naturally leading to the founding of innumerable publications that focused on rock and all its extensions.

Many hovered only a bit above the fan magazine format that typified the music media of old. Some large conglomerates got into the act. The Diners' Club managed to keep *Cheetah* afloat for a while. The Hearst Corporation's *Eye* held up for a year. The publications that survived gave the impression that they'd never heard of a market research report. Most powerful among them would be *Rolling Stone*.

Rolling Stone began as a local San Francisco

paper, dedicated to the proposition that nothing was equal to San Francisco rock. It was, moreover, strikingly noncommercial, which is not to say that it had a true disdain for matters of commerce, but that it *looked* that way—with its ornate logo, the flat, grayish matte of its paper, and the unorthodoxy of its layout giving it a deceptive similarity to the "underground" media. It talked a pious, anti-materialistic language as well, which added to its "underground" disguise. And all the while, under the guidance of its very ambitious editor, Jann Wenner, it grew to become the most financially successful in its field. It has, as its senior mentor, critic Ralph Gleason, who, in a fanatic loyalty to the paper, would have it that Jann Wenner is as heroic as Sir Galahad, when he resembles more clearly Hugh Hefner, if not in brains, then most assuredly in aspirations. Whatever its hypocrisies, *Rolling Stone* has maintained a tremendous prestige and has managed to attract some highly competent people to its staff. It has, moreover, drawn in a number of talented writers who publish free-lance in its pages and, on occasion, has been responsible for some astounding in-depth reporting. Still, just as often, at least in the past, it has been trivial and petty, displaying, in the headiness of power, a tendency to bitchy personal attack and an inexcusable amount of journalistic license. Always, it has operated deadpan on the assumption that rock brought the millennium. At the same time, that premise accounted for its fervor and the stick-to-it-iveness that helped it survive.

As for the free-lance writers, there were legions. Others of the "new journalism" genre would get involved in a range of subjects. The writers on rock wrote *only* of rock, partly because a good many of them could do no more. Some were merely obsessed and talented indeed. There were far too many to mention here. But Bob Christgau, for instance, had his *Esquire* column and Richard Goldstein contributed consistently to *The New York Times, Vogue,* and *New York* magazine, as well as *The Village Voice*. There was Jon Landau in Boston, Michael Lydon in California. There would be other writers later. These were the ones at the time. The point is that the entire bunch, from the best right down to the worst, would build their careers solely on rock. It was the very basis and thrust for their futures. Rock journalism was in its freshest, its most enthusiastic, and definitely its most influential stage. The established media took their cue. Underground, overground, younger, older, the entire press was speeding on the tracks charted by rock as a centrifugal force. That overnight stars would come from that was simply automatic.

To be sure, everyone who conceivably might be interested had been invited to Piraeus, My Love. Basically, however, the affair had been planned quite simply. We had assumed the party would attract a respectable number of people. In no way had we anticipated a multitude of crashers. But the Anderson performance and Bob Shelton's review had drawn everyone who could summon the minutest of credentials to get in. Piraeus, My Love was absolutely jammed.

Moreover, Arline, who had chosen the setting for the evening, had picked a restaurant where the food was scrumptious—and the experience in renting to large parties was simply nonexistent. That turned out as an unexpected blessing, causing the staff to be overly generous with the supply of food and drink. Press parties are usually indescribably dull. Somewhat due to the extravagance of the bar—Brandy Alexanders!—this one was a marvel.

Spotting Big Brother in the doorway, I excused myself from a conversation with Janet Rotter who, at that time, wrote a feature entertainment column for *Glamour*.

Robin Richmond blocked my way to the door.

"How soon can we set something up? *Life* hardly ever does things like this, you know! It's going to be a whole spread on rock! Just huge!"

I groaned. "I'm not sure yet, Robin. I have to check their schedule." I gave up trying to reach Big Brother and headed toward the hors d'oeuvres.

"This food!" Bob Christgau said, popping some exotic Greek item in his mouth.

"Isn't it terrific!" I said, turning to greet Richard Goldstein.

"It would really be better on the road," he nodded, discussing his idea for a story.

"I know," I agreed. "I just can't say when yet. I'll talk to you about it later."

Albert appeared at the door with Clive Davis, president of Columbia Records. Lumbering toward me, Albert nodded approvingly, a slight smile sneaking into the corners of his mouth. When Janis came bouncing across the room, his smile broadened and he hugged her paternally. I was already beginning to find him a much less ominous figure.

"How's everybody doing?" I asked Dave Getz.

"Ahhh! Gettin' drunk," he giggled. "This is ridiculous! I feel like we're putting people on!"

But Janis, in a black velvet minidress, had zipped over to the most active part of the restaurant, her colorful necklaces whooshing around as she shook her head excitedly. A group of people surrounded her.

"When I'm onstage . . ." she said. "It's a *feeling . . .*"

"Well, what does the San Francisco sound *mean?*" someone asked.

Janis turned around suddenly to grab at her drink. When I saw her face again, it was tight, masked in a splotchy pink that looked like the prelude to an onslaught of tears.

I pulled her aside. "What's the matter?"

"I don't know who that bitch is," she whimpered, "but my hair went into her face or something."

I looked around.

"She's gone," Janis moped.

"Well, what did she *do?*"

Janis pursed her lips in imitation. "She said, 'Who do you think you are!'" Mumbling something hoarsely, she stared forlornly at the floor.

"Oh, so what! It was just a remark! I can't believe you're this upset!"

"Well, let's face it," she moaned wretchedly. "I've got ratty hair."

In a few minutes, she was sufficiently recovered to renew the game of chatting with reporters. When I approached her again, she was yammering away breathily about her spontaneity, as if nothing had happened at all.

"I don't know *what* it is . . ." she exclaimed. It's just a feeling, something I can't help and I . . ."

"Hi!" I said. "Everything better?"

Frowning petulantly, Janis extricated herself from the group. "I don't know what this is all about," she protested. "I'm no star!"

I noticed that her eyes were darting expectantly around the room. A photographer named Dan Kramer raised his camera. Janis thrust her chin up provocatively and smiled, a resplendent vagabond with a look of triumph unmistakably imprinted on her face.

12

Just a few days after the press party, Big Brother left New York for performances in Boston, Providence, and Detroit. It was there, at Detroit's Grande Ballroom, that the first efforts were made to record. The results were disastrous. Hauled in from Chicago, the

recording equipment was completely inadequate for
the purposes at hand. Moreover, Big Brother played
terribly. The original plans, which were to record
them live, were more or less abandoned. The group
returned to New York to attempt studio recording
instead and also to be the headline performers at the
opening, March 8, of the Fillmore East.

Who could give a thought to the prospects of recording? The lobby of the Fillmore was bulging. The
streets outside were bedlam. Legions of people descended on the hall, fighting, streaming, swarming
toward the doors. It was only two and a half weeks
from that night at the Anderson, and the entire area
seemed to be overrun by an army of the possessed.

What happened afterward was media chaos. The
phones in my office screamed incessantly. When
could she be interviewed? When could she be
photographed? Could this one go on the road? Could
that one talk to her at midnight? One reporter would
settle for a hasty breakfast; another needed two
hours. None of us—Janis, Albert, the band, myself—
had a chance to catch a breath. The press had gone
absolutely amok, seized by a delirium of enthusiasm
and palpitating with an extravagance of language as
reckless and abandoned as Janis's own performances
and her outrageous façade.

Beads, rings, satins, sequins, she jangled as a blinding siege of color. Her speech poured out in an
avalance of multisyllabic combinations that set reporters crazy with delight. Janis was a *wizard* with
words, and they stopped only when she paused to
open her throat to the syrupy elixir of Southern Comfort that would, in no time, become her emblem. Yet,
in her very first interviews, Janis said nothing so
terrifically startling. She let the press know she'd been
a "weirdo" in Texas; she talked a great deal about
"soul" and "feeling." But she was natural, captivating,
and guileless; the animation in her face, the mobility
of her hands and body, the stream of vivacity that
rang through her statements creating the clip of a

tempo allegro that drove forward the character of the writing itself. Then, as she sensed this, did the pace and the heat pick up.

Janis took to the media interest with both childish pleasure and terrified awe. Responding to kindness with the most ingenuous candor, she reacted to threats with a bristling fury that was really just heartbreaking hurt. Only with photographers was she somewhat uncooperative, as if in pictures lay true exposure. So she fluctuated, complaining that she was no fashion queen, then facing the cameras with a defiant sauciness and a courageous proclamation of her curious glamour. Enchanted as she was with the attention, somehow it did little to sweep away an underlying bleakness. Always her eyes would drift off just at certain moments to linger in some haunted, solitary space.

On April 4, she wrote this letter to Linda:

Things still very weird here—recordings hard and we're busy besides. Got 2 tracks down though. Comb. of 2 and Piece of my Heart. It's gonna be a long hard drag, but we'll make it.

Things are looking a little better for me though. I took pictures for *Glamour* last week wearing your white lace things & everyone loved it. Going to be a full-length picture & I told her all about you—so get ready for the June issue. I'm also mentioned in the new *Vogue* &—this evening Nat Hentoff (!) is interviewing me for an article in the *New York Times* & then tomorrow (please let me brag—it's just about the only satisfaction I'm getting) I'm being interviewed for a thing in *Life* & *Look* is going to do us when we get back to S.F. So shit that makes Vogue, Glamour, N.Y. Times, Teen-Set, Life, Look, Wash. Post, the Voice, N.Y. Free Press—Jesus, I guess I must be happy! Well, actually, I even am a little bit—met a really groovy guy in Chicago. Really, really dug him. Tried to talk him into coming to S.F. & staying w/me. He may even show up one day. And also an Irish R & R band staying here at the Chelsea and I'm "seeing" the guitar player—fan*tas*tic & oh so charming. So things are a

little better. Really wish I could get————to come &
live w/me. He's from the N.Y. street gang school, really
smart & been through the same type shit as me. I was
really digging him (& in bed—SIGH) then found out
he's only 19!! Really dig him.

Hey, wanta do me a favor? Find a realtor or something & start looking for a house in Mill Valley—I'd
pay $100 or a little more. But dig this, if you can find
a bigger one with some sort of separate building—just
a garage or something (this is absolutely mandatory)
Dave will move in too & we can pay $200 more. Dave
& Nancy aren't together any more & he wants to move
over there—all he asks is a place to practice his drums.
So, start looking, please? Maybe the Blues Project's
house, or a lead through them . . . take the car & go
look, okay? Sure would be nice, wouldn't it babe?

Oh, & here's some money . . . oh wow, you could
have a sewing room & maybe a sun deck & 8 or 50
dogs & it would be so fine. . . !!

Wow, I miss y'all too—so much. We're leaving here
about the 8th or 9th, have a gig in L.A. on the 10th
and then to Winterland. Don't know—think it would
be more feasible to go to L.A. first then home so we'll
be there somewhere between the 8th & 11th SIGH!!

Oh, Danny Rifkin stoppd by yesterday on his way to
Paris—so good to see him.

Well bye, see you soon.

Love you all

Janis

The boy from Chicago to whom Janis referred was
a "jive punk," in Linda's terms, one of a type for
whom Janis had a sad and ruinous attraction. He was
also, back then, a sickly-faced junkie who gave off
the effect of having gangrene. As for Janis, she
looked now and then to be stoned on something,
presumably, besides liquor, on tranquilizers at worst.
Dave Richards was sure that during Janis's earliest
weeks in New York, it was only Librium dulling her
eyes. Nonetheless, John Simon overheard some talk
in Detroit. I was ignorant of the matter at the time,
but that was when Albert found out that his one con-

dition for the Big Brother contract had been violated from the first.

The letter to Linda was written two days after Big Brother opened for a week of performances at a club called Generation in the Village. It was that week I witnessed the first open friction between Janis and the band, although I took it as little more than a conflict extending from the circumstances of recording and therefore relatively minor. Less minor were the critical comments that came from a number of musicians who frequented the club that week. Janis reaped her share of the negative reaction a little later; it was plentiful and harsh. But prior to those days, the target was the group, Janis's flaws attributed to the family of musicians who played behind her: they were sloppy; they played out of tune; they were technically deficient. Their rhythm was imprecise, their volume unbearable. The remarks would gather in force. Meanwhile, Big Brother left New York to fulfill engagements on the West Coast and also to finish recording.

In between the days spent in Columbia's Hollywood studios and concerts in the surrounding area, Janis found some time to spend in her new apartment. Plans for a house had been delayed; she and Linda, instead, took a Noe Street flat. Altogether Janis had little chance to enjoy it. Her schedule, like all her activity, was simply too frenetic.

On the road, she pounded her way through performances like an overcharged Salome. She was a maddened scherzo of hips, feet, hair, and color, her shrieks and wails wrapped in an aggressive force that sprang from the stage to yank her audiences to their feet. They danced on the seats, they whooped down the aisles, they jumped on the stage, screamed, yelled, and carried on with an excitement to match her own. It was during those months of late spring and summer that the media deluge let loose.

A June cover story in *Time* on Aretha Franklin

made reference to Janis as "probably the most power-ful singer to emerge from the white rock movement." In *The New York Times*, Nat Hentoff said that she left him feeling that he had been "in contact with an overwhelming life force." *Vogue* raved that "she makes bunk of the history of singing the minute she opens her mouth," and ran an ecstatic article right next to an enormous photograph of Janis by Richard Avedon. In the same issue, Richard Goldstein crowned her "the most staggering leading woman in rock" and described her maniacally: ". . . she slinks like tar, scowls like war . . . she defies key, shrieking over one line, sputtering over the next and clutching the knees of a final stanza, begging it not to leave . . . Janis Joplin can sing the chic off any listener."

And so it went. Big Brother was left trailing as little more than a raucous background to her seething, surging light.

There were several things that were particularly odd about the entire phenomenon. One was its spontaneity, the fact that no publicity machinery was employed to create her stardom. Pictures were avail-able and a standard short biography, but no flood of press releases went forth from our office, nor from the offices of Columbia Records. I was fortunate to have a lot of close friends among the press, but I made no phone calls to generate their interest. Love was the imperative of Janis's existence, and she had seen the proof of what would bring it—even in the years before. Her talk began to thrash with more re-bellion; her bluntness gradually increased. An intui-tive phrase scored here, another worked well there, and Janis would meet expectations with sensational statements. The media whirlwind sprang from the ground quite on its own momentum, revved up by an anxiety to encompass that trend of which she was such an incendiary symbol. Had I *wanted* to "hype" her—it was not my style—I would never have had the chance.

What was most unprecedented was that all of it

occurred before the release of the Columbia album.
The press knew the story of the Mainstream record;
it might as well not have existed for the critical attention it was paid. For all intents and purposes, the
Columbia album would be the first. Janis Joplin was
the only pop singer in history to become a superstar
without even having what could be called a record!
Preceded by such heated expectations, the quality of
that recording would be more crucial than would ordinarily be the case.

Generally speaking, the aesthetic crux of the San
Francisco sound was dependent on its multimedia environment. Also, it was a music meant to be danced
to and, at its purest, it was absolutely radiant without
the pretentions of "art." For better or worse, the
recording medium required that the criterion of
having a good time be broadened to meet artistic
standards that could hold their own: no writhing
bodies, no steaming colors, nothing but the sound to
quicken the pulse. For better or worse, outside of San
Francisco there were other ideas about what constituted music. And John Simon held them.

"I always thought they were a great *performance*
band," he explained, "but I *didn't* think they made it
as a recording band. I *liked* seeing them; I *liked* the
excitement in the audience, but there was a time
when what was music and what the public *thought*
was music were very far apart to my way of thinking.
The drugs! That's how Janis Joplin could happen in
the first place. Everyone's mind was fried! Look, they
made a lot of people happy. That's *important* and it
counts and it shouldn't be held against them that they
couldn't make music! They had a cult and a following
and as a San Francisco phenomenon, they were in
their element and then . . . well . . . for some probably
sociological reason, Clive Davis forced them to make
a record! I'm *serious!*" John grinned wryly. "You
know, there's studied music and there's tribal music
and their stuff leaned more toward tribal music. What

they *should* have had was an Alan Lomax field recording from San Francisco! I mean, *that's* justice!"

Clearly there was not to be a meeting of minds. Knowing from the beginning that technical proficiency was not Big Brother's forte, John had nonetheless committed himself to produce the album with the thought of capturing them in actual performance. They were, after all, exciting. Another young producer named Elliot Mazer was originally to assist him in the business of recording Big Brother on stage. But John and Elliot came back from Detroit and played the tapes for Albert. As an understatement, no one was pleased. Elliot, for the time being, would not be needed. John took over in the studio alone, and it was murder all the way.

John's wicked sarcasm aside, he was quite serious in thinking of the band as a unique organic unit. He meant it when he stated that he thought them stupendously dynamic on stage. But he was in the studio to work, and Big Brother was not accustomed to professional demands or the display of professional behavior. They lurched around drunk; they insisted on trying foolish techniques with sound. Moreover, as Elliot put it, "John has more skill than anybody I've ever known. I'd watched him for years, but when you have perfect pitch, you can't stand to hear stuff that's out of tune and out of time, and they played out of tune and out of time."

What then happened as the sessions progressed was the rise of strife between Janis and the group, their unity shrinking as the energy of Big Brother was less and less a virtue, and as it became evident that the flaws absorbed so easily in the throes of visual excitement were unmercifully exaggerated on tape.

In the midst of the mounting strain that went on that spring and summer, Janis was frequently depressed. Her temper was poisonous, and whether in anger or in those moments that were taken for a lusty consumption of experience, she exploded not with vitality but with a shrieking, self-conscious crudity. It seemed to me too that she was grabbing at all the tools of gimmickry in some desperate effort to encapsulate an image of herself as a salty, tough, red-hot mama. "Well, man," she said to Linda that spring, "this can't last forever."

With that in mind, both her naiveté and her emotional needs had her steering the creation of herself in a way that previously she would never have considered—or so I thought at the time. If her sexuality, her uninhibited remarks and her intoxicating wildness had been embraced so thoroughly by the media, well, let them have more! Thus, while the recording sessions were going on in California, she called me and demanded that I publicize a fight she'd had with Jim Morrison of The Doors. She, Janis announced proudly, had been the victor, having slammed his skull with a bottle of scotch.

"He yanked a whole bunch of hair out of my scalp 'cause he was drunk 'n' I was stoned 'n' I had this bottle . . . so I clobbered 'im" she howled.

"Swell," I groaned.

"Maybe *you* don't like the story," she snapped, "but *his* people think it's somethin' and they want pictures and I want you to. . . ."

"Oooooh-kay," I said. "We'll spread it all over the country. I'll write up a jazzy press release! We'll take pictures . . . you can have his head on a platter! Jim the Baptist! How's that?"

Janis grumbled with doubt and the matter was dropped, but there seemed no question that she was of a mind to establish herself in a specific mold and, in some ways, was about as spontaneous as the Manhattan Project. Many months later—perhaps a full year—I suggested to her that it was time for a change. "That stuff made me famous!" she barked back. "Everybody loves it!"

Certainly nothing could have been more calculated than the artwork for the album itself, the R. Crumb comic strip cover. Witty, ingenious, and different it was, but it was gross and self-mocking as well. Not

Columbia, not Albert, just Janis alone was determined on that impression. Mulishly, she rejected some exquisite layouts prepared by Bob Cato, then head of Columbia's creative departments. It was a relief to the company that at least she was willing to have her original title suggestion of *Sex, Dope and Cheap Thrills*, abbreviated to *Cheap Thrills* alone. Sure it was funny, even hilarious; what would happen to Janis as time went on could hardly be called amusing.

Janis's development was occurring at the same rate as the transformation of the office. By midsummer Arline had married Dan Kramer and left. John Court had departed, replaced by Albert's second partner, Bert Block. By midsummer too, Vinnie Fusco's hair and his ambition had grown considerably. Stepping up to take charge of Albert's music publishing operations, he'd acquired, while he was at it, a southern amazon for a secretary and a manner that spoke an unquestioning assurance about his future. I'd been shifted to nicer quarters, and when Janis wasn't around I was trying to devote some time to the rest of the roster. All of this would have been fairly routine were it not for the bewildering congestion caused by Peter Cohon and Emmett Grogan, the first of them ambling, the second smashing, into the city that summer.

Emmett Grogan: the current one is the author of an autobiography, *Ringolevio*, *pu*blished in 1972. When I first got to know him in 1968, he was still riding hard his journey to the end of the night. A former junkie, actor, hustler, and, of course, Digger, Emmett had achieved some notoriety as a Robin Hood of the Haight-Ashbury. Actually, it was more than notoriety. In the American "underground" Emmett is as legendary and elusive as the Scarlet Pimpernel. They seek him here; they seek him there, and hanging over him is still the question whether he can best be found in heaven or in hell. In reality he resembles the Pimpernel about as much as does Sonny Corleone, except that he's gorgeous Irish, his features chiseled from a lucky heredity and an anger earned on the Brooklyn streets. He was also once a choirboy, all of that making for a combustible combination and a slightly alarming tendency he has to imagine, at given moments, that the entire United States of America has Emmett Grogan on its mind— negatively.

His reddish-brown hair was long when I met him, and he had a small gold earring in his left earlobe. He still has the earring, but his hair is now necklength. His eyes remain as dangerous and cold as two grenades. His walk has stayed a swagger, with an aggressive but reptilian grace. Emmett is astonishingly magnetic. As for the mystery? It takes a bourgeoise to figure it out. I once sent Emmett to my dentist, who performed on his mouth some elaborate work requiring much time and effort. Many months later the dentist gave me call. We both like Emmett; we discussed his appeal—and also his disappearance. "Charismatic!" my dentist agreed. "I know he's charismatic! I like him so much I almost left my wife for him three times! But what I wanna know is, where's my two thousand dollars?"

That aspect of Emmett aside, he is sometimes very serious. Peter Cohon is more so, possessed of a less melodramatic temperament and a superlative eloquence in his speech. In any event, the two of them were present that summer, almost daily in the office, making an enormous hoopla to hold back the kids who were planning to swarm to the Democratic Convention—that is, under the Yippie umbrella. The idea was to stop them by media persuasion: Emmett Grogan says don't go. To that end, he and Peter occupied desks and telephones throughout the office and raked in, to assist them, an assortment of lunatics from the street. The activity was noble; the motives seemed tinged with the air of internecine warfare, the underground shoot-out at the O.K. Corral.

I was tremendously relieved that none of our acts
had gone to the convention on behalf of the Yippie
interests, though requests had poured in all summer.
As for Janis, she was utterly apolitical, her concerns
as personal as the lyrics she chose, all the reflection
of a singular preoccupation with the matters of her
body and soul. That is not to say that she had no con-
victions; it was just that they stemmed primarily
from a fondness for the thumb-nosing zap. Once the
Voice of America called, dreaming, God knows, of
what they would hear, should she manage to find
some time. "Sure I'll say something," she quipped
when I told her. "How's this? 'Drop your guns and
run, boys!'"

That summer of '68, however, she was completely
uninvolved with the political events. The maneuvers,
the rumors, the whole gathering tension simply
passed her by. Her performances raged on like
Dionysian rites with bottles of Southern Comfort
passed up to the stage in ritualistic tribute. The
journalistic storm continued; her relationship with
Big Brother was deteriorating by the day.

Insofar as my own function was concerned, the
media demand had an unsettling effect. I could reject one writer with some certainty that another
would be assigned. I could insist on picture approval
with the knowledge that I would probably get it. I
could delay an interview with assurance that the in-
convenience would be tolerated. In brief, I had
power. Knowing that, I was determined to use it only
in her behalf. Unfortunately, one power I didn't
possess was that which could hold the media response
to some kind of reasonable level. With a personality
like Janis's, there was no moderate road, the only
alternative to the deluge being a complete refusal of
any interviews whatsoever. The pressure was of that
magnitude, simply indescribable. And what was happening, really by virtue of historical accident, was
that Janis was actually being merchandised as the
symbol of everything that was against the very idea

of merchandising. In effect, she was being *merchandised* for her *realness*. That, of course, is a contradiction, and contained the seeds for an institutionalized realness that would merely be another form of artificiality.

Janis and I, over the summer, had already become good friends. It was more than that; I adored her. No one who knew Janis could fail, in some way, to be affected by her vitality. Her speech was fascinating, the spatter of powerfully compelling impulse that literally drew people into the center of herself. The immediacy, the impatience, the *clarity* of her emotions, all were simply staggering. The slightest gloom would weight her as if it were the entire universe come down to crush her soul. The jubilance would rush out, a miracle of brightness, the original burst that made the firmament. She was intemperate, impetuous, kaleidoscopically wild, registering like a haywire neural encephalogram. That poor child was noisy even when she was totally *quiet*, so vivid were her feelings. But, in my presence, she did not seem so driven to display that raunchy madness, so that I found her frighteningly fragile, and something about that quality had a stabilizing effect on my own temperament, which could not exactly be called subdued. Then, back in those days, Janis's self-involvement was not as sharp as it would later become. She had charm, warmth, and a bewitching innocence. Even her temper was hit-and-run, her toughness just about the phoniest front I believe I've ever seen. And she had that *laugh!* What Nick Gravenites described as "the cackle-rap . . . like a demented cackle from an eight-year-old recluse, right? The boat comes into the deserted island, and up in the mountains in a cave, among the relics, way in the back, you'd hear this cackle?" That was her laugh. Then there were her eyes, as haunted as a ghost ship that creaks with depression, weary, alone, lost forever on a high and turbulent sea.

I was concerned about her always. She had, that

summer, gained an enormous amount of weight because of her heavy drinking. And if there was that
gorgeous rush of language, that dizzying shower of
feeling, that dazzling mobility in her face, they burst
from the same source as the nightmare of her self-
destructiveness and the terrifying demand of impulses that razed her spirit. It was that which led
Linda Gravenites to remark on Janis's recklessness:
"She was greedy, stone greedy. She wanted it *all!*
All at once, every minute. And it didn't matter if it
was good five minutes ago, if it wasn't good now, it
was shitty!"

Assuredly, that interior pressure did come to bear
on what most of Janis's friends took as an uncon-
flicted expression of gargantuan sexual appetites. Indeed, to hear Janis recount them, her escapades were
not only endless, but so shattering that the explosion
brought on by a million orgone boxes would be
diminished in comparison. Janis Joplin, she let us all
know, was the Aphrodite of our time. That she
couldn't stop telling us struck few as peculiar. That
sexual rejection brought on tantrums? Well, that was
just the way she was.

"If I turn out to be a lousy lay," Albert once told
her to sidetrack her approach, "I might not be able to
keep you as a client!"

That produced a contented cackle. Most men who
vetoed a bout with Janis were not so lucky. For one
thing, Janis was in need of an unrelenting testimony
to her appeal. Even in the days of her fame, she was
obsessed with a concept of herself as ugly. And, of
course, sex—the fantasy of it—in her early years had
triggered all that attention from her schoolmates, no
matter that it was consciously negative. As one result,
her success in tantalizing men was, in her mind, the
final measure of her desirability. Conversely, failure
she saw as the ultimate symbol of her worthlessness.
Sexual indifference to Janis was an intolerable blow;
her retaliation could be scathing. Nor could she permit herself to consider that there might be a range

of reasons for refusal. I recall an incident in which a musician politely declined an invitation, saying that he was in love with another girl, which very likely was true. Janis, infuriated, thereupon told me that he must, of course, be impotent. Even a willingness to have relations with Janis was not sufficient. Proof of her appeal must go further; the man had to be inexhaustible. Some suggestion exists that the fight with Jim Morrison had been basically brought on by her attack on his "performance." And, naturally, Janis's performances, she insisted continually, were not to be matched on this earth.

It would be almost automatic to attribute Janis's obsession with sex, and in particular her concept of self, to the socio-sexual scheme of things. The male chauvinism in the rock world is notorious. The definitions of femininity with which she grew up, her seeking approval through sexual channels, her star-status as sexual object, all give credibility to a legitimate-sounding view that she was the tragic result of an essentially political phenomenon. But Janis breathed, thought, felt, acted at a primitive level that was nearly absolute. Even in her twenties, she was still like a hurt and pleading child who wants exactly that very love complete in the physical embrace, and sex, in a way, was a valid synonym for what she was in search of. It wasn't love as an adult knows it: no sharing, no interest, no commitment, no giving, none of those things at all. But it really was love to *her*. In her hunger for affection, she was nearly amok. Her constant pursuit of physical contact resonated with echoes of infant longing, and frustration of such a need could not help but produce an unbearable anxiety. In that sense, sex was a palliative, an escape from tension that could not be endured, thus making sexual relief of inordinate, overbearing importance.

There was also the general temper of the age and the environment of erotomania which, in her suggestibility, Janis was beholden to embody. "Sex is

what it is!" Nick's wife Diane Gravenites remarked
in wise words about Janis's behavior. "No more, no
less! It's groovy, but it's not so much that you have to
be desperate all the time, so you have to fuck every
man and get every man wanting to do it constantly!
That's just crazy! I mean, talk about incarnations! She
was right on with the times, man! Look at everybody
—obsessed with it! They think, 'Well, if I can just get
a good fuck, I'll be better!' "

Perhaps, too, along with her infantilism, it was the
temper of the times that increased Janis's tendency to
act out in the first place and use sex as the prime
arena in which she dramatized all her difficulties. In
the same way that her loneliness, joy, craving, and
despair were highly eroticized in performance, so
were the troubles that pulled at her heart acutely
sexualized from day to day. The difference was that,
onstage, that eroticism provided a magnificent release
—for her and for her audiences. Offstage, it did little
more than drag her further into the darkness of confusion. So there would be moods in which Janis
would be the aggressor and frantic in her compulsion
to control, and then moods in which she would seek
to insure her passivity, playing games with the
machismo conquerors—the Hell's Angels and so on.
By Janis's declaration, expectedly that of her public's,
and also many of her friends', all of this was merely a
matter of Janis's fondness for "getting it on." It was
pitiable: a circle of anxiety, depression, liquor, and
drugs, the public salivating, and some of her
"friends" presiding over the walking tragedy of this
libertine creature who, in reality, did not exist.

"Why is it," Diane Gravenites asked me, "when she
was talking to a chick, she had a low, relaxed kind
of voice and when talking to a cat her voice got all
high and uptight?"

It was true, Janis, as a rule, was more comfortable,
more "herself," if you will, in the presence of women.
She was less on the rack of self-deprecation, less

prone to play buffoon, and because she was less driven to sexual priority, was less ridden with anxiety.

Heretical it may be, but there was enough about Janis's sexual behavior with men to suggest that its nature was counterphobic. Needless to say, that is not to be mistaken for courage. Her heartbreaking fear was merely rigidified by the recurrence of the pattern. Janis chose "jive punks." Her assaultive conduct was almost guaranteed to make things unsatisfactory, "jive punks" or no. She started affairs with men who were married or who really weren't interested in her at all. When there were men who might have cared, she rejected them. When there was a possibility of anything lasting, something would always interfere. That was Janis Joplin "getting it on."

According to some of her friends, "getting it on" naturally explained her sexual escapades with women too. "That's how free she was," Dave Getz was sure. "If somebody turned her on, like in a sexual way, it didn't matter if it was a guy or a chick, and if you can really be that free, that's really far out!"

Janis was so free, so uninhibited, so unconventional, that she was terrified that people would think there was something going on between her and myself. "Lissen," she said to me once, that summer of 1968. "Maybe you and I shouldn't go to Max's so much!"

I stared at her dumfounded. "What the hell is *this* about?"

"Well, ya know," she mumbled. "People might think . . . I mean, they might wonder . . . I mean, I don't have an old man and they might . . . I mean they must wonder why, like, ya know . . . I don't have a guy . . . and maybe . . . well, I guess it's silly."

Janis, however, most certainly from fear that I would disapprove, said not a single word more. Only once thereafter, in 1970, did she allude in my presence to any lesbian experiences she'd ever had. She was vague nonetheless and referred to the past.

While again, Janis's tendencies in that direction were most definitely not dominant, it is my opinion that her fear of homosexuality did play some part in an overcompensation the other way. It had certainly to do with her inclination to broadcast her heterosexual affairs—even beyond what actually occurred. The exaggeration was furthered by her need to manifest what was around her, her compulsion to proclaim her desirability, and her necessity to play to the fantasies of others. It was greatly exaggerated by *her* and, heaven knows, it was and still is greatly exaggerated by others. That goes for men as well as women, including the homosexuals. If there are twenty longhairs on every block of the country claiming their night of remembered bliss, there are the lesbian brigades placing Janis in innumerable situations that simply never occurred.

"You don't really know *what* she did, unless you were there, do you?" I said to Dave Getz.

"Yeah!" he replied suddenly, following his general insistence that there were simply no limits to Janis's sexual pursuits. "From firsthand experience, as a matter of fact." Somewhat disconcerted by his own memory, he began to reflect on those nights in the back seat of his car when Janis first joined Big Brother. "Exactly! It was usually her that would like get scared or something. Sure, she liked to present the image that she was balling everybody, but actually the number of people that she really got it on with was much smaller!" Giggling, he added, "Maybe a third!"

Dave Richards was shrewder: "Janis had her style *down*. Her riff in public was, 'I'm a good-time girl. I'm just a down-home drinkin' mama, and anytime you wanna knock on my door and split a bottle of whiskey and jump into my bed, I'll be glad to have ya.' But it *wasn't* just any fuckin' dude who pounded on the door with a bottle of whiskey! Janis was jive!"

My own impression was and still is that her activities were sporadic, periods of relative reserve, then, spurts of terribly indiscriminate behavior. Janis, when she was with men, identified with men as she thought they acted and sometimes did. She defined men sexually, as she defined herself, and then went at her one-night stands and sometimes orgies under the cover of a liberated style of life, taking her cue from the encouragement of those around her who loved to witness the show. She was left with little more than the yawning chasm of a tortured loneliness. Then miserable with that, she picked poor targets to bring her unhappiness to an end.

It was writer Lillian Roxon who recounted to me an incident of which I'd been only vaguely aware at the time: "You remember that guy she went around with for about three weeks that summer of sixty-eight? Well, I remember that at first he was just obsessed. It was, 'Ahh, the perfume of her body, her hair, her style.' Then one day he ran into her and she told him she was *lonely*. And BAM! That was it! He said, 'I don't want anything to do with her loneliness. I don't want to know anything about that!'."

Janis, of course, had her litany about fame: she was insulated behind superstardom. Only a little of it was true. Peter Cohon was right in saying, "She came on with such a pizzazz and amplification of media, and it had everybody so freaked that they couldn't get next to her."

Yet, as I remembered the incident that Lillian related, I also remembered the boy's face, pretty, anemic, and flickering with transience. Janis's rigmarole about fame was a convenient excuse for such obvious things as that.

Powell St. John saw it long before. "I think," he concluded, "that all she ever really wanted was somebody to love, but it just wasn't part of her nature to be satisfied or happy. A lot of it might have been the theatrical fantasy, but really, that was her natural way to find the world."

Complications of that nature were difficult for some people to discern. Janis was swamped in her own pizzazz and amplification quite apart from a word of print or even her stage performances. In that bellowing, bouncing, jangling clamor, there were those who saw a "self." But Janis was afflicted by an emotional astigmatism. Each second was clear, but there was no focus. She was disordered, decentralized, and *diffused*. As Mr. Giarritano, the psychiatric social worker in Beaumont, declared, "Most assuredly, when you get under the pressures of the profession, your behavior is going to get *more* diffused, which fed the other, the feeling and the emotional confusion."

Those pressures were always increasing. Even before the editing on *Cheap Thrills* was completed, the concert billing had been changed to "Janis Joplin with Big Brother and the Holding Company," and Albert had begun to make his disapproval of the band quite clear. If there was appeal in Big Brother's flash, fun to be had in their gutsy color and an air of spontaneity in the rhythmic inaccuracy, he thought those assets minor and that Janis's artistic potential would best develop in a different context.

The psychological factors that contributed to the impending split were greatly involved. Thus are the memories of many parties accordingly distorted. Albert and Janis, some still believe, were influenced by attacks on the band from the press. The media criticism of Big Brother, however, was almost negligible until after the decision was well in the making. One remark in *Variety* occurred when they played Generation. Other than that, the only critical words uttered early in print came ironically enough from *Rolling Stone*, which would later do an interesting cartwheel and land into Janis when she formed her second group. As for Big Brother, at a February date in Boston, "They were messy and a general musical disgrace." About their performance at the Newport Festival, Jon Landau had this to say: "Her melodrama, overstatement and coarseness are not virtues. They are signs of a lack of sophistication and a lack of security with her material." Big Brother, he wrote, was "truly lame . . . the band drags her at every turn." Albert would have thought those comments quite valid, had he seen them, which he probably did not. Anyway, the split was decided before that *Rolling Stone* article appeared. The criticism that affected Big Brother's direction was leveled by musicians, not by the media. Moreover, to the extent that those musicians were deploring the supplanting of technique by visual excitement, so was Big Brother literally ossified in the other direction, all of this representing a kind of magnified schism between the East Coast and San Francisco views of music, as they happened to stand at the time. Caught up in the glory of sheer energy, Big Brother was indifferent to anything *but* energy, and, most assuredly, their attitude was defensively calcified as the criticism of them increased. A malaise settled into their music; they could produce no new songs. Moreover, Big Brother became demoralized, not by bad reviews—they did not occur until later—but by the *attention* to Janis. She was affected by that attention too in some very complicated ways. The break was inevitable. It was also psychologically and musically necessary. Things had gone beyond the point where anything could have stayed the same.

The contention of the people who believed that Janis should never have left Big Brother was not only that she herself was no musician. That was patently correct. If later there was, unquestionably, the embryonic emergence of true artistry, it was not that apparent in those early days. The heart of that opinion, however, was that before the press began its attacks, Janis had no such ambitions; she was completely contented with the way she sang. Certainly in her early interviews, she betrayed no concern about musical matters. "I close my eyes and feel things," she told Nat Hentoff and, in variation, every reporter to whom she spoke. "If I were a musician, it might be a lot harder to get all that feeling out, but I'm really fortunate, because my gig is just feeling things." She was all shrieks, hollers, screams, and wails, with no thought of tempering her vocal technique—or so most everyone supposed. It did not seem to occur to anyone that some of Janis's protests about her fortunate lack of musicianship and even her refusal to practice came from fear that the unrelenting wallop was all that she possessed. Not incidentally, of course, she was voicing an outlook that seemed to bring applause.

Nonetheless, Elliot Mazer, who did most of the editing of the tapes for the album and the mixing of the sound, remembered that Janis's attitude toward the recording was an obsessive absorption in its quality. "She was *incredibly* on top of it," he said. "For two weeks, only Janis, myself, and the engineer would stay, from two in the afternoon until seven in the morning. Anything about her just having a good time and not working at it is just bullshit! I never *knew* an artist that worked harder. She was twenty times more serious than *any* of those people in that band!"

During the sessions themselves, Janis's efforts had even struck John Simon as antithetical to the blues. "She was planning out every single moan and shriek as she went," he insisted. "We'd do a take. She'd say, 'I like that.' The next take she'd do it the same. It was all planned out, like filling up the spaces in a double crostic."

That is a fascinating statement about a girl who talked constantly of her spontaneity. It is possible that Janis contrived effects onstage as well, without anyone ever knowing. On the other hand, such plotted phrasing, no matter how misguided, may also have been a striving for excellence and Janis's way of trying to please John—whether he realized it or not. John Simon is an outstanding musician. Janis must have been terribly frightened by his standards, much less his reserve, his seriousness, and his educated manner. As would be her way in the face of fear, she could only have stepped up everything, her temper as well as her coarseness. So, as she behaved, did he understandably see her, and she, sensing this, would in turn amplify her coarseness more. John is no prude; he thought she was funny, "a little like a character out of Zap comics." She *was*—with an underlying and very uncomical self-hatred. The whole studio situation was a bloody mess.

After months of work, the album was pulled together from an overwhelming number of tapes, approximately one hundred to two hundred reels. Moreover, because only one or two tracks had apparently been captured successfully onstage, Elliot and John ended up adding "excitement" effects to produce the impression of a live recording. Those "audience" screams? On most of *Cheap Thrills*, that's Elliot, John, and an engineer! The true live Big Brother tracks were only dredged up after Janis's death when, given some time, Elliot did a superb job putting together the material for the album *Joplin in Concert*.

Cheap Thrills, Elliot thinks, could have been better. The sound was terrible, and there was not time enough to polish the flaws. There were those mammoth stacks of tape. Above all, there was the unrelenting pressure from Columbia to get the damned thing out! "They'd already announced it had gotten a Gold Record for sales," Elliot laughed, "and I was still trying to figure out how to put the second side together! That album was produced by the uptightness of the industry!"

Cheap Thrills was finally released at the beginning of August 1968. The announcement of the split was made soon after. Essentially, the statement we released from the office was true: Janis was "pretend-

ing" onstage; there had been no new material for
months; the parting was "amicable." It was decided
that Janis would continue to work with Big Brother
through the fall. Sam Andrew would remain to be a
part of her new group. Who else that would consist of
was unknown.

13

Big Brother had been informed of the decision well
before the public announcement. That they'd known
it was coming made it no less terrible to be told, the
sense of finality throwing them into a state of loss,
confusion, and shock. When the immediate blow
subsided, they were left with the feeling of saddened
acceptance and even, in time, relief. Only Peter Albin
continued to consider Janis's act a betrayal, and while
his fury eventually diminished, he never really for-
gave her.

By the measure of emotional reaction, however, it
was Janis who really suffered. For all the musical
necessity and the rightness of the move in every
respect, she would have been insensitive not to have
experienced guilt. Hers was excessive, severe to the
extreme. She would force on herself a penalty too
for the not so paradoxical feeling that she, Janis Joplin, was very special. Emmett and Peter particularly
were afraid she was losing her perspective.

Yet, when Big Brother played the Fillmore East in
August, Janis betrayed an almost grieved insecurity
about her singing. The Staples Singers were on the
bill that night. Standing in the wings, awed by the
great gospel swoop of Mavis Staples's voice, Janis

whispered sadly, "I'll never be able to sing like that." Later in the evening, after she had exhausted herself in the voltage of her own performance, she crept onstage at the insistence of Pa Staples to join them in one song. It was not the grace of humility that had her awkward and shame-faced as she tried to sing, but the devastating terror of failure.

I noticed something else that weekend. Chalky-faced and drained from the adrenalin rush of her performance, Janis slumped dejectedly in the corner of the dressing room. After a few minutes, she got up and said she was going to visit the Staples, who were resting on another floor. If she did stop in to see them, it was not the reason for her departure. There was a tall, curly-headed visitor backstage that night; he followed her into the hall. When she returned, I saw something pass from her clenched hand into a handkerchief. A cataract of denial must have fuzzed my vision. A full year passed before I remembered, and realized what it had been.

It was the Southern Comfort that had me fooled, that and the fact that Janis's use of heroin was so sporadic for a while that there was nothing in her countenance to reveal it. Janis's drinking served to distract the public from an awareness of her drug use as well. With the bottle as a talisman, she floated in and out of Holiday Inns and backstage at hundreds of concerts without arousing the slightest suspicion. But if the public never knew about the dope, it was not because she was busy at hiding it.

"It was really weird," Dave Getz recalled. "She was *outrageous* about it. We played a gig in Cincinnati one time and we were invited to a party afterward and it was a house full of junkies and Janis did up in the kitchen. It was like, 'There's Janis Joplin and she's shooting up with all these Cincinnati hippies and isn't that funky!' She was like that all the time!"

Weird and outrageous it was. Heroin users are notorious for wallowing in the role of outlaw, the illegality, the separation from the rest of society part of the attraction in its use and, by some theories, an attraction that surpasses the appeal of the high itself.

In Janis's case, that seems to have been a lesser factor. Later, the range of functions that smack served for her became clear, but assuredly one of them was to provoke efforts from others to constrain her. Certainly her behavior around Albert indicated that she was looking to be controlled. "She knew how it really got him," Dave Getz continued, "so sometimes she'd talk about it openly." In the same fashion, during the mixing of *Cheap Thrills*, Janis pitched constant comments to Elliot Mazer about getting high. Could she shoot up the carbon tetrachloride used to clean the tape heads? How stoned could she get on the Freon, which was there for cleaning equipment? There were innumerable hints to me—which went right over my head; there were *always* confessions to doctors, with full-steam defiance but confessions still. Another member of Big Brother said that, alternately, Janis would worry about Albert's reaction and then would let him think she'd stopped, easily enough accomplished with eyes that looked bleary from drink. Twisting, turning, disguising, confronting, tormenting, relieving, joking, boasting, Janis was too bogged down in self-contradiction to make her signals discernible. Some members of Big Brother were hardly a help, falling— which they did—for her stated credo: she believed only in being stoned.

Janis's anxiety about hard drugs actually went by all of us, those who were aware of what she was doing and those who, like myself, were completely in the dark. At a Columbia press department meeting the second week she arrived in New York, she suddenly popped up with the astounding question, "What'll I do if someone asks me if I was ever a methadrine addict?" That reporters could be expected to make pointed inquiries about her attitude toward drugs was true. But "*Miss Joplin, were you ever a methadrine addict?*" Janis was not *that* naive. She was egocentric, paranoic, megalomanic, in fact, but not so much as to fancy that a reporter might go at the work of digging up her past with a special focus on her experience with drugs. I wondered at the time, "What a weird thing to say," and let it go at that.

Publicly Janis's name would be associated only with liquor, the connection sealed when Janis decided that Southern Comfort was obligated to bestow upon her a token of appreciation for her attention to its product. Southern Comfort was not so sure—until its offices were flooded with clippings, at which point the company succumbed and gave Janis a lynx coat, which was actually part of a twenty-five-hundred-dollar gift, though an extorted payment would be more the term. Just like any number of Janis's antics, that one was thought of as funny. The episode made *me* squeamish, but against her determination my negative feelings were absolutely useless. Whatever my skepticism, there was indeed something touching about her childish fervor the cold fall day I called her and announced the fur had finally arrived.

A half hour later, we were standing in a dusty warehouse and I was handing a shipping receipt to a man in grimy overalls. Janis had on no coat; she would enjoy her triumph from that moment on, and she was begging the man, could he rush, could he find it, would he please take the trouble, would he locate it right away.

"Joplin . . . Joplin . . ." He fumbled with the slip, peering with a baffled expression at Janis's red satin pants and the spangles that drooped from her waist. Frowning, he said, "Ten minutes."

Janis groaned as she began a skating motion around the floor. "OOoooooeeeee," she gurgled. "What a hustle!"

"I got it!" the man called, beckoning through the door that led to the back of the warehouse.

We next went to Max's Kansas City, where she

showed off her coat, then grabbed a cab and headed uptown; we were going to see *The Great White Hope*. With a positively voluptuous gesture, Janis locked the fur up high so that it almost covered her face and then said rather loudly, "What time's my interview tomorrow?"

"You don't have an . . ."

"Shhhh . . ." She nodded at the neck of the driver.

"Cut it out, Janis," I whispered.

She shouted, "Is it with *Life*?"

As the driver's neck twisted left toward some traffic, Janis's eyes shot anxiously toward the side mirror, where unhappily she failed to meet his glance. I made a clicking sound with my tongue and looked the other way.

"I just wanna see if anybody knows who I am," Janis sulked, then chuckled at her foolishness.

In the lobby of the theater, Janis grimaced at the array of striped ties and pearl necklaces. The odor of hairspray was stifling; hundreds of false eyelashes flittered in the mirrored ceiling above.

"Lucille says it's simply wonderful," one woman said, her eyes scanning Janis quizzically, then disinterestingly resting elsewhere.

"They think I'm a freak!" Janis pouted, clattering her bracelets.

I grunted, "Nobody's paying any attention."

"I *know* that," she said fiercely.

Throughout the evening, Janis sat quietly in her seat until the third act when, in response to one speech by James Earl Jones, she suddenly sprang to her feet. "Let 'em have it, mother!" she whooped, flailing her fist, genuinely oblivious to the cringing of the pearl necklaces and striped ties around her.

"Sit down, Janis," I laughed, yanking her back to her seat.

"Whatsa matter! What'd I do?"

I apologized. "Not a thing."

"Don't these friggin' corpses ever get excited about anything?" she protested.

"No," I grumbled, "goddamnit, they don't."

Janis was quiet on the cab ride back to the Chelsea, occasionally commenting about the play, which she had definitely liked, and the reserve of the audience, which she had definitely not. Then silent for a few minutes, she roared and came up with the remark she had been shaping all evening to ironic perfection: "This coat! What a hustle! Can you imagine getting paid for passing out for two years!"

Always there was a fluctuation in Janis between the uncontrollable burst of feeling and that which seemed spontaneous but was not that way at all. The fact is that she was becoming quite adept at aphorisms of all sorts; only later would I fully realize that they showed an obvious progression. The nature of her earliest comments about the experience of performing were not so very provocative: "It's like falling in love twenty times"; "I guess maybe having a baby would be something akin." By late summer and fall, they were quite a bit stronger: "It's like the 'rush' that people experience when they take heavy dope"; "It's like an orgasm." So did her proclamations about singing itself become broadened as time went on. "Why should I hold back now and sound mediocre just so I can sound mediocre twenty years from now?" was a common statement in the first of her interviews. It was a nine-month jump from that to the remark that was the one most quoted after she died: "Man, I'd rather have ten years of superhypermost than live to be seventy sitting in some goddamn chair watching TV." As some kind of tremendously over-simplified metaphor, the words were hardly a lie. There is no mistake, on the other hand, that her *Weltanschauung* was strikingly interdependent with the reactions it produced. Some of her statements were surely spontaneous. Others were amplifications of remarks that had successfully passed test runs. A few, I have not a single doubt, were secretly and shrewdly prepared. As Linda Gravenites said, "If Janis saw a look or a style that she liked, she immediately copied it." Janis admired what got attention, what drew, what evoked, what elicited love—or that which she could so interpret. The look she liked and the style she copied were now no other than her own.

Janis saw one other play that fall. *Hair* was made for the middle class, and Janis *loved* it. She loved it so much that she went twice, the second time going with the band. By the fall, her relationship with Big Brother had greatly improved.

As for my own attitude about the split, at the moment it happened, I was ambivalent. I used to wince at Big Brother's every out-of-tune note. When beat one splattered down at five different times, I cringed. The volume, I was afraid, would blow out my brains. Their ersatz blackness I found absurd. They were ludicrous, daffy, impossible, a violation of every musical standard that I held dear. But complaining in my mind at every second, I liked them all the same. Janis's break with the group would also mean an end to her amateurism. Somehow I found that inexpressibly depressing. The personal hurt to the band, as well, was a painful thing to observe. Still, Janis's talent was straining to develop and could not do so with the group. And I personally thought *Cheap Thrills* abominable.

For every reviewer who was a Big Brother loyalist and claimed to like that record, there was a writer who liked only the title—for its use as a descriptive lead-in. That was when the critical assault began, after the release of the album. Nor were the diatribes just directed at the group. Both Janis and Big Brother were a "a minstrel show." Janis was not original"; "instead of black face, she uses black voice," and other remarks to that effect started to become rather typical.

Most of the criticism I believed justified and, generally speaking, I had very little friction with the press. Undoubtedly I misjudged situations from time to time, but what I did have was a disposition to protect Janis from nastiness and a tendency to become extremely irritated when I sensed its presence. I once wrote an angry letter to a writer who did in *Cheap Thrills* with a special flair. On another occasion, I maneuvered an important publication to shift its choice of writers for a lengthy profile on Janis. And to the extent that its voice seemed to be that of its editor's, I had an out-and-out war with *Rolling Stone*, which was, among other things, the result of the paper's small-minded infractions in the area of reporting facts.

Never did I share Janis's belief that the press was beholden to treat her well. Janis's childishness reflected a completely unrealistic view of the world and how it was supposed to react to her, which she seemed to think should be with a constant shower of adoration. Again, there was contradiction: her feeling was also strong that would justice rule, she was due only punishment and rejection. Basically, however, she wanted immunity, and it was very difficult to make her understand that she could not expect such privilege. Even the most judicious criticism was prone to throw her into severe depression. She simply could not withstand the article or the review with the slightest hostile undertones. Behind a façade of confidence in her gifts, she held the conviction she couldn't sing *at all*; remarks she saw as proving that true tended to atomize her. Her personal insecurity in other areas was even worse. Her veneer was brash, her flamboyance the very substance to draw from some quarters the kind of attack that I couldn't teach her to take. Rough, loud, aggressive, crude, she was as fragile in her soul as the most delicate bone china. Unable to toughen her in any way, I simply took the other road, to protect her as best I could.

As an additional factor there was my powerful con-

viction that Janis didn't deserve to be hurt—and
certainly not in those days. It is true that she was de-
plorably self-centered and capable of being bruising
and calloused. Some of those qualities would really
get out of hand as her enchantment with fame developed. Still, such behavior was usually brought on
by fear (as well as the effects of drugs, alcohol, and
the complications of guilt). Threats needed not be
real for Janis to react with the venomous ferocity of a
wounded animal. Never did she forget the incident
with her hair at the press party and raised it in dis-
cussions from time to time right through the year of
her death, always with foul words for the person
who'd cast aspersions, so she took it, upon her appearance. Similarly she was gored by a photographer
who made the remark, "Isn't she quaint?" On the
other hand, Richard Avedon loved her sincerely, and
she reciprocated with an endearing warmth. She was
the same with Francesco Scavullo and David Gahr,
because of their attitudes toward her. These situations—with photographers—were especially significant because they were connected with her body and
appearance so directly and involved both her narcissism and self-hatred. The point is that when she felt
secure, her charm and graciousness were unmatch-
able.

   She was the same with reporters. There would be
occasions, with particular kinds of people and especially later on, when she would put on astounding
shows, but when her career was still in its beginning
stages, she was winning and lovable—as long as she
wasn't frightened. Moreover, Janis did not see the
world as ideally consisting of a divided humanity
with the "freaks" over here and the "straights" over
there, people over thirty best in their graves and the
remainder inheriting the earth. Excepting those situations in which she felt threatened, her judgment of
people was independent of categories. That is called
tolerance, and it is an astonishing quality, particularly

in a girl who symbolized a revolution that, whatever its merits, could not claim that among them.

Then, in those early days, her tenderness toward runaways and street people was overwhelming, as was her gentleness toward the deserted, the rejected, the ugly. One day I walked into her room at the Chelsea to find her sitting in bed, silent and miserable, studying the words of a negative review. In a chair nearby was a pathetic-looking young man with terrible skin and thick-lensed glasses, through which he kept staring at Janis. After he left, I said, "Jesus! Where in the hell did *he* come from! What a mess!"

Humbling me immediately, she answered quietly, "Myra, I don't know who he is. He called me from the lobby and said he just wanted to meet me. I know he isn't very pretty, but you shouldn't talk about people like that. He's a person too."

My overprotectiveness, if such it was, stemmed from such things as that. Needless to say, I wonder often how much did I err in this and would it have been better to let it all fall, however, whichever the way.

Janis's concluding performances with Big Brother were to wind up on the West Coast. The last one in New York was set for Hunter College on November 15 and was preceded by a hysteria of anticipation. The clawing for tickets became almost vicious; photographers were screeching for permission to photograph backstage; local CBS wanted to film the event. I was wrecked with exhaustion before the day of the concert. The day itself began at seven forty-five in the morning with the ring of my phone.

"Hi!" Janis said, or more accurately asked. Always her greetings—"Hi" or "Howdy"—were posed with the tone of a question.

"What's the matter?" I groaned.

"I can't sleep," she replied hoarsely. "I'm sorry, I'm

really sorry, but it's so noisy here at the Chelsea."
She paused. "Can I come sleep there while you go to
the office? I'll never get through the concert if I don't
get some rest."

I answered, "Sure . . . I have to get up anyway."

In fifteen minutes, Janis came trudging into my
apartment, nine blocks south of her hotel. She was
flittering strangely, her nerves clanging as loudly as
the bell that swung from her waist. "It was just that it
was so noisy," she said, "and I guess I'm a little nervous."

I looked at her suspiciously. "What happened . . ."

"It's nothing really." She waved her arms around,
then sank down on the sofa. "We got in late and the
goddamn noise . . . I couldn't . . ."

I nodded and started to get dressed. "How was the
concert in Hartford?" I asked.

"O.K. . . Myra, I have to get some pills to sleep
and . . ."

"Uh, oh," I said. "What d'ya mean you have to . . ."

"Some Seconal," she pleaded. "Please . . . I am telling you, I can-not sleep!"

I started to argue, then studying her pallor, reluctantly agreed. "*Two*. I'll call the doctor and get you
two."

"Just two!"

"You're goddamn right just two, and do you have
any liquor on you?"

"I won't take any, I promise. Just the pills. How
will I get through the concert if I don't sleep?"
Huddled on the couch, she moaned and sighed repeatedly.

I got a prescription for two Seconal and ran downstairs to the drugstore, returning promptly to give her
the pills. Just before I left for the office, I snuck the
bottle of Southern Comfort out of her bag and into
my own.

The morning and midafternoon I spent answering
calls from desperate reporters and trying to make
arrangements for last-minute seating. "Oh, my

God!" I cried, as I picked up one call to hear not
another reporter, but Janis telling me that she'd
gotten not a second of sleep. It was sometime
around three-thirty.

"I can't sing!" she whispered hoarsely. "I've lost my
voice or something! I've gotta see a doctor!"

"I'll get a throat specialist," I said quickly. "As soon
as I call you back, you grab a cab and get up here."
I slammed down the phone and ran down the hall
toward Albert's office, to find the door forbiddingly
closed.

"Myra," Liz said. "You can't go in there. He's got
some important meeting and . . ."

I raced back to my phone and finally reached a
friend, who gave me the name of a doctor specializ-
ing in treating singers. Shaking, I begged Johanna to
get a limousine. None was available. The doctor was
unable to see Janis until five; the concert was due to
begin at eight, and Janis had told me to tell Albert
that in no way could she carry the show alone, and
for God's sake would he get another act to go on first.
I was additionally panicked, fearing that her voice
just might have had it. The press was habitually wondering how it could possibly last. I myself often ques-
tioned its endurance.

Spotting Albert by the water cooler, I shot out into
the hall. "Albert, it's Janis, she says she . . ."

"I'm in a meeting," he said abruptly and,
whirling around, walked back into his office, closing
the door behind him.

I called Janis and told her to get moving. Taking
out the bottle of Southern Comfort from my bag, I
swallowed a hefty shot before I grabbed my coat and
went downstairs, where I waited for her so we'd lose
no time.

"Look," she said, as the cab raced to the doctor's
office, "what happened was someone put some speed
in my drink last night." She cackled that insane
laugh. "But I wrote a poem at your apartment."

"Thanks," I hissed.

"Don't be mad, honey!"

"I'm not mad!" I yelled. "I'm not mad! I'm fucking worried!"

"Well, it'll all work out," she pouted.

While I was in the doctor's office with her, Johanna got through to Albert, who telephoned to say he'd gotten James Cotton to go on first. Most reassuring, when I was able to think about it later, was the discovery about the condition of her throat. The doctor had found no nodes, and as far as anyone is aware she had none even at the time she died.

"Dig it," she laughed. "He says I should speak up! I talk too quiet!"

With the assurance that her throat was all right, Janis relaxed, although I did not.

"Don't worry, honey," she smiled sweetly, patting my arm as we sped toward my apartment. "Everything will be O.K."

It was amazing that Janis got through that concert, amazing that we got there at all. When we reached my apartment building, she disappeared into a store across the street and came out ten minutes later with a bag containing some lingerie. Inside, she decided to wash her hair, and while I was in the shower, she dashed out into the cold, her head sopping, to find a cleaners that could iron her new crushed velvet dress. Ready to go, we stood on the street while cabs zoomed by us full of passengers, and finally we burst into the dressing room at Hunter to face a roomful of relaxed countenances and the banter of nonchalance.

Janis was astounding that night. Seconal, speed, and God knows what else all pumping through her system, she lacerated that hall with notes that flew up from her dancing feet, spiraled from her pumping hips, and gushed from her throat. The melee in the auditorium was insane. But during the aftermath of screaming and the rush of fans to get backstage, she sat depressed in the dressing room and, except for a

frightening cough and the accompanying shudder of
her body, remained very still. She was in no condition
to see anyone. I believe it was my refusal that night
to permit a reporter backstage that provoked a comment in the *Daily News* that the Grossman office was
trying to wrap Janis in a "Garboesque image." In any
case, the madness of the weekend had just begun.
Janis went out and partied that night. Unbeknownst
to anyone, she was very ill.

On Sunday my phone rang early again. That time
it was Vinnie Fusco. "It's Janis," he said. "She called
me and I'm over at the Chelsea now! She can't
breathe! We better get her to a hospital!"

In the emergency room of New York Hospital,
Janis was told by my internist that she had acute
bronchitis. There was no available hospital bed. Because of the potential for pneumonia, she would
have to check into a hotel that provided room service
so she could remain immobile.

Sick though she was, Janis was done up in her
usual attire. Getting her into a standard New York
hotel wasn't so easily done. Vinnie and I looked like
a couple of Bowery tramps, altogether a rather dis-
reputable-looking trio with not one of us having any
money and little to convince a hotel clerk that Janis
was anything but some hooker or nut from the street.

"Don't you have any identification?" said the
manager of the Hilton.

"Won't this do?" Janis pleaded, slapping her San
Francisco library card on the desk.

Finally, we managed to get her into the Americana,
and the following Wednesday I went with her to see
the doctor as arranged.

· Speaking to me alone for a few minutes, he told
me that she was using—something he'd ascertained
because Janis, bellicose, defiant, downright unpleasant, had made a point of telling him. She'd called it
"dope," and because of that vague term, I was certain
that he'd misunderstood.

"She doesn't mean *that* kind of dope!" I protested.

Similarly, I had ignored a hint she had dropped to me earlier that year, also in a doctor's office.

"He's so square," she had said. "I said something about dope to him and he said, 'you mean herium'!"

I never gave it a thought, my anxiety and concern about Janis far more generalized throughout that year and focused only around an intuitive sense that something dreadful was in the making. The conditions of her fame were gruesomely clear. That she was doomed to incorporate them as the irreversible command of self-destruction, I could not have articulated at that time.

The reporters responsible for the stories on Janis had, most of them, been well-intentioned, particularly at the beginning. Few knives were raised to shred away at that onion-skin bravado. If the power of Janis's voice onstage was overwhelming, it was wistful when she spoke. No matter the blinding snap of her language, it was couched in a plaintiveness of tone that betrayed her vulnerability and carried an implicit plea for kindness. More often than not, she got it.

But as a collective force, the media works like a monster computer: plugs, buttons, switches, cords, a maze of technological perfection geared to produce a technological result. Receiving, coding, indexing, slotting, programming, dividing, multiplying, it condenses and subtracts, then collapses with simplicity, the process of it all too exhausting for its resources, the very immensity of size an obstacle to nuance. Janis fed it—her quotes, her heat, her repetitive bombast making her reality impossible. The accumulation of stories thickened into a pastiche portrait, the crystallization of a phosphorescent robot, and she offered herself as exactly that to her audiences, who then devoured her. Janis became renowned—and by far too many people, loved—for her wildness, her drinking, her loveless sexual abandon and all of that gobbling frenzy that fulfilled the fantasy of the age.

Everyone was sucking on it like a gargantuan leech. Her NOW was theirs. In no time, she was her raw and royal majesty, up on Mount Olympus, wrapped in her imperial lynx coat, with a bottle of Southern Comfort for a scepter and for a throne of glory, a deadly cage.

Brilliantly summarizing Janis's hopes and the drives that helped to trap her in that cage, Peter Cohon said sadly, "I *know* she wanted to be a big star, but what I'm sayin' is that she didn't really know what the life of a big star is about! That from the outside, a big star is access to any room, to any person you want to meet, to any place you want to go, anything you want to do. Sounds groovy! I mean, it's the same mode of force that has a cat walk down the street and see a woman and he goes through an imagining in his head of what kind of clothes that woman would wear and the car she would drive in and the restaurant she would be in, then going out and hustling the gig that would get him the jack to buy that car and buy this and buy that, *finally* so he can take *all* of it off and get into bed with that woman, you know. Like fuck-magnets, all of that!"

14

Janis used to call it the year of the Kozmic Blues. "You have to spell it that way," she'd say. "It's just too heavy to be taken seriously." The weight of it she lifted in a voice as craggy as an ancient pyramid.

Time keeps movin' on
Friends, they turn away

I keep movin' on, but I never found out why
I keep pushin' so hard an' babe, I keep try'n
To make it right to another lonely day. *

The style of it clanged around with a sputtering
madness as jumbled and loud as those clashing letters
and every bit as mocking.

Janis had acquired a Porsche by then, its metal en-
livened into one rupturing symbol of memory and defiance, an ingenious phantasmagoria created by the
imagination of Dave Richards. On one fender were
the faces of Big Brother; on its trunk, a bloodied
American flag. She had formed a corporation and
called it Fantality which, as a combination of fantasy
and reality, was meant to define the state of her
existence as she viewed it at the time. Her publishing
company she called Strong Arm Music, the title arising from the sense of justice that was part of her
puritanical core: Janis thought it unfair that she
could acquire copyrights to songs that she herself
had not written. She had a new wardrobe, and what
with the money to spend on personal splendor, those
tiers of satin, those fluffy plumes, the whole garish explosion of her attire took on a considerably more ex-
pensive cast. She had an identity, "the belle-ideale of
NOW!" implanted in *The New York Times* by writer
Michael Lydon, who was also privileged to receive a
series of socko-wham-bam quotes that popped out
from the pages of the *Times* as "The Janis Joplin
Philosophy." Then she had her new band, a jangling
staccato of musical incoherence, driven by a horn
section that, instead of a gleaming livery of brass,
was like the scattered intrusion of so much cheap
confetti, though certainly a great deal louder.

Janis had insisted on the horns, against Albert's advice and that of any number of others who were cer-

tain that their coloration would be wrong for the texture of her voice. Moreover, the band was pulled together with nervous haste and the participation of too many people. Albert had called on guitarist Mike Bloomfield, Elliot Mazer, and Nick Gravenites to help find the musicians and assist at rehearsals. The result was an aggregate of individuals who had no similarity of background. If Big Brother had been an eruption, its bond of unity a mangled primitivism that flashed and spewed without the necessity for a disciplined center, the new group was badly in need of a leader. The horns, the variety of views, the hurried nature of its formation, all were secondary to the most serious deficiency—that Janis was neither musically nor emotionally prepared for that role.

Elliot remembered that during the early rehearsals, which began in New York in 1968, Janis's anxiety about the separation from Big Brother was focused on acute feelings of inferiority. Had she extended herself beyond her ability? Would she be exposed as a minor talent? Perhaps she should have stayed with Big Brother, she'd say, and would demand from Elliot, too, reassurance that she was gifted, that she could sing, that she *deserved* to move ahead. Some of her attempts to prove her talent struck Elliot as simply pathetic. As she had done around John Simon, she deliberated effects; her screams and embellishments picked up, on occasion, from some very unlikely places.

"Lissen," she said, one day on the phone. "I just heard this dog do this outasight scream!" And "Ahhhhhooooooohhh!" she went.

According to Elliot, she was only half joking. "I mean," he said, "I was *upset* because she was a little *too* serious. It was groovy, but she'd say stuff like, 'How do you like my new scream?' She'd *always* say, 'Did I do it well? Do you love me?' And when one's thinking about someone like Janis Joplin, you don't expect them to be *that* concerned. It was her constant fear that she'd look bad behind a bunch of good musicians. Always, she'd say, 'I don't deserve this!' and she felt really doomed, like she should be *punished* for it!"

Moreover, there were only two and a half weeks of rehearsals before Janis and the band appeared at the Stax-Volt Convention in Memphis on December 21. On that occasion, the lineup of the group was still tentative, as was the commitment of most of the musicians throughout the entire year. Surely nothing was musically stable on February 11 of 1969, when Janis faced the test of a New York performance in the loaded atmosphere of the Fillmore East.

The kids had been letting the whip of winter lash at their skins since four in the afternoon of what was to be a very tense evening, the occasion of that Fillmore appearance. By seven-thirty, ragamuffins, dashing carnival outfits, thinly dressed hippies, conventional suits, and plush mink coats were staggered in a giant, grotesque corkscrew that twisted down Second Avenue for six to seven blocks.

As I ducked under the wooden barriers holding the crowd at bay, I heard a shivering optimist say, "I hear she kept Sam Andrew."

"It can't be the same," an embittered long-hair replied. "It's not Big Brother."

Backstage, Janis was moving fitfully around the dressing room, which had been newly painted in a smashing purple. Bill Graham had provided some other embellishments. There was a magnificently attired usher to do Janis's bidding, a bowl of guacamole, plenty of champagne, and some terrific rye bread from Ratner's Dairy Restaurant next door. The greatest embellishment of the evening was a CBS "60 Minutes" film crew, to whose presence we had not consented.

Janis smiled uneasily when she saw me, then started to chew on her nails. "Myra, is the crowd big?"

"Huge," I replied.

Terry Clements, Janis's tenor sax player, sat in a corner silently fingering his horn. The trumpet player, a self-designated mystic named Terry Hensley, was transcendentally facing a wall.

"Where's John Cooke?" I asked.

"He's in the office with Bill," Janis said. "What are we gonna do about this business with CBS? Man, I wish Albert was here."

The snow had trapped Albert in Woodstock, impelling him to wait until Wednesday, when the sun would hopefully soften the ice and he could risk the New York Thruway. Never had I wished more for his presence. I did not relish the prospect of opposing Bill Graham's will.

That kind of publicity, prime time on network CBS, is almost impossible to obtain, and I hardly blamed Bill for wanting it. The problem was that no one had *asked* us, until it was too late and the cameras were already there to film a show that would be called *Carnegie Hall for Children*, with Bill Graham as the costar. As Albert saw it, there were sound reasons for shunning the exposure on that particular night. The band was just too new and the performance was very likely to be shaky. In addition, the bass player, Brad Campbell, was from Canada, and we were not sure he had his work clearance. The immigration department is strict about formalities like that. If there was, in fact, a transgression, we didn't need filmed evidence. Furthermore, we'd already rejected an earlier request from the CBS local station for exactly those reasons. I did not like being tricked into a situation that was pressing me toward doing something I thought dreadfully unfair.

Moaning, I left the dressing room and headed for the Fillmore office. There a picture of a glowering Bill Graham giving the finger to the world looked down on the real thing, who was snorting around like a fuming bull.

"You! You!" Bill sputtered, flinging his arms madly in the air, then jabbing a finger with crisscross motions that came startlingly close to my eyes. John Cooke disappeared backstage to make sure everything was in order, and my only ally for a few minutes was a hopped-up character, new to the office, named Bobby Neuwirth, who was very, very crocked.

"I say no," I muttered, thinking to myself that maybe I'd call Albert. The CBS people were on one side of the room; I was on the other, and Bill Graham, his eyebrows thick black slashes, was screaming and ranting as if he were Rasputin trying out for the Moscow Art Theater. I knew I couldn't withstand the tirade and mostly the embarrassment of the carrying on in front of those people from CBS. If they would not film the performance, maybe an interview would be all right.

Bill yelled a hysterical "NO" at the suggestion and continued a dramatic march around his office. Actually, he was getting close to laughter—until Neuwirth opened his mouth.

"Hey man, the chick's too nervous, right?" Bobby growled.

Bill thundered toward him. "YOU STAY OUT OF THIS, YOU FUCKING SONOFABITCH!" He thrashed back toward me. Cooke dashed in to check the situation. Kip Cohen, then the Fillmore manager, was trying to pretend it wasn't all happening and sat staring at the ceiling. Mike Wallace and the producer of "60 Minutes" sat awed by the fury, no doubt convinced we were each of us insane.

Eventually, after calling Albert, we came to the compromise that had seemed the only thing feasible: an interview, but no performance. I sighed with relief and went backstage, where we proceeded to change Brad Campbell's appearance with every device at hand.

"Anybody got an eyebrow pencil?" Janis pleaded. The drummer, Roy Markowitz, stuck his head into the hall. "Eyebrow pencil! Eyebrow pencil!"

An accommodating groupie came up with a pencil, which Janis used to grace Brad with a Salvador

Dali mustache. She plopped her bushy fur hat on his head. "Needs more," Richard Kermode, the organ player, shrugged. "Here, take my sunglasses."

The disguise was complete, a precaution just in case the camera crew was tempted to violate the agreement, which was set at no performance shots, just a quickie of Janis when she hit the stage.

She hit it all right, charging down on her audience like the Four Horsemen of the Apocalypse, the microphone flailing in her hand. The old wood alcohol bite was there, her wails as improbable as ever. But Janis was horribly nervous and working too hard at her raunch. There was too much strain in the grind of her hips, too much deliberation in the wild toss of her head. To make things worse, the band was out of tune and the horns were overwhelming. Her self-depreciation was mortifying: she opened the set with a rabid version of a song called "Raise Your Hand," then introduced the band to the audience as "Janis and the Jack-Offs." The audience laughed; I felt sick.

Backstage, in between sets, Janis got drunk, and in preparation for the CBS interview told Mike Wallace he should just say "fuck" if she got out of line, then instructed the band to chant the same, if he should ask a silly question. A lot of people thought that was very funny. I did not. All in all, the evenings were packed away in a bag of sour memories. If the audience had seemed responsive, Janis was far from ecstatic. So was Albert, who made it into town for the next night's concert and complained about the band. Then there was the conclusion of the CBS drama, which wound up with Bill Graham threatening in the third act to decapitate Bobby Neuwirth.

My first encounter with Bobby Neuwirth came on a December evening in 1968 when, grumbling and hopping from one foot to the other, he reluctantly agreed to carry my shopping bag on the way to a party at Time Inc. The affair was to celebrate an issue of *Life* devoted to the "Winners and Losers" of the year, and Janis, presumably, was one of the winners. We walked to the party from the office, with Albert, Janis, and myself on the sidewalk and Bobby trudging curbside. Two panhandlers approached us along the way. It appeared that Bobby hadn't noticed. His head was down; his body was bent; he looked to be in another world. Then suddenly he did a little hop, up from the curb and in front of Janis.

"Hey, man!" said one of the panhandlers. "Can you spare a quart . . ."

"Here!" Bobby snarled, thrusting my shopping bag forward. "Ya wanna bag of shit?"

Once Bob Dylan's road manager, Bobby had been a luminary on the rock scene for some seven or eight years by virtue of his very noticeable presence and a series of revolving habits that include folk-singing, song-writing, fooling with film, and carving his role as a comic-in-residence with a humor as sharp as a vampire's teeth and headed quite often for exactly the place where the vampire's teeth are wont to go. Bobby was an old friend of John Cooke. He also knew Janis as far back as the mid-sixties, when he was hanging around Berkeley as part of the folk-music milieu. Somewhere between his religious immersion in being "with it" and his incommunicado hipness, there is an amazing amount of talent. But when I first met him, he was committed to nothing quite so much as the maintenance of his status as what *Esquire* once called "the stars' superstar."

Perhaps it was circumstance, but the formation of Janis's second band corresponded to an entire revolution in the character of her associations. Whether by accident, there was an intriguing similarity of tone. With the band, there was the flashy complexion of the horns, the bigness, the shape of professionalism, as opposed to the amateurish but much more natural spontaneity of Big Brother. And as that happened, everything around Janis took a jarring shift into super show business gear. John Cooke ripped out of his cocoon in the form of a fastidious dragon. Bobby

Neuwirth pounced into the office as a hired member of the team not too long before the night Bill Graham almost took off his head.

Around the same time there were other changes that had less of a bearing on the push to high drive, but were important to Janis nonetheless. Two new roadmen were hired: a fellow named George Ostrow replaced Dave Richards, who had quit but remained Janis's very close friend; and Marc Bronstein left, superseded by Vince Mitchell. The office heaved up in its annual fashion and thumped back down with new personnel, of which Bobby was only one. Vinnie Fusco was about to depart, and Albert employed Sam Gordon to take over the music publishing. Unsettled by the office environment, Sam hid for the first six months: "I wanted to systemize things, and Janis would come tripping in and let out some rip-roaring motherfucker or two and before I really knew her, I'd just jump in behind my desk and the boogeyin' was going on, the Neuwirths and all the games and I didn't know if I could *play* that game."

All mod bell-bottom pants, bright plaids, and flashing colors, Sam's clothes are as direct as the intelligibility of his speech. In his glistening Bronx brogue there was always a clarity of heart and thought noticeably missing in the likes of those who played the games Sam spoke of. Moreover, his reference to Neuwirth in the plural was not a slip of the tongue. Nor was he speaking of the layers of selves that exist in Bobby's character: lovable maniac, which he can be, and harlequin of papier-mâché. Bobby is very forceful, magnetizing not people so much as behavior—which tends to duplicate his own. As Dave Richards said in a different way, "Bobby's a choreographer." Sometimes what he choreographs is energy and appealing fun. At other times, he works up dances in quite another category, and so he did back then.

To be sure, they were fast and funny. With Bobby running the show, the whole office did indeed begin to tick to an ongoing competition for laughs—won by the cleverest at abuse. The extent to which people can be so choreographed depends on a readiness within them, of course, to have aggressions unleashed. John Cooke and Bobby seemed perpetually locked in what resembled a *folie à deux*. A fellow named Marty McGuinness strayed now and then from his more basically pleasant nature in a kind of temporary aberration. There was Michael Friedman, who came in as Albert's assistant. Blessed with a quickness of his own, he nonetheless steered rather clear of that particular race. Sam would have none of it at all. He is funny in his own right, but his humor turns to the whimsy of kindness, and when he heard the note of anything else, he retreated to his fifth-floor office. Albert was generally just droll, and Bert Block had an endless collection of hilarious but harmless stories about a legendary show-biz character named Joe Glaser. No, while it always had the cover of comedy, the fast-snapping repartee that went for the jugular remained in Janis's clique.

The fact is that most of the relationships in that clique were mobilized only by Janis's vitality and, of course, for those of us who were involved in her career, by a common function. Other than that, there were no relationships at all. If there was action on nonverbal levels, that which we call normal human speech went into a state of suspended animation, the constant jesting, the sideways language serving a definite purpose for people whose fear of being seen was as terrible as the trembling unto death. We never talked; we jibed. The sadistic content of the humor and the disengagement of the people constructed a barrier to the exchange of anything serious and settled around Janis's associates as a covenant of silence in the midst of a great deal of noise. The theme song was "keep on rockin'," which meant a lot of alcohol, a lot of laughs, and some occasional drivel about the new cinema, the new music, or the new personalities. The bonds of communication were

matters of business and humor, and those alone. The
commitment was to style—and a very particular one
at that.

Janis's entourage and the milieu it reflected was set
operative in an ambiance of common beliefs and
values endemic to the counterculture mentality. Its
members worried about the Indians; they were bitter
about the Corporate State. They believed in the com-
munal way, thought *Easy Rider* a masterpiece and
Woodstock the apotheosis of peace and love. Yet they
were "cool," thus uninvolved; "collective," thus imper-
sonal; "hip," thus uncommunicative; "free," thus
irresponsible; and much of the time "stoned," thus
usually incapable of making sense. Naturally there
were individual differences, but that was the tone of it
all, an insignia of manners and morals as salient as a
Legionnaire's cap, with "keep on rockin'" the
emptiest of prayers, and the style, emotional
atrophy.

A paralyzing listlessness and detachment atrophied
the mood of the band as well. By the middle of
February the horn section was expanded with the
addition of baritone sax player Cornelius "Snooky"
Flowers. If his barreling sense of humor made for
some good times on the road, they were overridden
by the soggy de-energizing lack of morale that
worsened as the months went on. A number of musicians were there to begin with only as a business venture. Nevertheless, Janis's state of mind did little to
lift their spirits and much to increase their attitudes
that backing up Janis was, after all, nothing more
than a job. Typically, she overcompensated for her
feelings of inadequacy with a demoralizing bravado
of self-assertion. Rehearsals capsized when she arrived. Her jokes were as funny as a pinched optic
nerve, her attempts at authority disorienting. Most of
all, there was the blanket of emptiness in her eyes,
occasional for a time and then like an immutable
nakedness.

After Janis died, the media, as a whole, could do no other than assume that she had paid the ultimate price for her gluttonous grasp of the instant experience. "Right now is where you are," she instructed Michael Lydon. "How can you wait?" To Hubert Saal of *Newsweek* she announced defiantly, "I don't want to do anything half-assed. I'm twenty-six and all I'm worried about is twenty-six, not ninety-five."

Despite her statements to the contrary, Janis was concerned about the future to an inordinate degree and depressingly preoccupied with the passing of time. "What's gonna happen to me when I'm not Number One any more?" she said to Albert one night at dinner.

Continually she worried about age and predicted a scarifying decline. "I'm afraid I'm gonna be one of those raucous old drunk ladies hanging out on Skid Row and picking up all the young boys."

Such comments were hardly inconsistent with an emphasis on the present, but one could not say the same about her attitude and approach to money. When it came to the matter of her finances, Janis betrayed a frugality that made her "today is all you've got" *Zeitgeist* appear downright ridiculous.

Big Brother's performances for the first half of 1968 had brought an average of $4500 a concert, and Janis, moreover, was only one of an equally sharing quintet. The members of the second band were salaried employees, and Janis's fees had climbed quite high. The Fillmore appearances had raked in $22,325; a weekend at San Francisco's Winterland in March would bring $30,000. While concerts like that were certainly not every day of the week, Janis's income increased tremendously during 1969. Not so the way in which she handled it. Her Porsche, her clothes, and even her Larkspur home, which she purchased later in the fall, were far from immoderate expenditures in proportion to the dollars at her disposal.

Nor was it true, as reported in several newspapers, that Janis was in the habit of opening bank accounts

around the country, the implication again being some
kind of free-wheeling attitude that was assumed to
permeate every aspect of her life. Quite the contrary.
As her lawyer Bob Gordon was fascinated to discover
in going through her papers after she died, there was
a scrupulous order to them all, and particularly to her
checkbooks, with the stubs a conscientiously kept record of every expense and deposit, subtracted or
added down to the penny in book after book after
book.

Moreover, no one who knew Janis well could in
honesty describe her as generous, though she could
be touchingly thoughtful from time to time. At Christmas she took an enormous and genuine pleasure in
giving me gifts, as she did Linda Gravenites and
some of her other friends. She usually honored the
birthdays of those who were close to her as well.
Sometime in 1969 she paid twenty thousand dollars
as an advance retainer to a team of lawyers hired to
defend one of her friends who was in serious difficulty, but the circumstances were unique (involving
a manslaughter charge and drugs) and evoked in
Janis a magnanimity that, holiday occasions notwithstanding, was essentially rather rare. Generally, when
she parted with her money, she did so with a grumbling reluctance, her fear of the future at work, to be
sure, but also that austerity that was hers at the core.
"She was *tight!*" Linda said. "You know that!" Indeed
I do. Hence, Janis's basic conservatism with money
gave very special significance to the mode of her dealing with one occupational hazard in particular.

Parasites flourished in Janis's presence. They were
there in droves—dropping in at her home, scratching
around at the bars she frequented, surrounding her
table at the restaurants where she ate. Always, she
was left to pick up the dinner checks and bills from
drinking bouts that occurred wherever she happened
to be. That she submitted was less from charitability
than confusion. Terrified to say no, she was unwilling
to risk the loss of love she thought her refusal might

bring and which, many a time, it certainly would. There was a more crucial reason. The actual exploitation aside, such situations were tools as well, permitting her to wallow in a grotesque and perpetual fantasy of Janis Joplin as victim.

"It was really strange," said one of her West Coast friends. "We'd go and sit down at a table and twenty people would come and she'd end up paying for the whole thing. She felt used, but she always *offered* to pay, you know. I could never figure that out!"

It was true, as Vince Mitchell remarked, "She didn't know who was her friend and who wasn't." It was just as true, as he further stated, "She had this block that people were using her—and the few who *weren't*, sometimes she'd come down on them like they *were*."

Vince had merely the wrong word, calling a "block" what was really a wish. So did her drug use pivot on a related emotional posture, a pervasive masochism made more acute by the needle's actual effects.

Janis had friends who speculated that at least when she started with heroin she might have done so for the sake of experience itself as the most unfortunate extreme in what they construed to be the philosophical quest that had her living so close to the edge. It was perhaps comparable in her mind to other activities that involve the risk of death and are enjoyed for the enhanced experience of life that such risks must certainly entail. One climbs mountains, canoes in terrifying rapids, skydives, and so on, and may easily die in the process. All the same, those endeavors involve the most active engagement of the body in a test against the forces of nature, the exhilaration of the experience extracted directly from a mental alertness and an aliveness of the senses to what is occurring, the very things that are obliterated in the anesthesia of the heroin high. Janis's dread of psychedelics stemmed from their tendency to intensify experience, and the most relatively innocuous drug around had a disturbing effect on her. "Grass makes me think too much," she'd say. Despite her early and disastrous methadrine habit, her overwhelming preference was for drugs that diminish awareness: the sedative, depressant, narcotic group, which lessened the magnitude of her anxiety, and much of that anxiety was conspicuously linked to the gratifications she proclaimed she enjoyed so free of guilt and fear. A related function was less obvious. In the emphasis on heroin as an analgesic and in the attention to its pain-killing properties, there is usually a superficial focus on what its effects wholly are. Heroin reduces affect completely, blunting more than the perception of pain. "It was boring, man!" said a friend of Janis's who tried it once. "Boring! You're perfectly tranquil and you're perfectly satisfied with sitting in a chair for eight hours gooned out and listening to boredom! I perceived, but my perceptions produced no emotional reaction at all. If I saw something terrible, I couldn't feel, 'Oh that hurts me,' and *if there was something happy, I couldn't feel, 'Oh, I feel joyful about that.'* I could react mentally, but not emotionally, because *I-did-not-care!"* And as Linda said to Janis repeatedly, "It may keep you from feeling bad, but it keeps you from feeling good too."

Certainly the reasons for heroin use as a widespread phenomenon are varied, with the orgasmic totality of the rush, the over-all placid euphoria, peer pressure, availability, the hideous conditions of the black ghettos, and a host of other factors coming into play, not to mention that once addiction is established, reasons may take a secondary place. Nevertheless, in Janis's case, if she cherished the ability of heroin to keep her from "feeling bad," she perversely valued even more the numbing of the senses and of mental states that had to do with "feeling good." In all its functions, her usage consisted of extreme aggression against her person. There is a certain gracefulness in using the term "self-destructive." More often than not, that is no more than society's palatable way of dealing with certain behaviors in a descriptive fashion, thereby sidestepping what sounds too purposeful, too motivated, too close to the truth. Chronic suicide is what Janis was engaged in throughout her life, the act taking this or that form along the way and penetrating all areas of her tortured existence. Janis herself would attribute her heroin use to the fear that accompanied her growing fame. There was indeed a connection; she had, after all, picked up the needle right after Monterey.

"I have to give her credit," organist Richard Kermode said, "for whatever she came up with, because she was tormented, all the time, just all the time miserable. What everything seemed to depend on was if she could have a man and, you know, I just couldn't be it for her."

Yet it was Richard Kermode to whom Janis became attached during the first several months of working with her second band. The fixation of fantasy, Richard felt, the filling of a need that had little to do with his own substance, born of loneliness, but something more, because it was clear that what was between them activated those tortuous poles in Janis's wretched depths and that Richard was a foil for their expression. He is not, by his own description, of a dominant nature, and Janis, it seemed to him, thrust upon him the heavy fury of aggression, trying at the same time to extract from him an intensity, not to match but to overcome her own. Then she would turn, become passive in some desperate attempt to shrink back into that delicate frailty that would give her the form of femininity, and the turmoil, the assault, the retreat into the whispering lisp that she would sometimes assume would gurgle up in one agonized sob of confusion.

"I wasn't about to assert dominance," he said. "And the kind of man she seemed to want, she couldn't have him. To be a star and to fulfill the image she was fulfilling meant being a certain type of woman that she didn't always want to be inside. Maybe she wanted to feel feminine sometimes, and the image just wouldn't allow it. But the relationship between Janis and me was just not real. In fact, *most* of Janis's things weren't real. And she would try to build them up so high to *make* them believable, but they *weren't!*"

It was disturbing to him too, because he felt terribly used, an object intended to fill her lonely hours after concerts were over and to be at her side in public places. After a while, it became too much for him, because it was complicated by her drug use: Janis, the symbol of all feeling, clutching to feel where there were no feelongs at all. That is, of course, one of the things that the needle does and also is one of its major purposes.* Richard was quite specific: "The junk didn't dampen her enthusiasm for sex. It was like she'd want to go on forever, but not *feeling* anything —or something. I couldn't get into it. It was weirdness. Pain was very much involved, very much. Just the sheer physical mash. It was a *pain* thing and that's what she dug about it!"

As for living in the present, certainly being on the road engenders the feeling that there is no future and no past. "Five minutes," John Cooke would say, and in five minutes the band would stumble into wherever the lobby happened to be, with Snooky Flowers' clothes all falling out of his suitcases and Janis ragged and unsmiling, because the days began quite early and her nights ran very late. John always sought the insurance of morning flights and as an extra precaution in case of any problems hauled the band to the airports way before takeoff. If the airports were dreary, the bars glinted with alcohol welcome. So there would be drinks in the morning, then drinks on

---

* Some recent studies at Phoenix House and Daytop Village in New York City indicate some variance in that effect. Daytop's study in particular revealed the majority of addicts to believe sex more enjoyable with drugs. The reasons, however, seemed derived from acute anxiety about sexual activity, which anxiety drugs served to diminish.

the plane, drinks while John collected the baggage
after landing, drinks in the motel bars. A sound check
in the afternoon, a concert at night, and the same routine the following day. Desolate airports, gray dressing rooms, colorless motels, and bar after bar after bar
—all were mere knots on a gnarled membrane of the
moment.

Janis made much of her loneliness on the road, and
God knows it was real enough in a way. "Sure," Sam
Gordon said, "Albert was there a phone call away
and the band was there for tunes and the wine store
was down the block and there were freaks in the
lobby for her entertainment. But after that, it was just
a situation with four walls, a chick laying in a fucking
hotel room with nobody and nothing."

Yet Vince Mitchell loved Janis, and simple and
countrified as he is, Vince has also what Emerson
called "moral charm," which is a great deal more than
can be said about most of the men in her life, roman-
tically involved or not. Consequently, Janis seems to
have found his feelings impossible to accept, halting
her relationship with him short of anything too serious.

"I can't have an old man on the road," she told him.
"The only way would be if he was traveling with me
—and then I couldn't get into it as much as I'd have
to."

No, there was something about the setting of the
road that was self-fulfilling for Janis. George Ostrow
stated it clearly: "It was like Janis wanted on the
road—or that's the way she approached it—to be 'one
of the guys.' Everything went, and she went to the
bars not just to get drunk, but she wanted to hang out
and be a part of everything." And so, since the men
around her pursued "little honeys" or "tender little
morsels," as some of them were prone to refer to
women, Janis went after "pretty young boys" and discussed her scores at breakfast.

"Sometimes it bothered me," Vince drawled. "Well,
most of the time . . . but . . . she was so mizzerble.

Sooo lonely, *vaaaree* lonely, one of the most lone-li-est
people I ever met. She just always felt down and
never really looked up. And she'd always say, 'Do ya
think I'm doin' good?' and *repeat* it and *repeat* it and
ask, 'How come you don't like me?' She used to think
that! She just wanted reassurance all the time!"

Reassurance was not exactly what Janis received during the first few months of 1969. The earliest concerts
had taken place on the East Coast and a few in Midwest cities. At best, they were mediocre. The songs
were new, the arrangements forced, and if Janis's
voice ripped out with the gleam of a savage scar, it
rose against a slopping, splashing background that in
her excessive self-doubt and lack of experience she
couldn't manage to direct. In a nervous reliance on
the stuff of mannerisms, she began cursing more onstage and toughening her Forty-second Street whore
veneer.

But if there was criticism of the band, there was
patience too, the reviews reflecting a hope for Janis's
developing musicality with some reservations about
the backup, and the flaws of that attributed to a lack
of unity, which time might possibly resolve. Not so,
however, in San Francisco, where Janis was left gasp-
ing from painful criticism.

The first performance at Winterland brought half-
hearted applause and, for the first time in Janis's career, no calls for an encore. What was worse was the
San Francisco press. Phil Elwood of the *Examiner*
called the performance "rocky," and that was a kindness. In the *Chronicle*, Ralph Gleason dismissed the
band as "a drag" and suggested that she dump it immediately and go back to Big Brother, if the group
would have her. And what certainly appeared a calculated assault began in *Rolling Stone* before Janis
had even gone on the road. Mocking Janis's love for
Tina Turner and the Ike and Tina Turner Revue,
summoning visions of a Memphis-style lineup with an
all-black chorus of "ooo-oooooh's," the paper stated

that the name of the group was The Janis Joplin Revue, the managing editor mumbling excuses about some never-revealed source for the false information when I called to protest. Corrected and told that at no time was such a name considered, the publication promptly proceeded to repeat it again throughout a writeup of the Memphis concert in December, topping it with a huge black headline: "The Memphis Debut of The Janis Joplin Revue"—all of this, of course, by virtue of the innocent carelessness that the paper claims is the only thing ever responsible for its mistakes. If the Fillmore East performance had been greeted with good-willed forbearance by the eastern press, *Rolling Stone* had to put her on the cover as "The Judy Garland of Rock and Roll." Janis was simply unable to tolerate the hurt, with the complication, the conflict, the agonizing tear between her voracious craving for acceptance and her unconscious need for punishment, creating within her an emotional *danse macabre* that was absolutely mutilating. Howard Smith of *The Village Voice*, who phoned Janis around the time that article appeared, was met with a deluge of tears and a hysterical plea for a postponement of his plans to interview her. Much more gruesome was an episode in which Bobby Neuwirth and Richard Kermode attempted to calm down Janis as she sobbingly begged a New York connection for more dope, a previous injection having failed to extinguish her anguish.

What is important about the suffering connected with that article is the way in which it came about, the piece based on an interview that Janis did with a *Rolling Stone* writer at the urging of John Cooke who, having met the reporter, was seized with the naive notion that the results of an interview would not be disastrous. My own contrary opinion was made very clear, as I recall it, in exactly these words: "Janis, you are going to get hurt and don't you dare turn around later and say I didn't warn you." Then Janis, who ordinarily always followed my advice in media matters, listened—in this situation, which was most crucial to

her—rather to John's well-intentioned but mistaken
judgment. Commencing to speak to the writer, she
furthermore handed him a series of groveling quotes
that no reporter could ignore and that gave considerable aid to the tone of the article, even to the point
where the Judy Garland number was irresistible, particularly to the editor of *Rolling Stone*. One might say
that Janis, in a manner of speaking, wrote the article
herself, then went for the needle to deaden the state
of excruciating misery she experienced over her masterpiece of self-damnation.

It was a relief, not only to Janis but to the entire
band, when they took off for Europe in April. The
most delighted was Linda Gravenites, who accompanied Janis on the trip. Where the climate of receptivity
to the new band would be more favorable, where
there would be the distraction of sightseeing, where,
above all, heroin was not so available, perhaps Janis
could be persuaded to stop before her still-occasional
use had tightened into the choking collar of addiction.

The tour was brilliant. Gone was the metallic spit of
the horns, the splotchiness of the rhythm section. Inspired by the warmth of the European audiences, the
band was a unified monument of ecstatic sound that
shimmered and pulsed behind the powerful soar of
Janis's voice. Leaving their audiences breathless, they
cut like a magnificent squall through Amsterdam, Co-
penhagen, Stockholm, and Paris before they hit London the third week of April.

Spirits were high, and they had some hilarious
times: crazy frolics in the Scandinavian discotheques,
loony adventures in the European hotels. Janis was
absorbed and seemingly happy. For a while, Linda
was hopeful. Then Janis, who had shown no withdrawal symptoms that anyone could notice, began to
talk about dope, though there was something quite
striking about her approach to the topic. Boasting,
taunting, praising its effects, she provoked, as if that
were part of the purpose, Linda's persistent opposi-
tion.

"Do you want me not to say anything?" Linda asked her, after an argument in Paris.

"God, no!" Janis replied.

Nor was it meaningless that Janis had asked her mother to go with her on the trip.

London proved too much, not only for Janis, but for Linda. After an astounding triumph at Albert Hall, Janis went to a party where she immediately shot up some junk. Linda could take it no more. Janis had overdosed once at the Noe Street apartment two months before the tour, a ghastly scene in which Linda and Sunshine had shocked her back to life with a salt solution, ice water, and the awful business of slapping her until there were welts all over her body. When someone else at that London party went into a temporary coma, Linda broke: "After I had to verify that the person in the next room had overdosed, I just freaked! When the person got conscious, I went to someone there and said, 'I'm getting the fuck out of here.'"

Linda remained in London when Janis returned to the States. Guilt-ridden and distraught, Linda was unable to tolerate what she was certain would be further deterioration, nor did she want to wake up one morning and find that brilliant luster all silent, purple and dead.

It was Sunshine who then moved into the Noe Street apartment. Today she is a senior staff counselor in the drug detoxification section of the Haight-Ashbury Drug Clinic. She was an ambulatory corpse back then.

15

What with the unanimity of spirit that had held so strong in Europe, the decline that began in the States seemed all the more disheartening. By June, when the group went into Columbia's Hollywood studios to record, it was just about ready for embalmment. As Brad Campbell described the whole procedure, "The *Kozmic Blues* recordings were chaos. Everybody was putting down everybody else. It was a mess, a total mess."

Basically, Gabriel Mekler, who produced that album, was stuck in the middle of converging circumstances: his own lack of admiration for the band, the discontent of most of the musicians, and a resulting round of arguments and frustrations, amplifying by the day. There were, moreover, new members in the group who'd not had time to adjust. A trumpet player named Luis Gasca had taken Terry Hensley's place; Maury Baker was the new drummer. Others were brought in just for the recording as a compromise of what Gabriel would actually have preferred: to dump the majority of the group for the sessions. As the man who would be responsible for the final results of the album, Gabriel could hardly have been expected to understand, cope with, tolerate, and overcome the psychological undercurrents that were one source of the band's failure. The band, of course, reacted in turn to his obvious distaste. Yet, in spite of the antagonism and bickering that occurred throughout those recordings, Janis pulled through to create some supreme moments: parts of the title song, "One Good Man," and, above all, "Little Girl Blue."

To Gabriel's knowledge, Janis stayed away from dope during the recording of that album. It was, in fact, to prevent her using and also to establish a comfortable working relationship that he had her stay at his home, and in that environment, with Gabriel's wife and the children affecting a temporary family, Janis periodically displayed some stunning transformations of personality.

To be sure, when out, driving around in her crazy Porsche, sauntering down the street, hopping from store to store, she was her harridan image, all silks and velvets and cheap gold shoes, dropping her ripened curses as fast as she swirled her body, and only changing to plead for reassurance. "Do you think they really love me?" she'd ask Gabriel when crowds would gather to receive one word from her lips and push in close to catch one twist of a smile.

At night she trouped around Los Angeles, exhausting herself in the panicked search for love, and if she refrained from deadening herself with dope, she butchered her vitality with liquor so that sometimes, in the studio, she had no voice and little energy to carry her through the day.

Still, around the house she was often subdued, and in private conversations with Gabriel and his wife she indicated that her experiences were not of the earth-shaking intensity that she led most people to believe. One evening, too, she underwent a bewildering metamorphosis, pulling her hair up in that prim bun of the past and dressing in a plain skirt. Gabriel recalled that she looked like a schoolteacher and that the occasion was something resembling a "legitimate" date. "I'm gonna be a *good* girl," she told her escort that night, although a few days later she returned to her more familiar garb, as if the other did not exist.

"She was fighting," Gabriel said, "fighting very hard. Fighting her background, because some people don't fit into that kind of background, except that if you're brought up that way, you can never really cut it off. And then she'd go and search for *anything* that was just so far in left field from that and it just ended up in more and more confusion!"

It was while Janis was recording *Kozmic Blues* that I was finally told she was using, thanks to writer John Bowers, who'd been on the road with her that spring, working on a piece for *Playboy*. Several weeks later, in July, Janis returned to New York. Over dinner at Max's the night she arrived, as I was nervously pondering some way to approach it, she brought up the subject herself.

"He can't even stand up anymore," she said in reference to another performer.

"What about you, Janis?"

Quickly looking away, she fumbled for cigarettes in her bag. "I ain't never missed a gig yet," she muttered uneasily.

That was true. Janis had never missed a performance because of dope. Indeed, it seemed impossible that such paroxysms of energy could well up from the paralyzing juices of heroin. Janis balanced it, chose the time of day to drowse her senses, so that when she hit the stage, she was able to draw only from the vibrant pump of life. If, somehow, there was less excitement than in the old days with Big Brother, it seemed attributable to musical difficulties alone.

And less excitement there was, no matter that the mood of the band improved once the recording sessions were over. One of the problems was the material itself, a repertoire of songs too similar in character. In a sense, the constriction was Janis's own integrity; never could she bring herself to touch a lyric that did not embody her most explicitly personal feelings.

> *They ain't never gonna love you any better, babe*
> *And they're nee-eever gonna love you ri-ight*
> *So you better dig it right now, right now*
> *Ohhhhhhh* *

Her enthrallment with this concept was increasing. Janis had found herself on the cover of *Newsweek* in May, the chosen figure to symbolize "The Rebirth of

---

* "Kozmic Blues" words & music by Janis Joplin and Gabriel Mekler. Copyright © 1969 Strong Arm Music & Wingate Music Corp., Suite 3100, 555 California St., San Francisco, Calif., 94104. Used by Permission. All Rights Reserved.

the Blues." Everywhere there was an accelerating media and audience emphasis on her lifestyle as the collaborator in the marvel of her performing intensity, the panegyrics ingested by her and serving to entrench her further into an emotional universe reeking already with despair and desolation.

> He'll say he'd make you very happy
> But he'll only make you cry*

On the surface, the theme would look to be no more than in the current of the blues tradition, stemming as it does from the black experience, wherein grief has been the inescapable condition of reality. But in black blues or white blues, with that reality as a metaphor, the music, excepting fashionable imitation, has always been a way of voicing the pain, but easing it too, the immediacy, the banal directness, and the sexual focus meant to express and relieve a greater anguish. That was not so with Janis. The day had passed when she was able through singing to exorcise her unhappiness. Blues had become her way of embracing it, her celebratory wedding with sorrow, and thereby her glad welcome of the marriage vow, the implicit commitment to self-destruct.

Without grasping the full significance, Janis herself understood that. "Interviewers," she told Mary Campbell of the Associated Press, "don't talk about my singing as much as about my lifestyle. The only reason I can see is that maybe a lot of artists have one way of art and another way of life: in me, they're the same."

Nor did she quite comprehend the whole circle of her partnership with the public, stopping at a frightening perception that did not include a recognition of her half of the bargain. "Maybe my audiences," she declared, "can enjoy my music more if they think I'm destroying myself."

As for the needle, I found it impossible to be certain of what was occurring. Throughout most of the summer of 1969, Janis was on the road, in New York for one or two days, out again for concerts. Her references to smack remained oblique, her responses evasive to my first attempts to discuss it. I would, on occasion, even get the feeling that she might possibly have stopped. The effects just didn't show for a while, or certainly not to me. First of all, Janis was not using daily as yet, that due very likely to multiple drug use. She was, of course, drinking always and may, at times, have used some speed, as was the case the night before Hunter. The multiple drug use may also have produced an idiosyncratic reaction wherein heroin, until her use increased, did not bring on a noticeably devitalizing effect. Most important was the fact that it was never openly discussed among the people around her. There was only the chasm of noncommunication filled by the argot of hipness, all spilling out in the impression that no one gave a solitary damn. And while that was not so, it was not I but Vince Mitchell who later called the extent of that concern into doubt. "I'd get mad at her," he remembered, "and she'd get mad back, but I kept at it. She really appreciated it when I'd *get* mad, but just anybody couldn't talk to her. If you're tryin' to help somebody you can't just come down on them with a roar. Cooke screamed at her sometimes. Bobby, he more or less could talk to her. But not everybody knew how to handle it and not everybody cared—not all *that* much. It was 'you do your thing and I'll do mine!'"

While Vince was right, the situation was also more complex. Janis was in the habit of enjoining other people to help her and then tyrannizing them with the display of some of the motives that had her using smack in the first place. Dave Richards described her pattern perfectly as it occurred somewhat later on.

"I don't want you to do that," he'd say.

"Why not?" she'd answer.

"Because it'll kill you."

"So what?"

"Because I love you and I don't *want* you to die."

"Do you really love me?"

"Yes, I love you."

"Do you *really*?"

Ad infinitum. "When I say she demanded a lot," he added, "I mean she *demanded*. It was really like either you took *full* responsibility for her or you'd have to back off one way or the other!"

Moreover, Janis could be extremely intimidating, and some of the people who tried to help were frequently met with a torrent of anger, although that anger may have facilitated the retreat to their more natural state of noninvolvement. I received mostly rage that summer, once she switched from evasion to defiance. Albert had experienced every routine she could summon. Nonetheless, she was responding to the evidence of concern. In early August she went to St. Thomas as the beginning of the struggle to stop.

"I'm goin' down there without anything, man," I heard her say to Albert when she called him in the country right before she left.

Nine days later she came back as pale as she'd been before and wouldn't admit when I picked her up at the airport that the attempt had failed. "It rained every day," she said gloomily.

In the meantime, what inertia was weighting her concerts was only indirectly related to smack. Both the arrangements and the repertoire still needed livening, and nothing seemed to work. "I'd put together tunes," Sam Gordon remembered, "and then she'd throw them out, and when she didn't rip me off with one blast of her mouth, she'd say, 'Well, that's wrong because of blah, blah, blah,' but beyond everything, being loved was most important, and she was looking to get that message across."

It was the quality of that need, only part of which

could be found in the lyrics, that was so difficult to meet. Janis could reject and choose songs only by instinct. She demanded, for one thing, the melodic room to linger on phrases, but there was no way she could explain the music that could convey that all-enveloping intensity with which she could engorge her audiences and cram them into herself. That is really what Janis meant when she talked about "oneness." "I'm into me, plus they're into me, and everything comes together."

At that particular time, however, Janis's insatiability was like a yoke on her artistic strivings, still undefined but very apparent. Gabriel Mekler was insistent that Janis was driven by more than those metabolic demons that preyed on her soul. "God! Did she ever want to sing rather than just scream it out. She didn't quite know the direction, but she wanted to develop her voice and go to a high level of art. She was just in a state of limbo."

Nick Gravenites was aware of that too. "She wanted to be respected as a great singer, not as a hippie freak. I don't know if that was way back. But people get new ideas, and they can't *get* new ideas until things happen to them. It sounds silly, but you can't grow unless you grow. And she *was* growing."

All of that—the unsettled internal argument, the conflict between the primitive yearning and the desire for control—were reflected in the arrangements, the songs, the character of the sets. The tone was sluggish, imposing, massive, and dismal. Audiences are notoriously resistant to new material anyway, and it was exasperating enough to have every new song met with cries for the old. In the past, Janis would have let her audiences feed on her excitement and convert it into their own, a sea of bobbing bodies, the wild flailing of open arms, the hysteria igniting without verbal encouragement from her. With that physical display no longer spontaneous, Janis had begun to exhort her audiences to action.

"Why isn't there anyone dancing?" she'd cry.

"The cops won't let us!"

"I said, 'WHY ISN'T THERE ANYONE DANC-
ING?'"

And up they would be, much to the consternation of
the guards and sometimes a nervous promoter. That
is, as Janis used to say, what rock 'n' roll is all about,
and she meant it when she'd yell, "What I'm tryin' to
tell you is get off your butt and *feel*."

More than that, she was after that symbolic embrace, and she would pull it out, even if it were im-
pacted in the recesses of torpor. Janis's concerts
gradually became spectacles, with audience participation a kind of theatrical routine. Never was there the
violence that later became associated with rock, although that might have been just plain luck. Even so,
Janis did seem to have a remarkable ability to contain
the more negative aspects of letting loose. Tensions,
when they occurred, were usually the result of the
uniformed garrisons who gathered to "protect" the
stage. But property damage was another story, and as
early as the summer of 1969 some promoters were
starting to get wary of what a Joplin concert might
mean. For the most part, however, they looked the
other way. One reason was that the economy had not
yet declined, and the dollars that could be reaped
from Janis's performances were a great inducement to
overlook the possibility of chaos. The other reason lay
in the psychological power of the rock culture. That
power was what reached its peak at White Lake, New
York, town of Bethel, where the Woodstock Festival
was held that August. That power was what made the
festival's myth.

Woodstock Wonderland. The festival, the press proclaimed, had been a triumph for music and peace over
the somewhat difficult conditions of overcrowding and
inclement weather. The sweetness of the kids had
evoked the goodwill of the surrounding communities,
who'd helped to avert a "national disaster." A few off-
duty cops had been present, but no one had even
known. As for the state troopers, they'd smiled and

stuck to directing traffic. The young were free to smoke their dope, and what wonders that had brought. Left to their own devices, nearly a half million young people had set an example for the entire country, conducting themselves like lambs under circumstances that would have turned a Kiwanis Club meeting into a massacre. The Woodstock film amplified its glories, giving the impression that the promoters had bestowed the weekend as a loving gift from their ever-loving hearts. The festival, in fact, was a cosmic moment in history. Only thirteen miles from Grossinger's!

Actually, a series of events had demolished the plans of the promoters to make themselves a mint. The fences were torn down early in the game, and except for those who'd bought tickets in advance, the festival was "free" by default. By the second day, it was a behemoth of four hundred thousand people with tentacles squirting out to choke the roads with crazy convoys that went as far back as forty miles on the New York Thruway. The stage looked like a tiny dot in the opening of a freaky forest glowing all over with flecks of orange, an asteroid belt of lit-up joints. On the perimeters, thousands and thousands of bodies, painted, nude, or wildly attired, merged together in one great rippling tattoo. Several times the sky opened up like a punctured ventricle and saturated the ground until it was an oozing crater of mud. By Sunday it was disgusting, the garbage rubbed into that thick wet acreage, making it as smelly and slippery as a rancid slab of bacon. Army choppers whirred in the sky; Max Yasgur's farm summoned a picture of a Vietnam delta under siege. The conditions were that abominable, and the peace that prevailed in spite of them was indeed very impressive. What kept the peace and the nature of it was preposterously underplayed.

Out on the roads converging onto the site, it was a vision from Transylvania: staggering bodies, bloodless faces, and expressionless, narcotized eyes. The hospi-

tal tents and the Hog Farm commune were kept busy
throughout the weekend, tranquilizing hallucinating
children. From the stage, Chip Monck periodically
announced the distinction between the "bad" acid
around, which was causing bad trips, and the "good"
acid (which was also causing some bad trips). If the
crowd jammed into the giant washbasin below was
astoundingly peaceful, it seemed to be so less from a
no-choice acceptance of intolerable conditions than
from the passivity of stupor. Half the people at White
Lake couldn't hear the music; no one cared in the
least.

Woodstock, everyone knew, was less a festival than
a religious convocation. Its ceremonies were the asser-
tions of lifestyle, and the lifestyle included a celebration of the mystical relationship between drugs and
rock, with grass the holy wafer. It was as if the dope
that everyone was free to use in the absence of the law
had been commandeered to take that very law's place.
No fences were there, no guards, no shower stalls.
What ruled was the rock world's *Realpolitik*: you are
only as good as the number of joints you smoke, only
as blessed as you are high. It was as if Woodstock was
the ultimate declaration of dope, not as an incidental
euphoriant, but as some kind of necessary virtue. The
old concentration camp image was unavoidable. So, to
my view, was some legitimate pondering that Woodstock was prophetic.

Criticism of the festival was almost negligible. Few
questions were raised about the promoters, not for
quite a while. Few qualms about the drugs dented the
almost uniformly enthusiastic reports. The press could
have been a crew of anthropologists who'd stumbled
across the missing link.

For one thing, the barrage of sights and sounds
hurled at the brain by that spectacle was overwhelming; the press was under pressure to translate its
meaning within hours, a challenge as tough as reading
a billboard of graffiti from a subway train with failed

brakes. Moreover, there were writers who did articles from the files of others and were not there to draw their own conclusions. Then, as one journalist told me, the press has a lemminglike instinct every bit as powerful as that suggested to be the force that brought the crowd. But as I witnessed it from hanging around the executive trailers and the media centers on the site, there was another element that affected the building of the Woodstock mythology: there was the sheer power of the cultural mood.

First of all, a lot of the reporting, both "underground" and "establishment," was done by people who were one with the rock culture to begin with, and none of them noticeable for an inclination to self-criticism. That situation was particularly striking at *Life*, where the bulk of the reporting was done by a clique with an apparent predisposition to bury any negative aspects to the weekend. On top of that, the press was drowning in information coming from the executive trailers. Facing the immensity of the view at Bethel, some writers relied less on the use of their own eyes and ears then they did on what they were told, the tendency to do that increased by a susceptibility to the rock mystique. After all, expressing reservations about Woodstock at the time would have been akin to complaining of gout in a nursery—stuffy and irrelevant. One had to look out for one's self-esteem. Either that, or have a lot of guts. Thus did Barry Farrell at *Life* dissent from the magazine's splendor-in-the-grass "Woodstock" supplement and indicate clearly that the festival had made him nervous about the future. A *Time* essay treaded water. As for *The New York Times*, it went absolutely schizy. In the front, its news pages were cloud-borne. In the middle, its ridiculous "Nightmare in the Catskills" editorial was ridden with the spirit of Lawrence Welk; somebody had to be possessed to dream up "maddened youths." Nonetheless, the following day, the *Times* came up with a retraction, a sort of apology to what would soon become known as Consciousness III. The final evidence of cultural power was in; Spiro Agnew never had it so good.

Naturally, all of that media glow (and then the Woodstock film) was responsible for the country's concept of the festival and also quite possibly for a reshaping of the event as it was experienced by the people who were there. A lot of them may not have been so accepting of the mud, the cold, the sickening sanitation, and the shortage of food, as they later claimed. How many, I wondered, were like this:

"I don't care what anybody says," a girl in my building complained when I saw her in the lobby after I returned. "It was a drag. It was polluted. You couldn't hear the music. Everybody was stoned out of their skulls. I hated it."

Three days later, having consumed the papers, she was dancing all over the building, singing another tune.

By the time of the Woodstock festival, Sam Andrew had returned to California to rejoin Big Brother and had been replaced by guitarist John Till. Janis had been mediocre at the festival, the backup a mess. Nonetheless, the band was slowly developing into a more cohesive group, though the joy of performance was shattered by Janis's increasing estrangement and the effects of dope on her personality. It made her ill-tempered and selfish. It rotted her vitality and sank her perky smile into the grimace of misery. Only her performances went directly unscathed, Janis continuing not to use before she went onstage. She also continued to pretend that she was not concerned. But when she started the negotiations for her Larkspur home, she called Linda in London to plead with her to return. Janis was unhappy. Her dog George had disappeared. The most important reason was Sunshine. At that time, she was hardly the roommate to have if Janis wanted to kick. Linda indicated a willingness to

THE METAMORPHOSIS FROM
JANIS TO PEARL
A PHOTO HISTORY

The little girl

PHOTOGRAPHED BY © DAVID GAHR

Janis inscribed this:
"To Mom and Dad.
From your daughter, Janis"

Her high school yearbook picture
JANIS JOPLIN—Art Club—59-60;
FNA—58-59; FTA—57-58; GRA
—57-58; Slide Rule Club— 58-59;
"B" Average Award—57-59

The solo performer

In front of the Chelsea

With John Cooke

All feathered and smiling

With Ken Threadgill

With Albert Grossman

PHOTOGRAPHED BY © DAVID GAHR

PHOTOGRAPH BY JOHN FISCHER

PHOTOGRAPHED BY © DAVID GAHR

With Richard Kermode, Sam Andrew and Snooky Flowers,
from the band of the Kozmic Blues

With Bobby Neuwirth

PHOTOGRAPH BY JOHN FISCHER

COURTESY OF LYNDALL ERB

PHOTOGRAPHED BY © DAVID GAHR

With David Niehaus

With Kris Kristofferson

With Ken Pearson and Brad Campbell of Full-Tilt Boogie

PHOTOGRAPHS BY CLARK PIERSON

leave London. Sometime in the fall, she received this letter from Janis:

I'm in L.A. for a couple of days to pick up an outfit that Nudie's is making for me. Did you read about him in the Rolling Stone? He makes the *incredible* flashy Western clothes—real gaudy stuff. Just what I wanted! I'm getting a pants & vest outfit. Purple w/flowers & scroll-work, encrusted w/all sorts of colored rhinestones. I'm so excited—real flashy colored rhinestones!

But I'd rather have something by you. Gosh I do hope you haven't changed your mind—I mean you didn't say all that about coming home just because you were depressed & you're gonna change your mind did ya? I hope not because it really feels right—I mean I'd been thinking a lot about you lately & was looking for a house. Wanted to find a little peace! The house—wow, what could be more perfect?/Except if we could find George. But I believe we will. I love him too much, he'll come back. I think someone stole him—he wandered away while we were rehearsing in a studio downtown. And it was night and there are so many lonely people downtown at night & he's so groovy. I think someone copped him. I've been to the pound & put an ad in the paper & it's been on the radio & I've offered a reward but nothing.

But let me tell you about the house. I've got it for sure—it's going into escrow & all the business is being done with the cat who owns it & I have agreed so it's set. It's in Larkspur on Baltimore Ave.—the last house, it's a dead-end so there's no traffic at all. No noise, it's the first thing I noticed—it's beautiful quiet. It's got an immense living dining room combination (all the rooms are huge) that has a stone fireplace that stands free & creates a little study on one side of it. This room opens onto the sun deck (this wall is all glass & I've got an idea for big arches w/stained-glass above.) The deck is large w/benches all around, a built-in barbeque, overlooks a stream, & has redwood trees growing right up through the floor. I'm going to have to lop some of them so will get sun in the afternoons—now it's all shaded. There's two big bedrooms, both w/bath, & the garage is practically finished as a den. It's wired for

stereo all throughout, has skylights in the bathrooms &
kitchen. It's real strong & rustic—exposed beams, etc.
And he's leaving me some furniture that I asked for—
a gorgeous old roll-top desk, a tapestry couch w/match-
ing chair, all the kitchen stuff, the wash'dryer (!!) &
a beautiful old (1906) Baldwin pool table. I'm going
to get a piano & I'm going to try the "other way" for
once. Y' know how we discussed the two ways of facing
the Kozmic Blues we discussed once? One to get stoned
& try and have as good a time as possible & two, to
try & adjust to it. Well I'm going to try #2. No dope,
walks in the woods, learn yoga, maybe (don't laugh)
horseback riding, try to learn to play piano—I think
all this & the excitement of having a house & the incredible peace you feel there ought to be wonderful.
We could really be happy there, I know it, & I really
need you. Please come.

As soon as I hear from you I'll send you some bread
so you can buy groovies for making clothes. I have a
place in N.Y. that's doing the most beautiful tie-dying.
I have a lot of velvets & they did me some satin sheets
that are just incredible. You'll love their stuff.

Well, I'll be in the mid-West for the next two weeks
(I'm going camping with Vince, one of my equipment
men in between weekends) then to the East Coast so
write me at the office c/o Myra & mark them Hold for
Arrival. Let me know your plans & feelings.

I do hope you haven't changed your mind—love.

J.

All summer, Vince had been talking to Janis about
going camping. What with the constant business of
concerts, it was hard to find the chance, but finally in
October the opportunity arose and they chose the hills
of Austin for Janis's best week that year. George
Ostrow, Vince, and Vince's brother parked the equipment truck in a Safeway parking lot and rented a station wagon, filled it up with supplies from an Army
surplus store, and waited there for Janis.

"You can't wear those!" Vince laughed, as she came
trudging toward the car in Levi's and a tall pair of
glistening silver boots!

Those boots were the only remnants of the stage

throughout those wonderful few days. They rented a boat. They fished, they swam, they walked through the woods. They did nothing but listen to the scurrying of squirrels, the rustle of leaves, and the gentle stroke of the Texas wind.

"Well," Janis cried, popping up from the sleeping bag one night. "You mean, this is camping!"

"Yep," Vince roared. "That's what it is!"

Never had Vince seen Janis so happy. "She set up the whole place, you know, just like a little house out in the open, and she cooked—in her silver boots. I'd never seen her like that. She didn't know you could have fun that way, but just goin' out and just campin' and doin' nothin'! Because I don't know, nobody ever really took time out to spend a little time with her and *make* her be happy."

That week came to an end with a performance at the University of Texas, one which was not attended, with the exception of Julie Paul, by her old Texas companions. Among those who were still in Austin, there was some feeling that Janis would not welcome their presence, should they try to go backstage.

"We had several reports," Jack Smith protested, "of people trying to get to see her and it was like, 'I don't want to know you because you knew me when . . . !'"

While Janis's memories of Texas were hardly happy, there is no question that she had a strong interest in the public picture of herself as more friendless in the past than was really the case. One of her cherished visions was that she'd been utterly unique. "There was no one like me," she used to say. Nonetheless, it is almost certain that the reports to which Jack Smith referred stemmed only from backstage turmoil. Also, what the overly sensitive may have interpreted as an attitude of disinterest was very likely no more than the tremendous seriousness with which Janis regarded her concerts. Only excessive drinking, in the instances that such occurred, affected her disciplined concentration. Janis was a dedicated performer. She was an actress as well as a singer, and before going onstage she was tensed by a mental state that most people couldn't fathom. Often her mood perpetuated itself throughout a given evening. Those unfamiliar with such factors would have been bound to misunderstand. Sometimes, for instance, it was her state of mind that led to her unavailability for interviews; sometimes it was backstage madness; sometimes, just her life.

Always it was amazing to me when reporters were unable to believe there were limits to Janis's endurance or when they could not imagine that she, like them, had a personal existence that called for her time. The nature of that existence, of course, made her schedule, on occasion, somewhat unpredictable. Now and then, I bore my own particular burden with that. For what possible reason could I turn someone down; perforce I must be horrible.

Generally, however, Janis was unusually accessible. Nothing prevented Julie Paul's appearance in Janis's dressing room the night that she played Austin. Perhaps it was the result of the camping trip, perhaps of the encounter with an old dear friend, but Janis was somewhat pensive, alternating between flamboyant chatter about her career and wistful comments about the stress it put on her life. "It's not easy," she reflected, "living up to Janis Joplin, you know."

Following the Austin date, Janis took off for Houston, where her old friend Philip Carter had no difficulty managing to visit her either. Philip was amazed that she was able to perform; she drank that much before going onstage. More surprising to him was what happened after the concert. He said nothing at the time about what Janis made sure he witnessed in her hotel room. Instead he sent her a letter. "Janis," he wrote, "you're my friend and I wish you would stop hurting my friend."

Did Janis not understand? In a sense she thought herself invulnerable. She couldn't get hooked; she couldn't die. When an overdose killed an actor she knew, Janis boasted to Linda, "Well, some people die and some people are survivors. I'm a survivor."

But when Nancy Getz told Janis that Nancy Gurley was dead from heroin, she got a different message. Janis naturally was upset. Then her reaction broadened with these curtly stated words: "Well, I guess I'll go score some smack!"

Ten days after the Houston concert, Janis came back to New York. She was centered there for the next two months, from October through December. So far as I was concerned, she might as well have been slumped, nodding out in a Harlem doorway, for all the resemblance to her former self that remained as the days went by.

16

Who cared when she was at her best and when she wasn't? Glitter burst from her gold vest, flash from the bracelets that climbed up her arm. There was the swirl of her purple tight pants and the hair that whipped over her face. There were curses and tequila and sex. Stomping, stamping, growling, groaning, she worked the stage. Attending her concerts was like mainlining an aphrodisiac right through the spine.

The jolt was marvelous, and it wasn't. There was little room for the reverie her talent deserved, little chance to sail with her on those great blazing wails that surged up from her throat. Neither her audiences nor Janis herself would permit it. She had carnalized herself too completely, had made the inciting of the crowds, the sex, and the booze, and the language, the substance of her presence. The pageantry was the point of attention, her developing musicality merely a small float in the middle of a wild parade. She was

compelled to be coarse, driven to create pandemonium. The audiences had to be swarming the aisles,
pressing toward the stage, whistling, yelling, shrieking, dancing, or it wasn't a Joplin concert; it wasn't the
testimony of love. She encouraged the crowds when
they were prone to be encouraged, and strafed them
with demands when they weren't. One way or the
other, they'd be roused and at it. Her performances
were like that throughout the fall.

Over the summer, the partnership between Albert
and Bert Block had dissolved, and shortly afterward
Albert had formed a new one with a man named Bennett Glotzer, an arrangement since terminated. Bennett had brought with him his brother-in-law Bobby
Schuster as part of the deal, as well as what looked
like a shifty approach to business and people that was
in startling contrast to Albert's style. Marty McGuinness had gone. Though no longer on the staff, Bobby
Neuwirth had made himself a fixture in the office.
John Cooke had quit—temporarily, it turned out—his
position, taken for several months by an affable fellow
named Joe Crowley. During that period, on November 16, Janis got busted for profanity in Florida.

According to Janis, there was nothing so startling
about her language that night at the Curtis-Hixon Hall
in Tampa—until she was provoked. The first of the
curses to roll from her mouth, she said, was only in an
attempt to cooperate with the authorities' wishes for
order. "You gotta remember," she instructed the audience as they packed the aisles and hopped madly on
their seats, "if we don't hurt nuthin', they can't say
shit!" What Janis was not about to do was conduct a
plea for immobility and, to her view, that was what
the police wanted: no one in the aisles, no one on their
seats, no one *moving* in any way at all. When a policeman came onstage with a bullhorn to command the
audience to sit down, Janis went berserk.

"That cop came on the stage with a foghorn!" she
said to me on the phone from Tampa, "a fucking foghorn! During 'SUMMERTIME!' "

After the performance, Janis had lashed out again at a policeman backstage and brought on herself two indictments for the use of "vulgar and indecent language."

"You know how it was," Richard Kermode recalled. "The test of the performance was whether she got the audience out of their seats. It was like Janis against the cops every time, and Joe couldn't handle it, or her. Man, he was beautiful, but he couldn't follow behind John Cooke."

The incident went flying over the wire services within hours of the arrest, and the affair was finally settled by the payment of a small fine. All in all it seemed a minor enough business at the time. It wasn't. Eventually—in terms of Janis's bookings—it had severe repercussions, compounded by the more serious matter of Jim Morrison's arrest for "lewd and lascivious behavior" in Miami the previous spring when, in an act of utter impotence, he had exposed himself onstage. Janis would have suffered consequences had the Morrison episode not happened. But both busts had occurred in Florida; neither person was prone to restraint. Well-founded or not, a link was established. In a sense, those arrests marked the beginning of a reaction setting in around the country, and bearing by no coincidence a similarity to the mood in Nixon's Washington.

I was more concerned that fall with what was happening to Janis in other respects. Yet, at last, Linda had arrived in New York from London the day before the Tampa incident. For me, it was the end of the stultifying refusal of everyone around Janis to speak about her drug use.

"Help me. Please talk to her," I'd said once to Bobby.

"Not me, man," he'd answered. "Last time I spoke to her she told me I was jealous."

What difference could it possibly have made that Bobby had indeed tried? As Sam Gordon described the situation, "O.K., I heard Janis was on drugs, but when her eyes were glassy, I thought it was booze. I wasn't that close to her, and if I was, how would I do it? Who would I talk to? To Albert? To Neuwirth? To Cooke? To you? It was always left to the *next* dude, and the people on the road were on the payroll, you dig, and maybe they didn't want to blow their good thing."

Sam did not have to mention that it was impossible for anyone to take the responsibility for what she was doing. What he said of the atmosphere was no less true. Treated like an insidious cancer, never discussed in the family, her drug use had become deadlier by the day, its growth even nourished by the lethal disease of silence.

As for Albert, there were those who felt that he could have been quite a bit firmer with Janis and that when it came to issues in her personal life he was a bit like a mild-mannered father who spoils and indulges a troubled daughter when the opposite is what's called for. That is not exactly false, just crucially incomplete. Albert's symbolic importance to Janis was such that her attempts to manipulate him were extraordinary. Seemingly, she was dedicated in her effort to outrage him, unnerve him, scare him, seduce him, drive him half crazy if she could. Those not subject to the same degree or type of maneuvering can speak easily and with self-righteous certainty about how they would have handled her conduct. Moreover, a man who exudes what George Ostrow accurately described as a "great deal of power presence in his being" might well be rendered especially anxious in regard to a problem so formidable as to arouse a feeling of helplessness. Rarely confused about business, Albert was, as I witnessed it, confused about Janis. But whatever his other relationships and dealings. his commitment to her was profound, quite above and beyond anything to do with her value as a client. Nonetheless, while his reasons were terribly complex and had never to do with indifference, he too made broaching the subject extremely difficult until that fall. I suspected he thought it pointless and that discussion would therefore amount only to distasteful gossip in which he wasn't about to indulge.

He was wrong, because the beginning of openness did make a difference. Two and a half weeks of joint understanding, of joint effort on the part of Linda, Albert, and myself, and Janis responded as she had not before. They were dreadful days, climaxed by an absolute horror show on Thanksgiving evening when the Rolling Stones and Ike and Tina Turner played at Madison Square Garden and Janis was so drunk, so stoned, so out of control that she could have been an institutionalized psychotic rent by mania. Then one night Linda and I took Janis into a Village bar. Janis retaliated viciously to what I had to say. Afterward, back at the hotel with Linda, Janis burst into tears. But when Albert spoke to her next, his words finally had an effect. Janis called me the following day. "I'm going to see this doctor Albert knows," she said, "and I just wanted to tell you that I know you wouldn't have talked to me like that if you hadn't cared."

That onslaught of concern from others appeared to be the prime force that had Janis in Dr. Ed Rothschild's office on December 9, 1969. What existed in the way of her own true worries, she did her utmost to hide. At best, she seemed ambivalent, dancing in to see him with her bravado at full flair and delivering her usual recitation honoring the ecstasies of being stoned. She was theatrical, provocative, and challenging, her attitude boastful and flip. "I don't think she was really committed at that time to kicking," Dr. Rothschild recalled. "It was, you know, 'I can do this. It's the best thing in the world. I don't know why everybody's getting so upset about it.' She indicated that other people wanted her to come and that she was here reluctantly, but she *was here* and then again she came back."

Ed Rothschild is an endocrinologist with a lot of experience in treating addicts. His hair curls down slightly below his neck. The walls of his lab at the Sloan-Kettering Institute are decorated with peace posters. He was clearly not the enemy. Yet Janis approached the encounter as if it were some sort of contest, her weapons persistent retorts to everything he said, her diversionary skirmishes typical attempts to test, to control, to shock. Dr. Rothschild tried to steer her away from the games of competition she seemed determined to play, but her extreme intelligence made the experience of dealing with her unsettling nonetheless. "Just intellectually bordering on brilliant," he said. "She really could think circles around most people. One of her problems was that intellectually she was so advanced and her emotions were childlike and uncontrollable. There was a constant pressure for speech. She couldn't be quiet. She was unbelievably 'on' most of the time. I let her talk herself out; I didn't think she would be able to tolerate my stopping her."

Some of that talkathon bluster—about alcohol, about drugs, and, of course, about sex—very likely erupted from the pressure of unconfessed anxiety. "I mean," he said, "one time she came sailing in and it was 'Wow! Fantastic!' She balled so and so and it was a pattern of hers that she would tell me about over and over again, that she was balling different guys from time to time. And I *didn't* think it was fantastic and it sort of bothered me as a human being that someone would take something that should be kind of personal and flaunt it. I got the feeling that the sex thing was uncontrollable too. She'd talk about drugs and back off, then about liquor and back off, and then about sex and back off. And she tended to be very flip in talking about serious things, and I pointed out to her that this was probably defensive, but that I didn't think she could understand what I was talking about, and, of course, she then immediately knew what I was talking about and we went around like that."

Ed Rothschild noted that her diet was terrible, that she ate a lot of sweets and had wide weight swings—she stated from 115 to 155 pounds. Interestingly, she told him that she was treated for alcoholism when she was seventeen, using that term specifically, which may have indicated a concern about her drinking that she was not prepared to admit. She was cocky about the results of the tests, which showed her liver function normal. "Well, that just shows I'm really a strong, healthy person," she announced, "because the way I've been drinking you'd think my liver would be shot!" He assured her that was not necessarily the case.

He repeatedly stressed Janis's need to manipulate the situation into some strange battle of wills. "I pointed out to her that it was a behavior pattern that was going to hurt her. I told her I could be helpful up to a point and beyond that, it was up to her, that I wasn't either rejecting her or assuming the total responsibility for her. I think what she wanted was one thing or the other, like she wanted to be kicked out, you're a crazy nut and nothing can be done *or* I'll take care of everything and make it all beautiful!"

Janis was not as unreachable as she pretended. She did try to cooperate to the extent of going on Dolophine, the pill form of methadone, for a ten-day period of withdrawal. The madness naturally went on. She blazed around town with Bobby and actor Michael J. Pollard, who'd become a buddy that fall. One night she landed up at Bachelor's III, where she managed to meet Joe Namath, assigned in her mind to the status of a goal post toward which she was running to score a touchdown. The fame game was creeping up; not everything crazy about Janis was connected with dope. But bit by bit, the heaviness lifted and the veil that had masked her vitality gave way, tattered by her old ineffable radiance and the infatuating warmth we had all so missed. Even her wackiness took on an appeal it hadn't held in the longest of times.

She had been off junk maybe six days when she swept into my office one afternoon and begged me to take her shopping. "Please," she whimpered. "Nobody'll wait on me. Not at Bloomingdale's they won't."

On Lexington Avenue, Janis stopped to look in the window of a cheap jewelry store. "Hey! Whatta ya think of that ring?" she asked. The sign above it read "Gen-u-ine Garnet."

"Janis," I urged, "if you want to buy some jewelry, let's not do it here."

"Well, I *like* it. Come on, I wanna know how much it is."

Janis charged clanging into the store. Behind the counter stood a swollen hulk of a man in a filthy blue shirt.

"You have a ring I wanna look at," Janis said. "That garnet in the window."

"You'll have to show me which one you mean, lady," he snarled.

"Well, there's only one there!" she snapped indignantly.

Grumbling, he pulled in the tray.

"I like the stone," Janis mumbled. "I don't like the setting too much. Myra, do you like the setting?"

"Janis, I don't like the store," I whispered. "Let's get out of here."

"Well, wait a minute," she said. "Hey, mister! Can the setting for this be changed?"

"No!"

"Well, why not?"

"'Cause that's the way it comes."

I backed over against a wall and bit hard on a knuckle.

"Well," Janis frowned. "How much is it?"

"Seventy dollars. You want it or you don't want it?"

"Seventy dollars! Well, is it real?"

"It says 'genuine,' doesn't it?"

"I didn't ask you if it was genuine. I asked you if it was *real!*"

"Lady, do you know what 'genuine' means?"

"Yeah!"

Convulsed, I watched her lean over the counter

and press her face close to the man's mean, blubbery features.

"I know what 'genuine' means and I wanna know if it's *real!*" she shouted, trying to hold back her laughter.

I grabbed her arm and pulled her outside.

"Boy," she giggled, "you know, they never treat me right until I start pulling out hundred-dollar bills."

"I told you, Janis. . . ."

"Oh, I know," she smiled. "I just felt like it. Hey, you like me today, don't you?"

"Yeah," I replied. "I like you a lot."

"Well," she beamed, "I like myself again too."

A few days later, Janis left New York for a concert in Nashville that turned out to be so spectacular that she made the front page of the *Nashville Tennessean*. She returned to New York for her closing concert of the year and her last with the band of the Kozmic Blues.

Jesus, I muttered to myself as I stood in one of the exit alcoves of Madison Square Garden and watched the crowd pour into the hall. Seven-fifty a ticket just to face Janis's back! Is the money really that important?

A few weeks before, when the Rolling Stones had played that mammoth arena, no seats had been sold behind them. A canopy had even been constructed to enclose all but the front of the stage in an attempt to make the best of the Garden's poor acoustics. Yes, I kept thinking, the Stones had a higher guarantee and could afford the loss of unsold seats, and yes, Janis was about to take a five-month vacation during which she would be earning nothing. But still it struck me, the unenclosed platform, which would have the sound bouncing from one concrete wall to the other, as a symbol of how very much things had changed. Walking down the corridor, I had an image of Janis jumping to her feet on "The Dick Cavett Show" a year and a half before. "I mean," she'd ex-

claimed, "how do you expect somebody to groove
sitting out there in Box X923Z, for God's sake!" I
sighed and opened the door to the dressing room.

In a corner, two cameramen, this time from local
CBS-TV, were readying their equipment. About
twenty other people were roving around, joking,
jabbering, tuning up instruments, slugging away at
tequila.

News commentator Scott Osborne approached me.

"Why don't we wait till things calm down a little," I
said.

"Oh sure," he nodded, glancing eagerly at Janis.
Seated at a long table, she was holding court in a blur
of flourishes, her speech rambling wildly, her features
distorted as hoarse, bellowing laughter rushed up
from her stomach.

"Honey, it was something else!" she gasped, shaking
the arm of Michael Pollard, who was slumped in a
chair to her right.

"Yeah," he responded with a troll-like grin.

Bobby Neuwirth was hopping around the room.
Linda stood quietly against a wall. Near her was a
young man named Toby Ross, whom Janis had
swooped out of a Bleecker Street bar called Nobody's. Attempting to look bored, he was indifferently
twisting the strands of his long, blond hair.

When Janis spotted me, she cried out anxiously,
"Oh! Do you think Joe Namath will get here? Maybe
he's here! Will you go look?"

The Namath caper was simply absurd, a fleeting
encounter built into a mountain. Janis meant to impress. Exasperated, I said, "Now, how am I going to
find him? There're seventeen thousand people out
there!"

"Well, you sent him an invitation to the party,
didn't you?"

"Janis, I told you before, but he's got a game
and . . ."

"Oh, all right," she moaned petulantly, then

bounded up from her chair to greet Albert as he appeared in the doorway. She did her interview with
CBS and in another ten minutes zoomed out onstage.

For all her gyrations, the damp strands of hair that
were flying around her face, the chomped notes, the
boiling emotion, there was something stale about the
performance that night. An avalanche of shuddering
moans flooded the hall as that eerie ensemble of
pitches seethed out of her in rattling shrieks. Gobs of
color rushed from her green chiffon blouse and crim-
son pants as she scampered around and pummeled
the audience with the great gusts of her voice. But
the sound was lopping too loosely around the hall;
the band was in terrible form, and Janis was bur-
dened by an intangible weight.

"What's the matter with her?" Toby Ross whispered
as we stood in the wings to the side of the stage.
"You should've heard 'Me and Bobby McGhee' in
Nashville. It was fantastic! All of it was fantastic!"

That was part of the problem, the success of the
Nashville concert and the expectation that this would
radiate a similar glory. Moreover, it was December
19. She'd finished the Dolophine just the day before,
and that afternoon I'd thought she'd seemed edgy.
Now she was doing ridiculous things. Someone had
told her Namath was there. "Joe, Joe," she moaned
into the microphone, "Joe, where are you, Joe?"

Between numbers, she shot over to the side of the
stage, turning her disillusioned face from the audience. Magnificence was reached only once in a
blues jam with Paul Butterfield and Johnny Winter.
After that, the music sagged, and Janis compensated
with a desperate determination to get the hall crazy,
no matter how. Frustrated, she stopped in the
middle of a song to challenge the crowd, "What's the
matter with you? What're ya sittin' down for? I ain't
supposed t' tell ya t' dance, but what the fuck are ya
doin'?"

Suddenly the whole Garden was shaking and rumbling as hordes of kids swept toward the stage. Janis, I thought, had gone too far.

"Oh my God," I said to Linda. "Wasn't Tampa enough?"

A boy near the front of the stage reached up and grabbed Janis's hand, then tried to pull her down to the floor.

"Now honey, that's not exactly what I had in mind," she said and stepped back to continue singing while chaos reigned in the hall.

"All the clothes are in the cars," our limo driver, John Fischer, called out. "Get ready! I wanna make a dash for it and get out of here the minute she's through!"

I nodded and glanced at the cars that were lined up backstage, shocked to notice that the wheels were bouncing at least two inches off the concrete floor.

"Don't worry," a guard laughed, "you should see it when the elephants are here."

A few minutes more and we ran for the limousines. I went with a group of people who were heading straight for a party that Clive Davis was throwing for Janis in his Central Park West apartment. Janis went back to the Number One Fifth Avenue Hotel with Linda and Toby to change clothes.

I could not imagine a more lavishly prepared affair of its kind. There was an elegant display of food in the dining area, a generous bar in the living room. The crowd was enormous, a mixture of recording celebrities, upper-media press, Columbia Records' executives, and people on Janis's list. But the party had been under way for almost an hour, and Janis hadn't arrived. I was going through the motions of being cordial; my mind was on her absence.

A reporter cornered me in the foyer to ask me about her plans. "Well," I answered, "she's going right back to California tomorrow to fix up her new house.

Then she's going to take a vacation and get her new band together after that."

Noticing Albert across the room, I caught his eye and looked at my watch.

"Where's the guest of honor?" Sy Rosen asked.

"Don't know," I said. "She ought to be here soon."

"Did you see Dylan!" Johanna Schier laughed.

Bob Dylan had been at the party over a half hour and still had on his coat and gloves.

Johanna's husband, guitarist-composer John Hall, quipped, "Probably wants to make sure he can make a quick exit."

The three of us went into one of the bedrooms to escape the congestion. "Listen," I said to Johanna, "I don't care if the *Voice* doesn't run the piece. I care that you're moving to California. That's much more important."

During the days preceding the Garden concert, Johanna had been working on a personality sketch of Janis for *The Village Voice*, which the paper now was not going to publish. She and John were among the few people who knew that Janis had been using smack and, of course, that she was trying to stop. I had welcomed their plans to move to California as a marvel of good fortune.

"Maybe you ought to call her," Johanna urged.

"I'm gonna wait ten minutes," I mumbled. "It's probably just taking her time to dress. Let's go in the living room."

I grabbed a drink. Albert came lumbering toward me. At his insistence, I phoned the hotel. Janis had already left. Albert lurched back into the crowd. Relieved, I went to get some food, chiding myself for worrying too much.

"She's left," I said brightly to Johanna. "Everything's O.K. She'll be here in a minute."

"Oh!" I heard Clive Davis exclaim. "Here she is!"

A cluster of people surrounded Janis. Bob Dylan came over to greet her. Then she turned and moved across the room, gliding very slowly. She had on an outfit Linda had made, a black chiffon blouse and black satin pants. I thought for a minute that she looked beautiful. The impression faded. The shine in her eyes was weird and sickly. Her face had a green-white glow, translucent or waxen or something like that, similar to the skin of a corpse.

17

Toby Ross flew back to California with Janis the following day, then stayed in her new Larkspur home for some three weeks thereafter. Several weeks' vacation had him free with time to spare. He was delighted to honor Janis's request that he spend that time with her. Did the glamour of it hold no appeal? He was piqued at the very suggestion. "I hadn't felt that way since the beginning," he insisted. "She used to say the most *unbelievable* things to me. She'd insinuate that the reason I was there was because she was Janis Joplin superstar!!"

Twenty-two at the time, Toby was raised in France and England. To him, he said, Janis was "the ultimate American girl." *That* was what caused his enchantment. Her lack of subtlety, her directness of feeling, was the summation, he proclaimed, of the entire American character: "I've always had the impression that bluntness is the way of American truth. Everything she did and said was a complete novelty to me. I just never met anybody like that before."

Janis had a few affairs like that off and on. They were more than one-night stands, but held no promise of being sustained. Still, her liking for Toby was genuine, and for all his star-struck fascination, he liked her in return. That was the extent of it; neither of them was the least bit serious. On the other hand, Janis committed herself to simulating an involvement of depth, referring to Toby as "my old man" in the presence of others and observing all the forms that go with love. Toby was amazed to find that she was consistently faithful during those weeks, though there was much opportunity for her to be otherwise. "It was just *not* the image!" he exclaimed. "She was *incredibly* faithful." He was struck by all her attempts at domesticity in the house. He had, of course, seen none of that in New York.

Toward the end of December, Janis gave a gigantic housewarming party. Most of the uncountable number of guests got very drunk. Some got stoned on smack, as did the hostess. Janis no longer had the incentive of refraining before performances. Excepting Linda and one or two others, all the girls she knew were using. By the time Toby returned to New York, around the sixth of January, Janis was considerably worse.

She had not wanted it that way. Those few days in New York, when the light had flowed back into her smile and she'd once more been able to reach out to her closest friends, had been marvelous, for us and mostly for her. It was by her own declaration that she saw being clean as a preferable way to exist. But she was a poor one for tolerating frustration, so that she had accepted quickly the dope someone had given her backstage at the Garden and in California would have to try stopping again, though her theme became "not yet." "I've got five bags," she told Sunshine. "I've been clean and I want to get rid of this, so let's use it up, because I'm going to be clean from now on."

Linda was especially disheartened, her unhappiness in living with it from day to day intensified by other changes in Janis's personality. Larkspur, Janis had said, was to be the environment where she planned to find some peace, where life would slow down and she could recuperate from the exhausting

year that had just ended, where, most of all, she
hoped to regain her sanity. She had meant it. But
even on junk, her way was to live at an energy level
that most people could hardly summon for a day, and
she lashed about in the house as if the quiet were an
intolerable restraint that would drive her mad. Im-
pelled to constant movement, she'd jump up to run
to the supermarket, whiz around Marin County in
search of things to do, blast into the Trident Restaurant in Sausalito to look for company, run here, run
there, anything to pound open the stillness, to ram
against the walls of boredom, to stop the beating of
her discontent. Linda was accustomed to that. It was
the special character of all such activity that Linda
was finding difficult to take.

Janis had sought too many answers in fame, had
looked to its glories for something so unnamable and
mighty that adulation, by contrast, was a meager gift.
Stardom was the divine prince who would pronounce
words of deliverance. It was the messenger of hope
who would hand her love and relieve her of her suffering. It was the celestial kingdom ringing with testimony to her worth, and while Janis was beginning to
know it was none of those things, she was rent by
terror that the kingdom would crumble. Fame had
played havoc with her instability. She was acting in
ways from which, a year and a half before, she would
have cringed with revulsion.

"This is Janis Joplin, J-O-P-L-I-N!" she had
shrieked at a switchboard operator in Nashville. "I
wanna speak to Johnny Cash! Just get him on the
phone! I'm the biggest singer in America you stupid
nut and he'll know who I am!"

Always Janis had shown flashes of temper, blasts
of rudeness, the tendency to behave on the premise
that the only needs in the world were her own. Yet
her charm and lovability had ruled before, and the
rest could be forgiven. But it was hard to forgive it
by then. If no one believed less in her talent than

Janis, if her outbursts were pathetically transparent,
that hardly reduced their effect. Janis, it appeared,
had become unduly impressed with her own stature.
Though the alcohol and the junk weren't solely responsible, they were intensifying the displays of a
Janis Joplin that only star-leeches could happily accept.

As it happened, the extent of Janis's addiction was
extremely difficult to determine. At least until the
winter of 1969, her usage had remained intermittent to
this degree, that for one day, for two days and sometimes for three, she could manage to abstain. Dr.
Rothschild had found the picture particularly cloudy
because of Janis's claim that she experienced no withdrawal symptoms, though he stressed that drug pa-
tients are inclined to lie or distort and that it was
possible she would start again as she began to feel uncomfortable. This seems to have been the case. Janis
was observably ill right before she went to St. Thomas.
Vince told me of several withdrawal bouts on the
road and said that even during the week they went
camping, she'd been unable to do without. Linda
agreed that there may have been days that Janis refrained from using, but added, "Not if she could help
it." Nonetheless, had her physiological addiction
been very advanced, the withdrawal would have been
much more severe and her abstinence nearly unbearable, which clearly it was not.

Janis's friends tended to attribute her relative
control of her habit to extraordinary willpower. "She
stayed behind junk," one of them said, "much better
than any of those people." One had to know Janis to
understand just how amazing her condition was in
contrast to her user companions. But there was a tendency even on the part of some who knew Janis
well to endow her with super-human qualities, to ex-
pand the concept of larger-than-life and more or
less imagine her larger-than-mortal. Exemplifying that
attitude, Toby Ross rambled on with fantastic de-

scriptions of Janis's amorous responses, which he
thought were intensified by junk, saying very much
the same thing as Richard Kermode, but interpreting
it rather differently.

"I was just a thin little English boy!" he exclaimed,
"and she, well, she was a Texan, you know! And
she couldn't have been acting! I could tell! I mean,
never in all my experience!"

"Oh, yeah," I said. "How much experience is that?"

What is most likely is that circumstance played a
great part in allowing Janis to exercise a control over
her habit, which otherwise she would never have been
able to maintain. On the road, she was only sporadi-
cally in contact with a direct connection and relied,
for the most part, on intermediaries. The supply was
therefore not always constant; that helped to slow
down the addiction process. Also, her craving for
liquor was in itself terribly powerful. Alcohol is not
cross-addictive with heroin. As a psychological substitute it surely enabled her to get through a day or two
if the situation so demanded. Off the road and staying in Larkspur, she continued somewhat the method
of getting junk from friends and sometimes from the
connection. No matter. Had she not stopped completely later that spring of 1970, she would have been
as strung out as any of the junkies against whose state
her own was so very favorably compared.

Nonetheless, her habit had previously been rather
regulated. Her physical need had gradually increased, but certainly up to the preceding fall she'd
not yet been driven to use for that exclusive reason.
Thus whatever control she was able to exert merely
clarified a significant pattern, as Dr. Rothschild saw it.
Janis never got stoned before concerts. For all the
pain and unhappiness that she was trying to escape
through smack, it seemed obvious to him that there
was more to it than that, and the fact that Janis made
a point of shooting up after a show had meaning
unto itself. "Getting off" he thought an appropriate
term.

"I pointed out to her," he told me, "that having gotten all that satisfaction in theory from what she did and from the audience response, that it was exactly at that point that she chose to turn herself off and insulate herself from what should have been a beautiful world. And I said that apart from the fact that life is full of difficult things that are hard to face, to me that bespoke something within her." Toby Ross had been mystified by the same pattern in quite another area. "Like she'd just get up from bed right away," he said, "and shoot up some dope *afterwards,* and it stunned me! I'd say, 'What are you going to shoot up *now* for?' and she'd say, 'What else is there to do!'"

Then, of course, the main area of satisfaction threatened by smack was life itself. Janis told Dr. Rothschild that she had overdosed six times; he warned her of the time there would be no return. That her emotional turmoil was so apparent—in the pattern of her drug use, in the entire battery of her responses—had then led him to suggest that she needed some psychiatric help. He had referred her to an analyst in San Francisco, and, much to his surprise, she followed through.

It is problematic enough for someone who holds an ordinary job to involve herself in such a procedure. For a person whose career is so tightly linked with constant mobility, the commitment is more diffcult still, but not completely unfeasible. Albert had told me he saw no reason why Janis's schedule, once she returned to work, could not somehow be arranged. "If she wants to do it, it can be done," he said optimistically. "She can perform a little less and travel back and forth."

As it turned out, the original doctor to whom Ed Rothschild referred her had no time available and sent her on to someone else. Janis saw him twice before she and Linda went to Rio for Carnival in early February. Prior to that Dr. Rothschild sent her another course of Dolophine. She withdrew from heroin again and was clean all the time in Brazil.

The vacation was spectacular. Janis and Linda took a large and elegant apartment with a glassed-in porch that faced the ocean, its scalloped beaches surrounded by huge round rocks that jutted up from the white sand like so many granite teeth. They splashed around in the rich blue water in the mornings; they relaxed on the balcony in the afternoons, chatting with the people who always strolled by on the broad promenade that ran underneath. The nights were lively, with samba bands in the streets and people all costumed and carrying on in the merriment that lifts, at that time of year, the more generally dreary spirits of the country. They went to the Municipal Ball, and through all the excitement that marked those days Janis seemed genuinely happy, particularly after she met David Niehaus one morning on the beach.

"He's just fantastic!" Janis told me, chattering rapidly over the telephone from Brazil. "He went to law school and he's traveling around the world and he's gorgeous and interesting and he wants to be a teacher and I can talk to him and . . ."

"Sounds marvelous! Why don't you just stay there?"

"Huh? Oh. Well, I'm gonna for a while. We're gonna go into the jungle and I mean it, man, I've never been so happy and I'm gonna leave all my clothes at a hotel here and I'm just not even gonna tell you when I'm comin' back 'cause I don't know and I'm getting my head together and I've forgotten about everything to do with the stage and show business and why don't you call *Rolling Stone* and tell them about it!"

Janis and David did not exactly go into the jungle. Rather they traveled along the north coast of Brazil up to the city of Salvador. Nor, obviously, had she forgotten about her career. Janis had received enormous attention in the Brazilian papers. She had held a press conference in grand Joplin style a few days after Carnival, and photographers and reporters had followed her all over Rio. She'd thoroughly enjoyed the uproar. Yet David Niehaus was in another category than most of her boyfriends in the past. Perhaps it was because her life was not then controlled by drugs, perhaps it was because of her increasing longing for something of true intimacy, but Janis had developed the only serious attachment I had known her to have until that time. All the frivolous encounters, the meaningless chaos that had twisted her life might finally have come to an end.

In the midst of those stupendously happy days, Janis had a motorcycle accident. She cracked her head, but received only a concussion.

Linda returned to Larkspur in late February to take care of household matters. Janis remained in Brazil with David for another week or so. The plan was for him to fly home with her after their jaunt into the countryside. Some trivial business with David's papers forced a delay in his departure, and Janis traveled alone. She took a flight to Los Angeles. There she went immediately to the connection. When David arrived at the house a day or two later, he was confronted with a joyless mockery of the girl he'd met in Rio.

David stayed and attempted to persuade Janis to stop, to abandon the career as well, to join him in the travels he wanted to continue, to find out from there where all of it might lead. He stayed until it was impossible for him to do anything but leave.

"David really loved her," Linda said. "Janis loved him too, but she was never satisfied. Even that, somebody loving her with all their heart and soul, wouldn't have been enough. She was saying, 'Stay with me,' and he'd say, 'Come with me.' She couldn't and he couldn't."

Some understanding did exist between Janis and

David concerning the distant future. He may have
taken it more to heart than she was able to do. Janis
talked constantly about quitting her career. She spoke
of being tired, of being scared. She told people that
Albert had said she need work for only two more
years if she wanted the money to retire forever. She
said that was what she longed for. But with David
gone, she lapsed back into a pattern of activity that,
if anything, was more frantic and capricious than before.

Marin County was the perfect setting. For all its
placid majesty, the imposing mountains that guard its
valleys, the sweet peace of its sylvan glories, it
rumbles with action for a certain segment of its population: the rock musicians, dope dealers, and male
and female groupies who are engaged in the suffo-
cating madness of one unrelenting group-grope.

"Living in this scene," Nancy Getz explained, "it's
like too many pretty cats, too many parties, too much
dope, too much alcohol. Everybody has done so much
with so many people that nobody ever gets it together
like to live with one person. And those cats in Marin,
they want a chick who stays home and polishes door-
knobs all day and is real dumb to live with, not to
have a good time with. So yeah, you go into the
Trident and you see someone and you ball him
again and you go around and just get it on all the
time. It's just gettin' it on—because you get so
lonely."

Apart from a handful of real friends, Janis's relationships were terribly narrow. So she had let them
become. There were a group of drug-tortured souls
whose own desperation led them to use Janis financially and prevented the real friendship they might
otherwise have been able to offer, as she was unable
to offer genuine friendship to them.

"It seemed to me like everybody was out for
what they could get," Vince said. "Sure, some people
have their excuses because they're junkies or were,
but she used to be ripped off. And like she'd give

them money and they stole dope and money and
wrecked her clothes, just really took advantage. I
don't know exactly how they'd be *not* junkies, because
the whole time I knew them, they were!"

There were the associations that resulted from her
stardom, and they were just as hollow. If the blood-
ties in the brotherhood of smack were solidified by
having shot dope out of the same needle (there are
people who still brag about that relationship to Janis),
the seal of fellowship among the others was the
empty affection for status. Though it was she who
was famous among them, Janis had taken to clutching
at a place in a small cadre of mutual predators feeding
on the emblems of celebrity. And that is where she
stood, caught between the world of junkies on the
one hand and a kind of third-rung jet-set triviality on
the other.

Janis's forays to the top were actually very rare.
Substituting symbols for people as she was, she was
often merely putting on a show, her feelings of in-
sufficiency driving her to displays of silliness that
she couldn't have taken seriously. Moaning Joe
Namath's name into the microphone at the Garden
had been downright embarrassing. Janis knew it was
absurd, as she did the gossip that followed.

"Now look what you started," I chided her one
day. "Earl Wilson's office called. They wanted to
know if you and Namath were getting married."

"What'd you tell them?" she gasped.

"What do you think I told them! I told them it
wasn't true!"

"You WHAT?"

"Listen," I snapped, "I told you a long time ago
how I felt about that kind of stuff. You were with
him exactly once, and that's exactly what I said. I
don't like to lie, and I can remember when you didn't
like it either!"

One up as always, she retorted quickly, "You
didn't have to lie! You could have denied it . . .
vehemently!"

By the time that rumor had materialized, Janis had all but forgotten the Namath incident. It was the delicious dream that lingered, some vision of herself and Joe Namath walking down a flower-strewn wedding aisle, no, a football field, so huge would be the arena in which this merger of the titans, so she saw it, would occur, and there would be millions of people screaming from the bleachers, and the whole country, the world, the universe, for God's sake, would be roaring with applause and astonishment and envy, and certainly *that* would grab them in Port Arthur.

It seemed that way, that everything Janis had done, the entire bizarre creation of herself, the crazily costumed eccentric she had become, even the career, much of it, had been undertaken to reach the folks back home. They had thought her ugly, and of all the feelings that oppressed Janis, that one was among the worst. Toby Ross claimed that he was amazed by her continual expressions of doubt, her references to her appearance and her implicit requirement that he repeatedly state his admiration.

"She was always talking about how ugly she was. 'I'm so ugly,' she'd say, or, 'You think I'm ugly, don't you?' and she'd say how in school they thought she was just an ugly girl of no significance, ugly and loud. I always had the impression that what she wanted to do was to go back to Port Arthur and be accepted and it didn't matter what she had to do to get that, but way in the back of the mind, that was basically the whole scheme."

At the same time, Janis's demands for attention had gotten completely out of bounds. She barged around Marin County, a swirl of plumes and bracelets, always in stage attire, the dazzle and the bombast never letting up for an instant. She hawked her importance and demanded special consideration. She became vexed if she was ignored and even threw tantrums if she didn't get an immediate table at the Trident. If all that carrying on was shorn of conviction at the heart, it was no less easy on Linda. Most of all, there was the dope, and bit by bit the relationship between Janis and Linda disintegrated to the point where, living in the same house, they hardly spoke at all.

Janis apparently had gone back at least once to see the psychiatrist she'd talked to before the Rio trip. As stated by the doctor in a letter to Ed Rothschild, she resisted his efforts to involve her in therapy and was interested only in getting more Dolophine. He was unable by law to prescribe it, and Janis therefore stopped going. At the end of March she informed him by phone that she was getting the pills from another source. She may have scrounged some up illegally. She got no more from Dr. Rothschild. "I would have cut her off from any supply of drugs by then," he said, "because she would have just been continuing to play the game."

Peter Cohon had already warned her about the tricks of methadone. "That's just getting strung out on the king's dope," he said, "and you're already strung out on the king's power and the king's money and the king's gifts, and I can't see just tradin' off!"

"But I need somethin' to get through the day," Janis pleaded.

Peter replied, "If your days are so bad, change 'em!"

In the meantime, a quiet, dark-haired girl named Lyndall Erb had become a frequent visitor to the house. She had known Janis off and on for several years. Something of a clothes deisgner, she was living a rather ill-defined existence at the time. Linda was refusing to blast around Sausalito and carry on at the Trident. Lyndall was less put off by making the scene and accompanied Janis on her rounds, whereas Linda simply would not. Moreover, she was more tolerant of Janis's habit than Linda could possibly be. "Linda got real funny about Janis's taking drugs," she said.

Aware of the strain in the house, Lyndall let Janis

know that should something happen, she would be glad to move in. The inevitable explosion occurred sometime in early April. Linda had already told me that she couldn't adapt to what Janis had become.

"It's the junk," she said. "And it isn't the junk. She's changed. I don't *know* her. If it doesn't stop, I can't stay!"

I hadn't tried to persuade Linda to change her mind.

One morning Janis came into the kitchen, where Linda was embroidering a purse. "I want to talk to you," she said gruffly.

"O.K." Linda answered. "I've been wanting to talk to you too!"

"Well," Janis barked, "either you change your attitude or you leave!"

"I'm not gonna change my attitude," Linda protested. "So I'll just be gone tomorrow."

Janis called me the following day, crying hysterically. "She left! She just left me! I said to her, 'You think I'm gonna be a junkie for the rest of my life, do you!' And she said, 'Yes!' That's what she said to me!"

"Well, Janis," I said, "she couldn't take it. I can't take it. Nobody who cares about you can."

"It's not true! I'm *not* gonna stay a junkie," she sobbed. "I'm *not!* I've never been any one thing in my whole life!"

Whether Janis kicked junk quite as immediately as she claimed—that is, right after Linda left—is subject to some question. Certainly while Linda was still in the house, she rode a typical seesaw with methadone, taking the pills for one or two days, sticking a needle in her arm the next. Thus on April 4, when she sang with Big Brother in a reunion performance, she deceived a few of her friends. But if that pattern continued after Linda was gone, it could not have been for long.

Janis had found Linda's action unforgivable, worsened by the fact that Linda had taken some

money, enough to settle herself somewhere else. Janis
was wrong. What Linda did was in a moment of
rage, an impulsive retaliation for behavior that had
become intolerable. Her departure altogether had
caused Janis the most crucial emotional experience
she'd undergone in the time I'd known her, representing some symbolic desertion that could hardly
be fathomed, so monumental was its impact. Her expectation that Linda would rescue her from all her
problems, that Linda would tolerate, guide, forgive,
advise, control, and even take responsibility for all
that Janis would do, had been demolished in one
night. The shock forced Janis to make up her mind.
She was *not* going to stay a junkie.

Lyndall Erb became Janis's roommate the second
week of April. She is positive that Janis, by then, had
once and for all stopped junk and was taking only
the Dolophine. I had one report to the contrary, but it
involved a single episode and could even have
stemmed from a date confusion in the mind of the
person who told me. Excepting that as a possibility,
however—that there was one other incident that
spring—she was finally through with heroin.

Those of us close to Janis made a horrible mistake;
we were certain it was forever.

Part Four

The Last Summer:
Pearl or Janis

18

Janis's third and final band was put together that
April. Just a few weeks of rehearsals, beginning
around the time that Lyndall moved in, and it was in
better shape than her previous group had been after
working on the road for a full year. Gone was the
strident blast of the horn section, the uncertain arrangements, the forced excitement of seven musicians
of seven different minds. From the year of the Kozmic
Blues, Brad Campbell and John Till remained. Janis
and Albert found drummer Clark Pierson in a San
Francisco topless bar. Organist Ken Pearson had
played with a number of Canadian rock and jazz
groups, and pianist Rick Bell was politely swiped
from the band of Canadian rocker Ronnie Hawkins.
Albert went to California several times and returned
ecstatic after hearing them practice. Janis called repeatedly to say that she'd finally found the combination of real musicians and family feeling that, until
then, had never coincided. They needed a name to
celebrate the mood; only Full-Tilt Boogie would do.

Perhaps Janis's second band might have been a
more successful unit had it not been saddled by the
burden of her addiction. Despite the proficiency and
commitment of the five musicians in Full-Tilt, it is
doubtful that Janis could have worked so well, even
with them, had she not managed to kick the junk. In
the first flush of that awesome achievement, her spirit
was plumped with more musical confidence than she'd
ever known before.

"I can do it!" she crowed. "I can tell those cats what

to do and they'll *do* it! It's *my* band. Finally, it's *my* band!"

But no metamorphosis had occurred. The truth was only obscured in the minds of those who, for various reasons, coveted the delusion that all was well. Janis's desperate behavior with men continued. There was her fuming around in her jazzed-up clothes, the snappy rashes of temper, the fear-ridden clinging to the symbols of fame. Everything plunged ahead of the music and the freedom from dope, coalescing as an independent force gone past the fail-safe point. And what underscored her entire persona took over where smack left off.

"I mean, you certainly know what her favorite drug was!" said John Cooke. "It was alcohol. Good drug, alcohol! Fortunately, it's legal!"

One does not have to think of the tormented letters of F. Scott Fitzgerald or glimpse the hell under Malcolm Lowry's volcano to shudder at the frivolousness of such a statement. At least nine million people in the United States are afflicted with a dreadful disease as a result of that "good drug" (alcoholism is classified as a disease, both medically and legally), which, as it happens, is a toxic substance ruining the lives of so many persons, creating so much social havoc, and causing so much direct damage to health that it stands, unchallenged, as the foremost drug problem in the country.

Any junkie, given his or her fix, can function better than an alcoholic. Any junkie, freed from the circumstances that produce dirty needles and lead him not to eat, is unendangered by organic damage; whereas alcohol can be destructive to the brain, the liver, the heart, the gastro-intestinal tract, the pancreas, and the whole structure of the central nervous system. Former theories that malnutrition was the cause of such destruction have been abandoned; sufficient quantities of ethyl alcohol alone are the source of the damage, proper nutrition notwithstanding. Withdrawal from heroin is not as hazardous as from alcohol: the former rarely causes death; the latter, frequently. Moreover, there is a strange phenomenon connected with heroin referred to as "aging out." For some reason, a noticeable percentage of drug addicts tend to stop their heroin use around their mid- or late-thirties. No such process occurs with the alcoholic. Due to the pharmacology of the drug, the problem cannot get better—only worse. In terms of social turmoil, there is no comparison between heroin and alcohol as they affect deaths on the highways, suicides, accidents, and drug-related crimes of violence. Indeed, to endow alcohol with unreluctant praise requires either incredible defiance of the facts or supreme ignorance of what they are. I do not mean to denigrate the alarming signs of a heroin epidemic or to underestimate heroin's terrible power. But in the magnitude of the respective drug habituations and in the specific effects themselves, alcoholism, realistically speaking, is without a doubt far more serious than addiction to heroin. The deterioration, the dysfunction, the devastation brought to the individual who abuses alcohol is that awesome. It is the socially approved drug, however, and for a very important reason: it has the edge as a "better" drug in a most significant respect, that its addictive potential is lower than heroin, and for centuries, the majority of people have used it as a mild—and sometimes not so mild—pleasurable inebriant without dire consequence. Janis Joplin was not among them.

John Cooke does not concur in that either. "I don't really agree that her drinking was a serious problem," he stated. "No, not at all. She had an extraordinary metabolism. Alcoholism is not solely determined on the frequency and amount of usage. Your attitude has to be included too. I think one judgment of alcoholism is whether it adversely affects a person's life. I didn't think she would ever stop singing because she was alcoholic, that it would affect her career. She enjoyed drinking. I think people that enjoy drinking should do it. Most people who are alcoholics don't enjoy it."

Denying heroin addiction is impossible. Denying alcoholism, on the other hand, is apparently part of the syndrome. The person who drinks is important to the next one who drinks and in a drinking society no one wants to recognize that a particular individual cannot handle what most everyone else can cope with. It is not unusual for the friends of an alcoholic to express shock over the amount that person consumes and at the same time to encourage the person to drink. "If I drank that much I'd be dead!" said a friend of Janis who happily shared in her drunkenness at the bars. "She was a good drinking buddy," said someone else, willing to brush aside the difference between her manner of ingesting and his for the sheer value of her companionship. Admitting the problem while minimizing what it means is common as well. "What's the matter with being a little alcoholic?" exclaimed another of Janis's pals.

The etiology of alcoholism remains mysterious. But along with profound psychological causes and contributing cultural factors, it is suspected to have a chemical basis; whether primary has not been absolutely established. This much, however, is understood to be valid: at a certain point, the alcoholic has crossed a line beyond normal drinking, and something in the chemistry has been permanently changed. There are some exceedingly rare exceptions. In the overwhelming majority of cases, the change is irreversible. That individual does not metabolize alcohol in the same way as others and never will. Relative to that chemical development, alcoholism is called a disease because it has a defined set of morbid symptoms, the major ones of which are tolerance, mental obsession, and above all, lack of control. There are innumerable secondary symptoms. One of them is *not* a failure to enjoy drinking, and all secondary symptoms—blackouts, morning drinking, gulping liquor, etc.—may be variable, as is tolerance, which decreases in the later stages. What is never variable is lack of control. And no betterment in mood, no emotional improvement, no brightened changes in one's life will alter the course of alcoholism as long as the person continues to drink. Alcoholism is progressive, and unless liquor is abandoned completely, it almost always ends in insanity or premature death.* Once alcoholism is established, the psychopathological bases become secondary. Drinking is no longer "a cry for help," as some sensitive but ill-informed people proclaimed about Janis. It has been called "a disease that is a flight from disease," and that is accurate, which is to say it represents a form of self-destruction that may be preferable to the intolerable destruction by feelings that contribute to its development and that are anesthetized by the very substance that destroys. But once alcoholism is a given fact, cause and effect are indistinguishable; symptom and disease blend into one.

The psychological rewards of drinking to the alcoholic are crucial. It induces the oblivion that the alcoholic seeks. It facilitates the regression that is his or her aim. That is why alcoholics are capable of periods of control; they are determined to prove it is a matter of choice so that they can continue to go on drinking. But even in straight society, the rewards the alcoholic is after are also shared by friends; some people enjoy seeing others act out the repressed impulses that they themselves would never dare to express, and there is no trigger like alcohol for the acting out of primitive instincts. In Janis's case, that was one

---

* There are research projects going on constantly to see if controlled drinking may be possible. On occasion, there are reports from those projects to the effect that it is. Nothing substantial has yet turned up, and the results of those studies are dismissed by most authorities. They have yet to test the alcoholic in his normal setting which, after all, is where he lives.

basis for her entire identity: in her lack of self she
bore the burden of embodying the fantasies of other
people; and all the situations in straight society that
make it so difficult for the alcoholic to stop drinking
were amplified threefold for her. Drunkenness was
the norm in Janis's world. Her drinking was an in-
trinsic part of her image. Whether some of the people
she knew could ever have adjusted to a Janis Joplin
without liquor is doubtful. In other cases, Janis
thought her drinking got approval, and that was
quite enough to aid her in continuing. This is not even
to mention the acquaintances and friends who drank
so much themselves that they had a particular interest
in denying the seriousness of her problem because it
helped them to deny their own. Janis was no innocent victim. She encouraged others to drink as they
encouraged her in a kind of group pathology that provided a circular reinforcement to constant intoxica-
tion. And because Janis was so dependent on the
approval of others (whether real is unimportant), she
was reluctant to express concern about her increasing consumption of alcohol. They were perhaps preoccupied. The great majority were merely naive. But
by that spring, at least in talking to myself and Vince
Mitchell, she had stopped all pretense that her drinking was anything less than deadly.

"Oh," Vince said, "it was worse than the junk. She
told me how scared she was about it. And I said,
'Well, shit, man, you gotta go to a doctor and get
something done about it.' She was getting sick from
drinking too much. She couldn't have just one, man. I
told her, but she couldn't cut down—no way."

"Sure," Janis admitted to me one evening. "If you
can call drinking a quart of tequila a day being better,
then I'm better!"

Delusion hung over everything but the music, including the atmosphere of her Larkspur home. What
with Janis's libertine image, one might have expected
the house to ooze at its corners with debauchery and
commotion, some madness in process at all hours of

the day. Occasionally, it was quite mad. Janis, really, preferred it quiet, with the comfort of her animals (three dogs, two cats), the serenity of the redwoods, the exclusively Joplin hip-antique decor, the rungs of stability to which she tried to cling for support. Yet the phone did not ring especially often, and while there was a noticeable influx of visitors, the motives of most of them were subject to question. To be sure, Janis's close friend Dave Richards was always around doing carpentry work. Vince, who never stopped loving her, came by all the time. Peter Cohon saw Janis whenever he was in town. There was Nancy Getz. There were Diane and Nick Gravenites. Other musicians dropped in to listen to rehearsals, and naturally she was busy with the band. Music or people, it made no difference. The house was swollen with the bounty of loneliness. I used to hear it pounding over the phone.

"Couldn't you just *feel* it!" Nancy Getz cried. "*Very* lonely. It wasn't that there weren't people over there. There were a *lot* of people, but I think she began to wonder why, if it was just because she was Janis Joplin."

"Well," I asked, "why *were* they there?"

"Because she was Janis Joplin."

Could Janis not help any of it? She was running on a two-way street, but less in command than ever to take another course. Nay to the junk and cheers for the drinking from almost everyone she knew. Her life raged on as it had, now tossed back and forth between efforts to maintain tranquillity and uncontrolled indulgence in all the other ways of dying. What people were going to discourage that on which they were emotionally thriving? Janis's sensitivity, her honesty, her vast well of feeling would reach out for the truth one minute. Confusion would rush in the next and have her preferring the lie. She got more lies, fed her by people who, for the most part unbeknownst to themselves, were driven by a need to have her act out their dreams and sometimes pull

them along, emboldening them to behave as she
herself would do, so that they could have a piece of
that lie, the substitute for whatever emptiness they
were trying to fill, the identity that, like Janis herself,
some of them didn't have.

Janis saw another psychiatrist until the middle of
May. She stopped using the Dolophine and consequently terminated the sessions, complaining to Lyndall that the doctor was square, giving me a series of
convoluted stories, none of which made true sense.
Lyndall accepted Janis's words; it was the psychiatrist's failure, not hers. "She really tried," she said,
"but she just couldn't talk to him, because he was telling her that her whole lifestyle was wrong."

Meanwhile, the band was having its own difficulties trying to adjust. Few in the group were heavy
drinkers under ordinary circumstances; they knew
nothing of hard dope. John Till was married; the
others were the kind that would be in the future. At
least John and Brad Campbell were accustomed to
the pace. For the three new members, the tumult
was foreign. Clark Pierson rode with it easily enough.
An ingenuous Rick Bell thought he was in heaven.
But Ken Pearson seems to have undergone some kind
of culture shock, which temporarily was so disorienting that he almost left. What brought that on was the
great tequila bash that began when Bobby Neuwirth
and Kris Kristofferson came charging in to become
part of Janis's household for several weeks that
spring.

Bobby and Kris had shot out of New York in a
moment of impulse born in the insantiy of a drunken
party in Manhattan. When they reached California, they crashed someplace in Berkeley, and at four
in the morning called Janis.

"This is yer rockin' buddy," Bobby growled.

"Hey, ya mother, what're ya doin'?" Janis rasped,
calling them back a few hours later. "Why doncha
start rockin'!" And with that, they rip-roared off.

There were piña coladas for breakfast; screwdrivers were for lunch. There was cocktail hour at the Trident; a late-night party at the house. They zoomed around Marin County; they lived it up at the Sausalito bars, and along with the consumption of unending amounts of alcohol, the party featured Janis's crush on Kris Kristofferson, the Rhodes scholar with the Nashville twang, movie star, country-singer, songwriter, and author of "Me and Bobby McGhee."

Janis was speaking more constantly than ever of the fear that people enjoyed her presence for the benefits of free booze and food, but what actually transpired during Kris and Bobby's stay was not so clear-cut as that.

"I'd a split there," Kris protested. "I dug her, but I had itchy feet. I'd get up intending to get out, and in she comes with the early-morning drinks and pretty soon you're wasted enough and you don't *care* about leaving. She'd definitely let ya know when she was being abused, and she thought so a lot. She was always jangling around talking about how everybody was living off of her, but she had people she'd bring into the house and then she'd bitch because she was giving them bed and board."

Whether that was all to what happened that spring, it was certainly true on many occasions. Always, Janis persisted in a belief that people were gorging themselves at her expense, and if they were not, she would create situations to insure that they did, wrapping herself in a delicious melancholy at the thought of exploitation. Even so, reality gouged its way right down the middle of her self-inflicted wounds. The bed and board were only symbols, and well Kris Kristofferson knew it. He liked her, Janis the star, she said, which very likely was true. But what of her feelings for him? They were air, thickened with fantasy. David Niehaus had been gone three weeks. Yet to hear Janis tell it, Kris had charmed her into working up a thundering passion and then would not return it. No, what developed was not his doing, beyond the mistake of letting

Bobby plant him in the house. "She had a hammerlock on Kristofferson," Nick Gravenites remembered, "that you wouldn't believe! He couldn't go to the bathroom!"

Well, the party rocked along for some three nutty weeks, and if it appeared to Lyndall and Bobby that it was another funridden blast, the display was not so appealing to all of Janis's friends. Nick and Diane were especially disturbed one afternoon when Janis came pouncing in with Kris and Bobby in tow, Janis decked up like a two-bit floozy with a peacock's tail on her head. "Ya know," Nick laughed, "her birdfeather costume. Drunk. And they were draggin' behind, wasted."

It was, moreover, the first time that Nick and Kris had met; they wanted to talk about music. Janis could think of nothing but running off to the Trident. "Let's get going, let's get to the bar, let's get a drink," she kept yapping. Agitated, pacing all over the living room, bouncing up and down on the couch, yanking at Kris's arm, she was unable to sit still and let them be. And so finally they danced off to the bars, Bobby, Kris, and Janis, with Nick refusing their invitation to to come along and left to ponder what it was all about, because Nick's affection for Janis was made of profounder stuff than the feathers that flopped from her hair. "I mean," he recalled, "she was gettin' kind of nuts! When she didn't get her way. *Real* crazy. You know, some people subordinate all those things, money, power, and fame to *other* things—like art! And what I saw happening with Janis with like Neuwirth, Kristofferson, and Joplin. The trio. They were drinking every bar dry in Marin County and it was all those people and Janis this and Janis that. She was such a good chick, a great chick, and that day she asked me to go, but I couldn't fuckin' stand it!"

Neither, in his own way, could Ken Pearson. It was culture-shock all right. That three-week bash climaxed with a party for Michael Pollard, and a few days before, Ken teetered off the roller-coaster,

having temporarily lost his balance. The girls got to
him; the pace got to him; the drinking got to him.
Passing time until rehearsal one day, he got very drunk
and bit through Janis's vest. Afterward he swooped
up one of the girls hanging around and ran into the
woods. It upset no one else. It thoroughly threw
him. He decided to tell Janis he was going to leave,
that he couldn't handle it, he couldn't adjust. "I told
Richard and John that I couldn't relate to the chicks
the way they did and I couldn't handle such heavy
drinking. It was crazy to me, the chicks and the
drinking and I thought rather than be a prick
about it and start condemning it, I should just
leave."

Ken was certain Janis would explode, be bitchy,
and demolish his sensitive heart. Nervous, he phoned
her from his hotel.

"I'm crazy, Janis," he groaned fearfully. "I can't take
it."

"What's the matter?" she asked softly.

Startled, he said, "Well, I'm just crazy!"

"Oh yeah," she murmured sympathetically.

"I'm gonna have to leave because I'm crazy
and . . ."

"Me too," she confessed. "I'm that way three days a
week, *every* week. Whadda you want? Pills? The
name of my doctor?"

Ken decided to try again. He liked her; he was
happy with the music. Only the atmosphere was
gettting him down, and while Ken did stay and eventually returned to his normal state, he was still unsettled by the day of the party.

The affair began at noon in a bustle of frantic preparation. A strange character in Indian pajama pants
arrived about three. He was some kind of acid-freak
and thought he was Jesus, though he called himself
The Phantom. He was very helpful, washing the
dishes, polishing the glasses, and sweeping out dust
wherever he could find it.

"Work is next to God," he kept saying.

"What isn't?" Dave Richards assured him.

Janis rushed off to the airport to pick up Michael Pollard, who was flying in from Los Angeles. She rushed back and busied herself at the phone, while Lyndall, Dave, and Bobby zipped out to do the shopping. By five, whoever was there was already soused. By eight, the house was jammed.

"What's that?" Brad said to Clark, as The Phantom went dashing into the kitchen with a handful of empty glasses.

"Don' know," Clark shrugged. "He calls himself The Phantom."

Rick Bell was hunched in a corner, watching a film projector someone was swirling around the room. A girl, topless, danced in front of the camera. Richard lurched over to the bar. Everyone in the room was roaring drunk.

A big drum of beer sat on the porch outside. There were hotdogs cooking on a grill. Clark walked out and nodded to Mike Bloomfield, who was leaning on the railing talking rapidly with a group of people, loosely clustered about. Nick was strumming on a guitar.

"Some party," Clark said to Vince.

"Yeah," Vince muttered. "Hey, you seen John Till?"

Clark had not. Vince went into the living room. "I don't know where he is, Dorkas," he said to John Till's wife.

Janis was running around the room, cackling. "Ya havin' a good time, honey?" she asked Vince. "If you're not havin' a good time, just keep on rockin' and you'll have one."

Vince put his arm around Janis. "Everything's fine."

She grinned impishly, then shot across the room to Kris, who was sitting on the floor next to Thurber, one of Janis's dogs.

Neuwirth was working out everywhere, snapping

his fingers, and hopping from one group of people to the next. "Hey, man," he was saying, "let's keep it goin' "—SNAP, SNAP, SNAP—"d-d-d-d" SNAP, SNAP. He crouched on the floor, rocking back and forth on his heels. He jumped up. He whirled around to check it all out. "Now I gotta song, man"—SNAP, SNAP—"it's like this—daaa-d-daaa-da." SNAP, SNAP.

A girl sat on the edge of the chaise lounge, staring at a cream-colored silk cloth that hung behind it on the wall. She gritted her teeth as tattooist Lyle Tuttle approached her flesh with a buzzing instrument to decorate the skin right over her breast with a heart just like the famous one Janis had.

"You better tell her what she's gettin' herself into," Janis said to Lyle.

"I d'n care," the girl grunted.

"Did you find John?" Dorkas asked Vince.

"Maybe he's found a new old lady," Vince teased.

Sometime during the evening, Rick Bell collapsed drunk in the fireplace. When he awoke, the tattooing had become more bizarre. Lyle Tuttle was drunk and a little shaky at his job.

Vince was standing on the porch when suddenly he heard a moan that seemed to come from the trees. He walked over to the railing.

"Ooooooh. Oooooooh," he heard.

"God, that sounds like John Till," he muttered, so he called out, "John? John?"

"Ooooooh. Ooooooo."

Dorkas appeared. "Did you find him?"

Vince giggled. "I think that's John down there."

Miserably sick, John was hidden in the trees near the balcony.

"John!" Dorkas cried. "What are you doing down there!"

"Ooooooh," John groaned. "I'm sick." Terrified of Dorkas, he pulled himself up and told her; he'd popped down some of her codeine pills along with a lot of booze.

"What'd you do *that* for?" she exclaimed.

"I don't *know*," he whined. "I'm sick. Ooooooh."

Back in the living room, Bobby was being tattooed. Michael Pollard had had his wife's name, Annie, lettered on his arm.

His pants down, Bobby was leaning against the chaise, very drunk and unable to stand still. A girl with long blond hair was pawing at his waist. People were running around with cameras.

"Goddamn it, man," Bobby snarled. "I'm not gonna have my ass photographed."

"Get those cameras out of the way," Janis cried.

"Whoops," Lyndall said, as she walked into her bedroom. A couple was balling on the bed. "Pardon me," she muttered and backed out of the room.

By that time, the party had begun to fade, had all but disintegrated by five in the morning. Some people had left quite early.

"We didn't want to stay," Johanna Schier reported to me. "There was this girl getting a tattoo and you could tell she was in terrible pain and was just doing it to copy Janis. And Ken looked pale. Janis was so drunk, she didn't recognize us, and there were some other people who left early because I guess they couldn't take it either."

"Sounds great," I said.

"I don't know, Myra," she sighed. "It's just not our idea of a good time."

A few days later, the house settled down to relative normality. Kris and Bobby left and Janis got down to the business of getting ready to go back on the road. The first concerts were set to start in Florida at the end of May. First Janis decided that she wanted to expose the new band at a "non-public" performance. She decided upon a Hell's Angels party for the occasion. Well, the Hell's Angels decided for her.

Janis's attitude toward the Angels had changed considerably by that spring. Even before the murder at Altamont, Janis had realized that hanging out with the bikers was a dangerous business and that she'd gotten in over her head. Early in the fall of 1969 she'd been socked by one raging creep when a bunch of the gang had charged in to make a party at her Noe Street apartment. They'd climbed through the windows, barged in at the door; they'd each grabbed a copy of *Kozmic Blues* as Sunshine had tried tactfully to usher them out.

Tact was never a Joplin specialty. "Hey, motherfucker!" she'd yelled. "Where you goin' with that record? Don't you *dare* leave my house with that record!"

And so this monster dude got indignant. "FUCK YOU, BITCH!" And WHAMMO! Janis had gone flying against a wall.

But as Sunshine later reflected, "She dedicated *Cheap Thrills* to them, right? Now, you don't take that kind of responsibility lightly."

After that night there were only one or two Angels whom Janis would have anything to do with. She stayed friendly with Sweet William. All sorts of people like him; they say he's basically docile and other nice things besides. For sure, he's docile now, having been shot through the head and paralyzed as a result, the very day of Janis's death.

Sweet William paid Janis a visit a few days after the party for Michael. An Angel named Moose and two biker girls came along with him. Moose shook Clark Pierson's hand. Clark made a point of not wincing as he felt his bones compress. Sweet William disappeared with Janis into her bedroom. The Angels would be having a bash. Janis would be happy to perform—wouldn't she?

"He didn't exactly ask her," Clark smiled. "He *told* her."

From Janis's view, it *would* be better to try out the band on an audience not inclined to run into the streets with a judgment of the performance. Whatever the street activities of the Angels, they are decidedly not verbal.

A week later, the party was held at Pepperland in

San Rafael, a huge, old-fashioned ballroom, great gilded mirrors on the walls and sofas, frazzled with wear, that went back to the Depression. Outside, bikes lined one wall of the auditorium. A battalion of rent-a-cops were on hand. "Check Your Weapons Here," warned a sign right over the door. Inside, some twenty-three hundred people were lurching drunkenly around in the dark. There were brawny Angels with Deaths Heads on their reeking jackets; there were girls, some beautiful, which startled Michael Friedman, who was in California at the time and, from curiosity, attended. Albert had flown out to be present; Bennett Glotzer was with Albert. Caution had detoured Bobby and Kris, but Michael Pollard took the risk, fascinated. Lyndall was there, of course. The West Coast distributor for Southern Comfort was there!

Big Brother was performing also that night and hung out in the dressing room with Nick Gravenites, who was singing with them at the time. Full-Tilt stayed backstage for most of the evening. But Janis was scampering around in the hall getting very, very drunk. Albert stood quietly in a corner, making that winding motion with his fingers and looking, Lyndall said, as if he wanted to wish himself out of that room. The party, Lyndall thought, was not so rowdy. Michael Friedman just thought it bizarre. Who can figure it: gorgeous girls slobbering kisses on the grease and grime, rubbing against leather, panting over the Deaths Heads.

Big Brother played their set and ignored the couple who were making it on the stage, nude, right next to Nick's feet. Full-Tilt came out to set up their equipment. Some forty Angels had assigned themselves to help, to make things comfortable for the band.

Janis began reeling toward the stage, carrying a bottle, slugging from it on the way. An Angel wanted some. "Gimme some of that!" he demanded. Janis clutched it tight and snapped, "No, man, it's mine!"

He snarled and showed his blackened teeth. "Yeah, well I want it!" Janis cursed, "Fuck you!" A girl approached the two and Janis told her to fuck off. They all tumbled to the floor. The girl and Janis clawed at each other, the Angel jumped in to slug Janis. Albert froze; there could have been a knife pulled. Bolting across the room, Sweet William came to the rescue, pushed away the assaulting Angel, and pulled Janis to her feet. She stumbled onto the stage.

It was ringed with Angels. While Janis was singing, Moose, short and stocky like a bull, leaned over and tapped a long-haired kid who was sitting on Ken's organ bench. "Can ya pay for that if ya break it?" The boy looked up nervously, answering, "No!" Moose commanded, "Then get the hell off!"

An Angel stood bodyguard over Clark and his drums. "Why doncha take yer shirt off?" The heat was overwhelming, and Clark continuing to play, said, "O.K., I will." Janis and the band started another song. The Angel tried to stick a popper in Clark's mouth to get him high. He shrugged when Clark spit it out. "Why doncha take yer shirt off?" he repeated. Clark took his shirt off. The Angel folded it neatly and placed it carefully on the amp. He wiped Clark's brow with a kerchief and loomed over him, protectively. Full-Tilt continued the set. A girlfriend of Janis raced onto the stage and threw beer on Clark's head—to cool him off. The band finished playing, and Janis staggered off the stage.

"I got the money for ya," an Angel mumbled.

"Give it to my manager," she said, slurring her words, her eyes rolling out of focus.

Albert, embarrassed, took the money, which was $10 short of the agreed-on payment, a token $250.

Janis passed out, and the band helped her to the car. Lyndall had to drive.

Lyndall did not think that Janis was upset that she'd been punched around or that she'd gotten so drunk she was unable to remember the performance. She shrugged: "It had happened before."

Janis phoned me the day after the party to give me a report. "I don't know what to do," she cried. "I'm drinking so much and I had this fight and it was awful. I don't like the Angels; I don't *like* them." She started to whimper. "I couldn't remember anything. I couldn't remember how the band played. I couldn't remember how I sang. I don't know what's happening to me!"

The same day, Janis also dropped in to see Michael Pollard at his hotel: "She sat down on the edge of the bed, you know, and she asked me if she'd been any good, that she couldn't remember how she'd sung. I told her, 'Yeah, you were good.' Then she lay down on the bed and started to cry."

"Why do you think she cried?" I asked.

"I dunno, man," he grunted. "I dunno. I mean, she was just cryin'. But don't put that in the book!"

19

The long tequila bash aside, the depression over the Hell's Angels' party too, everything else seemed marvelous. The band was not without flaws. But it was still the finest she'd ever had and was helping her to carve the first signs of artful subtlety from the gritty but spectacular material of her talent. Janis and Full-Tilt were ready to ship out for their Florida concerts. One matter dangled: they needed a road manager.

What I'd noticed most during John Cooke's "sabbatical" was the absence of his white-toothed sneer. But strangely enough I prayed for his return to the job. Joe Crowley had certainly been easier to work

with. Yet I'd maintained the conviction that had
Cooke been around, the Tampa bust just maybe might
not have happened. Here's why: John was the only
one who could yell louder than Janis. Also, he could
sweet-talk cops and promoters like nobody's business.
And you couldn't beat that efficiency of his. I even
harbored some personal reasons for wanting him to return. Cooke was part of the team. If the concerts
were going to be as exciting as everyone seemed to
think, he just ought to be along. An amicable fellow
named Stan Rublowsky was willing to give it a try.
But he wore a plaid blazer. Cooke was a hip aristo-
crat. Wouldn't be caught dead in a jacket like that.
It might actually have been that blazer, which
Cooke had spotted, that got him going. Anyway,
John went out to San Francisco, was properly delighted with Full-Tilt, and went marching back home
to his old job. I mean marching.

At the end of May, the crew, which included Vince
Mitchell and George Ostrow, took off for the University of Florida at Gainesville. They played Jacksonville
next, and on the road, traveling from Jacksonville to
Miami, where a concert was scheduled at the Bar-B
ranch, Janis got very drunk again. She got so drunk
that a helicopter pilot refused to transport her
to the concert site, invoking FAA regulations against
carrying intoxicated passengers. The band and Janis
were instead taken by bus, and Janis passed out on
the way, waking up some twenty minutes before the
performance, almost unable to go on. Ken Pearson
told me that he didn't think Janis would make it.
John Cooke prefers to believe that she fell asleep, exhausted, which she was. But it was Janis herself who
called me from Florida, distressed and worried about
the incident. "I can't sing anymore when I'm drunk,"
she said.

She then explained that she was trying to pace her
drinking to keep it under control. She would, she
told me, develop a routine. She'd start in the morn-

ing; she'd pass out in the afternoon. She'd recover by the time of her concerts; she'd get drunk later. The next day she'd start again. Drink. Pass out. Sing. Drink. On the days of no performance, she'd break the routine and drink straight through. "Listen," she continued, her voice quavering poignantly, "I saw this doctor down here and he said I might not be able to have babies because I . . ."

"Janis! That's crazy! You got penicillin right away and you're all right. That doctor's just a sonofabitch. You'll see somebody in New York."

A few days after the Florida concerts she was in my office, slumped despairingly in a chair. "When do I see that doctor?" she murmured sadly.

"The week after next."

"Well," she groaned, "maybe I oughta see a doctor that specializes in escapism too."

"Ya mean it?"

"Yeah . . . I guess . . . oh . . . yeah, I mean it."

"Why don't you go back to the hotel. I'll give you a call."

Newspaper writeups slammed around in my head: "100 Proof Janis Joplin!" . . . "Onstage, the lady pauses between songs to swig from a bottle of 100 percent proof Southern Comfort" . . . "She alternated chug-a-lugging individual bottles of tequila, liqueur, and Galliano!" I thought about her adoring audiences. "We luv ya, Janis! Here's a quart of Southern Comfort for ya, Janis! Have one on us, Janis!" I thought about her friends. It was impossible, all of it, impossible. So I sighed helplessly and called the National Council on Alcoholism anyway. I was referred to a Dr. Richard Perkins.

"Does she want to stop drinking?" he asked me, when I phoned him for an appointment.

"Oh sure!" I laughed. "By *magic*, she wants to. . . . But she did ask to see someone. That's gotta mean something, doesn't it?"

Kindly, he answered that it did and agreed that he would see her.

"Ecccccch! Listen to this!" Janis said, as we sat in the lobby of Dr. Perkins' office on the morning of June 9. Janis was reading a review of *Zelda* in *Time*. "Good Chr-rist!" she choked. "This letter! Listen to it! 'We didn't destroy each other, we destroyed ourselves'!" Janis would afterward take those lines and make them a flippant part of her routine in babbling to reporters. That morning her voice was shaking, and she was very, very pale.

When Janis came out of the doctor's office, we grabbed a cab on Park, heading downtown. "He's groovy," she giggled. "He's a Scorpio! I said to him, 'Scorpios are good in bed.' He said, 'That's what they say.'"—*basso profundo* voice from Janis, imitating doctor. "He told me alcohol's a depressant, and the best stimulant is coffee." She mumbled, "Jesus, I can't stand coffee."

"Is that all he said?"

"Nope," she answered, staring out the window. Silent for a few minutes, she turned and began shaking an instructive finger in the air. "You know what he told me? He said, 'Well, I had this man who came to see me. Now, he stopped drinking. He'd been drinking a quart of vodka a day for forty years and he stopped and in three days he went into convulsions. But the thing is that he was sixty-five, soooooo, maybe you could figure, well, all right, you're sixty-five. But *Janis!*' he said to me, 'you're only *twenty-seven!*'" She settled back in her seat, looking tiny and contemplative. "He said, if I could kick junk, I could kick this!"

"If you want to!"

"Yeah, that's what he said."

When we reached the office, Janis came with me upstairs and hung around for a while. Maybe it was an hour before she asked, "What time does Aux Puces open?" Then she hopped across the street to get herself a drink. Janis liked Aux Puces. It was small, plush-hip, and run by a couple of Madison Avenue with-it types who were also Joplin fans.

But there is also this huge Chinese restaurant on Fifty-fifth Street called Sun Luck East. Albert's office was right next door. "Where's so-and-so?" someone would ask. "Must be in Sun Luck." On the day Janis saw the gynecologist, we scooted in there first to pass some time, Janis saying, "The appointment's at five? I'll take it easy. I promise."

Janis nodded when the waiter asked if she wanted a vodka and orange juice.

The scene was getting too heavy for me and I said, "Just a Coke today."

Trying to sip slowly at her drink, Janis again expressed her worry that she would be forever childless and said softly, "I know all this being stoned and making it with strangers isn't just for kicks. I know there's something wrong and I wanna . . ."

"How ya doin?" yelped Bobby Neuwirth, diving into the booth next to Janis.

Janis gurgled, "Hi ya, honey!"

"Waiter! Tequila! Waiter!" Bobby motioned to a figure on the far side of the room and turned his head toward Janis. " 'Nother vodka and orange juice?" He grinned.

"Sure," Janis chuckled.

"Ahhh!" Bobby popped down the contents of his shot glass and gestured again to the waiter, who promptly went off for another tequila.

"Booze is where it's *at!*" he said, throwing down his second shot. "Juice is where it's *at!*" His words were delivered like that, with a rhythmic punch at the end. "Booze is the *greatest!*" The cadences kept rolling. They really had a songlike effect. Very tuneful.

No one could have been happier than Bobby that Janis stopped junk. It was just that he had this theory, you see: alcohol was an energizing drug.

"Isn't juice *terrific!*" He motioned for another, hopping up and down in his seat.

Janis was all laughs now, her eyes clouding only when she looked at the glass she raised occasionally to her lips.

"Janis," I urged, "we've gotta go!"

"Hey, let me get Sam!" Bobby chortled. "We'll go with you!"

Full-bellied women. Crispy-proper maternity outfits. And sedate! We walked into that waiting room . . . BAM! Hands shot out to grab magazines. Heads went down. Not an eye in the whole place was going to look at that vibrating creature with the shaking feathers and the ringing bells who'd just made the entrance. I slumped in a chair and tried to look at my feet. Sam struggled to maintain some dignity. Bobby had gone ape, trying to make us laugh. The more serious the ladies, the crazier he got. Bobby distended his stomach. Their eyes stayed on the print. He did it again, sucked in this huge gulp of air, and whammed it against his abdomen muscles. He looked ready for the operating table. I collapsed, just about went to the floor, howling. Sam lost all control, doubled up in his chair, laughing hysterically. I bit my lip and it bled! Pregnant Bobby just sat there. Only Janis really stayed somewhat together.

Suddenly Sam grabbed Bobby's arm and dragged him out of there. "Listen," he giggled, "you know that bar on Lexington. We'll meet you there." Janis disappeared finally into the interior office. Some of the ladies looked up as she went through the door.

Janis was more relaxed when she came out. The Florida doctor had been merely cruel. At the bar on Lexington she had more drinks, as did Bobby. Sam stayed cool and the four of us then took off to have dinner at a bar and restaurant called Bradley's in the Village.

We took a round table in the front of the restaurant and ordered food and drinks. "Hey, hey," Bobby stammered, "hey, yeah, right, I know what lez do. Lez call Dylan! We can just scoot over to his place, right?"

Bobby had given up on eating. Drunk, he'd almost gotten into a fight with a guy at the next table. Then, at the precise second Bobby had started to cut

his steak—the knife and fork poised over the plate—
zip, the meat had sailed right onto the floor. "Sam,
you call 'im," he said.

I was not enthused, nor was Sam. Bobby and Janis
were well on the way to the total whack-out stage,
and family-man Dylan, I had this idea, was not going
to take to that. I guess Sam figured we had nothing
to lose. From the bar, he phoned Dylan and
beckoned to Janis.

"You know what he said to me," Janis muttered,
returning from the phone, dejected. "I said, 'This is
Janis,' and he said, 'Janis who?' and I said, *'Janis!
This is Janis Joplin!'* He said, 'How do I know you're
Janis Joplin?'" Disconsolate, she stared at her plate.

Janis's first meeting with Dylan had been a
disaster, at least as she related it to me. "I said
'Howdy' and then I passed out," she'd reported. Now
he didn't want to see her, or so she interpreted his
attitude. I interpreted it as a simple wish for a quiet
evening.

"He has to do a TV show," Bobby said, ordering
another drink.

"I'll bet," I mumbled.

Out on the street, the mood snapped up as Janis
and Bobby wrestled each other to the ground in some
silly pseudo-rape drama.

"Let's take your knickers down," Bobby grunted,
"I'll give ya a poke, jez a lil' poke."

"If ya win it!" Janis shrieked, pinning Bobby
against a wall.

A Village freak with wild, bushy hair and a beautifully jeweled vest walked by.

Janis stopped tussling with Bobby. "Hey, honey,
where ya goin'?"

The Village freak grinned. Janis stumbled after
him, fading small into the night.

Janis couldn't cut down on liquor. What she did was
to polish her drinking routine and stay sober enough

before performances to bounce vigorously around onstage. Musically, the concerts she gave that spring were marvelous. There was the same old swagger, the hips swiveling, the body spinning, the energy lathered into what seemed an impossible release of the body. There were the bells, the satins, the feathers. But there was the band and, most of all, the change in her singing. The voice was richer, more open. Notes were now stitched into meaningful phrases, and if they were hurled with devilish savagery, if she thwacked here, shattered there, grunted, hissed, screeched, and yowled, there was an inflamed and masterful unity through it all that had never been there before.

Unfortunately, there were not many people who heard those performances. A series of concerts in the Midwest had been put, by Bennett and Bobby Schuster, into the hands of a promoter who was simply terrible. As a result, the concerts were poorly attended. A few were even canceled, because of inadequate sales of tickets.

Possibly Janis's five-month absence from the stage had some effect on the size of the crowds. Nor had she had a record since *Kozmic Blues* the previous fall. The economy, moreover, was shaky, to say the least. But from my view, the paltry attendance was due to lousy promotion, the other factors just not enough to have an effect of such dimension. Smaller crowds perhaps. But no crowds at all!

I'd flown out to St. Louis in the middle of June to hear Janis with the new band, and arrived to find out there would be no concert. The Grateful Dead had sold out Kiel Auditorium one week before, so it was hard for me to buy a teetering economy as the reason for her cancellation. It was true that Janis was not doing much herself to help. She was balking at interviews that could only be done on the phone; they interrupted her drinking. But mostly it was the promotion. I'd noted the awful advertising in the St. Louis

papers. I'd checked into the radio spots, and while the
promoter claimed a sufficient expenditure, no one to
whom I spoke seemed to have any idea she was expected. I reported the situation to the office. No one
listened. Albert was in the country, occupied with the
studio. As for Bennett and Bobby, well, they had
chosen the promoter. Later, when the crowds picked
up for concerts promoted by others, they admitted to
having made a mistake. At the time, they were admitting nothing, and Janis was led to believe that her
prestige was diminishing.

"What is it?" she said fearfully to Vince. "They
don't like me anymore. I must be slippin'!"

Unable to hear the new band in St. Louis, I went
on to Kansas City, where, while the ticket sales were
hardly spectacular, the concert would at least pro-
ceed.

I found Janis in an especially tense mood. Before
the performance she was bitching away about the
size of the crowd and was upset too because she
thought her gold-threaded vest had been stolen. A
couple of teen-age girls came to gawk worshipfully
through the window of the dingy dressing room we
occupied.

"*Can't ya see I'm gettin' dressed?*" Janis screamed.
"*Goddamn it! Get the hell away from here!*" That
was not like Janis at all.

The kids scampered away, shocked and hurt. I said
nothing, but watched Janis as she began to make
herself up in a mirror. She was wearing a tight black
leotard with net-stocking legs. Those dumb feathers
were flopping around her head. Scooping a jar of
rouge out of her bag, she planted on each cheek a
blazing blotch of red and turned toward me for my
opinion.

"Yaaaaaah!" I cried. "What the hell are you
doing?"

"Well," she whimpered, "I like it."

"It looks *awful*!"

She stamped her foot and said testily, "I don't care! It's my new thing! You won't ever let me do anything! I wanna look like a painted woman!"

"Well, you look good and painted," I laughed. Then unsmilingly, I asked her, "Did you ever think of just singing?"

Turning back toward the mirror, Janis squeezed her features tight and rubbed off some of the rouge. "Better?"

"Yeah," was all I could say. "If you gotta have 'em, that's better."

Onstage, Janis faced the half-full house as if it were jammed. Not a sign from her of disappointment. Janis was always like that. There could have been three people there or twenty thousand. What threw me was a rap she laid on the audience before one of her songs. One version can be heard on the *Joplin in Concert* album. It was pretty much the same that night:

It was about a year ago, I lived on the third floor of this apartment in San Francisco. Lived on the third floor, right? And I had these two rooms and I always thought I had my shit together. But things just weren't right. Wasn't getting any. . . . action . . . know what I mean? No talent comin' around. And I used to see this chick on the street and she didn't have much and she was doin' all right and so I said to myself: *"What's wrong, Janis?"* I mean, how come you ain't gettin' any?" So I thought I better check it out, see what *she* had that I didn't! So one day, I got up early and looked out my window and I saw this chick, see, and I saw what it was she was doin'! I mean, she was *hustling*! She was on the streets at NOON! So, I said to myself, well, Janis, honey, you ain't tryin'! And any time, you want a little talent, ya gotta try. Try—a little bit harder.

And the music started: Shuka-boom—shuka-boom—bam, bam, bam. . . .

Triiiiiiii, Trii-iiiiiiii
Just a little bit harder

So I can love, love love you
I tell myse-elf *

Her singing was spectacular. Her fuck-me-in-the
alley rap made me feel sick. I decided to say nothing about it. On the phone from Miami, Janis had
said, "I can't *sleep!* I go to bed worrying and I wake
up worrying every morning, worrying that they'll have
found out I really can't sing!"

Back at the Holiday Inn, Janis asked me, "Ya
wanna come in my room and talk?" She sat propped
up against the headboard of the bed, looking miserable, stringing beads. Her speech kept breaking into
a choking cough, which I thought a little alarming.
She spoke of being lonely, of fearing the future, again
of her inability to sleep. Repeating what she'd said
before, she cried, "I *can't!* I'm scared they're gonna
find out!"

She spoke, most of all that night, of her fear that
Albert was deserting her. He was, she thought, turning her life over to Bennett and Bobby, had lost interest in her future, and no longer cared. She had
even sent Albert a cable from Brazil, which he'd
shown me, his face grim with concern and also mysti-
fication. It had said something like, "I know I'm not
The Band or Dylan, but care about me too." Albert
had clearly been disturbed. Janis could have been
his own child, so much did he love her. But he had
indeed become tremendously involved in the building of the Bearsville studio, was hardly ever in the
office anymore, and while, I was sure, he was not
dumping Janis into anyone's lap, he was permitting
some business on which he might have maintained a
tighter rein to be handled by that pair. I was still convinced that, in regard to her, he saw himself only in a
temporary bind. But Janis, so morose, so childlike,

---

* Words & music by: Jerry Ragovoy & Chip Taylor. Copyright 1968 Ragmar Music Corp., 353 West 48 Street, New
York, N.Y. 10036.

took it as if she were an abandoned infant, helpless on someone's doorstep.

"Janis," I pleaded as she started to cry, "I wouldn't be surprised if he dumped that whole office, but he's not gonna dump you and maybe it's time for you to start thinking about quitting anyway!" I'd not said a word about that since David Niehaus left. "I mean, you could record and give a few concerts, and start thinking about *other* things! This is killing you!"

Janis sobbed, these horrible, wrenching sobs, and said over and over, "I don't have anything else."

I went back to my room. On the way, I heard laughter. In one of the rooms, a couple of musicians and groupies were yakking it up, partying.

The next morning I found Janis down by the pool, sipping a vodka and orange juice. It was about ten-thirty, and there was some time to relax before we were due to catch our plane. We watched Vince Mitchell and Phil Badella, who'd taken George Ostrow's place, swim and splash around in the water. John Cooke leaned over the balcony and called out, "Time to get ready!"

Janis was wearing a black bikini. Getting up from her chair, she sauntered across the cement, her hips rotating in such an expansive swing that I laughed, "Janis, you're walking like a nineteen-thirties hooker!"

She nodded, "I know. I'm an anachronism." That was the moment at which Janis shaped up that particular riff, and talk of being an anachronism began to invade her public conversation.

There was something true about it, some quality that emanated from Janis that seemed timeless, unrelated to the sixties in innumerable ways. It was a manner of looking at things, her lack of cultishness; because Janis, when it came down to it, participated in few of the rites that marked the age she lived in. She did not smoke grass; she did not take acid. She talked about her "Capricorn" friends but clung not at all to any real belief in astrology. She took her heroes

and heroines from the past. She identified with
Bessie Smith. She read literature of the thirties. And
over that last summer she was beginning to cultivate
a rather spooky concept about her image, with just a
slight shrewd ear for the way it all sounded as well.
That concept generated the "Try" rap.

Was she to be Pearl, or would she be Janis? Sometime
that spring Janis had given herself another name.
The idea had come from Dave Richards, who'd meant
nothing serious at all. Janis developed it from there.
Her "friend" Peggy Caserta would call herself Ruby;
she would take Pearl. It began as a joke or, at most,
a playful fantasy. A honky-tonk woman should have a
honky-tonk name. Yet, for the entire time of her
career (and before), there'd been a great deal more
involved in her game, of which Pearl was only the
climax, than would apply, say, in the case of most
other celebrities. Except for the representatives of the
"new Hollywood," who are just another contingent of
the rock culture in the first place, most stars are not
bitten by the compulsion to be real anyway. Like
politicians, those old Hollywood fossils field their
mythologies with distance, "onstage" when required,
retreating, when opportunity so affords, to a private
role with a fairly comfortable awareness of the difference. Nor are their fictions so hazardous to begin with.
    But Pearl was another story, a hard-drinking-
swearing-always-partying-fuck-anybody-get-it-on-get-
it-off-stay-stoned-keep-on-rocking-floozy,   flourishing
under the tyranny of an applause that didn't come just
from the galleries. And still, lurking like an amorphous
ghost behind that "public" persona, there was another
Janis, in that last year asserting herself in equally clear
definition, but thriving in an isolation as scaldingly
painful as the most solitary of prison confinements. No
loud cheers for *that* girl, bored with the dreariness of
the turnover in her bed, weak from the shallow laughter, rebelling against the regalia of hipness surrounding
her, and sick to death of being drunk. There seemed,

in fact, little recognition of her existence. Well, Janis knew who would applaud what.

As for her role-switching, it took place with an alarming quickness, her adaptations to the demands of the moment smooth to the point of being almost undetectable. Symbolically, I found the "Pearl" business just too eerie. Actually, none of Janis's friends bestowed her with that name very often, but I refused to call her anything but Janis and sometimes J.J. After her death, I thought the name Pearl appropriately poignant. While she lived, I couldn't stand it. The schism in her personality was quite visible enough, exceeding anything that could be construed as the common contradictions in human nature. As far as I was concerned, hers needed no embellishment to suggest the ominous coexistence of two entirely different people locked in the tortuous movement of a weird fugal dance. And while that was not so, it was too goddamned close for me.

It was Pearl who hung out at a Village bar called Nobody's. I couldn't stomach it, or the hungry creatures that littered the place. That was where she went for her "pretty young boys," the term interchangeable with "talent." Well, her references to "talent" depressed me. Besides, I had some suspicion that those "pretty young boys" were not as "talented" as she kept proclaiming and was pretty certain that was at least one reason she chose them.

There was one rainy Sunday that June when she called me at ten in the morning, having been at Nobody's the night before. She sounded manic-morose, and when she said "Howdy," her greeting as always was posed as some sort of question.

"Whatsa matter?" I said.

She cackled madly for a minute. "Uh, uh, uh, uh, I got drunk at Nobody's last night and ooooooooeeeee, there's this uh, pretty boy right here in mah bed! Wanna talk to him? I call him the Artful Dodger."

"No, I don't wanna talk to him, Janis. What's wrong?"

Janis sighed heavily and the anguished whisper came out, "I'm lonely."

"Well, why don't you come on over."

In an hour, Janis walked in with the Artful Dodger trailing behind her. He looked about sixteen, his eyes moronically dull, his delicate face cast in the blankness of low intelligence. Janis sank onto the couch and sighed repeatedly. The Artful Dodger pawed at her arm. She shrugged him off and went into my kitchen to fix herself a drink. She had brought a quart of vodka.

"You have any tomato juice?" she called.

I went into the kitchen and said, "Janis, you're here, please, there's tomato juice, but you don't. . . ."

"I do!" she insisted. She came back in the living room, slugged down half the Bloody Mary, and placed the glass on the coffee table. "Lissen," she said, "I think maybe I wanna see that doctor again. I wanna see if there isn't some way I can control this!"

"I'm sure he'd be happy to see you, Janis, but if you, I mean, he's gonna tell you . . ."

"I'm not gonna stop! I'm not gonna stop!"

It was about one when Janis said, "I wanna leave. Let's go to a bar. Is Bradley's open?"

The three of us went out on the street and walked over to University Place. A light drizzle was falling, and Janis's gold sandals were squooshing noisily on the wet pavement. The feathers in her hair looked wilted. She was oblivious to the Artful Dodger and so, for sure, was I.

Outside of Bradley's, Janis told him she'd rather he'd split. She had become increasingly depressed at my house. By then her despondency was frightening. As the Artful Dodger walked off, she moaned wretchedly, "He wouldn't fuck me this morning."

In the bar, Janis was unreachable. She neither wanted me to leave, nor would she talk. She couldn't, was able only to muster the voice to ask Jerry the bartender for a drink. The rest of the time she simply sat there, staring at her glass or raising it to her mouth, her expression distant and funereal.

Back at my apartment, Janis had made this one remark in the midst of talking about drinking. "You don't have to worry about the junk," she had said. "I'll never touch it again—not unless I do it deliberately to go out!"

Vince Mitchell, Richard Kermode, several people had heard similar statements during the days she was using. It was the first time she'd said anything like that to me. Shaken, I'd looked at her and had probably paled.

"Oh no," she'd said. "I won't."

Within days, her mood, on the surface, picked up. Never did Janis seem to waver in her conviction that stopping heroin had been the greatest of triimphs. Her comment that Sunday was overridden by a much more frequent emphasis on a determination to remain free of dope forever. "There's no such thing as a weekend junkie," she'd say, then would shake her head glumly and speak about the foolishness of people who thought they could play with that most powerful substance and most insufferable killer of feeling.

She took such pride in telling people she had kicked. It was the first thing she said to Toby Ross when she called him in New York. "She was so proud of that," he remembered. "She seemed so happy and confident about it."

She was scheduled to appear on "The Dick Cavett Show" June 25 and was ecstatic, because Janis had never been on that program except stoned. Clasping her hands and grinning that radiant smile, she cried, "Oh, he'll be so pleased to see me straight!"

The evening prior to the Cavett show Janis and I went to the premiere of *Myra Breckenridge*. My friend Jay Cocks, a *Time* magazine movie critic, had invited us to the event. It would be a movie premiere in the grand tradition of movie premieres, and it sounded like it might be fun. None of us, not even Jay, had been to one of those before.

"You ready?" I asked, walking into Janis's room at the No. 1 Fifth Avenue.

"Yeah, yeah, yeah . . . in a minute. Gotta put my feathers on."

Peering into the mirror, Janis turned her head into an ostrich tail, placing the boa feathers just so. One purple, one green, and a wide, fluffy stream of the wildest hot pink in the world.

"Hey, c'mon, we'll be late," I finally pleaded.

"O.K.," Janis rasped, raising her hand to her mouth as she coughed, then coughed again. She glanced quickly in the mirror once more and drew back a little, wincing. We walked fast to the elevator.

When we hit the street, Janis waved, "Hey honey, how ya doin'?" to Johnny Winter. She'd asked him along to be her date. He was wearing black velvet, and it was absolutely burning in contrast to that platinum albino hair. Jay was already in the back seat of the limo, which was not driven that night by our most favorite person, John Fischer. The cat at the wheel this evening! Six joints at least, I was sure.

"Wait-wait-wait," Janis said with a riveting staccato. "Gotta get somethin' to drink!"

Janis shot into the hotel and came back with a large thermos full of vodka and orange juice.

When we reached Forty-ninth Street we could see that Broadway was mobbed. Thousands of people were held at bay by police and wooden barricades. The traffic was impossible, and it seemed wise to walk. It was all right with me, but not with Janis, because we goofed her entrance by not sticking it out and entering by the center celebrity path, the area a bright afternoon in the arc of mammoth klieg lights.

"It would happen to me," Janis muttered, as we passed unnoticed into the theater.

There were movie stars all over the place, old-time

ones, Joan Bennett and people like that. Janis and
Johnny leaned against a wall of the ornate lobby. Jangling her bells, Janis swooshed her head around nervously in search of attention. She got it, when Jerry
Lewis walked by, pointed at them, and howled. Janis
was hurt, but forgot about it as we entered the theater
and Mae West was ushered down one aisle, tawdry,
ancient, tired. Jay thought Janis was taken with the
artificial sexuality. She was, though the endurance got
her too.

"Hey, mama! You're lookin' good!" Janis whooped.
She had hopped up on her seat and was jumping
around like a dazzled teenie-bopper. Suddenly, she
looked serious and said, "She's the real thing."

Jay grunted, "Oh yeah."

The movie was so abominable that I got up and left
to wait it out in the lobby.

"That movie is *dirty*," Janis complained afterward.
"Really dirty, ya know what I mean!"*

"Yep," I agreed. "Hey, there's the car."

We inched along in the track, then turned up Sixth
Avenue—with half of the limo on the sidewalk.

Jay had been quiet, but whispered, "Hey, Myra.
Uhhhh. We're on the sidewalk!"

"I know." I tapped the driver's shoulder. "Hey, man,
you're driving on the sidewalk!"

"Oh," he said, and we bumped back into the street.
Janis and Johnny hadn't noticed.

"Hey, let's stop for a drink!" Janis pleaded. She and
Johnny had polished off the thermos during the film.
The traffic was slow. As an excuse, Janis said, "I don't
wanna get to that party so soon." She pointed to a
sleazy bar. "There!"

Janis liked bars like that, bleak gin-mills full of

---

* Early in 1969, a writer named Henry Edwards had visited
Janis at the Chelsea, wanting merely to meet her. Some fellow
had been there and had said to Henry, "You New York guys
always think you can just ball San Francisco chicks!" Janis
had admonished him, "Don't use language like that!"

bleak, far-gone customers. Swing, swirl, clang, jangle,
she waltzed to the back of the place. The sad, scrawny
necks lined up at the bar snapped in an in-sync twist
toward the vision that skipped by.

"Must be better than what they usually see, huh?"
she said with a decidedly edgy titter.

"Heavy," Johnny nodded.

We sat at a dirty formica-topped table in miserably
uncomfortable chairs until, fortified with a few drinks,
Janis was ready to leave. We scooted on to the party,
which was held at the Time-Life Building and was for
Raquel Welch. I thought it was very dull.

The next evening on the Cavett show, Janis sang
"Get It While You Can."

> Don't you know when you're loving anybody babe
> You're taking a gamble on a little sorrow
> But then who cares, baby,
> 'Cause we may not be here tomorrow.*

She hung weakly onto the mike when she finished.
Her face was blanched. Janis had sung as if the rattle
of death were already in her throat.

On the panel itself, she was animated, even unusually so. A gorgeous Raquel Welch seemed to be doing
a hippie number. Chet Huntley was also on, gray as
ever, being a six-thirty news broadcast. Janis was unaffected, except by Douglas Fairbanks, who was a
guest as well. That elegance! She was in awe of it.
There was something else. I sat in the front row of the
audience, as I always did when Janis appeared on the
show. While Douglas Fairbanks was talking, Janis
looked at me for reassurance.

Dick Cavett asked him why he'd stopped making
films. Fairbanks replied, "Well . . . I felt if you're a
gambler you might as well stop while you're ahead.

---

* "Get It While You Can" words & music by Mort Shuman
and Jerry Ragovoy. Copyright © 1967 by Hill and Range
Songs, Inc., and Ragmar Music Corp. All rights administered
by Hill and Range Songs, Inc. Used by Permission.

And I was very lucky. I had a long string of good luck, and when the time came, I thought, this is getting to be a strain to keep the standard up. Maybe the thing to do is to quit now before somebody says, 'Why *don't* you quit!' "

Off camera, Janis, at that very moment, mouthed something to me that I couldn't grasp. I shook my head, gesturing that she'd have to tell me later.

When the show was over, she asked me, "Did you get what I was saying?"

"How could . . . what was that all about?"

Janis answered, "I was trying to tell you that I want you to let me know when I'm ahead so I can quit!"

An hour after the taping, we sat at a Village bar called Remington's, Janis, myself, and Toby Ross. The band members had gone back to the hotel, to the movies, to dinner. We would meet them later at the No. 1 Fifth Avenue Hotel to watch the telecast.

Janis was prattling lightly, referring to the show, jabbering about her pleasure with the band and dropping it to Toby that, yummy, there'd been this "pretty boy" earlier in the week and that "pretty boy" the next night. "Oooo-ooo-oooooeeee," she squirmed, and Toby sat enchanted. Occasionally, she commented about her drinking, her words flippant, but her eyes tightening painfully. She talked about her career, and her voice dipped bleak and hoarse as she mentioned a once-famous singer who was now forced to take whatever she could get, was singing in some dive Janis thought to be in Texas, and what if it would come to that for her? "Never," she mused. "Never."

She had two drinks before dinner, three with a light salad. She jumped up to call Lyndall Erb and scampered back to say that the dogs were fine, but missed her. Then she sighed, "My mother's gonna kill me for what I said about Port Arthur." (Janis had announced on the show that she was going home for her high school reunion: "They laughed me out of Port Arthur, they laughed me out of the state," adding with an evil chuckle, "and now I'm goin' home!") She went to phone her parents and talked to them for twenty minutes. Back at the table, she said, "The Cavett show doesn't get seen down there, thank God!"

Janis belted down about five more drinks before we left the bar. By then she was severely depressed and hideously drunk. When we reached her room, she passed out cold on the bed. One by one the members of the band came in, except for Clark, who never did appear. Janis came to, in time to watch the telecast. Afterward we took off for Nobody's. Janis got very drunk all over again and went for another "pretty young boy." The wretchedness in her gray sad eyes was unbearable. That night, I believe, she went home alone.

Janis's call that evening to Port Arthur was not unusual. She'd never lost touch with her parents; if anything, she was phoning them more than ever during the last months of her life. Those calls were memorable to Mrs. Joplin; Janis claimed she was severely exhausted. As Mrs. Joplin told it to me, Janis would repeatedly say, "Mother, I'm so tired . . . I'm just so *tired*." Mrs. Joplin would advise her, "Janis, why don't you just work less. The money has never mattered to you." And Janis would reply, "Well, no, but it matters to them."

Of course, it just wasn't true that the money didn't matter to Janis, and it wasn't true that she was the victim of an entity *them*, working her into the ground against her will. Whatever the case with Bennett and Bobby, they couldn't push her around—not in *that* way. Albert wouldn't have wanted to. The almost inhuman schedule she'd kept all through 1969 had been a result of her own demands. At one point, she'd even dragged me into the booking situation with this order: "You tell Albert and you tell Bert Block that I wanna work every single date they can get me! Maybe they think I can't do it, but I can!" The amount of bookings could be overwhelming, and still she protested that they were not sufficient. Part of the reason (though only part) had been money. What Janis said to her mother was dishonest when it came to that, and the entire wording was a detour from what was troubling her. But the torment and conflict were tearing her apart. No wonder she was exhausted.

Furthermore, her career appeared, at the time, to be in jeopardy, and the small attendance at those badly promoted concerts in the Midwest was the least of it. It had nothing to do with the music. Janis was very much affected by the deterioration occuring in the rock scene as a whole. Large concerts had become, in many instances, the setting for bad vibrations and sometimes violence. The Altamont Festival had featured murder. The drug situation had worsened. Audiences were no longer restricting themselves to grass, but were popping reds, blues, and yellows the way health-food enthusiasts down vitamins. Heroin had become downright faddish, and the mood of the country had changed, reflecting little fondness for the members of Woodstock nation. Janis's Tampa arrest was now giving her difficulty. Above all, her exhortations to get audiences on their feet were frightening promoters, and while the whole matter got a great deal more menacing later in the summer, she was already having trouble getting bookings for the fall and winter. Had Janis lived, the *Pearl* album would certainly have affected that trend, the promise of huge box-office receipts making promoters much more amenable to taking chances. Even so, more restraint would have been required in Janis's stage demeanor. And that summer she was faced with the prospect of performing without that frenzied response. Janis, it was demanded, must keep her audiences under control.

There's a lyric in "Half-Moon" that goes like this as John and Johanna Hall originally wrote it:

> *You move me like the mountains, yeah, yeah*
> *You fill me like the sea* *

Janis changed it:

> *Fill me like the mountains*
> *Fill me like the sea*

No man, she would say, could ever give her that, the running down the aisles, the jumping onstage, the clasping for a touch of her hands, the screams for more, the *rush*, the *filling*, the geyser of love, utterly unapproachable except in that grand reciprocal swallowing, Janis of the audience and the audience of her, the cosmic moment to dispel her Kozmic Blues.

That visible hysteria now must cease, and she was tremendously threatened. But there was the career itself. The loss of that was just as threatening. There was the gratification from the artistic growth and the conflict of hanging onto all that opposed it. There was the house she was struggling to get out of while its bricks were getting higher and higher. She was threatened by Pearl and unable to discard her. She was threatened by drinking, threatened by stopping. She was threatened by sycophants and terrified to dismiss them. She was threatened by the very continuance of her career—the *price* of it—and threatened to set herself at sea. She didn't want to quit. And she did. She was lonely. She'd always been lonely. It was becoming worse.

That spring in Larkspur Janis had done a few odd things, apart from the partying and carrying on. She had proposed quite seriously to a musician who was already happily married. Nor was he someone with whom she was having an affair. The man's wife was also a friend of Janis. That was typical. Janis wanted something. (Oh! Would it bother your wife?) Gently reminded of the facts, she dropped her pursuit, but

---

* Copyright © 1970 Hall Music and Mojohanna Music—Divisions of Open End Music.

went on to make proposals to others. By summer, marriage was frequently on her mind.

One afternoon that June in Aux Puces, she was having a drink with Sam Gordon. He'd been complaining about life in suburbia.

"Ya wanna know something?" Janis cried. "Just give me an old man that comes home, like when he splits at nine I know he's gonna be back at six for me and only me and I'll take that shit with the two garages and the two TVs."

"Janis! You're fucking kidding!"

"No, I'm not, man," she said. "I'm not kidding at all."

A little while later, I came downstairs from the office and was just walking across the street as Janis came out of Aux Puces. She was done up like a goddamn flower shop window. The bracelets were prancing all over her arms. The feathers were squirting around in the air; the gold sandals were squooshing on the street; her vest was sparkling, her pants were gleaming, and she had those two awful blotches of rouge on her cheeks.

On the sidewalk right in front of the office building there was a man in a clown costume, collecting money for a children's hospital. He had on a wild jumpsuit. His face was clown-painted, with a huge white nose and a circle of smashing red around his mouth. Janis hopped toward him and stopped.

"Hawww, hawww, hee, hee," she cackled and pointed at his face.

The clown looked her up and down, chortled madly, and pointed right back. People walked by and gawked.

Clutching her stomach, Janis howled, "I bet I get paid more for my gig than you do!"

Then Janis and the clown just jumped around laughing. They were laughing to beat the band.

20

By all accounts, Janis had a marvelous time on the Festival Train that went through Canada the first week of July. I couldn't go. My plans were for a vacation a little later that month, and I had work to clear up before I left. Janis told me she enjoyed herself, and I believe it true, in the sense that her conscious despondency was temporarily buried. Delaney and Bonnie were part of the event. So were the Grateful Dead and a host of other performers. Rick Danko of The Band was along. There was a great deal of partying and a lot of "in" camaraderie. There was, of course, an enormous amount of drinking. Janis and Full-Tilt performed superbly. She laughed a lot and stayed drunk. Two reporters were also on the trip, and Janis had David Dalton's tape recorder into which she was able to sound off for endless hours in a razzle-dazzle discourse on the subject of Janis Joplin.

I had an astonishing conversation with Janis some four weeks later that July. It concerned a *Newsweek* story on the declining festival phenomenon. I'd made arrangements for a reporter in the magazine's Los Angeles bureau to talk to Janis, and she had several days' notice before the interview. Afterward the reporter was kind enough to read me the long, colorfully ornamented quotes he'd succeeded in obtaining. What was left in the final editing, however, were a few sentences only: Janis dispensing with gate-crashers in high Joplin form—"Sell your old lady. Sell your dope. Look at me, I'm selling my heart!" Often Janis was crude when she wanted to make a point and also naive, constantly assuming her words would never be taken out of context. I thought it best to let her know exactly what had appeared in the issue before she saw it herself, so I called her on the Coast.

"Goddammit, they've done it again," she protested. "That's not all there was to it!" And zippo, she raced verbatim through the long paragraphs I'd already heard from the *Newsweek* correspondent.

Stunned, I remained silent for a minute, wondering if that had been total recall.

Then Janis said, "Whatsa matter, whatsa matter?"

"Uhhhh, it's just that . . ."

"Well, it's a good rap. Or it *was* a good rap, before they cut it up."

"Yeah, Janis," I muttered, "It's a good rap."

When dealing with the media in the past, Janis's way had been to crash into a phrase, garnish it with a little more garble as time went on, then plant it in a notebook or tape recorder at the moment of a reporter's most obvious pleasure in the general run of her chatter. There is hardly a famous Joplin phrase that was not issued in some other context before it went into print. She was never as spontaneous as people supposed or as I myself had once believed. Such calculation as seemed to have occurred in the *Newsweek* incident was another matter. I still imagine that rather rare. Nonetheless, although Janis had always been a talker, in that last year she had become polished in verbal pyrotechnics, absolute filibusters if encouraged, sometimes even when not. As her career progressed, moreover, she became less and less scrupulous about the honesty of her remarks and even while Linda was still living with her had become inclined to long-winded distortions of the truth. Linda recalled, "As far as phrases, she copped them definitely. But I was noticing she'd change facts to make a good story. I remember my saying, 'But it didn't happen like that.' She'd grit her teeth and whisper, 'It doesn't matter.' You know, this happened, blah, blah, blah. That went down, hooray, hooray. I objected, because it was negating one of the finest things about her. The honesty."

A few of those stories predated her fame, such as the "I-was-fucked-into-joining-Big-Brother" garbage. Still, by 1970, her fabrications had become frequent. Some were really whoppers. She had created a preposterous tale about her visit to Dr. Perkins, telling even Dave Richards that she'd seen a specialist, had given him her history, and that he'd dismissed everything she'd told him with approving words to the effect that it was all "groovy." "It doesn't sound right, does it?" Dave Richards exclaimed. It didn't sound right, because it hadn't happened. Janis had *hoped* Dr. Perkins would tell her that her drinking wasn't dangerous. As in the past, her inventions were not so much dishonest as they were elaborate daydreams, expressions of wishes or ways of playing to the fantasies of others. That was always true when it came to her sex life. If Janis had no real escapade to relate, damned if she wouldn't make one up. Then the fame, the attention to her every word, the exploitation of her sickness, had increased the focus of her interest in herself—which was already nearly total. When Janis hit the spaces in her soliloquies, she was simply compelled to keep on talking. Anything would do, as long as the topic was Janis. But while she was egocentric and self-absorbed, a lot of that came from an introverted melancholia burst out in a manic splash over which she had no control whatsoever. That may have enamored hot and panting reporters, her public, show-biz-minded comrades, and certain buddies. People sensing the emotional isolation behind it and her growing unhappiness thought it tragic.

However, in contrast to what I'd witnessed that June, Janis's mood seemed temporarily improved during the Canadian jaunt. On July 4, she was in Seattle and impressed an old friend as being in excellent spirits. James Cotton's road manager, Eddie West, ran into Janis at the Edgewater Inn. They spent the evening shooting off firecrackers from the balcony outside Eddie's room. Janis was relatively low-keyed, he thought, and not too obviously tormented. At one point, however, Eddie said, "You're such a shriek *now*! What're you going to be at thirty?"

"I'll never see thirty," she said.

Her sexual stories were wild as usual. "Goddamn," she announced. "There were three hundred and sixty-five people on that train and I only got laid sixty-five times!"

Eddie believed it. "Why would she lie?" he cried.

Janis returned to Larkspur for a day or two, then took off for Hawaii, where occurred one of the more memorable insanities of Full-Tilt's summer.

They arrived—Janis, the band, Lyndall, the crew— in the Honolulu airport, spinning drunk. Lyndall had passed out in the middle of the movie on the plane. Even John Cooke had gotten a little crocked, which was unusual. It was all so corny, going to Hawaii, cornier still when they hit the airport and debarked down the ramp. Flowers were waving. Cameras were snapping. Aloha, aloha, the works. Cooke was trying to keep order. Contending with hundreds of people milling about, he was also attempting to get the rent-a-cars lined up, to scoot everybody to the hotel. He yelled, "EVERYBODY STAY RIGHT HERE! NO-BODY MOVE!"

As Vince summarized it, "I mean, fucking John, man, anytime you'd leave the group, fuck, you don't *leave*."

They left, a few of them, to travel a wee distance of some six feet to a soda stand. Brad, Vince, and Ken wanted some ice cream. Ken trailed a little on the re-turn to the spot where Cooke had everyone else glued to the ground, and John let loose: "*Now, I'm going to tell you right now! When we go somewhere, you're to stay put un-til I say OTHERWISE!*"

Ken was reeling from the drinks on the plane and he screamed, "WELL, THAT'S A LOT OF FUCK-ING BULLSHIT! WE'RE NOT ROBOTS! YOU DON'T HAVE TO TREAT US LIKE THAT! WE'RE NOT ROBOTS! WE'RE NOT ROBO . . ."

"Uhhh," John said, taken aback by Ken's defiance. "Uhhh, uh, let's not have a scene here."

By the time they got to the Hilton hotel, all was amicable again. Cooke went to take care of business. Janis, Lyndall, and Richard shot off to the bar. Ken headed with Vince and Brad for the cafeteria. Very bombed, he accidentally stumbled into the ladies' room on the way. Afterward he was eating his food

when a very large Samoan cop with a very large billy
club and very large murderous eyes approached the
table. Apparently he'd been told this character had
slipped into the female john and there they were, the
three of them, looking like a bunch of drunken freaks
anyway, and who knew they were in Janis's band and
registered at the hotel?

"What room are you in?" the cop inquired gruffly.

The Hilton had something like twenty-three floors.
Ken said, "Forty-second floor! Room 1209!"

The cop went crazy. *"You fuckin' chuck that food
down and get the hell out of here!"*

A sweet little old lady was sitting next to Ken,
clutching a teddy bear. Leaning over, she whispered,
"Young man, you better do as he says."

"Why doncha take your teddy bear," snarled Ken,
"and get the hell out of here?"

"Uh oh," Vince muttered. "I think I'll get Cooke."
He scooted out of the cafeteria.

The cop swung his club threateningly, as he stood
there glowering at Ken. "Ya heard me!" he repeated.
"Chuck that food down and *get out!"*

Sweet, lovable Ken would have crawled under that
table had he been sober. Instead, he looked up and
barked, *"You see that gun! Well you chuck that fuckin'
gun down and beat it!"*

Cooke came charging in to the rescue and things
settled down once more. A morose and wrecked Ken
Pearson plopped out on the beach to sleep it off. Everyone else rocked on, having a lot of fun. The next
day, Janis called me at something like four in the
morning New York time, sounding better than she had
in months. She was not drunk, and I sensed nothing
forced in her mood when she said she was happy, that
they were all having the time of their lives, and the
concert, she just knew, was going to be terrific.

It was indeed. Janis swirled up enough intensity in
that house of seven thousand to get the *Honolulu Ad-
vertiser* blaring "Dazzling Delirium" as a headline. A
little trouble occurred with the police, who, again, did

not take kindly to the mass of bodies that engulfed the area near the stage. One Honolulu reporter, however, thought the police, not Janis, provocative. Another article mentioned that her language was tame.

Janis talked amiably with a reporter or two backstage. "I used to go into concerts completely stoned," she told one of them, "but now I stop at four if I have a concert and start again an hour before I go on. I went into a couple of concerts smashed and when I came off, I couldn't remember them. I can trust Janis Joplin. I know she'll come off okay, but I can't trust Southern Comfort to put on a good show."

On July 10, Janis flew from Hawaii to Austin to attend a birthday celebration in Ken Threadgill's honor. She had canceled an engagement in order to be present, and she took along John Cooke. Most of her superstar veneer slipped away. There was to be, she stated to her old friend Julie Paul when she first arrived, no press coverage at all. She had come from love. It was Ken Threadgill's day, not hers. Nor did she go early to the Jubilee concert that evening, not wanting to detract from him. She was, of course, onstage, but asked that there be no fanfare. Naturally, she was urged to sing.

No routines, no tough-babe voice came out when she spoke to the audience. Rather, she slid into a noticeable country accent, very sweet, very Texas. "Gimme a git-tar. Whar's mah git-tar? Help. Help. I cain't tune it. I cain't play any rock 'n' roll tune without mah band, and mah band is in Hawaii."

She then sang, "Me and Bobby McGhee," and also "Sunday Morning Coming Down," which she preceded by an ironically drawled, "And that's almost as bad as Tuesday morning coming down—or Thursday morning coming down."

Mr. Threadgill said some deeply meant words about Janis's presence. Responding shyly, she stepped forward, holding a big wreath of flowers.

"Now," she announced, "I was in Hawaii and I brought him one thing that I knew he'd like." The flowers went around Mr. Threadgill's neck and Janis laughed, "A good lei!"

He chuckled, "Now, that's one thing I wouldn't know what to do with."

Julie and Janis had some chance to talk alone, though not for very long, and Julie thought Janis in a better frame of mind than she'd been during her previous visit to Austin. Janis laughed about her dependence on John Cooke, which was frequently striking. She did mention that she was tired of the road and wanted to go rest in Larkspur. She said too, "I only live to perform. That's the only time I feel." The confession wasn't new to Julie, and her impression remained that Janis was in "as good a shape as I'd ever seen her."

One other incident occurred. An old friend named Carlos Santos approached Janis and asked her, "Are you happy in what you're doing?"

Janis told him, "I wrote the part!"

Janis's only good days that midsummer had totaled not quite two weeks. Hardly had she left Austin when the depression and anxiety closed in again, all the worse for the trickery of the intermission. On July 11, Full-Tilt and Big Brother shared a bill in San Diego. Between sets, Janis whisked Richard Hundgin aside and ran down one of her sex story numbers, the details of a quickie in a backstage bathroom at a concert the night before. Maybe she got her dates mixed up; no such incident could possibly have happened in Austin, which is where she'd been the night before. Then, done with her anecdote, she said, "I hear a rumor that somebody in San Francisco is spreading stories that I'm a dyke." True to her part, she added, "You go back there and find out who it is and tell them that Janis says she's gotten it on with a couple of thousand cats in her life and a few hundred chicks and see what they can do with *that!*"

"Was she sober?" I asked.

"No, she was drunk."

On the flight back to San Francisco with Full-Tilt and Big Brother, she was especially extravagant in her gestures and speech. Ordering rounds of drinks for everyone (including herself), she carried on loudly and "held court," as Dave Getz put it. She probably laughed a great deal. She babbled unceasingly about her happiness with Full-Tilt. James Gurley was sitting next to her. He believed her about the band, and otherwise not at all. "Oh," he said, "she was very happy musically. *That* way definitely. It was something deeper. Lonely but . . . I don't know how to say. Just a kind of despair or something. *Heavier* than lonely."

Chet Helms saw Janis that July too, at a Grateful Dead concert in San Rafael. There, at Pepperland, she was appallingly drunk, and, as so often happened when she was morbidly depressed, the alcohol made her shrewish, the bitterness raging out in coarse attacks and insults. Janis created a scene inside and almost caused the Dead to stop playing. Outside, trying to get into the hall, she put Chet through a nightmare, brutalizing him, typically, with sexual demand. "Too bad we never got it on," she snapped sarcastically, and in a seizure of drunken aggression kissed him so violently that he was left with a bruise on his mouth for several days. Her face was gaunt, bony, actually green, he recalled—"like a vision from *Naked Lunch*."

Another evening, drinking at the Trident with Richard Hundgin, she spotted a musclebound long-hair and wound herself up for the capture, descending with a socko, bang, whop, crash, "Come on home with *me*, honey." He responded, a score for a score, and swaggered toughly to his MG on the parking lot while Janis and Richard hopped in her Porsche. Speeding on the way to Larkspur, she kept saying, "We gotta race him, we gotta beat him home, we gotta win, we gotta get there first." She got there first. He left in the middle of the night.

Yet, throughout that time, along with the amplified Pearl flamboyance, the charging forward of the superstar flash, the aggression pushing out of her almost more than ever, Janis's transformation in quite the other direction was just as apparent. Bob Gordon and his wife Gail noticed it one evening that summer when Albert, it happened, was in town and the four of them were having dinner. Janis was dressed more conservatively than usual. One bell dangled down from the waist of her white dress. Her hair was once again up, and she seemed to be making a special effort to maintain a subdued demeanor. That night she commented to Gail about the two small spots of paint that were reddening her cheeks. "I'm putting on rouge like little old ladies do," she said, "because I'm losing my figure, and when I get old, I'm gonna have skinny little legs and the rest of me is going to be all round."

At dinner she let Albert order and was generally quiet, behaving with a demure reserve. Somewhere along the line she talked about David Niehaus, which she frequently did when her heart would ache for stability and closeness.

Some of the attempted transformation in Janis had to have been engendered by the problem she was having with bookings. But her efforts went so much deeper, rising right out of that terrible pounding longing for love and a growing loneliness from which she was simply bleeding to death. Had Janis been set afloat in space, lost somewhere in God's infinite, lonesome universe, it could have been no worse. It was total, the most complete abysmal empty isolation that the heart can know, and I would never underestimate the role of that loneliness in her horrible, wretched life and in its grim conclusion. And yet I believe that something was occurring in her that went beyond, that the loneliness was causing the change, that the change was sucking to the surface old and buried quarrels that were ripping her apart.

It may have been during those midsummer days that Janis met an aspiring actress and persuaded her to abandon her ambitions. Janis even took her to the bus depot, bought her a ticket, and sent her packing

back to the small southern town she came from. Surely
Janis identified. Surely her disillusionment with fame
bore on that gesture, as did her basic tenderness toward runaways and people confused about the direction of their lives. That aside, and quite apart from
whether the girl is better off for having hopped that
bus, Janis's advice was in keeping with a very particular mode of thinking. "She told me once," said Tary
Owens, "that she couldn't understand how I could
function in the straight world and the hip world at the
same time. She couldn't do that. For her it was either
one or the other. There wasn't any in-between." Always the reason had been her inability to restrain herself without extraordinary impositions. It had been
another important function of the dope to deaden the
terror and guilt brought on by her impulse-driven life.
Shackles and chains had been the alternative to hold
her back at all, the Janis with the tight neat bun
placed just so at the back of the neck, the one who
wore a proper dress with a proper bit of neckline, the
"good girl" from Port Arthur. Now she was fighting to
change, and everything was working against her. The
loneliness was making her more desperate. The fear
about her career had her more scattered. Perhaps
most of all there was her alcoholism, which was independent of the rest and not really a symptom of anything so much as a symptom of itself. The loneliness,
the fear, the drinking, they were torturing her enough.
They were also plummeting her toward less and less
control and so more and more anxiety. In turn, the
anxiety made it even harder for her to cope with everything that brought it on, and the horror of that circle was narrowing to crush her soul, just as she was
struggling the most to climb out of her own ruins. "I
feel," James Agee wrote in a letter to Father Flye, "as
if I were disintegrating and 'growing up,' whatever
that means, simultaneously, and that there is a race of
bloody grappling going on between the two in my
head and solar plexus." That is not all, but something
like that was happening to Janis. "For a little fucking

peace," she used to say to Linda Gravenites. She'd had more of it at the time.

That summer Nancy Getz noticed that Janis had become considerably warmer than during the previous spring, when she'd been bopping around Marin County. In July, she phoned Nancy frequently, asking her and David to visit often. "You know," Nancy said, "to tell us her problems." Janis spoke continually of fear, saying that she was worried about the booking situation, about Albert, about everything. Then Nancy named the worst of it: "She'd get really down and lonely and she wouldn't understand what was happening and she'd need people to talk to and . . . well, you know who I mean . . . she liked them, chitter chatter . . . but underneath, on a human level, it was impossible. She'd need people to talk to and she couldn't *talk* to them!"

Sometime that month, John Clay ran into Janis at a party in North Beach. Six or seven years had passed since their last encounter; for a minute what went on between them shot right back to their days at The Ghetto. John fired off a "one-of-our-boys-made-it" comment. Janis sneered, "Huh! I see you're still wearing jeans and a T-shirt. We'll have to do something about that!" The sequence of the remarks wasn't made clear, but as Tary Owens said, "A lot of people felt she disliked them, like John Clay. I know personally though —*he* didn't know it—but she was trying a lot to help him. She had a tape of his stuff and she was playing it around, trying to get people interested." John may or may not have known, his relationship with Janis so fixed in a history of mutual put-downs that he could hardly help his ambivalence. In spite of that, it came through to him that she was as if weakened by a tremendous emotional weariness. At one point in the evening, Janis sighed, "John, you don't want to be a star."

Most of that month I'd been on vacation, having left a day or so after Janis called me from Honolulu. I returned in late July. Janis was by then in Los Angeles

for the first recording sessions of *Pearl* and was staying
at the Landmark Hotel, as she would be doing when
she died some two months later. The results of the few
songs she and the band recorded pleased her no end.
She was also delighted with producer Paul Rothchild
and thought him perfect for the sessions. But she
glossed over it quickly when she spoke to me, everything that concerned the music. Her voice, her words
were weighted with wretchedness. Janis was slipping
deeper and deeper into the blackest of despairs.

The surface looked merely foolish, her infinitely
genuine suffering often attached to people, events,
worries, fears that had little or nothing to do with the
real source of her hell. This time it was Kris Kristofferson who was also, that week, in Los Angeles. Janis was
shattered, she told me, because Kris refused to see her.
According to her, he was busy with "stars" and she,
Janis, was not important enough for his attention. Over
and over, she grieved, "Who am I?"

Kris didn't refuse to see her, he claimed. He tried to
attend some of her sessions, but getting there late
would then be assaulted with a barrage of criticism
for his failure to arrive. Following that would come a
stream of childish apologies: "Hey, baby, I was just
kidding; I didn't mean it," and phrases like that.

What was so inexpressibly sad was the unreality of
her own feeling, because Janis was not in love with
Kris to pine as she did that he only liked her and
wasn't torn asunder by passion. "Love to Janis," Linda
said, "wasn't what it is to me. If you love somebody,
you love *them*. Not from your own needs. And Janis
needed. She didn't love. She loved what filled her
needs." So that Janis would have a love crackling like
the lightning of Thor to force her to feel what was
never there, except when she was on that stage. Some
friends of Janis joined in her fantasy: all she needed
was a man to love her. But if Kris had loved Janis,
what then? Well, she *wanted* to love.

Janis complained that week too that actor Jack
Nicholson had told her Albert had been approached

about the possibility of her being in *Five Easy Pieces* and had summarily dismissed the offer. I pointed out to her that such an incident made no sense and that there must be some misunderstanding, which, as it turned out, there most certainly was. (We were never able to clarify all the confusion in back of that situation, but it appeared that some agent in California had spoken for Albert with no authorization to do so.) Through all her talk about the film, she was whiny and bitchy, some quality in her complaints once more angling off into a depression unrelated to the issue itself. Dave Richards, who was still doing his carpentry work on the house, noted that Janis would always get feisty when she was severely despondent. She'd snap at him, and, shrewdly, he'd say, "You wanna know if I love you? Yes, I love you."

"Do you really?" she'd ask fearfully, "or is it the money?"

"No," he'd answer, "it's not the money."

"Do you *really* love me?"

"Yes, I love you."

"Do you *really*?" And so it would go, exactly as she had done when she was using junk.

Then one day that week, Janis called me at the office, and without so much as a "Howdy" to precede her words, cried, "I was just sitting here and figuring things out, and I realized that the only people who love me are on my payroll!" Her voice was sunk in a morbidity as heavy as death itself.

"Good God, Janis!" I said. 'What's the matter?"

"Well, you're the only one who has pictures of me in your office!"

"Aw c'mon, there're pictures of you in Albert's office, and you know it!"

"But it's true!" she mourned. "Nobody really loves me, *nobody*!" Pausing for a moment, she made horrible whimpering sounds and muttered again that no one loved her. Suddenly, she said, "The only people who love me are the junkies I used to know!"

"Now waaait a minute," I said. "Don't pull that shit

with me! Those people love you about as much as they love themselves, which is mostly zero, and you know that too. . . . Janis, what's going on? . . . I mean . . ."

"Oh," she apologized, "I don't mean it. Honest, I don't. I'll never do it again. I told you. Never. I got troubles enough!"

From the time that Janis had kicked, she had vowed, at Albert's persistent urging, to see no more of her addicted companions. That decision was easily adhered to while she was on the road. After her death, however, I found out she had not exactly honored her promise, hanging somewhere between completely severing those associations and retaining a degree of contact, though it was certainly minimal and involved no smack. Lyndall might have been smarter—or something—than to have dropped it to Janis in a letter that Peggy Caserta, one of those companions, was a little upset; it had been so long since she'd seen her. Ironically, it was Sunshine—the one who finally succeeded in stopping—whom Janis consistently refused to have anything to do with. But Janis had done some rather strange things in regard to that relationship too. "She'd do these weird trips with me," Sunshine said. "She'd call me and say, 'Are you clean?' And I'd say, 'No,' and she'd say, 'Well, I don't want to see you,' and then hang up!"

Had I known that, I doubt that I would have reacted much differently to Janis's call that afternoon. Were there no smack to consider, I would have been just as concerned. Janis was *continually* despondent. She had said something (as she had in June) suggesting that along with the other motives so obviously in back of her words, the needle might really be on her mind. That, I said to myself, is not the same as picking it up, which indeed it wasn't. And, after all, it was almost a matter of hours before I would see her.

I met Janis at the Chelsea the evening of July 31, when she arrived in New York. She seemed to be feeling considerably better, claiming that she was looking forward to the next night's concert at the Forest Hills Stadium in Queens. Janis's moods changed by the second, and the appearance of lightness meant nothing. Still, something significant occurred. Someone Janis knew, who'd previously been a user, was staying at the hotel. When I told her, she frowned, "I don't want to see him." I assured her the person was clean.

"Are you positive?" she persisted.

"Yes, I am."

"Oh yeah!" she said happily. "Then, where the hell is he?"

Relieved by her reaction, I discarded the idea of dope altogether. The rest was bad enough. Janis, I knew, was in a state of crisis. But she would be East for half of August; I would try to help her to the extent that I possibly could. I hoped, I believed, that "bloody grappling" was a plunge into hell where the battles of the soul need not always be lost.

21

"Look at that, Janis," I said, pointing to the ground under the block of rows that stretched back from the stage of the stadium. The area had been covered with huge pieces of asbestos. On top, the legs of the folding chairs looked like so many open pairs of scissors, and where the slabs curled at the edges you could see tiny patches of the sweet tender moss that was smothering under their weight.

The protection was necessary. The previous summer that gentle roll of green had been brutally gutted when ten, twenty, a hundred or more kids had jumped the barricades to dance. The damage had cost Janis some several thousand dollars and had placed the future of the summer concerts in jeopardy.

But it looked so wrong, the chairs set evenly like that and the floor of the field so ugly. Stark and geometric, the corners of the back row cut stiffly into the rising spoon of boxes and balcony seats that receded in an easy curve beyond them. And as I read it, that chair-covered field spelled a great deal more than "No Dancing Permitted," just because of the grass. If, as always in the past, promoter Leonard Ruskin was obliged to guard the lawn (previously only with wooden horses and a routine crew of gendarmes), he was now beholden to oversee an atmosphere of restraint. There, at the Forest Hills Festival, as everywhere else that summer, the public mood was demanding that rock concerts be conducted with a minimum of excitement and a maximum of control.

"Such an easy solution," I grumbled. "I wonder why he never thought of it before?" Still, I thought, it was nice that the distance between the audience and the stage had been lessened. "Janis," I added, "it's gonna rain and don't you understand, there are thousands of kids up at Powder Ridge."

Her expression sullen, Janis whirled around without replying and walked back into the dressing room.

The turnout was terribly disheartening. Some twelve thousand people can be seated at the Forest Hills Stadium, and the crowd was nowhere near capacity. Thin audience attendance in the Midwest was one thing, but Forest Hills was right over the Queensborough Bridge, thirty minutes from Manhattan, and the meager box-office sale could be interpreted as an ominous sign for Janis—if one knew nothing of the facts.

It happened, however, that there were some thirty-five thousand, perhaps fifty thousand kids camping out at Powder Ridge, Connecticut, obstinately refusing to leave, although the festival for which they'd bought tickets was not going to take place. Moreover,

Janis had originally been booked for another festival at Mountaindale, New York (also canceled), for the afternoon of this very evening at Forest Hills, and she was advertised to appear at Powder Ridge the next day as well. A festival at Randalls Island, New York, had yielded, in part, to pressure demanding that the concerts be free; and with the gates thrown open to be entered without tickets by those who'd not purchased them in advance, the promoters, short of expected income, had refused to pay a number of acts who, as a result, simply refused to appear. The crowd had expressed its displeasure, menacingly. Threats of similar "trouble" along with general concern everywhere had resulted in community injunctions against the other festivals.

The pressure on festival promoters, in many cases, was largely motivated by radical groups who undoubtedly would have persisted in their activities had the festival been judiciously planned in all respects. But at Powder Ridge in particular sanitation facilities were wholly inadequate, and traffic control was practically nonexistent. Admission to the festivals ran generally about twenty dollars a head for a weekend. Of course, money due the acts was high, but the festivals seemed to have been conceived as if the price of admission obligated the promoters to offer nothing more than the music itself—and if there would be no music, the hell with that too. So that if the radical tactics of stirring community fears (the White Panthers supposedly sent letters to residents of Powder Ridge promising rape if not pillage) were born of a mechanical shrillness and the invocation of reflex dialectic (music belongs to the people and should be free or not at all), the general conduct of those behind the festivals, Powder Ridge especially, and also of some agents and managers who took and may have kept deposit money that should have been returned to the kids, bespoke, nonetheless, a criminal contempt for human needs. Later it was revealed that there were Mafia connections among the promoters of Powder Ridge, one of whom was sentenced to four years in Sing Sing for perjury in connection with that event.

In any case, a mysterious organization called The Ryp Collective was supposedly instrumental in opening the gates at Randalls Island and in creating the climate of community anxiety that doomed some of the other festivals. Ryp was for "rip-off," and, the radical inclinations of the pressure groups notwithstanding, that is exactly what was happening.

The effect of all this was cumulative. A rollercoaster of rumors and facts was crashing right into the nervous mood of alarm kicked off at the mention of large gatherings of the young. While a number of kids were prone to scrounging up the bread for those events by hustling grass, panhandling, and perhaps, here and there, a job, a good many went straight to the source they had always depended on when the chips were down. Except this time money was short, and damned if Ma and Pa were going to empty their pockets for their kids to get a lump on the head or a case of hepatitis.

That was part of it. The kids who remained in the city were the children of parents who were hearing the reports from Powder Ridge, and yes, my dear, you can go to the movies but not to any rock concert. Most of all, there were those asinine bookings: Janis had been advertised to appear at three different nearby places in one weekend, and she was not going to show at two of them. Moreover, there was that crowd in the Connecticut mud, sticking it out in some fantasized simulation of Woodstock unity. Those people would otherwise have been in the city, besides which a percentage probably deluded themselves that Janis would arrive at the festival site; why in the hell should they leave Powder Ridge and trek back in to Queens?

Albert had been spending most of his time in Woodstock. He may have known what was going on; my impression was that he didn't (not then). Bennett

Glotzer and Bobby Schuster were responsible for the bookings. They were not exactly going out of their way to glue Janis's attention to the realities, or any one else's either. In all fairness, it is also possible that they themselves were unable to comprehend the situation, some of it involving social complexities that may have been beyond them. Of course, Janis was given assurances: it would change when her album was completed. But again, as had been the case in July when her Midwest concerts had drawn poorly because of an inept promoter, the emphasis as to the reason was shifted: Janis needed a new record, and her absence from the public eye for five months had affected her popularity. While she was somewhat aware of the booking idiocy, for the most part she believed it. Those things had the least to do with that small crowd at Forest Hills. That was all I had heard the week before, a record and her goddamn vacation.

"Look," I'd protested to Bobby Schuster, "Al Aronowitz is a reliable reporter and he's got it right here in the *Post*. There are thirty-five thousand kids up there at Powder Ridge, for Christ's sake, and some cases of hepatitis and skin disease!"

Now, it is true that the mention of Mafia involvement had not yet appeared in print, but rumors were flying all over the place, and any fool in the business knew there was something mysterious about the people behind that festival. Standing on the field of Forest Hills that night of August 1, I thought of Schuster's reply: "I just spoke to the promoters and they say there's nobody there!"

"Oh shit," I mumbled, and returned to the dressing room area.

There were nicer quarters in a rear brick building, but Janis preferred the rooms near the parking lot. They were two brightly lit oblongs, sort of funky in a way. One had a mirror and dresser, but for some reason, we restricted ourselves mostly to the barer of the two. Well, it had a little more space, and that night we needed it. Two artist friends of Bobby were present. Just everybody was there, including Janis's old friend Emmett Grogan, who was in New York that summer, beginning work on his autobiography, *Ringolevio*, which, he said, would tell the waiting world exactly who he was. The book, among other things, turned out to be a highly colorful tribute to Emmett's self-effacement on behalf of the "revolution"—of which he is the true leader. It failed in the other mission. But Emmett had changed in a number of ways. He also looked terrific; those grenade-like eyes were clear, and that was very good to see.

"Hey," said a guard, beckoning to me. "There's a fellow at the gate who wants to get in. He says you're expecting him."

I walked toward an anxious but pleasant-faced young man bearing a camera. "Hi, are you Jerry Tobias? The photographer from *Circus?*"

"That's me!" he replied. "Is it gonna be O.K.?"

"C'mon," I motioned. "You can get some backstage shots, but I don't think there's going to be a performance."

"Yeah, it's already raining," he noted.

The sky rumbled forbiddingly. Bodies scurried to leave the stadium as the downpour finally hit.

Backstage, nobody seemed prepared to leave the premises.

Janis was walking back and forth, swigging on a bottle. Between drinks, she'd let out this wheeze of unprovoked laughs. "Man, who cares if it rains?" she rasped. "We'll just have a party."

Our limo driver, John Fischer, said, "Yeah," and giggled amiably.

A chorus of voices followed his: "Yeah!" Everybody laughed at that one.

Bobby Neuwirth was crouched in a corner near a small table, its surface covered with several six-packs of beer, an assortment of liquor bottles, and a torn bag of potato chips. "Hey, man," he called to Sam Gordon, who was standing across the room. "Wanna beer?" A beer sailed through the air. Sam's hand swung back to catch it and almost hit Bennett in the face.

Sam said, "Whoops." All of us roared, "Hah, hah, hah, hah, hah!"

Cooke had been storming around and shouting a lot about something or other. He stopped to announce crisply, "I don't know about this."

"We'll go with the flow," Albert mumbled. He grinned at his own remark, which was truly funny, since the field outside was drenched.

The members of the band were ambling around, exchanging seats. Emmett and a beautiful Tuesday Weld sat on a couch.

Neuwirth came over to me and whispered, "Hey, hey, what's Emmett doing with Tuesday Weld?"

I shrugged, "Why not?"

Jerry Tobias was kind of crawling around on the floor, trying to be unobtrusive. A poet named Patti Smith was also in the room.

Janis cackled and sat down, snuggling next to Albert. "How's about it tonight, honey!" she grinned.

Albert smiled, "The moon's not out! I can't do it without the moon!"

Janis roared. Everybody else snickered.

"Hey you!" Emmett said suddenly.

Jerry Tobias peered up from the floor, startled. "Who, me?"

"Yeah, you!"

"What's the matter?"

"Nuthin's the matter. I just wanna make sure ya keep it that way!"

"What am I doing?" he stammered.

"You're not doin' nuthin,'" Emmett snapped. "Just don't take no pictures over here!"

"But I'm not! I'm not!" Jerry protested.

"Well, don't! 'Cause if I hear a click in this direction, you're gonna hear *another* click and *that* click is gonna be the last click you're ever gonna hear!"

Everybody howled—except Jerry Tobias, who whispered to me, "Hey, who's that guy?"

I almost said "The Scarlet Pimpernel," but thought better of it and told him the truth.

Jerry's eyes got very large. "*Boy!*" he said, "I knew he had to be *somebody* to talk like that!"

"Oh yeah?" I laughed. "Well, don't let him bother you, Jerry. He used to be an actor."

With no chance of a concert that night, Albert decided to shift the scene and take everybody out to dinner, at Remington's in the Village. We split up into five or six cars and headed into Manhattan.

I went in John Fischer's limo and sat in the back with Rick Bell and Neuwirth; Janis was in the front. Nobody is as safe to drive with as John Fischer—ordinarily.

The rain had stopped by then, but the roads were hazardously wet. As John spotted Sam Gordon's Olds, he whizzed by a sign warning, "Thirty Miles an Hour," and took the street at forty. We were sweeping along Queens Boulevard, nearing the turn onto the Long Island Expressway. I sank down in my seat. Pressing down on the accelerator, John began a crazy snake-dance around the other cars on the road. Sam's Olds was still ahead of us. In his car was a guy named Paul Fishkin. He jerked around as he noticed our limo, and I could see him urging Sam to cool it as Sam, caught up in the night's racing juices, hopelessly tried to keep ahead. Now we were parallel with the Olds. The distance between us was narrowing . . . three feet . . . two feet. . . . I froze.

Janis rolled down the window, yanked a can of Budweiser up from the floor, and swung her arm toward Sam. "Wheeeeee!" she cried. "Hey, man, have a beer!"

I hid my face in my hands, then made a V-opening in my fingers. We had to be going fifty. Out shot Sam's left arm. He grasped the beer, almost dropped it, and grabbed at it again. With his right hand, he clutched the wheel, ripping his car back to the left, having veered a bit close to the other side of the road. I sucked in my breath and hissed, "Let's cut this out." Bobby Neuwirth howled merrily. I found myself laughing.

"Let's race to the toll bridge," John Fischer shouted.

Regaining his sanity, Sam said wearily, "No way. That's enough for me! See ya at Remington's." He waved and dropped behind us. John Fischer calmed down as well and we drove ahead, on and into the city.

At Remington's Neuwirth arm-wrestled Bennett. Everyone horsed around. We ordered a lot of food and a lot of drinks, but the high had been too much, the laughs teetering on a mountaintop weighted a little too long on one side. I had simply had it; my mood was sinking, mostly from watching and listening to Janis. As the hour got later and with no way to sustain the night's earlier pace, she was again becoming depressed. She was also extremely drunk—and was beginning to talk in a very peculiar voice.

It was supposed to be an imitation of Michael Pollard or W. C. Fields or some friend of hers in San Francisco she had told me about. Starting that spring, Janis had taken to doing that when she got drunk or just when she was being "Pearl." Her voice would get sort of nasal. She would take the consonants and, like a pliers, use them to compress her vowels right out of her words. So a word such as happy would come out "hpy" or "sad" would sound as "sd." Almost the only vowel sound would be "oh," which would come out in a whistled "ooo" rhyming with "you," except it was "yewwwww." All of her words would chug around in a sing-song intonation, jumping from a low garble to a nervous treble squeak. Just a tinge of that phony voice crept in to make even sadder the tough-babe stage raps recorded on the *Joplin in Concert* album. That is because it increased or lessened depending on the amount of alcohol in her system and how much wretchedness possessed her.

Right then, Janis was very drunk and utterly despondent, speaking in that voice to a marvelously gracious Tuesday Weld who, all evening, had made no point of her own celebrity.

"I'm a big star," Janis was telling her, "and I can't even get laid." It was bad enough, but it came out, "I'm a bg str 'n' I cn't evn gt ld."

Albert was nine or ten people away. Of those closer, no one except Tuesday seemed to notice—which was typical. After a while Janis stumbled over to the bartender and said, "Whr' 're all the prtty yng boys? I wanna gt ld." She was far too drunk to be reachable. I excused myself from the table and went home, feeling heartsick and indescribably helpless.

The next day, Ken Pearson, who'd not been at Remington's, ran into Janis walking alone on the street in front of the Chelsea. "Where can I get breakfast and a drink?" she said. It was nine-thirty in the morning.

We returned that night to Forest Hills for the raindate performance. The evening started out with a dynamite spat between Janis and John Cooke. That was not particularly uncommon. Frequently, a screaming match between the two would be followed—after John's infuriated departure—by Janis's ecstatic cry, "I love it! I love it!" This time, however, Janis was holding up the limousines, parked in front of the Chelsea, waiting for some creep she wanted to bring along to the concert. She'd found him at Nobody's or in the Chelsea Hotel lobby or someplace, and he was a cocaine nut.

Cooke wanted to get going. "O.K.!" he yelled. *"You just lost a road manager!"*

Stepping out of the car, Janis slammed the door and screamed back at Cooke. Just then, the cocaine freak appeared on the sidewalk. He had filthy hair, jumpy black eyes, and slimy, narrow features. I thought him the worst of Janis's street finds and made some gurgling sound of disgust to myself. Nor did Janis really want him, but she wanted the coke; she

had some idea that the shit would counteract the
deadening effects of the alcohol she was consuming
daily in ever-increasing quantity. She was not really
one for cocaine, though she got a sniff or two off him
before we left.

As it turned out, for some reason or other, we
departed without him. Janis calmed down, and so did
John, who'd been right, we had to leave. The creep
received instructions from Janis to find his own way
to Forest Hills, Janis then telling me to make sure he
got through the gates when he arrived.

"Christ," I mumbled, but she didn't hear me.

The crowd at the stadium was, if anything, smaller
than the previous evening's, and the mood backstage
was generally low-spirited. Also, a pair of groupies had
latched on for the evening. They were ghastly, having
about as much class as a Queens sidewalk. "I'm so
excited," one of them panted. "I love you all."

Her head looked as if it had been pierced with a
thousand tootsie-rolls—corkscrew curls, I guess. She
had a milky coloring and milky blank-blue eyes. While
she talked, which was often, she chomped on bubble
gum. The other one had stringy hair and sat glumly
in a corner.

Paul Butterfield came into the room. His band was
playing the first half of the bill. I declined his teasing
request that I dance onstage while they performed
and told him I'd much rather listen.

Somebody told me the coke boy was at the gate, and
Janis again insisted I get him in. Fortunately, he left
quickly enough, with or without his coke supply. I
never really knew. There was always plenty around
at concerts, though, if you wanted it.

The character with the tootsie-rolls on her head
jabbered, "Hey, hey, I'm gonna get some coke. Yeah,
ya wan' some, ya wan' some. Hey, d'ya wan' me to see
if I c'n get ya some coke, hey?"

"Yeah, sure," I said. "Go, go, get me some coke."

"O.K.," she said, thinking I meant it. "I'll go see if
I can get some."

In the meantime, John Cooke was outdoing himself, acting as if he were Field Marshal Rommel, stamping around and yelling. Possibly he was under some strain, about equipment, about time, or something like that. Albert approached him to have a few words. Cooke eased down. I remained exceedingly tense. Janis's mood of the late night before seemed to me still with her. There were a lot of reporters around. Press people were at the gates complaining that their complimentary tickets weren't there.

The tootsie-roll head reappeared. "Hey," she cried. "Hey, there ain't enuff. I really tried fer ya."

I waved her away. "It's all right."

"Hey, sumpin' the matta wit cha? Ya look all uptight!"

I glared. "Listen, you dumb groupie broad I'm working. Go get stoned, go get laid, go do whatever you want! But get the hell away from me!"

Much to my relief, she looked crushed and disappeared. When she returned, she was limping and had scratches on her face. Stoned out of her tootsie-roll skull, she'd apparently taken a fall.

Janis's performance that night was neither extraordinary, nor was it bad. She socked into "Tell Mama," her colors zinging around in a gaudy blur. She strutted and joked with the audience. She pounded out a fairly exciting "Try." As always, her body throbbed with astounding energy. Still, the slow songs weren't really working.

> *Maaaay-be*
> *Maaaay-be*
> *Maybe, maybe, maybe dear*
> *I guess I might hav' done somethin' wrong*
> *Honey, I'll be glad to admit it*
> *Ooooooooooo-ooo-ooo*
> *Come on home to meee-e-eee-e* *

"Maybe" was very strained, but it was evident throughout the set: the cocaine and liquor had combined to work like a caustic on her throat, and her voice was fighting for the high notes. She was also tired, having been up so early that morning. The band, on the other hand, played very well, and the audience seemed enthused.

On the drive back, Janis muttered, "We've done better than that," her words coming out between gasps for breath and heavy gushing coughs. No matter her energy output, I had the feeling she was more exhausted than she was ordinarily prone to be.

When we got to the Chelsea, some of us headed for El Quijote bar. Brad, I believe, left almost immediately. Clark stayed, and possibly Rick Bell. There were myself, Ken Pearson, Cooke, and Neuwirth. Janis slumped into a chair next to Bobby as Bobby and John began chattering about films.

"I'm lonely," Janis whimpered plaintively.

"Join the club!" Bobby yipped, whooping down a tequila.

Standing up, Janis leaned slightly over the table toward Cooke. "John," she pleaded, "will you marry me?"

"Sure, Pearl," he grinned. "I'll marry you." John rose to kiss Janis lightly. He sat down and went on talking to Bobby. Janis sank heavily back into her chair. Her face was puffy, her eyes a wasted gray, grief-dim and frighteningly remote.

A few minutes later, she murmured, "I'm gonna give it eight and a half months . . . and if it doesn't get any better . . . I'm gonna end it."

As it happened, Janis had recently seen 8½, and if only in respect to that I was a little amused, having guessed that the movie had inspired the figure right at that very moment. "How come eight and a half months?" I asked.

Her head again down, she answered in a choking half-whisper, "I don't know. It just sounds right."

As Ken recalled it, however, she'd said, "A year

from last April," which eight and a half months would
have been. Obviously, she'd said both.

I'm not sure anyone, besides Ken and myself, even
heard her, though most of her words were quite loud
enough. She said no more, sighed three or four times,
and left the bar to go to her room.

The following evening, August 3, when Janis
made her final appearance on the Cavett show, she
wasn't feeling much different. Though she sang well
in spite of it, her state was obvious enough to produce
some post-mortem speculation that she'd been dope-
stoned on the show. Her eyes indeed were glazed—
with the effects of liquor and the depression that
hadn't dissipated since the previous night. Cavett
himself, accustomed to Janis's more common effervescence, seemed to me a bit uncomfortable and definitely aware that something was wrong. Because Janis
was saying little even when called upon to do so, he
attempted to shift the conversation to the other
guests, who included Gloria Swanson, a young actress,
and football player Dave Meggyesy.

Through a member of the program's staff, I had
requested that Cavett ask Janis about two upcoming
festivals planned to raise money for the peace movement. One was to be at Shea Stadium, the other in
Philadelphia. The latter, however, had to be scratched,
due to right-wing elements in that city. Benefits
were also affected that summer by the scare mood
connected with all large rock concerts, and Peter
Yarrow, who was to emcee the events and had gathered most of the talent, had expressed to me a special
concern that the turnouts would be small. Could I get
Janis to give a plug? Surely that could only help.
Shortly before the taping, I'd reminded her that she'd
promised. Janis had nodded in reluctant agreement
when I'd said, "Dick will bring it up. Just give the
dates. Say they're gonna be terrific, and everyone
should go."

Stumbling through the program, humorless, talking
in that fake godawful voice, Janis became confused

about the dates of the festivals. From the audience, I mouthed, "August 6, Shea; August 9, Philadelphia." She caught it, but it came out garbled and without much impact, though she mentioned Peter Yarrow's involvement, which was not the purpose of his request. When Dave Meggyesy came on, her mood brightened somewhat. Generally it was dismal.

Afterward, while we were still at the theater, Janis asked me sadly, "How was I?"

"Well, uh . . . you sang beautifully, but well . . . it doesn't matter."

It wasn't unusual when Janis was drunk for her to get very nasty. "Lissen," she snapped, "talking about the peace festivals isn't exactly fascinating!"

"Forget it, Janis, but you could have said a little more. They're important."

"I mentioned Peter Yarrow's name, for Chrissake! What the fuck else does he want!"

Losing my temper, I snapped back, "You just don't understand, do you? *Some* people care about other things than having their names mentioned! That was not the goddamn point!"

Janis stamped away from me and went to talk with Cavett. In a few minutes, she returned. "I'm sorry, honey," she rasped softly. "Let's go to dinner. There're all those people waiting. I'm just so down."

It was not the moment for me to say what was really on my mind, because Janis had *not* understood. But I let it go and nodded instead, "I know, Janis."

Taking my arm, she said, "I know you know."

In late August and early fall, right on to the moment of her death in October, Janis's spirits would definitely improve, and her tampering with heroin was assumed, by many of her friends, to be the result of the pressures of recording and circumstance. The end, of course, was termed an accident. But no lack of conscious intention erases the significance of her state in all those preceding months. I was unaware of it, then, that Janis had also threatened Kris

Kristofferson. "If it doesn't get any better," she'd warned, "I'm gonna go back on junk," and along with that had talked of suicide. "*Often*," he told me. Kris had naturally become very upset, and Janis, in response, had retorted bitterly, "You won't be around. None of 'em will be."

As for the threats themselves, Janis was so despondent during those summer weeks that serious suicidal fantasies were inevitable. That night in El Quijote she'd not said a thing about junk, and except for twice when speaking to me, once in June and again in July, she'd referred to it only in the most rejecting terms, even when depressed. Moreover, I had been very misled by my assumption about 8½. When Janis had said, "It just sounds right," I hadn't realized what she'd meant, believing the number to have just spurted out as an idea provoked by the film. "A year from last April," on the other hand, had a very particular import. That related to when she'd kicked junk and had also formed the new band. Had I heard it the same as Ken, it might have struck me as something with which she'd been steadily preoccupied and thus quite a bit more alarming. Not that I'd doubted right then and there she'd meant it, every word. I'd felt exactly like Ken, that "it was really heavy." Still, feeling her fantasy to be so sudden, I was affected mostly by the imploring itself. Others at the table, if they'd caught what she'd said, might have brushed it aside as a bid for attention. I would have agreed; *real* attention indeed was what she'd wanted.

On the basis of what I knew then, it was Janis's call in July from Los Angeles that I should never have ignored. The unconscious wheels that were turning when she'd spoken of her user friends had been more indicative by far than any threat of suicide. Janis had also referred to junkies at the Landmark, and later I would burn with guilt for my failure to protest her return to that hotel. Months would pass after her death before I would fully realize that the Landmark had nothing to do with it. And still it would make little difference. It is a troublesome question whether one may be dreadfully guilty by virtue of having cared, because that carries with it (or should) the concept of responsibility, or if guilt lay with the indifferent (of whom there were naturally none, once she was dead). Some, of course, would say that there was *no* guilt because nothing could have been done, as if to infer in all seriousness that the first can be concluded from the second and to imply, beyond that, that her death was all that mattered.

Yet Janis whipped up the behavior agreement between herself and others. Her intimidating manner made it very hard for many to sense the tremendous dependency underneath or, in fact, to understand her at all. The dependency itself was often tyrannical, no less so in the voice of soft anguish. "If *it* doesn't get any better," she'd said, and *it* was meant to be bettered by anyone around except Janis. Besides, it wasn't *it*, but *her!* "An emotional twelve-year-old," Linda called her. She was being much too generous.

Janis lit my life in innumerable ways for almost three years, as she dominated it too. If the zany creature that the public saw, all that campy, trivial bluster, was real enough in its way, it was far from the substance of her deeper glow. The hysteria, the extravagance, and the foolish noise were a barren fuss embraced by barren hearts, and it was a lost child who would kick up such rubbish to gain entrance into rooms so empty. She was a girl with a dazzling intelligence, and separate from the nonsense was a life in her that blazed like the wonder of creation, as beyond explanation as the talent it was her fortune to possess. She was my friend; I loved her.

But those other things about her still stand as true, so that the situation was a tough one for the few who were deeply engaged emotionally and forbidding enough to prevent more than a peripheral involvement for most, though they'd be loath to admit that they were anything less than her dearest friends.

But some did as much for Janis as their relationship with her permitted. Several merely played the parts she assigned them, more destructively perhaps than they might have done were they fully aware of what they were doing. There was an incredible amount of naiveté around Janis, and people were caught in their own private traps. They were products of their own histories; their intelligence varied, and for some reason there are always those who seem, as if by birth, to lack a certain savvy when it comes to the human heart. In that sense, the question of guilt really goes into an unanswerable quagmire, and no one is to blame for anything, much less the end.

In any case, rather than focused on a fear of suicide or even a return to junk—I didn't believe that would happen—my growing concern about her was much more generalized. I was certain only that she needed help, and that I wanted to talk to Albert. Neither thought was new.

Speaking to Albert at great length had been very difficult for me during all that spring and summer. He was ever more in the country and always I found it impossible to talk to him on the phone about anything except business matters. When he was in the city, he was bogged down in work: calls, meetings, appointments, they seemed to go on forever. Also, while the anxiety I once had felt in his presence had faded considerably, a bit of it still remained, enough to give me cold feet if he seemed pressed in any way. Just the same, when he was approachable (I only wish it had been more often), there was simply no one like him. Then his influence on Janis was matched by no one's—more profound, I used to suspect, than he fully realized. Something about the changes in Janis, so stunningly apparent when she was sober, led me to think that she might be more amenable to seeing a doctor than she'd been before. Again, I thought her in a sort of crisis that could go one way or the other, and in that respect, it seemed to me that things were rather hopeful. Of course, they were also abominable; there was this additional reason: Janis's depression was enormously intensified as a direct result of alcohol, a problem so monstrous unto itself that it left little room for the possibility of solutions to anything, were there no solution to that. By comparison, encouraging her to stop junk had been easy. Well, I didn't know the answers to any of it. I knew only about trying. I felt no hysterical urgency. I had decided that I had to get into his office, but I would wait for the moment and the mood. After all, it was not a matter of life or death. And given the circumstances at the time, it wasn't, it really wasn't.

The day right after the Cavett show brought a brief moratorium on Janis's gloom. Mostly, it was due to her plans for the evening, "a *real* date," she told me, "and with *real* stars." Emmett was taking her to dinner with Rip Torn and his wife, Geraldine Page. From dinner, they'd be off to the Garden for a little of the old ultra violence in the ring. But for Janis, the night would be spectacular, a glorious departure from a routine that, minus the relief of concerts, was as dreary as a Skid Row doorway. She was terribly excited when she phoned me that morning, and also rather frightened.

"What'll I wear?" she gasped. "She's a star! She's a *lady!* Christ, I'm just a weirdo freak! What'll I do?"

"You have that black velvet job Linda made for you?"

"Oh yeah!" she answered airily. "I hadn't thought of that!" Some weird mumble came through the phone and then a cranky whine. "Maybe I'll just be as freaky as I can and wear my plain old crazy clothes? . . ."

I said, "Black velvet."

"Well," she whimpered, "will you come over tonight before I go and tell me how I look?"

In the evening, I met her at El Quijote, where she was waiting for Emmett and the Torns. She was sitting alone, and as I'd expected, had done herself up in black velvet. Her face was also glowing, touched with a bit of makeup, but no harsh blobs of whorish rouge.

I told her that she looked beautiful.

"Huh!" she grunted toughly, trying to hide the shyest of smiles with a three-quarter turn of her head.

A few members of the band came into the bar and sat down at the table, as did a strange, mousy-looking girl with a flat look in her eyes and a very wan complexion. The girl began rapping away about acid, and she apparently had a special fondness for those who dose the innocent. Janis and myself, on the other hand, did not. Making her attitude clear, Janis had some choice words for the Grateful Dead in particular, around whom it is common for people to receive sanctification whether they want the blessing or not. Snooky Flowers had once been victimized by a vat of dosed wine during a Dead performance and had landed up in a hospital, raving, with Janis holding his hand for six tormented hours. On the train trip through Canada, somebody connected with the Dead had seen to it that a little enlightenment was put in Delaney's birthday cake. Janis fortunately had known it and had told him before he celebrated another year by going right out of his noodle.

"Well," the girl said, "maybe it shouldn't have been done to *Delaney*, but *some* people, I mean, they should, I mean, it's groovy when . . ."

"Hey," Janis said, "if somebody wants to screw up their own head, maybe that's their business, but I'd like to know what the difference is between people who fuck with other people's brains, and cops who get called 'fascist pigs' when they go around smashing skulls. Now you wanna tell me the difference?"

The girl, however, had to leave the bar. Trembling before she'd started her rap, she was then perspiring and shaking violently in a withdrawal state from pills.

"Fantastic!" I said to Janis when we again were alone at the table.

"Yeah, well," she said kindly, "I shouldn't have been so rough on her. I know who she is. She was in a terrible automobile accident and her head got banged up and maybe it did something to her so she can't think so good."

Then the Torns and Emmett arrived. Discovering that Rip and Geraldine had never seen Janis onstage, I asked them to join us at the Capitol Theater in Port Chester, where Janis would be performing that coming Saturday night.

Wednesday morning Janis phoned to tell me she'd had a great time. "If I just wasn't so ugly," she added.

"Janis! Stop that!"

"Well, I *am* ugly. I am!"

Janis's concert that Wednesday night at Ravinia, in the Chicago suburb of Highland Park, was almost canceled. What was happening all over the country by way of anxiety about rock concerts was kicked up further in Chicago by a couple of incidents confirming the fear to which it might be assumed the Windy City was basically predisposed. In late July, however, there had been a hideous riot in Grant Park, where a performance had been scheduled by Sly and the Family Stone. The week before Janis was expected, there had also been trouble at Ravinia. Dionne Warwicke had been late; the audience had demonstrated its annoyance by creating general turmoil, nothing like the melee in Grant Park but sufficient to increase the edginess of the Highland Park community. Ravinia was under pressure to have done with rock events altogether, and there was special pressure to cancel Janis.

Fortunately, the concert was salvaged, due to efforts by the office to convince the Ravinia staff that they need not fear any trouble. I myself had a number of conversations with the public relations director. What I said was not quite the same as what I thought. John Cooke's efficiency was one thing. "Late!" I snickered, in answer to her concern. "That'll be the

day!" With great conviction, I had assured her that
John would be in control. I was not so certain about
Janis, not in the long run, anyway. The anxiety in
Chicago was very real. I had visions of a nationwide
boycott of Janis were she not to stop lashing up her
audiences into such active adoration. After a particularly nerveracking talk with the Ravinia PR lady, I
walked into Albert's office and said that the atmosphere
was a great deal worse than I, at least, had
realized. "Either she stops it," I added, "or the career's all over." More aware, I was sure, than myself,
Albert merely nodded in agreement.

I went back to my office, my mind whirling with
mixed thoughts about the whole matter. No, I didn't
always like it that she felt driven to have the stage
rushed. And while there had never been any violence,
that didn't mean it could not occur. But still, what
she did seemed so minor. For a minute I felt sad.
"She'll never do it," I thought. "She'll never keep those
kids sitting down." Then I grinned: "Shit, maybe it'll
make her quit the whole trip!"

To the surprise of the huge police forces, the extra
crew of ushers, the Ravinia management, the community of Highland Park—and myself—Ravinia went
off smoothly. Eighteen thousand people attended.
They stomped, they danced, they clapped, they
yelled, but at no time did anything veer toward
getting out of hand. The sound system, however, was
horrible, and Janis had done some terrific professional
joshing with the crowd to keep everyone cool about
that.

"Can you hear me out there?" she yelled.

"NO!"

"Well," she said, signaling to Full-Tilt, "that makes
six of us!" Poor sound system notwithstanding, the performance was electrifying, and after several encores,
the audience still shrieking for more, John got Janis
and the band out quickly, to avoid the rush of the
crowd.

Exhausted and breathing heavily, Janis complained

a bit about the sound as they drove away from the grounds. "There wasn't a fucking monitor working on that stage, man. . . . I need a cigarette [pant]. Who's got [pant] . . . John, d'ya . . ."

"There's something in that back seat," John said. "A hungry bear."

"No," she cackled. "It's that singer dying of cigarette withdrawal." Janis began to cough. "Take that air off me." Her hacking got worse. "Hey," she continued, "did you hear my line—you know, that guy who said, 'What about the poor people who are on the outside?' and I said, 'I wish I was out there doin' it, man.'"

"Yeah," Cooke replied. "What'd you say about the sleeping bag?"

"I said, 'They're all there in their sleeping bags gettin' together. Goddamn, I just get to sing the next song.'" Janis let loose with a breathy cackle, broken up by more coughing.

Backstage at Ravinia, Janis had chatted with a few reporters. She had been drinking, but refused to have her picture taken holding a bottle. "Keep those bottles out of the picture!" she barked. "My manager says my national image is bad enough already!"

An interviewer asked her, "How is it with you now that you've made it?"

"Made it?" she laughed. "It's been so long, baby, I don't know."

Talking to another reporter, she was more somber, and reflected, "Why not sit back and enjoy it, as long as you know you're gonna crap out in the end anyway?"

Janis and Full-Tilt arrived back in New York the next day, just in time for the Peace Festival at Shea Stadium. Hearing that some twenty thousand people had shown up, Janis, of a sudden, got very interested and decided she ought to appear. This, after all, was a New York audience. If twenty thousand was a small crowd for Shea, it was still a goddamn lot of people. Scheduled or not, she wasn't going to miss the opportunity to perform.

The festival, produced by Sid Bernstein, was a terrible strain on all the people working behind the scenes. Peter Yarrow was onstage for the entire day and night, pacing the show and entertaining between the acts. Although those acts were playing for free, a few were childishly arguing over the order of their appearance and were hardly displaying the spirit of gentleness that should have ruled the day. Financial concern added to the tension. Advertising had been costly; the turnout was disappointing. There was the rental of Shea itself. Should the festival pass the time limit for that rental, more money would have to be spent. The quibbling of the rock acts was causing a delay. Janis's appearance, while a boon for the audience, was going to add time to the show. Peter was delighted that Janis was there, but he was also very nervous. How long would she stay on that stage? And would she keep the crowd serene, or try to get it crazy?

John Cooke had not come to the stadium. Just before it was Janis's turn to perform, Peter said to me, "Please don't let her stay on there for more than ten minutes, and try to get it through to her that the audience has *got* to stay cool."

Attempts were still being made to save the Philadelphia benefit. Peter had cautioned the crowd that what it did was crucial to the future of all such events. Thus far the audience had been terrific, restricting itself to a fervor that did not include any jumping of the wooden barriers and hopping around on the lawns. The police looked relaxed, even happy. Peter had good reason to worry that Janis might possibly blow it. Whatever her state in Chicago, it had certainly worsened. She was on a nightmare drunk. Her mood was vicious, and what she would do, onstage or off, was simply unpredictable.

"Janis," I said, "for Peter's sake, please try to keep those kids from jumping the barriers!"

"I'm not stoppin' 'em," she snarled. "I'm not gonna tell 'em to get out there and dance, but if they do it, man, I won't say a word! If they break those barriers, I *ain't* tellin' 'em to sit down. I won't! I won't!"

I stood on the side of the stage and prayed as Janis's voice ripped into the audience, sharp, fierce, magnificent.

Peter was looking at his watch. Then he looked at me.

I stepped over to Janis and tried a soft persuasion. "You've gotta get off, O.K.? They're really having a time problem."

Janis grabbed the mike and gave me a look the Medusa could barely have summoned.

"It's gonna cost ten thousand dollars extra if they go overtime!" I pleaded. "Do just one more. Why don't you do 'Move Over'?"

"Move Over" had the audience clapping along but, thank God, not roused to hit the grass. Then enraged that she could do no more songs, Janis marched off the stage. A policeman smiled and gave her the peace sign. She glowered, raised her right hand, and slammed it into the crook of her elbow, giving him a foul "Fuck you."

An hour before she'd been in the dugout, attacking people for being at the festival and saying they were all full of shit. She'd trooped through the halls swigging on a bottle, telling this one and that one that she couldn't get laid. She'd moaned that she was ugly. Sometime during the evening she'd run into Joe McDonald and had carried on in a self-pitying tirade.

After her performance, she refused to leave the stadium. To get her away from the crowd I persuaded her to come with me to a room being used by the festival staff. A girl named Pat Kelley from Sid Bernstein's office was there. A few people were wandering around, among whom was disc jockey Scott Muni.

Janis sat at the end of a table, bottle in hand and mostly in mouth, ranting in her Michael Pollard-W. C. Fields voice that she, Janis, had spent a hundred dollars to get there and all she got for it was a shortened performance, and that was some way to be treated. "It cost me a hundred dollars!" she kept saying. "A hundred dollars! For what?"

I glanced at Pat Kelley, who was cringing in shock. I would call her tomorrow and explain that Janis had been in a drunken depression and didn't mean what she was saying, but I was becoming furious. Scott Muni's presence was also making me uneasy, though I do not believe he heard her.

"Janis," I whispered, "stop talking like that and *stop* talking in that voice!"

"ALL RIGHT!" she shrieked. "THIS-IS-MY-OWN-VOICE! YOU-LIKE-THIS-BETTER?"

"Listen, honey," I hissed. "You better calm down. You've already done enough, and that man wandering around is Scott Muni, the disc jockey. Do you want him to hear you?"

Turning paler than she already was, Janis mumbled that she'd be quiet, then got up and left the room.

Janis's behavior that Thursday evening of August 6 had been witnessed, at one time or another, by at least a hundred people. When I spoke to her Friday morning, I said, "You're gonna be awful lucky if nothing appears in print, and the chances are that it will."

"Do you really think so?" she asked me and went on to say that it would be justice—because she was "so ugly."

The sound of pleasure in her voice was simply unmistakable.

Janis's comments about her physical appearance were increasing. So were her proclamations to almost everyone she met that she couldn't get laid. She talked constantly about her lack of beauty, complaining that she was not Tuesday Weld or Raquel Welch, saying maybe that was the trouble. Her body, as always, bore the burden of proof for all she understood of her worthiness, and now it had become the focus of an obsession energized by her shattering loneliness, the pressure of which was also behind her thickening,

primitive language. The more she was famished for
closeness, the more her speech would resonate with
an infantile emotional blur, so that the business of
getting laid had become to her totally indivisible
from the matter of being loved, which it decidedly
was not. (That kind of talk, by the way, predated any
actual experience. As Karleen Bennett told me, "I can
remember her saying things like, 'Why can't I get
laid?' when she had never *been* laid!") Unable to
grasp her predicament, Janis was aware only of the
loneliness itself and the anger and the grief and the
scourging hurt and that nothing seemed to help. Thus,
no matter the number of her sexual encounters, she
would say the same, reporting to others what sounded
like a round-robin of erotic activity and going into
horrible depressions about the absence of sex in her
life.

"Yeah," Vince Mitchell sighed. "I remember that
shit. It was ridiculous. I mean, it was kind of crazy! It
used to get me mad. I'd say things to her about it,
and she'd say, 'Aw, you're old-fashioned. You remind
me of my mom or my father.' And she'd say, 'Well,
how come nobody wants to be around me?' and I'd
say, 'It's not that nobody wants to be around you,' but
she sort of scared some people. I thought she'd make
a fool of herself. I don't know if anybody else
thought that, but I cared about her, so naturally I
took it another way. You know, she just wanted to see
if somebody cared, that's all."

When I spoke to Janis, she cried, said she was lonely and didn't know what to do. In a moment of delusion, I thought Emmett might be able to talk to her.

"Yeah," he nodded. "I know what ya mean. Ya mean
she should stop fucking nobodys and start fucking
somebodys."

"No," I groaned. "That's *not* what I mean. She
doesn't mean she wants to get laid. She means she
wants to be close to someone. She wants to get
married. I think she wants to quit and get married."

"*She* doesn't wanna get married!"

"You're sure of that, are you?"

"Huh!" he grunted, "maybe you're right," though the look on his face clearly spelled a *macho* incomprehension.

But, characteristically, her conversation was perforated with laughing tales of sexual victories and, characteristically, a good many of the reactions she got were cooperative, even encouraging. And while there was in some cases, merely a lack of concern, per Vince's summary of the grand old ethic, "You do your thing, I'll do mine," there was, in addition, a dread of interference, an incredible romanticizing of her behavior—and a deficiency of the mental ear. Again, at least some innocence ran through the pattern of response. She was the queen, after all, and regarded with great subservience. So there was this unspoken pact between Janis and court that her talk, her ways, her style, should receive ceremonial homage. The reactions, then, were to some degree by way of a curious deference, and the harm to her was quite unrecognized, as was the nature of the actual tributes: shock, wonderment, humor, and the gleaming eyes that betrayed the covert chill of titillation that ran sneakily up the spine.

Staying at the Chelsea Hotel was a gifted and powerfully attractive musician named Toby Ben, who had an undigestible stomachful watching the scene during those August days. Toby wrote a beautiful song to Janis, called it "Pearl" (with saddest irony), and also made it a waltz. He thought life had twisted her up, forced her to clang along in a fortissimo rocking madness when she really wanted to amble on through, graceful and easy, in three-quarter time. Toby met Janis in El Quijote a day or so after her arrival in New York. During that first encounter, Emmett Grogan had charged into the bar and expanded his fine hello to her with a hefty grab of her breasts. When Toby later asked Janis, "How could you let him just do that to you like that?" she answered, "Well, Emmett's a holy man."

The memory of another incident turned his black eyes wrathful. Two loving freaks had come into the bar to revel over a bout with Janis, having just come down from her room. "It seemed to me," he said, "that she had no command over it, that she thought that kind of stuff was expected of her. And the guys came down to the bar. They thought it was hip, funny, a gas, a good free ride. Like she was a good washing machine or something!"

One night that first week of August, poet Patti Smith was witness to a pathetic scene. Huddled up tiny in her room, sitting on the edge of her bed, Janis had started to moan and cry that she'd had to come home alone. Her feathers fell from her hair to the floor, leaving her small, unadorned, a helpless, whimpering waif. Startled by her appearance, Patti said, "God! You look so little!"

Janis was very drunk. Lurching up, she staggered across the room to the mirror and, having picked up her feathers, began to put them back in her hair. "Man," Janis said gruffly, "that's 'cause I don't have my feathers on, man." Her voice had slipped into that weird intonation. "That's all mn. I'll put them on . . . and then I'll be *real* big!"

Janis sat back down on the bed and began to strum her guitar. "Hey, here's this song I wrote," she said.

> *If you wanna be a big woman star*
> *You gotta sleep alone*
> *If you wan . . . wanna . . . be . . .*

She started to choke. Her face got all squeezed up until it was purple, blotchy, and swollen. Massive spasms seized her body as the tears assaulted her wasted face, and in between the ragged sobs came forth the pitiable cry, the lament that she couldn't get laid.

Some were oblivious to the state she was in; some were not. "Sure," Dave Richards mused, "she was happy with her band, but that was her *work!* She had a lot of other things happening!" Certainly the improvement in the music and Janis's genuine enthusiasm when it came to Full-Tilt Boogie were distracting. Thus John Cooke, with typical insight, was adamant that Janis was in a fine frame of mind. "Yeah! Absolutely!" he announced crisply. "Better than ever! She was happy onstage and a good deal of the rest of the time, because she was having such a good time with that band!" Furthermore, her natural volatility almost guaranteed moments of what looked to be high spirits, even though they were seldom more than manic outbursts as loaded with depression as the most blatant kind of melancholy. "You know," Vince said, "when Janis was happy, she *still* wasn't happy." And as Ken Pearson put it, "Motion, motion, motion. And it wasn't the concerts, it wasn't the music, it was how she *herself* was doing." A few others knew; perhaps there were understandable reasons that others did not. Nonetheless, the atmosphere was very similar to that which created Janis's awesome aloneness at the University of Texas. "She made good times for *them*," Tary Owens said, "but it wasn't for *her!*"

On a sunny afternoon that week, the day that Janis went to the fights with Emmett and the Torns, Jerry Tobias finished taking his pictures for *Circus* magazine. We'd arranged to do the photos somewhere near the West Village studio where Full-Tilt was in rehearsal. She wanted to do some shopping; we could meet the band when she was through. So Jerry, Janis and I went first to a shop in the garment district, and Janis rummaged around, happily absorbed in picking out plumes and glitter. We took off from there in a cab, which went south on a route through the Bowery.

"Please God, not yet," Janis grimaced, as she stared glumly out on the street. Suddenly, she jumped around and howled, "Look! Look! Did you see that?" Pushing aside those zany feathers, which were falling over her eyes, she pointed toward the rear window. "That cat

flat on the sidewalk saw me, man, and raised his
arm and said, 'Right on!'"

Downtown, Jerry took some of his pictures outside
on the sidewalk, the rest in a rundown corner saloon.
There a charade in which Janis played barmaid, serving drinks to the band.

"Wouldn't this be great for the album!" she cried,
but remarked to me in a hopeful tone that Albert perhaps wouldn't like it. Then she shot right back behind
the bar and asked that Jerry take more.

When the photo session was finished, she said,
"Oh! Did I show you this?" and with that handed me
an article from a Philadelphia paper, which contained
the item that Janis had contributed to a tombstone for
Bessie Smith.

Janis's fantasy about Bessie Smith, the web of
identification she had formed, went back many years.
Bessie, of course, was one of her major influences, and
Janis had made it a point, even in her adolescence, to
familiarize herself with Bessie's life. From Janis's own
darkness of heart came the enchantment with Bessie's
style—hard-drinking, hard-suffering, loser to men, and
the victim of early death. The buying of half the
tombstone—the other half paid for by a Philadelphia
nurse—did not occur, however, with the drama
woven around that event after Janis's death. Far from
it. Janis had been drunk one afternoon in her Larkspur
home and had gotten a call from Philadelphia, requesting the contribution, which is not to say that
she would have refused, had she, in fact, been sober.
These were merely the circumstances under which
her commitment was made.

"Sure, why not?" she'd said drunkenly. "I got two
hundred dollars to spare."

Or such was the story she told me that afternoon
while we were sitting around that grubby bar. But
while she was definitely flippant at first, she abruptly
underwent a noticeable change in mood.

I said, "Well, let me have the article, Janis. I'll put it
in the file."

Janis started to hand me the clipping again, frowned instead, and held it back. She scanned the item, and possessed by some instantaneous depression—I saw those gray eyes turn inward—shook her head and said, "No." Her face was set firm, and she looked off into the distance before studying the paper once more.

"No," she repeated, her voice low and remote. "I'll keep it. I wanna keep it."

22

Wear this, wear that, don't bother, forget it, and the hell with it all, who cares? Janis had a gold mesh vest made of the same material as a sweater I'd bought that summer. On Saturday, August 8, getting dressed for the Port Chester concert, I went through an hour of crazy turmoil before I slipped on that sweater (worrying about her reaction!), left my apartment, grabbed a cab, and headed on up to the Chelsea. Was I actually hoping to provoke her? Certainly I was feeling a bit resentful. The week had near done me in, and if she reacted to that stupid sweater, well, that was just too damned bad.

"She's the star," I muttered. "I can look good if I want to. She's gotta grow up sometime." Then I thought as I reached the hotel, "If it really upsets her, I'll give it to her." Oh, martyrdom! She, of course, wouldn't take it, and I'd be left with the satisfaction of having made her feel guilty. "Aw shit," I moaned. "Why didn't I leave this goddamn thing at home? . . . Well, maybe she won't even notice."

Most of the guys in Janis's band were in the Chelsea lobby when I arrived. I waved and walked into El

Quijote, where I ordered a sandwich to take in the car.

"Always in a rush," the waiter remarked.

Looking around for John Cooke, I said, "Let somebody else be late, not me!"

Late! We were going to be excruciatingly early. The first show was scheduled to begin at eight, the second at eleven-thirty. With two acts set to go on before Janis, she couldn't possibly be onstage before ten. It was now a quarter to five. Port Chester was an hour's drive out of the city. There would have to be a sound check, and John had set five for the hour of departure which, considering late-afternoon traffic, was reasonable enough. Still, it was going to be an awfully long night.

"Oh, hi," I said, as the Torns appeared.

Rip asked, "Is there time for a drink?"

"Looks like it. Janis isn't downstairs yet, and I haven't seen John Cooke."

Neuwirth came lumbering through the door just then, and slapping Rip on the back—"Well there you are, you silver-tongued devil!"—nearly jolted him off his bar stool.

"One tequila, man," Bobby said to the bartender, who accommodated him very quickly. Just as quickly, the drink disappeared. "Ahhhhh, wake-up time!" Bobby grinned, smacking his lips and ordering another.

"O.K., let's go," Cooke called, entering the bar to collect us. "Janis will be down in a minute. Let's load up."

Out on Twenty-third Street, John Fischer was leaning against one of the limousines. The members of the band were already in the cars. The rest of us stood about, waiting for Janis.

When she came downstairs, the first thing she did was look at me and glare, "I'm not sure I like you wearing that!"

She herself had on a simple purple dress with one string of beads around her neck, not a feather or a bell in sight. She also looked very little and absolutely wretched. To the Torns, she nodded, but said nothing.

"Come on, Janis," I pleaded. "You don't really care about this sweater."

Walking by me without a word, she handed her stage clothes to John Fischer.

"What's the matter now?" I sighed.

She turned to me and snapped, "Leave me alone! I just don't feel like talking!"

I backed away and went over to talk about nothing in particular to John Fischer. My rapping was automatic. What was on my mind was Albert again and when I'd be able to speak to him. I believed he was in California that weekend. Nor did I know when he was due to return.

Just as we were about to get in the cars, Janis approached me and whined bitterly, "It's not the sweater! You know it's not the sweater! I'm sick of these gigs. I just found out there are two shows. For *what?* For what, man? How come I'm playing some crappy theater in Port Chester? Two fucking shows! We'll be there 'til three!" Her voice started to rise. "I can't take it! I can't! I can't!" Then speaking more quietly, she hissed, "And I won't be able to drink."

By the time we reached the Capitol Theater, Janis was feeling slightly better. She agreed that we'd had to get there early and seemed resigned, with less anger for the moment, to the fact that there were hours ahead before the evening would end. Then too, Neuwirth's antics had begun to amuse her; it was obvious also that the sound would be excellent, as it so rarely was. Rick Bell was at the piano, improvising. Janis sat on a stool next to the piano, smiling sweetly as she listened. The reality, the *truth* of her, in that plain purple dress was overwhelming.

The sound check completed, we packed into the limos to find a place to eat dinner. Janis sat in the front of John Fischer's car, the Torns and myself in the back. Shifting around to face us, Janis began

talking about Albert, whizzing off in a nonstop mono-
logue that seemed to rush up from nowhere.

"I'll do anything he tells me. Anything. It's yes,
Albert, no, Albert, anything you say, Albert. . . . He
told me not to wear dresses onstage, I stopped wearing dresses. . . . He told me not to carry a bottle onstage. I said O.K., O.K., I'll drink from a cup. We were
driving toward Cincinnati and the concert wasn't sold
out and I didn't know if it was canceled because the
promoter didn't tell us what was happening so we
stopped on the road and John Cooke called Albert
and then I talked to Albert and it was but, Albert, no,
Albert, yes, Albert, what, what, yes, no, Albert. But.
Yes. Yes. O.K., Albert. Anything you say." She took a
breath and faced front again. "And that's the way it
is," she sighed.

As we rolled into the main part of town, she pointed
out the window and chuckled, "Oh, let's eat *there!*"
Obligingly, John Fischer parked. The other limo
pulled up and we all trooped into this joint she'd
picked called The Terminal Bar and Restaurant.

Janis remained at the table, possibly for twenty
minutes. But the misery was stuck to her like flypaper.
She left without touching her food and walked back
to the theater alone.

At the hall an hour later I found her in a dingy
dressing room, one of three ill-lit cubicles on the
second level of the building. Down the hall, the
toilets weren't working. The floor had the smell of a
wet cigar butt chewed on for a week.

Still wearing her simple purple dress, she was
sitting in a soiled red chair and reading. I hesitated at
the door.

"O.K.," she said gloomily. "It's O.K. Come on in. I
don't know, Myra. I just can't take it anymore."

"Then *quit*, Janis."

She said nothing, but reached over to a shelf opposite the chair and picked up a quart of Southern Comfort, a loving gift from a loving fan. The bottle was

unopened. "I can't drink," she groaned. "Not this early. I'll get too crocked." Her voice became strident again. "I wanna know why I'm playing this dump, why I'm doing two shows, and I'm fucking sick and tired of Seatrain being on my bill all the time. I don't give a fuck if they're good. They're *always* on my show. I'm being used and I don't like it. Is Bennett gonna be here tonight?"

"I guess so."

"Well, I wanna see him! You tell him to get up here when you find him. I want an answer to this crap! That house isn't even half full!"

In point of fact, it surely wasn't, what with the overbooking of Janis in the area and this, the Capitol Theater night, a week after Forest Hills and the Powder Ridge debacle.

"Hey, Janis," I said. "You dig John Hall, and Johanna's here. Why don't we go downstairs and hear his set?"

'Yeah, all right." She put the bottle back on the shelf. Sticking the book in her bag, she placed it in a corner of the chair.

As she walked into the corridor, I lingered for a second and glanced in her bag to see what she'd been reading. It turned out to be some philosophy anthology, but I didn't want her to see me looking, so I quickly slipped it back and followed her out of the room.

Janis was standing in the wings downstairs, still in her little dress. Johanna kissed her on the cheek. After a while, Janis sighed, "Well, I have to go and change into Janis Joplin. She's upstairs in a box!"

She returned, a marbelized package with a sizzling array of boa feathers slightly askew on her head. Onstage, she stood very quietly, looking down at her feet. She paced around in back of the mike, then whirled around and grabbed it. "This song calls for a little audience participation," she announced. Her face turned up transformed, and the body began to roll and bend, she clapped her hands, d-boom, d-boom,

that corrugated rumble rose out of her, wicked, tough,
gutty. . . .

> *You say that it's over baby*
> *Ya say that it's over now*
> *And still you hang around, now come on*
> *Won't you move over* *

I could recall only a few renditions of "Ball and
Chain," going back to the early days with Big Brother,
that approached Janis's performances that night. Her
voice had nuance and stretch from every shriek, moan,
and shudder, the brilliant sparks from the fume of an
intensity quivering up from her toes. She pounded on
through the rockers, roaring like a hopped-up car-
buretor about to explode in its heat. In the sweep of
the slower songs, her throat opened in a liquid lament
shaped with consummate authority . . .

> *So come on . . . come on . . . come on . . . COME ON*
> *. . . COME ON Criiiiiii Baabe* **

. . . a wailing rainbow of pitches. Who could fathom
the source of that sound? It was an hour of sheer glory,
and almost dreadful, moving from the drive of that
fantastic sex into a migration of feeling so shattering
that it seemed to take her and suspend her, unrecover-
able from a paradise of grief.

As awed as I'd been, I was also irritated, because
Janis, in her raps with the audience, had talked again
in that pinched inflection, spattered full of those
noxious squeaks. The several times I'd said something,
she'd been defensive, to put it mildly. "The hell with
that," I thought. "I'm gonna tell her again. That's the
whole trouble. Nobody ever says a goddamn thing!"

---

* "Move Over" words & music by Janis Joplin. Copyright ©
1971 Strong Arm Music, Suite 3100, 555 California St., San
Francisco, Calif., 94104. Used by Permission. All Rights Re-
served.
** "Cry Baby" words & music by Burt Russell and Norman
Meade. © 1963 by Robert Mellin Inc. & Rittenhouse Music Inc.

Trembling and pale, Janis was huddled in a dressing-room chair. Her feathers had been replaced by a towel wrapped turban-fashion around her head. She looked no less forlorn than she had two hours before. A stream of people came filing up the stairs, to congratulate her on the performance. The Torns, of course, were there; Geraldine Page went into the room and threw her arms around her. Temporarily rejuvenated, Janis stepped out into the hall. Mobility showed on her face, and her eyes were wide as she cried excitedly, "Do you know what she said to me? She said, 'Janis, most performers give just a fraction of themselves. I can't remember the last time I saw one who gave everything they had!' She said that to me! Geraldine Page said that!" By now she was beaming and jumping around, a whirl of animation. "Come on, everybody!" she shouted. "Let's get it together! Where's the nearest bar?"

The Torns had to leave. The remainder of our crew sailed off to a gin mill on the corner. When we were seated and drinks had been ordered, I said to Janis, "Listen. She's right. You've never been better. I just wish you'd pay attention to me about talking that way. You don't need stuff like that. It's phony."

Gulping on her vodka and orange juice, Janis said sarcastically, "*You're* not the public. *He's* the public." She pointed at John Fischer, who was sitting across the table, happily high and, as usual, totally agreeable. "You're the public, aren't you, John?"

"Yeah," he giggled.

"Well, wh't do you thnk of th' way I tlk? I mn whn I do this?"

"Oh, it's groovy, Janis!" John answered. "I dig it! Anything you do is terrific!"

"See," she said to me, "he's the public and he likes it."

"I don't give a damn if he's the public," I said, "or if he *thinks* he's the public, or if *you* think he's the public or even if the public likes it! It sucks!"

Surprisingly, Janis didn't get angry, though she refused to continue the conversation and went on

downing her drinks. The table, in the meantime,
became quite crowded. People were hopping all over
the place in a bizarre game of musical chairs, which
spared everyone from the strain of talking to each
other for long. There was, however, a lot of laughter,
with spirits up, those served and those affected. Before
we left the bar, Janis and Bobby Neuwirth added
the last verse to her famous *a cappella* "Mercedes
Benz":

> *Oh Lord, won't you buy me a night on the town?*
> *I'm counting on you, Lord, please don't let me down*
> *Prove that you love me and buy the next round*
> *Oh Lord, won't you buy me a night on the town?* *

Back at the theater, Janis looked crestfallen. "I
thought you felt better," I said. Ruefully, she scowled,
"I'll feel better in hell."

The audience for the second show was larger—and
spaced. Backstage a blond boy of about seventeen was
tripping. Right behind the curtains, he was writhing
on the floor in a prostrate St. Vitus dance. Occasionally
he'd jerk to a sitting position or somehow twitch to his
feet. His features were a smear of spasmodic tics, and
he was smiling. I retreated from the wings and went
out front to hear the set from there. Half the crowd
looked to be in a cataleptic trance. "What the devil's
going on here?" I muttered and collapsed, mystified,
in a seat.

Janis was beginning "Piece of My Heart," after a set
that was simply inspired, a siege of emotion that had
burned through the hall, surpassing the marvel of the
early performance. The audience had summoned the
strength to applaud and bring her back for more. Still,
it was a motionless bunch if ever there was one, with
what seemed to be pills for eyes. Applause or not, from

Janis's view she might as well have been confronted
with a mass case of rigor mortis. Her reaction, however,
was extreme, steaming out of her in a blast of curses,
a wild anger at the entire world. Infuriated, she was
marching around the stage on a rampage right in the
middle of the music. "Come on, come one, gimme a
little piece of your heart," turned into, "Come on, what
am I up here for, goddamn you . . . get the hell off
your asses. What d'ya think I'm fucking knocking myself out for? A fucking eleven hours for this!" Once
she'd succeeded in getting them up, her rage subsided.
But when she stamped offstage, she said, "Man, I ain't
never goin' through anything like this again."

It was around 3:00 A.M. when I settled into John
Fischer's car again, in the back with Clark and
Neuwirth. A cool breeze was stirring in the air. Slung
over the front seat was Cooke's leather jacket, which
I took and put over my shoulders, since I was quite
lightly dressed and freezing as a consequence.

A few seconds later, Cooke hopped in the front.
"O.K.," he said, "let's split."

Until eight or so minutes out of Port Chester, total
quiet prevailed in the car. Then just as we were nearing the highway, this ungodly yell slammed through
the silence.

"M-O-T-H-E-R-F-U-C-K-E-R! GODDAMN SHIT
FUCK I LEFT MY . . ."

"John, John," I tried to say, "John, I've got your . ."

". . . WE'VE GOT TO GO THE FUCK BACK!"

"No, no, John, I've got it." Cooke kept on screaming,
so I said it louder. *"John, I've got your jacket!"*

Snap! His torso went stiff as an ice pick and without
a bend in that brittle posture, he jerked around so
rigidly that by the laws of skeletal formation, he should
have broken right in two. "Gimme that jacket!" he
snarled.

"John, I'm cold. . . . I *am*."

He bared his teeth and snarled again, "Give-it-to-
me!" The words shot out in a riveting crackle, like
the stuttering rage of a machine gun.

"Christ, John," I pleaded. "I'm freezing to death . . . look what I've got on . . . you're not cold." It would have been easier to reason with a Doberman pinscher, foaming rabid at the mouth. My teeth chattering, I removed his jacket; he yanked it roughly from my hand. He rolled it up in a very tight ball and held it lovingly in his lap.

The car lapsed back into routine silence, cut here and there by the bumps on the highway: ta-click, ta-click, ta-click.

Neuwirth stretched back in his seat, slugging from a bottle of Southern Comfort and looking out the window.

Cooke's spine, I noticed, was strangely curved, thrusting his head aggressively forward, but also making a hollow in front for the nesting of the jacket, which he was clasping tenderly still. Anger, however, radiated from the tension in his body. My mental picture of his face had it a big fat prune.

Ta-click, ta-click, ta-click.

Suddenly Bobby said, "John Cooke is sucking on his jacket."

"Oh Jesus," I thought, "there he goes," and started feeling sorry for Cooke.

Bobby continued. "He's got the corner of the lapel in his mouth . . . he's started to chew on the sleeve . . . pretty soon, he'll swallow the whole thing."

No laughs. No words. Ta-click, ta-click.

"When's that *Esquire* thing coming out?" Bobby asked.

"October issue," I replied.

"Did you draw a mustache on my picture?"

"Nope. Just sent it the way it was."

"I told you to draw a mustache in, you dumb Madison Avenue flak!"

That brought Cooke to life. "Yeah, Myra," he said gleefully, "I told you I wanted a blank space with my name under it. I bet you sent my picture."

"I can take you out completely, John," I said. "I'll be more than happy to do that."

The top 100 of Rock. Jesus Christ!

The subject was milked. There were no others, making for a ride that progressed in utter silence until Bobby started in on Cooke once more. When we dropped John off at his uptown apartment, he slammed the door and said to Bobby, "I notice you come around when you want a good meal!"

Following that denouement, we zipped on off to the Chelsea, where I said goodnight to Janis before John Fischer drove me home. "Life's a rotten bummer," she said despairingly.

Right before I'd gone on vacation, I'd bought some blouses Janis had liked. Borrowing one in the hope of wearing it for the concert at Forest Hills, Janis had been disappointed because it happened to be too small. Actually, the blouses were body shirts, snapping between the legs, which meant they were great with slacks, and ideal, Janis felt, for the stage. She'd also thought them hilarious. "I wanna get one of those things with the snap-in crotch," she'd cackled.

To that purpose, in part, she called me Monday morning and asked could I get away early from the office and thus be free to take her shopping.

"*Take* you shopping!" I laughed.

"Yeah!" she answered, without a tinge of comprehending humor.

Her voice, however, was loaded with mischievous affectation when she stated sadly that if I didn't go, well no one, of course, would wait on her, and she might as well not leave the hotel. She would stay there and pine away.

"Hey, come on! What is this?"

"Well, I want your company. . . . I'm trying to get my fucking head together, man!"

Janis's remarkable resilience had overcome her depression, or so it seemed that afternoon when I did indeed go with her to Bloomingdale's, which was where I'd found the blouses. As we walked up Lexington Avenue, she was warm, ebullient, quiet, pensive, the emotional stances spinning as usual, but flowing from her in an intimate manner that had her—I'd call it "in contact," as she hadn't been for ages.

I told her about the episode Saturday concerning the leather jacket.

Shaking her head, she commented wryly, "Man, can you imagine scrambling an egg for John Cooke?"

She asked me about my vacation too and a lot of other matters, coming out of herself as was definitely not her more common self-absorbed way. Her eyes, of course, were clicking like a metronome, an unrelenting to and fro, fixed quickly on every face that passed us, for the light of recognition.

Then as we were about to cross the street near the store, she suddenly said, "Hey! Did you see that awful business they're trying to do to Martin Lurther King's reputation?" (This involved the FBI's claiming information about King gleaned from wire tapping that revealed alleged adulterous activities.)

"I mean," she said, "it's just shocking! Can you imagine them being that low?"

A car that I failed to see just about took off my feet, before Janis grabbed my arm. Pulling me back to the curb, she huffily continued, "Now, you know Martin Luther King never did anything like that!"

Actually, I was no more than momentarily startled by the remark in terms of its nature. What surprised me most was her awareness of the incident itself. Janis's book-reading I took for granted. Newspapers and magazines she rarely touched, unless they contained news about her. Occasionally, a conversation might spark her interest in something other than her immediate concerns, but it didn't happen often. She must have sensed my reaction. When we emerged from the revolving doors that led to Bloomingdale's lobby, she grinned and said, "Well, it's about time I find out what's going on in the world, isn't it?"

Janis's claim that only the flash of many bills would get her attention in New York stores was, at one time, true enough. This day it was clear that things had changed. On the second floor, a salesgirl asked her for her autograph. A middle-aged lady rushed over to where we stood, saying, "Miss Joplin, can I help you? We have lovely robes over here." From nowhere, a fellow appeared, holding out paper and pencil. A small mob gathered, asking wasn't she Janis Joplin and wouldn't she just sign this or write a few words here or tell them where the next concert would be. Janis complied politely and bestowed on the crowd a very reserved and ever-so-dignified smile. And all the while, those kooky feathers were drooping over her face and her bells were clanging and the rattle of her bracelets must have been heard in the shoe department on the sixth floor.

When they had all gone, she looked at me and sighed with determined apathy. "It sure is a drag not to be able to go shopping like anybody else."

Solemnly, I agreed. "Oh yes, Janis, I know. It's simply terrible."

"Oh, all right," she protested. "I love it. So what?"

"So what, nothing. Come on. Let's see about the blouses."

We ended the afternoon in a Lexington Avenue cocktail lounge, quite a bit fancier than Janis's style, had it been a typical day. "Let's try this place," she'd said, after peering through the window. "It looks nice. I don't feel like going anywhere scummy." No one knew Janis there, which didn't appear to bother her much, although she was briefly infuriated that we weren't permitted to sit at the bar. "You see how they treat beatniks!" she cried, poking a pugilistic finger in the air. She smiled then with satisfaction. "You see! You see!" she cried again. "You didn't believe me, did you?"

Without any further ado, however, we settled for taking a table, which as it happened was much to my preference. Save for a second's glare when the waiter came by to take our order, Janis herself seemed through with the issue. Her mood was soft and confidential; she was far too interested in talking to make any kind of a scene. Cumulatively, what she said to me that afternoon was extraordinary.

Janis spoke for a while about her imminent visit August 15 to Port Arthur for her high school reunion. Courtesy of her own bankroll, Cooke, Neuwirth, and John Fischer were also going along. That Janis should want a male escort made perfect sense to me, and my feelings would have been sympathetic were she to have settled for taking Cooke. For Janis, that wasn't enough. She was going to show them: the evidence, mind you, the evidence—not one man, not two, but three, all of that planned with a great deal of bravado about blowing the minds of the people back home. She had, of course, made her bitter but funny remark on the Cavett show, and in a few newspaper interviews had intimated that she was well prepared to hand out some whopping derogatory remarks when she hit Texas. Even Linda said to me, "You know, she only went to that reunion to thumb her nose." I thought quite otherwise, that Janis was returning for that event, her beseeching heart bursting with the prayer that now they might finally accept her, that love (from whom?) might finally be hers. It is academic to say that an enormous anger was in her and that the despotic conflict that ruled her had cooked up the choice for the self-defeat that would come with her entourage. Cooke would observe proprieties, perhaps, one could say, to a fault. But Neuwirth and John Fischer were bound to raise hell, and Janis certainly knew it. "*She* is gonna act like a lady," Sam Gordon had said. "*They* are gonna blow it!" The outcome was absolutely predictable. Still, she said to me that afternoon, "You know I'm not going to do all those things I said I was going to do . . . laugh at everybody and say stuff like, 'What are you doing, still driving a truck?' I'm not going to do that."

She went on to talk about her family, her wish to get married, her fear of aging—a lot about that—and as she spoke, which she did slowly, in contrast to her usual way, her eyes did odd short darts to nowhere and back. Saying virtually nothing about her career, she made an affectionate comment or two in reference to the members of the band and in particular to Ken Pearson, about whom, she said, she was worried. "There aren't enough decent chicks on the road," she muttered sternly. Occasionally, she remarked she was "growing up," adding at one point introspectively that the change had taken her by surprise. "Man," she smiled, "I never thought it would come to that!" Whenever she'd say "growing up," she'd also voice her ambivalence, every time in just this way: "I can't *stand* it," she'd say. "Ah that's not true. I love it." All afternoon, through the shopping and the attention she'd received, she'd been doing that: "I can't stand it; I love it; I can't stand it; I love it."

Only when she talked about men did her tone begin to get frivolous, and even that passed quickly enough, giving way to the sober admission, "I get ridiculous when I'm scared, don't I?"

I nodded. She growled, "Sheeet, what a fuck-up!"

She spoke then about weariness, with special emphasis on her "pretty young boys," but mostly she bemoaned the transience, insisting nevertheless that she didn't think it was "in the cards" for her to have anything else.

I told her I didn't agree. "That's not really true," I said. "I mean, you keep going into Nobody's and you go after what you go after and you get what you get and you've had opportunity, Janis, like no one I've ever known. It's not the cards."

"Well, I know," she answered mournfully, "but I get so lonely and it just seems like I'm driven and I don't know, I just do things and I don't know why. . ."

"For beginners, seems to me if you had a little more respect for yourself, you wouldn't do it."

With all the relish of her masochism, she naturally jumped in on that one, though she recognized the truth of it too and reflected on it well. "Yeah," she said, "maybe you're right. Hmmmmmmm. I guess I don't respect myself very much." Her face brightened. "O.K.," she smiled. "I'm gonna think about that!"

I smiled back and shut up. "There's something else," she rambled, returning to the subject of her family. "I haven't quite made up my mind about it yet, but you know my kid brother?" She sighed, "Well, he's kind of wild and that's good you know . . . or maybe . . . or I used to think so. But he wants to drop out of high school and I thought that was really groovy once, but I'm not sure he should do it now, and when I go home I'm gonna have a talk with him and tell him I think he should finish. I haven't made up my mind, but I think that's what I'm gonna do." She paused and asked me, "What do you think about that?"

"I think that might make sense," I replied.

She grunted, "Yeah," and said again, "I'm growing up, aren't I? I can't stand it; I love it."

Briefly, we discussed my doing a book in the future. Janis said, "It can't be yet. I want it to be the truth, Myra, about the drugs, about everything. I mean really the truth."

Continuing to talk about her family, she moaned. "Oh God, my mother. She's just like I am—or, I mean, I'm just like *her*. It's murder when we get together. We're both so strong-willed, you know." Then she commenced to speak of her father. "I'm afraid to see him in a way," she mused. "You know, he hasn't been well. And he's got this horrible rheumatism. I've always been afraid of that. It runs in the family. I don't want to get old like that, all scrounged up in pain." The pace of her talk picked up, accelerated by thoughts of her father's past vitality. Her eyes were shining with adoration. "You have no idea," she said, "how active he was, physically and mentally. He encouraged me to read, you know. He was fantastic, energetic, and he went his own way in what he thought."

Her speech became weighted again, and with a quirky smile she said, " 'Get It While You Can.' Everybody thinks I mean sex." She shook her head very slowly. "I don't mean that. They always expect me to mean that. My father. He had a life of the mind. That's what he wanted, and he got it while he could. Whatever's for you. That's what it oughta be. Man, they can never believe that there's anything else on my mind."

"I wonder why," I laughed.

Janis made a face at me, but laughed too. Becoming serious again, she reminisced about her childhood, mostly the very early years, recalling some incident of singing in the kitchen when she was about three. Very little came up about her adolescence, except that it had been painful. As she rambled on, she said that she thought her family, all considered, had been very understanding, that her eccentricities must have been impossible to bear, and while there had been hard times and much strain, they had come a long way in accepting her for what she was.

Her eyes wandering sadly around the room, Janis bowed her head for a second before she spoke again. Several times during that conversation I'd glanced at those crazy boa feathers and the necklaces and the rings and the bracelets and had stifled the tightness in my stomach as it had started to rise to my throat. Several times I'd felt it, the swelling urge to tears. Only this climactic statement really jolted me that afternoon: Janis told me that the last time she'd been in Port Arthur—which, I believe, was September of 1969—she'd gone to church![*]

I cupped my chin, my fingers partially covering my mouth to hide my reactions, and said not a word as she elaborated. "I didn't do it because I really wanted to go. I haven't believed in anything like that since I was ten. It wasn't that. It just seemed that since my parents had learned to accept the way I am, I ought to do the same with them. So I put on straight clothes, you know, a really straight dress, and I put my hair up so I wouldn't embarrass my mother, and I went."

---

[*] Trying to verify this incident, I asked the Joplins about it. Janis's mother said that it did indeed occur; Mr. Joplin did not recall it.

Again, I said nothing. Janis shifted in her chair and waved to the waiter, who truly didn't seem to like us. Bringing over the check, which was something like $2.50, he dropped it rudely on the table before he walked away.

Janis's eyes tightened hard, then glinted. "You have to make at least fifty thousand dollars a year to have an American Express card, right?"

"Something like that."

"Well, goddamn it," she cackled. "I'm gonna pay this check with my card! Ooooo-eeeeee! That'll get him!"

A few minutes later, we flagged a cab. Janis zipped back into her usual banter. It was I who stayed very silent.

That evening, Toby Ben, Janis, myself, and several members of Full-Tilt went to dinner at Bradley's. The plan was to go afterward to the Fillmore to hear Santana, then uptown to Ungano's, where Tony Williams' Lifetime was playing. Before we took off to eat, Janis began to complain about the routine that the evening would typify. "Does it always have to be Bradley's, Remington's, Max's, Nobody's, Bradley's, Max's, Remington's? . . . Can't we ever just go to a nice quiet little Italian restaurant or something?" I made an enthusiastic gesture and then subsided into torpor. Our imaginations were dragging terribly. Bradley's was closer to the Fillmore than any place we could think of. "We'll do it another night, Janis," I said. "Besides, I can write a check there, and I don't have any cash."

So off to Bradley's we went, Janis accepting the situation without further protest. In some ways, during that dinner, Janis perpetuated her mood and thoughts of the afternoon. She spoke again about the Grateful Dead and what she called "hippie brainwashing." "I don't see where they've done any better," she grumbled. "They're frauds, the whole goddamn culture. They bitch about brainwashing from their parents and they do the same damn thing. I've never known a one of those people who would tolerate any way of life but their own. I'm sick of 'em; I'm sick of everything they think and all that spouting off!" She shook her head sadly, "Nobody ever seems to learn anything."

Unfortunately, however, as the dinner progressed, Janis was downing a great deal more liquid than food. By the time we reached the Fillmore, she was horribly drunk. On the way she'd bought a bottle, which she'd guzzled on greedily in the cab. Backstage, she raced around, offering slugs of booze to everyone in a sloppy, drunken blather. Pearl to the hilt.

One slightly amusing incident occurred. Janis went out to the front of the Fillmore and plopped herself down on the stairs. That being against the fire laws, she got an usher frantic. "You've *got* to move," he pleaded. "Even if you *are* Janis Joplin, you're not allowed to sit here!"

"Honey," she said sweetly, "you're doing a wonderful job and I want you to keep it up—but I ain't movin'." The usher dashed off to the Fillmore office for help. Janis turned to me and said sincerely, "You know, I really like it when I'm treated just like anybody else. But I *still* ain't gonna move."

Full-Tilt remained for a while at the Fillmore. Janis, Toby, and I took off for Ungano's, discovering when we got there that we'd arrived far too early. Janis's increasingly drunken madness had gotten me simply distraught. I complained of a headache and a queasy stomach.

"Whatsa matter with you?" Janis griped.

"You're giving me an ulcer."

Apologizing, Janis seemed obviously pleased nonetheless that her behavior was having such a decided effect. Unable to bear the night anymore, I left, with assurances from Toby that he would make certain Janis would be all right.

After my departure, Janis dragged him to a bar called the Embassy Lounge. Toby remembered that it was all very weird for many reasons, but especially this one: the whole place was full of women with crazy feathers on their heads.

Nothing else about the scene at the Embassy Lounge was funny in the least. Janis whipped down three screwdrivers, which increased her drunkenness and brought on an outburst of grief-ridden angry self-pity. She told Toby she'd rather play concerts attended by smaller audiences; it was easier that way to get laid. At the large halls, it was too overwhelming. "They get scared of me," she whimpered. Speaking about David Niehaus, she blabbed to Toby some poor excuse for having sent him away. She seethed about that for a while, than raged on about her appearance. Her looks were suffering, she cried, from the wear and tear of liquor, and she was getting old. At one point, she grabbed the skin under her arm and pulled at it viciously. "Nobody wants an old chick like me," she screamed bitterly. "They want young girls, can't you understand that! They want young girls!"

Toby began to plead with her to get out of the whole thing, to stop, to quit, to do anything. "What are you doing this for?" he said. "Pull out! Stop!"

She was afraid, she moaned. "They'll *forget* me. They don't love me, man! *Nobody* loves me!"

He cried, "How can you torture yourself like this! Look at the position you're in! Everybody loves you!"

"Doesn't it occur to you that I just don't believe that?" she shrieked.

He pleaded again with her to walk away from the career, and Janis said that she couldn't, that she didn't know how to do anything else.

By the time they got back to Ungano's, Full-Tilt was in the audience and Janis was a great deal worse. During Tony Williams's set, Janis sat screaming that her band was better, that she, Janis Joplin, was the greatest. Over and over, she yelled and kept yelling, "I'm the greatest! My band is the greatest!" Janis had another bottle, which she'd nearly polished off. Storming backstage, she thrust it forward to bass player Jack Bruce, snorting drunkenly, "Hello, fellow superstar!"

Things were to get still more grotesque. Janis had lurched into the sexual number, intent on landing Toby, who'd not pursued her in that fashion, the pity of her freezing out any of those impulses, and he had a girlfriend to begin with. That girlfriend happened to be in the audience and became upset that he was with Janis; Janis went berserk, because she had competition. Working herself into a frenzy, she began screaming at Toby, "Are you gonna ball her? Are you gonna ball her?"

The evening ended with a cab ride back to the Chelsea. Toby, his girlfriend, and Toby's manager sitting in the back, Janis slumped miserably in the front. Janis slammed into El Quijote, sullen and mean, not saying a word. The sexual rejection intolerable to her, she promptly went after someone else, who had no mind to be concerned as to what had driven her to do it.

Sometime around noon on Tuesday, Toby brought Janis some flowers. Janis was deeply moved, sweet and penitent as she thanked him. "Was I really out of it?" she inquired.

"Uhhhhhh," he answered. "Yes, as a matter of fact, you were *very* out of it."

"Well," she replied flippantly, "just chalk it up to the Janis Joplin style."

Some several hours later, Toby ran into Janis in the lobby of the hotel. "Listen," she said, "I asked all my friends how I was last night and they told me that I was just fine!"

That evening, August 11, Janis played the Garden State Arts Center in Holmdel, New Jersey, an outdoor arena in a placid setting, with grassy hills surrounding the area, the landscape rich with green.

Arriving early, as usual, we had plenty of time to relax. Full-Tilt, Vince, and Phil horsed around playing

Frisbee on the parking lot while Janis and I watched them from a hill in back of the theater.

When we'd stopped for dinner on the road, Janis had swigged down a drink or two. The bottle she'd taken with her, however, she'd left untouched in the dressing room. "No heavy drinking for me, man," she frowned. "Not before the performance." Suddenly, she said, "There are the guys I've had," and she started to spew off a list of names: "I've had this one and that one . . . and him . . . and him . . . and . . ."

I said, "Come off it, Janis! What are you doing?"

"Oh," she moaned. "I don't know. . . . I was just . . ." Then flipping it off as an afterthought, she launched into a discourse on men. Remarking that she wanted a "strong" man who would "dominate" her, yes, even "knock her around," she added immediately that she wasn't sure she could tolerate that, that she had to do the controlling.

"What a view of a relationship," I muttered.

Ignoring my comment, she said, "That's what I want. . . . I don't know if I could take it. . . . That's what I want. . . . It would never work. . . . Maybe it would work. . . .I need somebody like that. . . . I'd never put up with it."

In the dressing room, once we'd retired there, Janis's mood became more contemplative. She fiddled around with her feathers for a bit, shimmying in front of the mirror, but her face had turned sad and her voice, poignant. There was a couch on one side of the room. Janis sank down on it slowly and started to speak about David Niehaus. "He's the only one I could ever really talk to," she sighed. "I mean, I could really talk to him, and he's just so fine and bright."

"Then why not?" I pleaded. "Why not?"

"I don't know," she groaned. "Can you see me married to a teacher?"

"Yeah. I don't think that's why you let him go."

She looked at me quizzically, but I said no more as to what I meant. Rather, I changed the subject from David directly and brought up the topic of her career.

"You know," I said, "after you make the album, you could start cutting down a bit. What would be the matter with making recordings and just being less on the road? 'Til you figure other things out?"

Janis, of course, had talked about that often and had discussed such a plan with Albert. Certainly, at times, she meant it. How often is somewhat doubtful. At Garden State, all she did was sigh, "I can't do that. . . . I'm afraid." Her statement to Toby Ben about playing smaller halls was not consistent either with this particular exchange:

"Listen, Janis," I said, "at least, maybe to come back to a smaller scale. I mean, Madison Square Garden and all this stuff. You haven't played the Fillmore in ages."

"But Myra, I can't make as much money!"

"Aw, Janis. Enough with the money! The album oughta make you a mint if it's good! How the hell much do you need?"

"Yeah," she mumbled, "maybe you're right. Sure would be nice to play for a hip audience again."

Janis donned a pair of sleek blue pants and slipped on a rhinestone jacket. "Well, here I am again!" she laughed, as we left the room and went back outside.

On the lawn, Rick Bell was relaxing, chatting about going on a camping trip before the recording got under way.

Janis said, "Richard thinks I look younger without these feathers. What do you think?"

"He's right. You wanna be Bessie Smith, be Bessie Smith, but yes, you look younger without them." She nodded and very soon after sauntered off to go onstage.

Driving back to the city later, I was in a limo separate from Janis. When we pulled up in front of the Chelsea, Janis had already entered the bar. Outside on the street, John Fischer said, "Hey, Janis got sick in the car."

"What do you mean?" I said.

"I don't know, man, she had to throw up."

I walked quickly into El Quijote to see what was

going on. Janis was sitting on a bar stool, a vodka and orange juice in front of her, the members of the band, John Cooke and Emmett, and a few other people gathered about.

"What's this about throwing up?" I asked.

"It's nothing," Janis said. "It happens sometimes."

That was news to me. Nor was it "nothing." Janis's face was mottled a weird sickly pink, and the cast of it was pulpy and swollen. I thought she looked terrifyingly ill.

Nobody else seemed to notice a thing. There was just a lot of laughter and the sound of clinking glasses. Somebody said, "Keep on rockin'." Everything as usual.

A wad of fear jamming my chest, I said, "Call me after Boston, Janis. I don't like the way you look."

She shrugged, but not with an air of indifference. Giving her a quick hug, I took one more look at her haunted eyes and the pulpy swell of her face. Then I waved goodbye to the others and walked out of the door. There were uncountable times I spoke to Janis thereafter. That parting moment in El Quijote was the last time I ever saw her.

23

One glance at the gigantic mass that poured into Harvard Stadium on August 12 should have dispelled Janis's concern that her celebrity was endangered. Some forty thousand attended, half with tickets and half by vaulting the walls. The size of it had to be gratifying. Regrettably, on the other hand, the night nearly erupted into a nasty full-scale riot.

The static in the air that evening was not provoked by Janis. Trouble began in the afternoon when the sound equipment was swiped. Other equipment was found, once again to be stolen before the gates were opened. The first band on the bill was late; a local group was slapped onstage while the hunt went on for the necessary system so that Janis could be heard at her best. When the musicians billed to precede her arrived, they obstinately insisted on playing, though the crowd was absolutely seething, restless with waiting for Janis. To make matters worse, the cops on the streets of Cambridge were of a most unpleasant species: mean as they come and armed to the teeth as if hopeful for a clash. Cambridge, it happened, was nervous, what with a recent siege of street action. But the riot squad had gone nuts: this to prepare for the concert—helmets, clubs, dogs, grenades, and, one write-up had it, machine guns. None of that could do anything, of course, but rile up the mood in the arena. And radicals of the lunatic fringe were also up to their stuff. Suspicions were very high that it was they who'd done off with the equipment; supposedly a gaggle of hate-freaks was working its way through the crowd, trying to whip up anger. And the delay was bad enough. Ken Pearson said, "It was like a football stadium full of people who've been told the teams can't show because their uniforms didn't come back from the laundry." By the time Janis got onstage, the whole place was one tensed and dangerous coil, ready to spring in an instant.

It didn't, though the spirit of the crowd remained alarming through at least part of Janis's performance. In spite of the eerie vibrations, however, she was in blazing and magnificent form. That was fortunate for those who were there. Harvard Stadium was the final concert of Janis's life.

Janis took a flight to Texas the following day. I phoned Port Arthur that afternoon, and Mrs. Joplin told me that Janis's flight had been delayed.

"Why, I thought you were coming to Texas!" Mrs. Joplin said warmly. Wary of discussing my concerns, I mumbled that I just couldn't do it.

In answer to a question of mine, Janis's mother then told me that the press was ready and waiting—like a flock of vultures. I bit my lip as she said with anger, "My daughter is being used!"

My irritation with the reunion affair and the way that Janis had planned it increased upon that conversation. The Three Musketeers—Cooke, Neuwirth, and John Fischer—would blast in to Port Arthur on Thursday and the vision, in a way, was uproarious. Just how funny, of course, depended on the point of view. Mine stemmed from the certain knowledge that Janis at bottom didn't want a comedy or to zap it to the folks back home. In one crazy way or another, something was bound to happen, the potential of it even more loaded by the expected commotion with the press.

When Janis called me from the Houston airport during a stop-over, I brought up the subject. "You know, Janis, you maybe should have thought about this a little more. I spoke to your mother, and there are going to be reporters climbing all over you."

"Well, come on down!" she said. "You can come if you want to. I never said you couldn't!"

"I don't have the money," I answered, telling her the truth, but backing away from making it clear that I didn't see that particular trip as comparable to a pleasure cruise.

"Well, call Albert in the country and tell *him* to pay for it."

I had no intention of doing that. She'd flushed her dollars down the sewer for plans she was going to regret. I was bristling and close to saying, "Not on your life. *You* wake up and pay if you wants things to go right."

I said nothing to that effect, however, offering instead an excuse. "Well, I have to be at The Band concert."

"Oh," she replied, resentfully. "Well then, if you can't come here, you can't."

Dropping the entire business, I asked her how she

felt, and made a reference to her sickly appearance
the night that I'd last seen her.

Replying that she was all right, she said she'd had
several drinks in the airport, but was trying, she added,
to take it easy. "I don't want to be crocked when I get
to Port Arthur," she said, her voice a whimsical rasp.
If she was a little high when she called me, she was
far from being drunk, and I prayed she could keep her
intake moderate throughout the days of the trip.

All things being relative, Janis did exactly that,
though for weeks after she left Port Arthur there was
much drivel to the contrary. Nearly everyone there
that weekend was doing well enough at the bottle,
and many of her former classmates, in fact, slurped
away quite heavily. Then, having been good and
drunk, they oozed from their pores with sweaty stories
of Janis as staggeringly blasted—which she was not.
What the local press conveyed (and the national
media as a result) was an almost exclusively bene-
volent atmosphere. To be sure, there was a basis for
the character of those reports. Naturally, Janis was
encircled by a hoopla of attention. The pretense of
pleasantry reigned, and from a handful of sensitive
souls there was definitely extended to her some honest
heartfelt warmth. But true decency at the reunion
and in the talk that followed was about as common as
a Port Arthur snowfall. A few of the remarks were
merely ludicrous; most were riffraff crude, occasionally
out-and-out loathsome (At least two suit-and-tie
citizens down there properly belong on a dunghill.
Smirked one to the other as Janis walked by, "Well,
there goes your claim to immortality.") And right up
from those backwater frustrations came the typical
disgorgement of elaborate fantasy about Janis's behavior during her stay.

Some of the sludge got dumped on Karleen Bennett,
who, sadly, was unable to attend. Janis, she heard, had
been sloppy drunk and talk with her impossible:
incoherent from alcohol, Janis had obviously been on

pills as well—and had brought in all sorts of dope.
"No," Karleen chuckled, "I didn't believe it. I didn't
think she'd come all the way to Port Arthur just to do
that."

Moreover, the Port Arthur cops, I was told, had been
buzzing around with bravado: what a coup it would
be to bust her. Said arrest was not attempted, as it
happened, which is certainly lucky for them, because
Janis, of course, had no dope on her: no pills, no weed,
no nothing. Nevertheless, the investment in believing
that she was dope-ridden to every feather on her head
was powerful. Other talk went around town. One
Port Arthur woman said, "They called her a 'pig' in
high school; they were calling her a 'pig' at the end."

In Port Arthur for a visit at the time, Philip Carter
knew nothing either of the reunion or of Janis's presence until the event was almost over. Hoping to see
her, he dashed to the hotel where the final festivities
had occurred; Janis had already gone. The girls especially were all in a lather. Janis has been *outrageous*
. . . *wild* . . . *cursing* . . . kookier than ever, they
babbled. Mournfully, he said, "I don't think that
anything Janis could have done, conforming or otherwise, ever would have made Port Arthur accept her."

The truth was that Janis's behavior was generally
irreproachable, and the real breaches in dignity
hardly forthcoming from her. That is not to say that
all went smoothly. Quite to the contrary; everything
happened exactly as predicted.

Janis had to have been enormously conflicted by
the attention she received, coveting the sense of her
importance on the one hand and fearful of it on the
other. What was always so under any circumstances
could only have been more acute that week-end, with
her self-deprecation and the anxiety of her guilt
causing her to cringe from the surge of pleasure she
must have felt in being so at the center. Hence, in
what undoubtedly was a more highly charged emotional state than anyone realized, she shunned exces-

sive contact with the media and instead gave a single press conference—which boomeranged.

The over-all tone of that interview was exceptionally gracious. Though her attitude was somewhat predicated on her hunger for the town's acceptance, that made what she said no less mellow and expresssive of a tolerance toward Port Arthur that few Port Arthur inhabitants had ever displayed toward her. Rarely was there a word of bitterness. "Did you entertain in high school?" she was asked. "Only when I walked down the aisles," she quipped, but immediately followed that remark with a serious statement that no, she hadn't, she wasn't then singing in public. Mostly, the interview was full of forgiveness for what, in Janis's adolescence, had surely been unforgivable, and of her emphasis on a willingness to find some grounds for communication with almost anyone, would they have the heart to try the same.

All that aside, in the midst of a half hour's talking, she also shot off three or four sentences that deviated a bit from the general character of her words. She planted a light phrase about dope (by which she meant only grass) in terms of Port Arthur loosening up. At worst, that was incautious, no matter that she might have been right. Two other remarks, however, seemed to take aim at her parents. One concerned her sleeping conditions at the house that weekend. "They put me on a cot this wide!" she said, holding her hands about a foot apart. The other was this: "It's nice to be home, though. They've been very tolerant. When all my friends came over this morning for breakfast, they left." Uttered waggishly, these comments were decidedly quite innocuous as part of the whole, and in no way reflected the dominant nature of her thoughts. That is not to say that they were empty of motive, light sparks, I would think, from Janis's underlying determination to sabotage the weekend. It was unfortunate that she had the enthusiastic help of Port Arthur's Channel 4.

If the station was unable to run more than a minute (which is very unlikely), it surely could have managed an editing job that retained the heart of her words. Instead the locals listened to Janis take what sounded like sideswipes at her parents. The Joplins listened also. Not having been present when the press conference was held, they were ignorant then of the whole. The *Houston Chronicle* would print the entire interview and later the *Port Arthur News*. At the time, the Joplins knew only what they heard when they turned on the tube.

And that was only the curtain-raiser. When Neuwirth returned to New York and I asked him how it had gone, he garbled a series of nervous hip syllables, designed to evade an answer. A little bit later in the day, after I spoke to Janis, I would know why. The weekend indeed had been topped off by the anticipated grandstand performance.

The same night that the interview was telecast, Janis, her sister, Laura, and the entourage skipped out to a place called the Pelican Club, where Jerry Lee Lewis was playing. Backstage, Janis had a clash with Jerry Lee, who made a remark about Laura's appearance. Because Janis's sister is very appealing, the comment was just plain silly, and had reason prevailed would have been dismissed for exactly what it was. Janis, however, had become very fond of Laura. Moreover, the "insult" touched deeply on her own hellish experience, so that Janis took exception to his words, *extreme* exception. In short, she swung back her arm to belt him.

"If you're gonna act like a man," he snarled, "I'll treat ya like one."

That drove Janis wilder still and precipitated some heavy drinking on her part, the only time during that Texas jaunt. Bobby Neuwirth and John Fischer, on the other hand, had been at the tequila since the beginning of the trip. The fault, nonetheless, was Janis's for asking them to come in the first place. With Bobby, I suspect, as the prime inspiration, they'd set off for

Port Arthur as if Janis had issued them an injunction to do what they damned well pleased. Which, in a way, she had. "We were gonna whoop it up," John Fischer told me, "so we were pretty wasted when we got to the airport."

They got more than pretty wasted that night. Although what they did was hardly criminal, it wasn't so terrific either, and by any standards was in sophomoric disregard for what they might provoke. The Joplins had already viewed the TV debacle, which was humiliating. It dug right into their entrails when, on getting up in the morning, they found John Fischer in a drunken snooze on their living room couch and Neuwirth zonked out in the car outside. Had Mrs. Joplin a pesticide for humans on hand, she would have sprayed them on the spot. Lacking that, the pair was invited to leave—quickly. Mrs. Joplin was understandably very angry at Janis, and there ensued a particularly fractious argument, though the relationship between Janis and her parents was healed within days after she returned to Larkspur.

That, on the surface, was what had happened in Port Arthur. Janis had enacted all the ordinary courtesies, had been raucous here and there, but mostly well-mannered. She had given a press interview that was not understood. She had sped through one night of wildness and had worked events toward a fight with her mother. And then she had departed, relieved perhaps to go home to Larkspur, where she would think a lot about the visit, then less, then not at all. So it appeared, and the journey struck no one of great consequence.

But a mixed and crucial purpose had taken Janis to Texas for that foolishness. It had started as a mission of revenge, and her warpaint and her tribe were its instruments. It had turned to a mission of atonement and a trembling hunt that would test for love. The hope for acceptance was burning in her, and it is impossbile that she could have done other than look back on the past as in no previous trip to her birthplace. The memories stirred up had to have been painful, the emotions mobilized, devastating; the shame, the hunger, the guilt, the rage, the cruelty of it all, overwhelming.

Janis had been severely disturbed by the clash with her parents and was the first to say that she'd been responsible for the unpleasantness that had developed. After telling me what had happened, she groaned, "I should have known it, man, I never should have taken those people." Making an attempt to shrug it off, she murmured an indifferent, "Well, you can't go home again, right?" Then she sighed and turned her thoughts again to the friction with her mother. Mrs. Joplin believes that in the immediacy of the situation she overreacted and said hostile things to Janis she did not really mean. That is most certainly so. The way in which Janis may have incorporated her mother's anger is altogether separate.

One other incident occurred during the four days of Janis's stay. According to Mrs. Joplin, there was a quiet moment between her daughter and herself in which Janis said, "Mother, you were right and I was wrong!"

Mrs. Joplin did not elaborate as to what Janis may have meant.

Sometime in late July Janis had met a young man named Seth Morgan, the scion of a wealthy, prestigious New York family and a student at Berkeley. The encounter had been characteristic: casual of feeling and brief. He'd stayed a day or two; he'd left, whisked off by Janis into a mental haze with uncountable quick affections, another one of which, in fact, had been abruptly terminated on the night that Seth materialized. At the time, she'd also been in the throes of carrying on about Kris. During the days she'd spent in New York earlier that month, she'd gone through her melancholy reflection about the loss of David Niehaus, which had not deterred her from the longing reference to other men as well. Seth Morgan, however, had not been mentioned.

Yet hardly had Janis returned to Larkspur following the trip to Port Arthur when Seth reappeared to resume the affair, and overnight, as it were, she was smitten. Perhaps a day and a half had passed before she and Seth were exchanging vows of love. In less than forty-eight hours they had begun to speak of marriage.

A little over six weeks would pass, all the rest there would be to Janis's life, and the great portion of those days she was in Hollywood recording. Seth remained in the Bay Area, excepting weekends, when he flew to Los Angeles to join her. He thinks he attended possibly eight recording sessions. Twice, though the trips were brief, he also went to New York. Some question further exists as to the extent of his presence in Larkspur, even while Janis was still there. According to Lyndall Erb, Seth maintained his own apartment in Berkeley for at least a while and could not really be said to have been living in the Larkspur house until Janis was already in Hollywood, at which point it hardly mattered which quarters he called his residence. Whatever the case, the amount of time in which their felings were established was clearly very short.

All year Janis's mind had been reeling with thoughts of permanence, and the men were, in many ways, no more than the shadows of an elusive symbol to which her free-floating fantasies affixed themselves in all but random fashion. Relatively speaking, her most recent lovers were decidedly of a different breed, more mature, more independent, more on her level than the types to which she'd been drawn before. That signified, in theory, a change in Janis, a disposition to involve herself as she hadn't been able in the past. Her attachments, nonetheless, had been tenuous at the very best. In some instances they were impossible, as was so with Kris and with a lover in 1969 who—it simply happened—was married. At all times her sentiments lacked the ring of the genuine, no matter

the passion of her words. One does not interchange
the objects of real love so rapidly, as was her habit.
Even her feeling for David Niehaus, perhaps the most
honest she ever had, seemed to be rather shallow, a
fantasy brought alive by the commitment to the *idea*
of love, but too inconstant, too replaceable, to be considered love at all. Janis's aptitude for the sudden
switching of affections was absolutely astonishing. As
for the affair with Seth, he naturally does not like the
idea that it might have been less than deep. Naturally,
too, he does not like being dismissed as just the last
object at the end of the line, which is how some of
Janis's friends are inclined to regard him. They are
both right and wrong.

Press references to Seth as an "affluent easterner"
after Janis's death disturbed him, he says. His reasons
essentially are vague, because he himself believes that
his potential independence was crucial to what developed between them. If Seth did not yet have money
to what could be called a substantial degree, his
family most certainly did. He would be very well-off
in the future, and Janis need not brew up the terror
that he was around with a mind to financial exploitation, always one of her greatest, or most oft-spoken
fears. Seth also was not a Joplin fan, proof at least as
he saw it that it was not her fame to which he was
drawn. But the money aspect made a difference indeed. To any number of her friends, Janis drew attention to Seth's ability to pay the dinner checks. When
she seemed to be serious about marriage, she stressed
that it wasn't her income he would rely on for support.
They'd wed in Mexico, then go on a cruise. And the
cost of it wouldn't be hers. "He's gonna use *his*
bread!" she told Dave Richards. "How about *that*,
honey!"

Janis was taken with Seth's background too, that
financial and social status something she could speak
about to others with pride. Seth said that Janis urged
him to stay in school. She wanted to be married to a
college graduate—she wanted to be "respectable."

Beyond those most visible aspects leading to Janis's apparent involvement were some personal elements about Seth, just as important in triggering the affair and more so in dictating its fundamental character, which was anything but smooth.

Janis had a conversation with Bob Gordon in August —she could have known Seth no more than a week— in which she somberly voiced her concern that career and marriage could be combined, her words to the effect that to make it work she'd need a "very strong man." Seth, she said, "treated her better" than anyone she'd ever met and made her feel "more like a woman" than any man had done. Seth, however, had this to say about Janis and one of her previous paramours: "She loved him in a way. . . . He was mean to her." Perhaps he needed the disclaimer he offered as an explanation. "She was just very romantic," he said.

There is nothing retiring about Seth Morgan. He has a burly kind of attractiveness and an earthy aggression in his manner. As the embodiment of Janis's fantasies that made him especially suitable. He, in turn, most certainly had needs of his own, which emerged to join in that very explosive delirium that Janis and he would name as romance. One would surely have cause to wonder at a flame ignited so quickly. But then who is to say that the imitation of passion is any less vivid than passion itself or to question, with Janis in particular, that she could not work her emotions into an intensity as powerful as those nurtured slowly and brought to life by the more common sympathies that make for love.

Janis appeared to be tremendously happy. The house during those August days in Larkspur was quiet, which Seth found rather surprising. When their relationship was tranquil, Janis padded about contentedly, attending to domestic matters sometimes, but being with Seth most of all. They talked properly at breakfast, lingering over coffee, then discussing events as couples do, after reading the morning

papers. They ambled around the woods, spent time at
the beach and the movies. Seth thought Janis was
a prude. At the drive-ins, she wouldn't mess around
in the car. As for Janis's conception of the future, it
could have been gardens and white picket fences.
Marriage, of course, would be passion eternal, not an
hour of boredom to blight its perfection. Mostly, it
would be held together by an inviolate loyalty. That
was at least one issue that brought turmoil to the relationship, its moments of calm merely clouding the
fitful tempo that pounded heatedly underneath. Seth
was twenty-one at the time. However serious he might
then have believed their affair to be, he later admitted some doubts that he could have accommodated
himself to what he apparently felt were her puritanical restrictions. Nor was he above testing them out, to
see what Janis was willing to take. Their days were
turbulent in many ways. Janis was caught in the
middle of friction between Seth and Lyndall, who
was still living in the house. Each regarded the other
as a nuisance, and each was facile with a host of
solid-sounding excuses to disguise the competition
that was the basic source of the clash. Lyndall, however, was more on the defensive, which made it seem
that Seth's motives might have had a double edge.

Apart from that, Seth and Janis were engaged in a
variety of dramas, an episode always handily arising
to sustain the *Sturm und Drang.* Janis, of a sudden,
would worry if once again she was being used, but if
that caused her a genuine fear, she must have
cherished it too—because there could be anger and
remorse and victories and defeats, the lunacy of
melodrama on which she thrived. Then the turmoil
would recede and she would be happy again.

Their time together was interrupted when Janis
went down to Los Angeles to start selecting material
for the album and was gone for several days. Seth also
made a trip to New York and was supposed to call me
during his visit. Preceding his absence from Larkspur,
Janis had phoned me and had made a great point of

her wish that Seth and I meet, coyly unspecific, however, in refusing to say just why.

"Now lissen," she'd said. "About my BOYFRIEND! He's not like the others!"

"What's that supposed to be?" I'd laughed. "An apology?"

"No, no, no. I just don't want you to be surprised when you meet him. He'll call you and I just want you to know, he's *different*. . . . I mean, he's not a pretty young boy."

"Is he ugly?"

"NO! He's just not a pretty young boy. . . . Ya know what I mean!"

"Hey, Janis. What's going on?"

"Oh, nothing special. . . . I just want you to meet him, that's all."

Whatever his reasons, Seth failed to call, and I didn't meet him at that time. While he was still in New York, Janis phoned me again, wanting to know if I'd heard from him, taking the fact that I hadn't to mean that Seth had permanently left her. "Oh, well," she sighed, "I guess he found another girlfriend." Somehow, her voice lacked the tremor of profound disappointment. Nonetheless, within hours, Seth was back in Larkspur and Janis was once more madly in love.

During one of our conversations about Seth, however, Janis had said something extremely bizarre. She'd offered to share Seth with me. Putting it in her inimitable fashion, she'd said, "You can fuck him if you want to," and had said it very brightly at that.

Had I, at any point, been attracted to one of Janis's men, I wouldn't have given him a flirtatious glance, much less encouraged a tumble in the hay. Janis's jealousy of other women was extraordinary, except when they were homosexual. Given the inflexibility of my heterosexual orientation, which she well knew, and considering that Seth was more than a passing fancy, what she said to me was simply astounding. Consistent with her jealousy, she should have issued me a venomous warning and, in any case, hardly an offer. It is true, of course, that she had to expect that I would quickly decline.

"Jesus Christ!" I'd said. "This is *me*. What in the hell's the matter with you?"

Janis then laughed and quickly added that she didn't know why she'd said it.

Terribly startled, I took her remark at that moment as an impulsive outburst of gross self-mockery but was puzzled still as to what in the world could possibly have provoked such an outlandish comment. But Janis's candor was primitive always, which is to say it was primal. What was "up front" was her infant psyche; her most active emotional life was at a level most of us leave behind. The self-mocking aspect notwithstanding, the remark was very suggestive of the original *ménage à trois*. Janis frequently referred to me as her "Jewish mother," and it is hard to avoid the thought that her words represented a conciliatory gesture toward someone for whom I was merely a surrogate. It is not my role that matters, however.

Seth said that Janis talked some about the reunion. She referred to her mother's anger and said she was sorry she'd put on that show, by bringing those people to Port Arthur. She told Seth little about her father, saying only that the two of them had the same first name. She joked about it.

Meanwhile, Janis's demeanor revealed scarcely a sign that anything was wrong. Her general behavior flickered madly, as always. Around Seth she was soft, impressionable, reserved. But the Pearl façade could spring up in an instant: the feathers, the beads, the car, the yelling, the cursing, the crude, tough bluster, the dizzying splash of the superstar. Surely there was nothing unusual about that.

Janis, Seth tried to tell me, even cut down on her drinking, although in no way could she have contained it for long. Actually, the extent of her control, by Seth's contradictory account to me, sounded very dubious. He recalled an evening when Janis watched Kris Kristofferson on TV and worked herself into a state, using that as an excuse to get drunk. Apparently, she now and then celebrated her happiness by doing exactly the same. It seems, in general, that the period of control was ludicrously short, appearing impressive to Seth only by contrast with the routine he'd observed in July when Janis got drunk in the morning, passed out by midafternoon, and got up in the early evening to start on the bottle again. Moreover, it still seemed vague that her pattern was really modified. "Well," Seth finally attested, "at night she'd drink, but that was a big improvement. She was really happy, and she said how extraordinary it was that I was making her happy. And she said she didn't feel that she needed to drink and that she didn't want to." In the same flow of words, he said, "See, she got me into it—drinking. I drank before that, but I mean that all-day-long drinking routine. . . ."

This, however, is definite. There was, as yet, no other drug use at all. A vial of low-milligram Valium was in a medicine cabinet, but Seth cannot remember her taking any of those and, as he stated, "she swore against heroin."

And so the August days went by. From Janis's opulent imagination had poured the dream of love, and to the degree that her feelings were illusory, illusion would suffice. There was ahead of her the opportunity to be like others, or so she fancied. Marriage, according to her concept, would also be a form of restraint, which she'd seemed to be seeking on the one occasion in her life when she'd planned to marry before. Surely, the timing of her marriage plans was striking, following months of despondency and severe emotional turmoil, and then the trip to Port Arthur. Seth came along at a moment of stress, his uniqueness, his traits, his character, his being, who he was in his own right, secondary to that fact. Her mental manipulation was sufficient to make him the anchor of her longing. The emotional experience of the affair was what mattered; Janis was happy. Others might wonder and not believe, so she spoke of it always with lightness. Probably she was fearful of looking foolish. Perhaps she was bothered by her own chafing doubt . . . and more.

Janis saw Julie Paul and her husband that August, when they were performing at the Matrix. She told them of her impending marriage but mocked herself as usual, and there was something about her laughter and certainly her words that carried a conviction of imminent disaster. It was all very humorously put, that ripping around the roads on Seth's motorbike she would have a fatal accident. "Think of my career!" she yelped. "The short and happy life of Janis Joplin ending crashed on a motorcycle!"

I cannot believe that there was never a helplessness in her eyes or one brooding sigh to give a clue that something might be amiss. I suspect that the opinions of those around her who insisted that nothing showed were grounded in poor perception. Recovery for Janis had its limits. Nonetheless, there is just no question that her mood had definitely improved by the measure of what it had been. Certainly nothing she said to me was cause for extreme alarm.

Janis, for one thing, did not state to me that she actually planned on marriage, an amazing omission, considering our relationship and also the frequency with which we spoke. Normally Janis would never have failed to tell me of a major decision in her life, or even a minor one, for that matter. However, her first talks with Seth about said wedding included ideas of media coverage. "Well, we'll get married," she said, "and we'll get someone from *Time* to be there." Seth had objected. Janis, perhaps to oblige him and thinking that I might tell the press, never directly said to me exactly how involved she supposedly was. It is possible, moreover, that she might have feared my reaction. She yammered to me constantly about being in love, but hedged at the mention of marriage in any serious context. Once she joked that she might do it; I ignored the hint. I cannot imagine that had she told me, I would have been frightened as a result. It is only likely that I would have felt something was very unusual. Needless to say, I would have been curious to meet Seth Morgan.

The point is that I had no reason to consider anything out of the ordinary and only cause to be relieved —which I both was and wasn't. My acute concern of the months before had definitely subsided. My thought of speaking to Albert remained the same: Janis might be feeling better; but she was still an appalling mess, and my tolerance of her social environment, I'll call it, had nearly come to an end. Also, once in a while, I had one troubling memory, and that was of the way she'd looked the last time that I saw her.

John Cooke was offended that I might mention that Janis had vomited in the car that night. "I hope you're not going to put anything in the book about Janis throwing up, are you, Myra?" he sniffed with indignant distaste. "Maybe she ate a bad hot dog. All people tend to look pale after they throw up. I don't think it's important."

But Janis had not looked pale. And it is impossible for me to regard her appearance as having been unimportant, not in view of the following incident:

One afternoon at the office that August—it might have been the very end of the month—I received a call from Toby Ben. His voice was agitated, simply loaded with noticeable anxiety.

"Myra," he pleaded, "isn't there anything you can do? I mean, did you see the way Janis looked that night in El Quijote? Did you see it? That funny pink!"

Shaken to hear confirmed the reality of that ghoulish coloring, I replied, "Yes, I saw it," and nervously added, "Why?"

"Well, you have to do something!" he demanded. "You're the only one who cares!"

I protested that such was not true, that others

cared, but just failed to see. "That's not true, Toby," I said. "It's more complicated than that. You don't know . . ."

Toby snapped, "It's *not* more complicated! Does that girl have any real friends? I mean *real friends!*"

"Well," I started to say, "in California, there's . . ."

"What does *that* mean? One big party!"

"Oh, Toby," I groaned, "I don't know. I don't know what goes on or who . . ."

"Lissen," he retorted abruptly, "you better talk to Albert, because that girl is going to die!"

Toby reeled off the remark with an insistence that was absolutely chilling. I was aware of a sudden clamminess; my mind resisted what he said. It wasn't that I rejected his words as being wholly absurd. Indeed I did not. The abnormal flush in her face had been awful, and watching Janis at any time should have summoned feelings of eventual disaster. To know that someone else had noticed how ill she'd looked that night inevitably boosted my anxiety. His urgency was what I balked at. Toby wasn't thinking of dope at all. He knew that Janis was clean, and nothing he expressed had anything to do with a suspicion that her state might change. I couldn't believe that such a catastrophe was imminent. Maybe it was his very certainty that made me feel it was impossible as something that could happen in the immediate future. From somewhere it popped into my mind that she had about a year. So I told him exactly that: she'd die too soon if things didn't change, but still, I protested, there was time. I said yes, that I would talk to Albert, as I'd intended all along.

Several times, Toby repeated the warning. "She's gonna die if you don't do something! She's gonna die!"

Uncomfortable, I nonetheless assured him. "Not yet. She's not going to die yet. A year, Toby, and we'll do something way before that."

For all the possible exaggeration involved in

Toby's specific warning, he had made me very uneasy. If I'd been inclined to be skeptical of the prediction of imminent death, I wasn't about to ignore it in terms of the over-all context of that call. Whatever I planned on telling Albert, it had been decidedly expanded. Feeling shaky, I walked down the hall and asked his secretary if she knew when he would be in. She didn't.

Janis went to Los Angeles to begin recording the first week of September. She stayed at the Landmark Hotel, as did all the members of the band, and John Cooke, Phil Badella, and Vince Mitchell.

The recording sessions were a strain, but no more than had been expected. In some ways, they were actually less arduous than the studio situations of the past. Partially, that was because of the band, partially because of producer Paul Rothchild, who certainly worked well with Janis. Just the same, he did not have the obstacles that John Simon or Gabriel Mekler had been forced to deal with. If everything in the studio went well, it was due to all involved, as was the artistic superiority of the *Pearl* album itself, though Paul did a brilliant job of getting on record what was recorded after Janis was gone.

There was a problem in the choice of material. Paul and Janis spent an extraordinary number of hours listening to tapes and making decisions as to songs. With the potential there for an album of a quality beyond anything Janis had previously achieved, she was especially anxious about the results. The repertoire would be crucial, the tension of choosing it considerable.

Seth, of course, came down to Los Angeles periodically. Drama continued between them, thrashed up most often over the issue of Seth's refusal to be with Janis as often as she wished, with Seth enacting his role quite well in Janis's fiery theater. His claim, however, is surely true that he felt like an outsider in Los Angeles because everything was directed toward music. Janis would become jealous and angry, her passionate propensities demanding that her needs be continually met, but burning also to foment the visions of betrayal, without which she was strangely uncomfortable.

"I had this dream," she told me one day. "And you know how when you want someone, you overdo it! And you're just all over them and you land up pushing them away! It was something like that, and I woke up crying!"

In our frequent conversations, though, there was nothing in Janis's voice that betrayed the despondency I'd witnessed all summer. Yet, at least in early September, the memory of that swollen pink face had not left me; Toby's call burned in my thoughts, unforgettable.

Speaking to Albert about Janis on the phone struck me as impossible. On the one hand, I was inclined to dismiss my own concern. On the other, it had built dramatically. On the basis of what Janis professed by way of her state of mind, my worry might be out of proportion and was bound, I thought, to seem so to Albert. In a sense, it *was*—in terms of the reality as we presumed it to be. I stuck to my decision to speak to him anyway. Toby's warning specifically might have been without foundation; the same could not be said about what he'd intimated in the rest of that call. And the prediction, in any case, mattered, if only as part of his other words and the many things that were on my mind.

I was pestered by a constant feeling that Albert or myself should go to California, and I had more time than he. My ideas went further than that. She needed a saner environment, and the disappearance of several people would be a great improvement. She needed professional help, perhaps even to be in a hospital. Of this I was simply certain: Janis was more susceptible to changes than she'd ever been before. Well, there she was in the midst of recording, this to be her outstanding album and, after all, there was her career.

This happened in 1969: before Albert spoke to Janis and got her to see Dr. Rothschild, I called one of the state agencies concerned with addiction and spoke to a psychiatrist on the staff. I explained the difficulty of dealing with Janis without saying exactly who she was, and asked him what he suggested.

"Well," he said, "if you can get her to do it, she'll just have to go into a halfway house and register as an addict like everybody else." His particular directives as to methods of help are not what was important.

I said, "But she'll never do it! She just bought a new house; she'd have to stop her career, which she'll never do, and she's going to form a new band!"

He said, "Listen, miss, I don't know who it is you're talking about, but not her money or her house or her career or her band is going to make one bit of difference when she's dead!"

Dr. Rothschild said something similar, adding, "I thought if she could have stayed in New York . . . but all she could talk about was her house and the new band."

The needle, of course, was not now in question, making what I planned on saying of an altogether different nature. So there would be moments I would think the whole thing foolish. To say the least, I was also very nervous at the prospect of explaining to Albert. I simply couldn't guess how he would react to such drastic words.

Janis was already in Los Angeles—I don't think for very long—when Albert came into the office one day, and I requested some of his time. What hadn't been possible for months finally seemed about to happen: he was definite in saying we would talk before the day was over. A lineup of appointments had him busy throughout the afternoon. The phone calls he received must have mounted to a hundred. By six-thirty, all the office personnel had left. Albert was still on the phone. I waited. It was nearly eight before I got into his office.

Scared half out of my wits at what I was about to

say, I thought I'd tap out his mood first and went over a few minor things that had nothing to do with my real purpose. Albert, as it happened, was especially gracious. So finally I said, "It's really Janis I want to talk to you about."

Albert peered at me with interest and sat back comfortably in his chair, everything in his presence and manner conveying an unusual receptivity.

"Well," I began nervously, "the thing is, she's getting better and she's getting worse."

To my astonishment, he answered, "I know."

The deep, relieved breath I took at that moment just before opening my mouth to speak was interrupted by the ring of the telephone. The call was from Mo Ostin, at that time president of Warner Bros. Records.

"Let me get this call over with," Albert said, "and then we'll talk."

He walked out of his office to finish the call at his secretary's desk. It must have been an hour he was on the phone, maybe even longer than that. I had not eaten dinner; neither had Albert. Wearily, he lumbered back into the office and sank down in his chair to resume our talk. His exhaustion was apparent. Shaking his head, almost painfully, he mumbled, "Listen, I really want to talk about this. . . . I'm just too tired now. . . . Do you think we can do it later?"

I said, "Sure," and rose from my seat to go home.

After that my fear waned. In the general sense, I felt no different. Janis's nonsense jabber, her happy laughter, I'd heard it all before. An alleged love, a great band, a fine record, I dismissed those things as superfluous. She was exactly what I said to Albert, both better and worse. But the immediate panic dissolved. My thoughts of going to Los Angeles never really disappeared; mostly I merely pushed them aside. I would talk to Albert when the chance came up. What matter if it was next week, in two weeks, or three. Off and on, I would say to myself that if that passed, well, it could wait until I saw Janis again, as I would when she'd be in New York in the late autumn. As Toby later cried, "My God! I didn't really think she was going to die! I don't know why I felt that when I phoned!" I had no reason to take Toby's words seriously, no cause to think myself anything but overly alarmed and suggestible. It was like this: neither Albert nor I had the vaguest notion that Janis had picked up a needle again until she was dead. There were people in California who knew! . . . No one said a word to us.

Obviously, there is no way to know if something could have been done, and certainly no way to be certain that the same thing wouldn't have happened at another time in the future. Still, I, at least, was unable to help but manipulate events as they might have occurred, to say no, it needn't have been.

As for the silence, it stemmed from innocence, naiveté, and disbelief. There was the circumstance of Jimi Hendrix's death and the natural assumption that such a repetition was too extraordinary to occur. But death aside, she was using, and wasn't that enough? Well, there was hardly any time to think—for most. And even for those who had some time, there was a conviction that it was an inconsequential tampering that would certainly pass: Janis would stop as soon as the sessions were over. There was a host of reasons. The silence came from human frailty. But so had the silence before.

Many months later I was talking to Toby Ben and explaining the exceptional circumstances that bore so greatly on that most understandable and final failure to speak. "O.K.," Toby said. "I believe you. Honestly, I really do. But I just want to know one thing: even before, did anybody *ever* call you like I did, did anybody *ever* talk to you, did anybody ever say *anything* that they were concerned about her at all?"

Confusion still exists as to the exact date that it all began. Some, in California, found out before others. A few, in reality, may not have actually known at all, but merely thought so in the aftermath. There were those who were completely ignorant, had no more idea than we. Certainly a mental cloudiness descended in the anguish of emotional reaction to what ultimately happened. Nonetheless, I am fairly certain that what I report here is correct. Janis picked up the needle possibly as early as the eleventh of September, definitely before the death of Jimi Hendrix, which was on the eighteenth. The question, of course, is not the precise minute when, but the dreadful, mysterious why.

Staying at the Landmark Hotel was Peggy Caserta, one of the addicted girls whom Janis had refused, for the most part, to see through all those previous months when she hadn't been using. The connection who supplied Peggy and sometimes Janis in the past, came around periodically, the goodwill merchant about his business. I had not known it before, but Peggy had been in New York on one occasion that summer and had visited with Janis then. I dismiss it as the most outside of possibilities that something, unbeknownst to anyone, might have happened at that time. Peggy has sworn to me no; it would seem final that Janis did not start shooting up again until three weeks, add a fraction, prior to the date on which she died.

Before Janis stopped using, there had been, between the two women, something Peggy believed to be a profound friendship.* They had also sexual bonds. Seth Morgan blithely said, "Peggy was the girlfriend Janis most admired. . . . She was very much like Janis." It is not incidental that Janis also had ties with a girl in New York whose physical resemblance was such that she was sometimes mistaken for Janis herself. As for the former relationship, it was consid-

---

* The nature of Peggy Caserta's relationship with Janis has been distorted (and its importance to Janis greatly overemphasized) in a book by Peggy and Dan Knapp published in the spring of 1973, crudely titled *Going Down With Janis* (Lyle Stuart).

ered a close one in California. I do not doubt that in a
way it was, as I do not doubt the feelings shared between Janis and her other addicted companions. But
it clicked to the rituals of needles and cottons and the
jabbing of veins, and there is no escaping that fact. It
strikes me as rather questionable that real friendship
can thrive in a context like that, although its founda-
tions were not that much gloomier than a good many
of Janis's other relationships. Peggy believed she loved
Janis, and, by a certain definition, she did. Let us say
there was *emotion* between them, and complex emotion at that. "I got comfort from her," Peggy said. "I
thought if she digs me, I must be groovy. She was so
much hipper. A lot of people sought me out, because
she was my friend. . . . Her death took my confidence
away." She said she didn't quite mean that. "We were
like butterflies into the flame," she sighed.

In any case, Janis had not quite severed the association, but relatively speaking, it had come to an end.
Then she saw Peggy at the hotel and set herself to a
process like the one she'd enacted with Sunshine five
or so months before.

She called Peggy, indignantly demanding that she
move to another hotel. I gather there were several
calls of that nature. Predictably, the plea for heroin
came next. Peggy said no; then finally succumbed.
Later, she would torture herself with guilt and name
that as a reason for the continuance of her own habit.

There must indeed have been enmity in that trans-
action. In Janis, there was most assuredly venom in
making Peggy feel that she held the cards to what
Janis herself would do. In Peggy, there was anger as
well. Janis had rejected her. Moreover, when Janis
had kicked, she had left Peggy a large amount of
dope. Peggy had stopped using at the time. Walking
away clean herself, Janis had bestowed on her "friend"
the means of destruction. That was a gesture of hatred, quite apart from the fact that Peggy had the op-
tion to discard it. Such was the nature of the exchange
between them in September. Those hostile implica-

tions hardly bypassed Peggy, or she wouldn't have re-acted negatively to Janis's first request. The fault, however, wasn't hers, her eventual agreement to Janis's plea, an enabler to a choice already made. Were there not the circumstance of her presence, Janis would have found another source, perhaps not that day, but the next. What Janis said to Peggy was, "If I can't shoot one shot and stop, then I don't have it together."

Janis danced on happily, noticeably down at times, but only in the way of her ordinary moodiness. She was lonely in Los Angeles when Seth wasn't there. The members of the band did not really like to go bouncing around town. Janis was left with nothing to do. In solitude, perhaps, may have lurked the shadows of a brooding melancholy.

In August, of course, Janis had expressed her conflict over the choice between career and marriage. If that indecision remained, and it undoubtedly did, she said little of it in September, but rather proceeded with marital plans and discussed those at length with Bob Gordon.

The first of those conversations occurred at a dinner with Seth present, and it focused on the financial conditions of matrimony. Janis joked about Seth's trust funds. Wouldn't she get half of that money? Indeed she would not, Bob laughed. But, Bob said, he would get half of *her* earnings, current income, and trust-fund moneys not categorized the same under the community property laws of California. The humor faded— for Janis. Bob thought Seth looked amused. Later, Bob told Janis that a premarital agreement could be made to waive mutual property rights. Janis requested that such an agreement be drafted.

Janis's decision seemed to be firm, if one could judge by what she said. To Seth, Janis indicated that she wanted to wind down her career. They would have a child that year. She had made her choice. She would record and perform occasionally but wanted done with the constant insanity of the road.

Apropos of that particular subject, that was the time of year, that late summer and fall of 1970, when promoters and hall managers around the country had reached a height of anxiety about presenting Janis. To counteract it, an open letter was prepared in our office that the booking agency would use as expected resistance arose. In all likelihood, the hall managers were gripped by at least some specific fears. A few perhaps were afraid of violence. None looked kindly on the possibility of property damage they thought might result in the midst of stirred-up disorder. But in a realistic light, those reluctant to book her would not have seen such a serious threat, since no real trouble had ever occurred. Rationality, however, was not ruling their mood. Rather, Janis had become a symbol. The hall managers, in many cases, bent to the will of their communities, and in conservative communities there stirred unnamable fears ill-understood by the communities themselves. That became especially clear to me when I saw an article from Texas that a ban on rock groups in Houston had been lifted with these exceptions: "The Doors, for one, because of the trouble they had in Miami, and Janis Joplin, *for her attitude in general.*" (Italics mine.)

The letter, in any event, was to be accompanied by statements from sympathetic promoters, anything to quiet apprehension, quotes if they could be found. On the very afternoon that I was working on a first draft, a bunch of reviews from Janis's clipping service was delivered to my desk. Hoping I might find some usable words. I opened the package immediately. A write-up in the *Cambridge Phoenix* of the Harvard Stadium concert lay right on top the pile. Its opener was a quote, all right, dear Janis's own: "My music ain't supposed to make you want to riot! My music's supposed to make you want to fuck!"

That remark was grimly invoked by writer Jon Landau after Janis's death in a brilliant reflection about Janis's willingness to be the person of audience fantasy, which she was much more than he knew.

But good grief! For that quote to land before me as it did on the day I first saw it!

"Oh, Jesus Christ!" I howled.

Albert walked into my office. Giggling, I showed him the article, saying, "How's *this* quote? I'll use it right at that beginning!"

Albert snickered, "No, send it to Spiro Agnew and be sure to tell him to show it to his kids!"

That very day I almost tried speaking to Albert again, then suddenly changed my mind. The incident with the quote was just too ludicrous, too incompatible with such somber thoughts. Another time would have to do.

In the meantime, my impression that Janis's spirits were up, continued. That feeling was not consistent, but by the measure of the summer's depression, there was nothing inordinate about the occasional moments of melancholy here and there. Most of our conversations had to do with Seth—in one way or another.

"Hey, I wanna ask you something," Janis said one night. "Did you read *The Sensuous Woman?*"

"WHAT?"

"You don't have to get all huffy," she snapped. "I just asked you a question!"

"Well, what the hell are you reading *that* for?"

"Lissen," she said testily. "I didn't ask you to ask me why I was reading it. I asked you if *you* read it."

I hadn't, as it happened, but sort of guessing what was coming, I said, "I skimmed it in a bookstore. How could you buy stuff like that? Did you buy it?"

"Well . . . uh . . . what I wanna ask you is, was there anything in there you didn't know?"

"Nope!"

"Hmmmmm," she muttered. "Hmmmm . . . well, there wasn't anything in there *I* didn't know either."

"Oh, there *couldn't* have been." Under my breath, I snickered, "You phony."

"What'd you call me?"

"Noth . . . Janis . . . I called you Janis."

"You bitch! You're laughing at me!"

"I'm not laughing at you," I choked.

Quickly, she changed the subject and said she was reading *Little Big Man*, at John Cooke's suggestion, John being big on Indians, for whom he feels great compassion.

"I'm sure it's better than *The Sensuous Woman*," I said.

During another call, Janis did tell me that she was drinking too much and that it was affecting her voice. Once she phoned worried about the polls, her anxiety stimulated by a report from *Melody Maker* that she had slipped to third place. Another day she called and said, "Now, I don't want you to think badly of me because I want to know this and I'm not worrying or anything, but do you think I'll still be first in the *Playboy* poll this year?" She told me, on occasion, that recording was hard; she spoke of her concern about repertoire.

Was it the career? Was the drop in the polls so terrifying, a symbolic withdrawal of love that her heart just couldn't bear? But the polls did not appear until after she'd started on junk again. Well, then, the anguish of deciding between career and marriage? The tension of recording? The pull of addiction itself? An independent power that flicked up to compel her, for no reason but its own? Five months is not a very long time to be off heroin, and there was the presence of Peggy to tempt her. With the pressure of all those circumstances, would that not explain it, that to still all those myriad conflicts—the stress, the pull, the worry —she would jam a needle in a vein and with that gain some quiet?

Six times in the past Janis had overdosed, five from heroin. She knew people, of course, who had died from smack. There was Nancy Gurley in particular, with whom Janis identified so acutely that her death could not help but have provoked in Janis a vivid sense of her possible own. Granted, it is doubtful that anyone can really comprehend his or her own mortality. Granted, the infantilism of the junkie, which may lessen that comprehension more, which may also make for a concept of death as just a going to sleep. (The term "nodding out" is pointedly derivative of exactly what the child believes death actually to be. In a way, every heroin high is a death of sorts and, beyond the metaphor, a certain reality. The death of feeling is undeniable. A junkie is quite literally "out of this world.") That Janis conceived of death to be such, the never-never land of dreams, I would think almost certain. And yet the prospect of death through the needle was anything but beyond her grasp. Intensifying her awareness, there had been Dr. Rothschild's warning, stated with extra emphasis to make it clear to her just what she was doing. He hadn't said she might die from junk as long as she chose to continue; he'd told her it was certain, and the variable merely when. The infantile belief that she was invulnerable may not have passed completely, but it had been mightily shaken. That was part of the reason she'd stopped. She could not have opened that door, not at the first prick of the needle, without a powerful alertness to the possibilities. There were these distinct differences from the days of the past: her attitude toward junk had changed, and she deplored it; she no longer was under the delusion that one could use and not get addicted; most of all, she was keenly aware of the risk of death. Indeed, she was *so* aware that she'd been stating the connection between the needle and death in her threats throughout the summer. But Janis had really done no more than spell out the nature of the beast.

What I am saying becomes very sticky, so that I wish to make one thing extremely clear. No information I have contradicts the validity of the coroner's ruling of accidental death; I regard it, in fact, as inarguable on the basis of what I know, which is a very great deal. What I mean to say is that the term "accidental" is only a legal technicality, limited to the conclusion that at that decisive moment when Janis used the needle for the very last time she had no conscious

intention to do herself in. But accurate though that
conclusion may be, it has nothing to do with what
happened. One tells the truth or one lies, to begin
with. Also, the truth is important, in this case especially. That is because of the astonishing and
widespread refusal to recognize what Janis herself
acknowledged at any number of times, not only in a
personal regard, but, barring the circumstances in
special milieus, in regard to the entire phenomenon of
addiction.

Grace Slick offered the analogy of being hit by a car,
that also to serve as a lesson in how Janis's death
should be viewed: Drugs? "When someone gets killed
in an auto crash, it doesn't make me stop driving."
Summoning himself to his full stature, the Richelieu of
Rock, Jerry Garcia, proclaimed that accidents happen
to everybody, driving an auto, walking down the
stairs, and portentously (what else?) the payoff for
life is death, and besides that, her life was a good one,
he said knowledgeably, because, after all, she went
out happy; Janis would have preferred people partying, so no one should take her death as a downer. Such
comments among the rock community were not the
least bit unusual.

Closer to home came the denial from Janis's friends.
"Why else was the moon in Scorpio that day?" said
Sam Andrew. His opinion was later retracted, but Peter Cohon cited this to illustrate her death as fate: he
knew someone who was shot at from a very short distance; the bullet missed him. Seth Morgan was convinced Janis had no "premonitions . . . or that sort of
thing." Insisting "it was accidental through an error in
judgment," John Cooke, as I recall it, was angered by
the obituary in *Time*. "They might as well have called
it *suicide!*" he exclaimed with outrage. But what the
Time article had done was not to imply suicide at all.
It had merely endowed the act with activity, graphi-
cally pictorialized that fatal injection as having come
from Janis's hand. What disturbed John could only
have been that inescapable image. And in that image

lies the obvious significance of all those reactions.
Whether it be the addle-brained shallowness of Jerry
Garcia, through Peter Cohon's lapse in the use of his
normally high intelligence, or John Cooke's angry rejection, even if just for a moment, of the image summoned by *Time*, the theme is the same: her death
came from *outside*—like a boulder that fell from the
sky. Where the responses were not quite so foolish as
that, they were not that divergent. With a few exceptions, even the media failed to perceive the nature of
what happened: her death was an accident in only the
most marginal use of that term.

The thought of picking up the needle had been
idling all summer, and in the months of an excruciating despondency had stayed an idea in her mind.
She drank, and that was bad enough, even though
legal and slower. With the mentality of addiction still
there, she could have veered, at any point, right back
to heroin. But she didn't. The fears about her career
had been gnawing at her all summer, much more so, in
fact, than at the end. The *Melody Maker* poll, as I
said, did not appear until after she'd already picked
up the needle. Nor am I sure that Janis actually knew
of the letter concerning her bookings. Were she greatly
concerned in any case, she would surely have said so
to me. She knew the album would probably be an artistic success, certainly more so than any recording
she'd ever made before. She had confidence in Paul
Rothchild. She was aware of the improvement in her
singing and was happy with the band. Janis was *never*
secure, but relatively speaking, anxiety about her career could at the very most have been no greater than
before. As for quitting the stage, she had struggled
with that thought all year, and the anxieties about
that too were already present. Pressure, terrible conflict, and horrendous depression, all of them were at
the utmost earlier that summer. And temptation had
not been absent, not in New York and not in California. After all, she'd mentioned the junkie friends she
knew who were staying at the Landmark in July.

These things only were different in September: she was thinking of getting married; she was feeling better. It was *then*, at that very time, that she chose to do what, in all those terrible months, she had fought against so well. In a general sense, it would seem as if the insufferable depression of the months before was sufficient to satisfy her need for punishment. Without it, no longer so depressed, she was compelled to seek another strategy, a means for her damnation.

Some six or seven days before her death, Janis complained to me that Seth wasn't with her in Los Angeles. "But he's called me three times today!" she admitted.

"Well, good grief, Janis!" I cried.

"I know! But he isn't here!"

"You know something," I said. "I don't think you can stand being happy."

Janis sighed, "You're right."

The psychological conditions, or so I believe, were narrower than that generalized impulse to self-destruct. What Seth Morgan might have brought Janis in the way of real happiness doesn't matter in the least. Symbolically, he was a way out. He was a means of escape from the career and what it had done to her; he was symbolically a means of escaping Pearl, whose impulses were totally rampant. He also represented an attempt, no matter how feeble, by Janis to form a genuine attachment. In that sense, the affair may have been something of a rear-guard action to prevent what eventually occurred. Given the other elements in Seth and what he seems to have symbolized, he was also, or so I believe, an unwitting vehicle for bringing about what happened.

There seemed no sense to what Janis did, in picking up the needle. To be sure, her friends said, she knew the risks. She merely took them . . . to tranquilize herself . . . perhaps . . . to . . . to . . . drinking too much . . . sleep . . . her career . . . temptation . . to . . recording . . to . . . uh . . . she ignor . . she just . . . uh . . . uh . . .

no reason! But there was. In the paradox of her mood
and the more hopeful conditions of her life was the
very sense to it all, the precise tragic logic of guilt.

It is Janis's ambivalence, in a way, that is the most terrible of all, speaking as it does for the great possibility
that what happened was not inevitable. Janis immediately told Lyndall what she was doing and blamed it
on the strain of recording and the difficulty of finding
material. Janis claimed, of course, that the temptation
was too much, what with Peggy and the connection
around the hotel. "What could I say?" Lyndall remarked blandly. "I said I didn't think it was a very
good idea. I thought she shouldn't do it." Janis assured
Lyndall she would stop when the recording was over.
At that point, she was only using once every three
days. Janis insisted that Lyndall tell no one, so Lyndall
did not. If Janis no longer believed in her invulnera-
bility, others apparently did: she was some kind of
superhuman, a deity to whom it couldn't happen.

Janis pleaded with Seth to make her stop. "Why
don't you lean on me?" she demanded. Seth thought
Janis was indulging herself with him, trying to get attention.

Then, on the eighteenth of September, came the
death of Jimi Hendrix. The following evening, I spoke
to Janis; the Associated Press wanted a quote.

"I don't know what to . . ." Janis said. "How 'bout,
'There but for the grace of Go . . .'"

"Janis! Come on!" I cried. "That's *not* funny!"

"Well, it seems so. . . . O.K. Lesseeee. . . . I can't
say I was shocked . . . because I *wasn't* shocked, I
wasn't!" After coming up with some words of eulogy,
Janis added, "They're saying it was pills."

The cause of death was not yet verified; there was
still some question at that time. I said, "I know, but
maybe it's a coverup. . . . Listen, I gotta go."

Janis sighed, sounding extremely hesitant about
ending the conversation.

"What is it, Janis?"

"Oh, I dunno," she replied. "I was just thinking. . . .
I wonder what they'll say about *me* after I die."

How could one even fathom the cavern of emotion
that must have opened after that event? I myself find
it almost impossible to believe that a conscious thought
of suicide never entered her mind. The sheer omnipo-
tence in the possibilities, the vision of power in it all!
To create herself as so memorable! The thought of it
must have been irresistible. At the same time, there is
no doubt in my mind that it also frightened her terribly, giving her much motivation to drop such ideas as
insanity, giving her also the feeling that she ought to
stop using right away. *What am I thinking? I don't
want to die!*

There were a number of statements that Janis made
in reference to Hendrix's death. A few, indeed, were
to the effect that he was stealing her thunder. Her remark to me, for one. She also said to Brad Campbell,
"I wonder if I'll get as much promotion as he did."
Those comments, however, were very soon after Hendrix's death, at which point, I would think, such ideas
would have been at their strongest. Far more comments she made indicated a reluctance to die and the
same disbelief—bearing so much on the silence of
others—that such a thing could happen twice. To Seth
she said, "I can't go out the same year because he's a
bigger star!" To Peggy she remarked, "It just decreases
my chances. Two rock stars can't die in the same
year." A little less than a week before she died, Janis
told John Till she had "no intention of pulling any
tricks like that."

Right then, it dawned on him what she was doing.
"Janis! Why? How can you mess with that shit? Isn't
life groovy?"

Janis replied. "Yeah, it's groovy. Sometimes it ain't
groovy enough."

She spoke rather similarly to Kris Kristofferson. The
subject of dope came up between them. He said,
"Man, you got everything going for you. You got a

man you love; you got a producer you love. Chicks, artists, never have either one. Why blow it?"

Janis said, "What's it all worth?"

Sometime during the last two weeks, she told Richard Bell. Once she had said to him, referring to herself, "You don't care about *anything*," and had explained that the lack of feeling was exactly why she'd stopped. She didn't want to live like that, she'd said. Richard thinks that he may have been naive, that if his reaction had been firm enough, perhaps she could have been stopped. "I think if I'd known more," he mused, "if I'd a slapped her across the face or something, she wouldn't a done it anymore."

Janis assured Richard that she was going to stop as soon as she finished the quantity she had.

Vince Mitchell found out and became enraged, though not, in his heart, at Janis, feeling that Peggy and Seth were more deserving of his anger. He went to Janis nonetheless. "After all this time!" he yelled. "You've stopped, and now you're just gonna blow it again!"

"I just did it to see," she said.

"TO SEE WHAT?"

"To see if I wanted to do it anymore."

Vince is the only one who expressed any feelings about failing to call Albert. He'd gotten through himself. " 'Cause she said she wasn't gonna do it anymore. She *swore* to me she wouldn't."

Clark and Ken never knew at all; it's hard to know if the others really knew or only thought so in retrospect. "It's like is the movie in black or white," John Cooke announced. "I could tell when Janis was using!" I'm sure John did not really intend his words to sound a point of pride.

Among those who knew or didn't, almost all were impressed with Janis as being extraordinarily happy. On one occasion toward the end, however, a severe morbidity was apparent, at least to Dave Richards, who was in Larkspur working on the house, not in Los Angeles.

A few days before she died, she called Larkspur. Dave is uncertain whether she told him she was using, whether she threatened, or whether he guessed. He remembered, though, that she was consistently bitchy and that her irritation was thick with the tone of a heavy and overwhelming depression. Dave had a friend who was a former junkie helping him out at the house. He asked him to come to the phone.

"She's really fucking down," Dave said. "I think she's using. Talk to her."

When the friend hung up, all he could say to Dave was a feeble, "Whew!"

In spite of her mood, Janis did discuss her future plans with Seth during that conversation.

The weekend before Janis died, an extremely dramatic scene occurred between Seth and Janis. It focused originally around the buying of a shirt, then generated into hysteria, with Janis plunging into a rage that Seth was trying to use her. He says he thought he was joking, when he fingered a shirt in a store and said, "Thanks a lot, that's really nice of you," implying that Janis would buy it. "I'm not going to buy that for you," she said. It worked itself up from there and got rather nasty for a while, with Janis making a number of bitter remarks about money. Back at the hotel, Janis became more upset still and went sobbing to her room. Seth went out to the pool. Then Janis came out as well. She was extremely emotional, crying and stricken with terror that the relationship might be over. "She looked so scared," Seth said. "I'd never seen her look so scared." Seth did not seem to think the incident very significant. "Everything was cool after that," he said. That was the last time he saw Janis. The week before her death he remained in the San Francisco area and may also at that time have taken a quick trip to New York. Anyway, he was not in Los Angeles, but planning to go there on Saturday, October 3.

The Wednesday before she died, I spoke to Janis about doing an interview with Howard Smith of *The*

Village Voice, which he would tape for a radio show. We spoke later again that day, and on both occasions she sounded fine. I spoke to her on Thursday too, just to tell her my plans for the weekend. I would be in Woodstock, I said. Sarcastically, she snapped, "Oh, you're going up there too! *You* gonna move to the country next!"

I informed her that I would be back in the city on Saturday. At the time, I thought her voice sounded odd, which is to say somewhat sleepy, but it was also early in the day. I recall saying, "What's wrong with you?"

She pepped up immediately and cried exuberantly, "Nothing! I'm just in love, that's all!"

That same day, Thursday, October 1, Janis went to the beauty parlor and had her hair streaked. She had been losing weight purposely and had also acquired a tan, from spending time at the pool. It was not common for Janis to do such things. Everyone was struck by a very special attractiveness and an intangible aura about her.

Janis also signed her will that Thursday. This incident was mere coincidence. A previous will existed from 1968. That will, however, designated her entire estate to her brother and also a bequest of some money to Linda Gravenites. Janis's parents and sister were excluded. Way back in July Bob had suggested a revision of the will. There was a great deal more money involved than before; Linda was now out of Janis's life. It was Bob, not Janis, who brought the matter up when she returned to the Coast. Bob asked her if she wanted to perpetuate the provision that her brother receive the entire estate. Janis said definitely, "No." She indicated a closer feeling to her parents and sister than she had in the past. The disposition accordingly was changed: one half the estate to her parents, a quarter to Michael, a quarter to Laura. Should anything happen, the contents of the house were to go to Lyndall—to be distributed to Janis's friends. It was all quite routine that the will was revised and routine

that it was signed. The purpose of her visit to Bob's office that day was to scrutinize the draft of the premarital agreement. The will was ready. Bob presented it
for her signature. She automatically signed it. The will
is of no significance at all. On the other hand, it is foolish to say that no feelings were stimulated by signing
it. She did say that she wanted a provision for a party
in the event of her death, and allocated twenty-five
hundred dollars for that purpose. She asked Bob to
promise that the party would take place. How could
that have been frivolous? She knew the possibilities.
That may, in fact, have been the same day she spoke
to Dave Richards and sounded so depressed. I would
take her mood to be indicative only of the exhausting
nightmare below.

In Bob's office, she read the premarital agreement
carefully. Satisfied, she asked that it be typed up and
sent over to the Landmark. On Friday, she called Bob
and wanted to know about signing it. He told her
they needed a witness, and he could serve as notary.
Janis replied, "Baby, this isn't going to be signed before any notary. Seth and I are going to be alone, and
you know where."

Janis was adamant; a compromise was reached.
They could sign it alone and acknowledge it afterward, at which point Bob could notarize the papers.

I stayed in Woodstock only until Friday evening,
October 2. That morning from Albert's house I spoke
to Howard Smith and listened to the interview he'd
taped with Janis. He had complied with her request
that I hear it. It was, for the most part, a standard
Joplin interview. Howard did ask her some questions
about the women's movement. Janis was very anxious
that she might have alienated some people, and insisted that Howard check those particular remarks
with me. There were several pleas of that nature on
the tape.

Howard and I chatted a bit about her concern, neither of us thinking anything offensive about what
she'd said. I, at least, was puzzled and unexplainably

bothered. As I went back into the city that night, Janis was very much on my mind. Nonetheless, I merely decided I would call her sometime that weekend. Sunday, I thought, would do. On Saturday evening I went to a Gordon Lightfoot concert at Carnegie Hall. A party was held for Gordon afterward, and I went to that as well. It was extremely late when a friend took me home. At my apartment, I said, "I think I'll call Janis." He said, "Yeah, let's call her." We tossed that around for a minute. Changing my mind, I said, "No, she must be asleep. I don't want to wake her. I'll call her tomorrow." I would suspect my impulse to have sprung up in reaction to the sound of her voice and things she'd said through the weeks before, my response at a level of which I was completely unaware. Nothing excludes the possibility that it was eerier than that—or that it also was just plain coincidence. In California, it may have been two-thirty, perhaps a little earlier when I considered making the call. Her time of death was later estimated at one-forty of that exact Sunday morning, October 4, 1970.

A record of the calls Janis made on Saturday, October 3, was kept at the Landmark desk. The first was to City Hall, presumably to inquire about a marriage license. There could have been no other reason. City Hall, of course, wasn't open; she would have to try on Monday. That day, too, she called a seamstress who was making her some clothes. Her second call was to the connection, whom she failed to reach. Twice more she phoned him. On the last call, she was successful. She had perhaps a little dope on hand, and maybe even none. By that time, her habit had surely grown; probably she was edgy. Lyndall spoke to Janis several times that Saturday. Janis told her she'd gotten more dope, but also some Dolophine to stop. Apparently that was true, since a few Dolophine tablets were found in her room. Certainly a wish to stop would seem indicated in her reference to getting the pills.

Sometime that afternoon the connection came to the hotel, and one could have high praise for his goods by the measure of quality. He left Janis a supply of heroin that was very special; it may have been exceedingly pure. Having used for only three weeks, in all those months, her tolerance would not have been very high.

At an undetermined hour before evening, she did up. What she shot into her vein at that time may have been cooked from some smack she'd had before. It may have been what he brought her. But Janis, due to be at the studio and not wanting her energy affected, would be particularly cautious in any event, using less than usual.

Earlier Janis and Seth had had an argument on the phone. That, of course, was the day he was to come to Los Angeles; he had decided that Sunday would do. Janis was very angry. The flare-up seemed routine, nonetheless. What impressed everyone that night when she arrived at the studio was the exceptional brightness of her spirits.

"You're smiling and jumping around, Janis," Richard Bell remarked as he and Janis walked toward a Chinese restaurant during a break.

"Well," she teased, "I've got a secret." The members of the band knew she was serious about Seth, but she'd told none of them she actually intended the formalities. No one knew she'd called City Hall.

By the time they returned to the studio, it was jammed. Nick Gravenites was there. So was song writer Bobby Womack. Bennett Glotzer was around. All in all, there were perhaps twenty to twenty-five people present. Janis did not sing that night, but merely listened to the instrumental track the band had completed that day. It was Nick's song, "Buried Alive in the Blues."

Janis was exhilarated by the prospect of doing the vocal on Sunday, a light like a sunburst in her smile and eyes.

Before she went home, Janis called Lyndall. She

was very agitated that Seth wasn't with her, but her
voice was otherwise exuberant.

Only Vince sensed the tinge of a slightly strange
mood; he thought she had "a funny gleam."

The session was called to an end. Most of the band
took off in the truck they called "the boogie wagon."
Janis hopped into her Porsche with Ken Pearson and
some other fellow who tagged along. She waved goodbye to the others and zipped off to Barney's Beanery
for a drink, to which Ken agreed. At the bar, she drank
vodka and orange juice, only two. The fellow who
tagged along pestered her with some questions about
her singing style and such. Janis paid little attention
and spoke only with Ken.

"Did *you* play that?" she asked him, when she
heard one of her hits on the jukebox.

"Well, yeah," he admitted.

"Shit!" she said. "I wish someone else had done it."

They left Barney's Beanery and headed back to the
hotel. As Ken recalled it, Janis talked excitedly about
some of the cuts for the album and wanted only assurance that everyone in the band was as fond of her as
she of them. She stated her affection for the band several times. "If any of you guys ever leave me, I'll kill
ya," she said. Her talk, however, was geared to the
future, her demeanor charming and warm. It was October 4, approximately 12:30 A.M., Ken believes, when
they reached the Landmark and Janis went alone to
her room.

The rush could only have been jolting as she sent the
smack through her vein with the jab of that needle.

When Janis was through, she placed the package of
heroin in the dresser. She put the works in a Chinese
box and laid it neatly in a drawer. Janis usually left
it on the night table. These gestures could reliably be
taken to mean she really intended this hit to be the last
and wanted no reminders in the morning. *This* time,
she meant to stop. There is something about the magic
of mornings. Rebirth with the pale blue dawn.

The heroin in her system might have killed her im-

mediately. It did not. When, after a while, she walked
out to the lobby, she could not have known she was
dying. There she chatted with the hotel clerk for a
second and asked him to change a five-dollar bill for
cigarettes, which she purchased.

Then she walked back to her room. Closing the
door, she stepped forward a foot or two and fell, like a
puppet hurled down or kicked over.

Epilogue—Revised for this Edition

According to official records and statements of the office of Thomas T. Noguchi, M.D., chief medical examiner-coroner of the County of Los Angeles, Janis died of an accidental overdose of heroin (which converts to morphine after entering the body). Alcohol was also present in the blood, and her liver showed the effects of long-term heavy drinking. Additional tests for barbiturates, phenothiazine, amphetamines, Librium, Valium, Noludar, meprobamate, methadone, soma, Quaalude, and codeine were negative. When John Cooke discovered Janis's body, her nose appeared to have been broken in the fall. The examination, however, revealed only a cut lip, obviously sustained when she collapsed. The coroner's record lists no evidence of injury or of violence.

Much mystery surrounded the fact that Janis did not die immediately. Some people insisted that a heroin overdose could not have happened in that manner. But the Medical Examiner's Office of New York informs me that there is nothing uncommon about a delay between the time of injection and the moment of death.

For the sake of technical accuracy, it should be stated that the term "overdose" is frequently used to describe the cause of heroin-related deaths even though no conclusive evidence of an actual pharmacological overdose is present. The *Consumers Union Report on Licit and Illicit Drugs*, for example, cites research to the effect that massive amounts of heroin are usually required to end life. The great majority of deaths following an injection of heroin are really the result of an adulteration of the product with various substances or of other mysterious elements: what is called a "synergistic reaction" to a combination of drugs in some instances, or of other toxic factors.

In the spring of 1974, during an insurance trial related to Janis's death, it was revealed that the amounts of morphine found in Janis's body were not overwhelmingly large. Accordingly, it remains possible that the alcohol in her system contributed to her death or that something unknown triggered a fatal reaction. On the other hand, the morphine quantities reported do not rule out the possibility that an actual overdose occurred—from an amount that was more than her body could tolerate or from heroin that may have been exceptionally pure.

Private services for immediate members of the Joplin family were held at the Westwood Village Mortuary, Los Angeles County on October 7, 1970. According to her wishes, Janis's remains were cremated and scattered by air along the coastline of Marin County, California.

ABOUT THE AUTHOR

MYRA FRIEDMAN was born and raised in St. Louis. She majored in music at Northwestern University, worked with Decca Records and then for five years as a writer with Columbia Records. In 1968 she went to work for Janis Joplin's manager, Albert Grossman, and remained there until Janis's death in October 1970.

FREE!
Bantam Book Catalog

It lists over a thousand money-saving best-sellers originally priced from $3.75 to $15.00 —bestsellers that are yours now for as little as 50¢ to $2.95!

The catalog gives you a great opportunity to build your own private library at huge savings!

So don't delay any longer—send for your catalog TODAY! It's absolutely FREE!